HOOKED

Kevin Markham, born and educated in Ireland, started playing golf at the age of six and has played ever since. After a Business Degree at Dublin City University he lived in London for eight years, working in direct marketing. When he returned to Ireland in 1998, he worked for Esat Digifone. In 2000 he became a full-time freelance copywriter. He contributes articles on golf to newspapers and magazines.

This book is dedicated to my father and my grandfather, without whose efforts and patience I would never have learned to swing a club.

HOOKED

AN AMATEUR'S GUIDE
TO THE GOLF COURSES OF IRELAND

Kevin Markham

The Collins Press

First published in 2009 by
The Collins Press
West Link Park
Doughcloyne
Wilton
Cork

This revised edition published 2011

British Library Cataloguing in Publication Data

Markham, Kevin.
Hooked : an amateur's guide to the golf courses of Ireland.
— New updated ed.
1. Golf courses — Ireland — Guidebooks. 2. Ireland —
Guidebooks.
I. Title
796.3'52068415-dc22
ISBN-13: 9781848891067

Typesetting by Carole Lynch
Typeset in Rotis Semi Sans
Printed in Ireland by Watermans Printers

FSC
www.fsc.org

MIX

Paper from
responsible sources

FSC® C084572

CONTENTS

ACKNOWLEDGEMENTS

My biggest thanks go to the golf courses of Ireland which have allowed me to play their eighteen holes. General Managers, Secretary Managers, Directors of Golf, Professionals, Captains and Honorary Secretaries have all been most accommodating on my quest to play every course in Ireland. Some of them have been amused, some bemused, but nearly all of them envious.

To all the golfers with whom I have had the pleasure of playing, thank you for your patience. From hackers to professionals, I have enjoyed your company tremendously and many of you have shown me how some of Ireland's most difficult courses should be played: Philip at Ardglass; Martin at Lahinch; the boys at Castlerock.

To my agent, Jonathan Williams, for opening the door. My friend Julie, for her creativity. My thanks to Brendan at Daysha Consulting, without whose support this book might never have happened.

To my mother, father and sister. And FAM. I could never have done this without you.

NOTE TO THE SECOND EDITION

The first edition of *Hooked* was written at a time when Ireland was, to put it mildly, exuberant. As any Irish golfer will tell you, the country's green fees were similarly exuberant. These days the majority of green fees have fallen, sometimes by over 50 per cent. The courses have changed very little and remain as thrilling and challenging as ever, so there really is no better time to enjoy some of our 350 courses.

This second edition sees considerable changes to green fee rates (Northern Ireland less so), as well as the Value for Money scores. There are numerous course updates, from new clubhouses to new holes, and three new courses are included (Bunclody, Cobh, Killeen Castle). Two courses no longer qualify (Carnbeg, Citywest Lakes) and Mount Ober, the only club not to let me review their course, has been removed (Map Reference: Map 3/B2/230) due to space restrictions.

There are well over 3,000 photographs of Ireland's golf courses on my Flickr page: www.flickr.com/photos/kevinmarkham and these are being added to all of the time. They'll give you a great taste of what to expect.

Green fees correct at the time of writing.

Please note that during 2010 and into 2011, several golf courses were facing closure. Some will survive; others won't. I apologise if you decide to play one of the clubs listed in this book, only to discover it has closed.

LIST OF GOLF COURSES

INTRODUCTION

I love golf. Always have and always will. It can frustrate the hell out of me but when you're kicking up the dew on your way down the fairway, or watching your ball disappear into dappled evening shadows, there's no better place to be than on one of Ireland's golf courses.

Here's a simple question: what makes playing a golf course a great experience? Is it holes tumbling through ancient woods and around lakes, or coasting through the dunes with the roar of the sea in your ears as you absorb beautiful mountain views? Is it the reputation of the course, whether old or new? Ballybunion and Royal Portrush conjure up images of flat caps, plus fours and wooden clubs, as well as a host of famous faces and victories. Knightsbrook and The Heritage at Killenard emphasise how golf has changed in the modern era, and how landscapes can be moulded to satisfy designers' every whim.

Do you want to play a course because of the designer? Do you favour the old (Old Tom Morris, Colt, Vardon) or the new (Christy O'Connor Jnr, Nick Faldo, Pat Ruddy)? Are you impressed by the ingenuity of clever features, be they man-made lakes or mounds, or do you prefer the natural beauty of the landscape to express itself across a course?

What about your playing partners? How much does a friendly round of golf add to your overall golf experience? Or would you prefer to play head-to-head for hard cash?

Even if you answer all of these questions, there are still two crucial factors that can only be determined when you play the course: how well you play and the weather. Each is as temperamental as the other. If you come in with a score of 48 points then you will love the course, no matter how good or bad it is. And vice versa. That is the nature of a golfer's competitiveness. The weather is a different matter entirely. You'll often hear of Americans playing the great links in force eight gales and driving rain because they will never get another chance. That's the nature of a golfer's love of the game.

PURPOSE OF THIS BOOK

There are 350 eighteen-hole golf courses in Ireland. Not only is that one of the highest number of golf courses per capita in the world, it is also a world of choice for Irish and international golfers alike. Yet try and get some independent information on these courses and you might hit a brick wall. The big, famous courses have plenty to say and are praised at length in numerous books. Smaller courses, however, are given a cursory glance and pushed to the side with a couple of lines of lethargic copy. How could the description '*a pleasant parkland course on undulating terrain with fast greens*' possibly capture your imagination? This is wrong. We have too many great courses that rarely get mentioned in the top tier of Irish golf courses. Obvious ones include Enniscrone and Tulfarris. But what about Portumna, Portarlington, Scrabo, Strandhill and Rosslare? They all offer an amazing golfing experience, in one way or another.

On the other hand, there are numerous courses that claim to be wonderful and/or of 'championship' design that will leave you wondering how 'championship' is defined. When you visit their website or read an advertisement in a magazine, you'll be salivating at the prospect of a round of golf, only to be utterly let down when you arrive. Having read their website and then played their course, I found Castle Hume to be one such disappointment. Fernhill is another, and there are plenty more.

This book gives every course its own detailed review, one that cuts through the hype or gives credit where it is deserved. The objective is to introduce you to the course, outline what makes it special, say why it's fun to play and set realistic expectations.

Yes, of course it is subjective, but I try to be consistent and I try to be honest. I have no doubt that people will disagree with me. That in itself makes this book worth writing, because you can't beat a good debate. Look at the furore caused by the K Club hosting the Ryder Cup.

I hope you enjoy the reviews, but most of all I hope you enjoy playing the courses you find in this book. Ireland has some of the best courses in the world and some of these you have probably never heard of. From links to parkland, from healthland to farmland, you'll find something in here that will inspire you out onto an Irish golf course.

I started my blog a bit late in the day but you'll find over 100 courses on there. Mostly it is the story of my visit, what happened on the day, who I met or played with and how the weather affected the course conditions. And maybe the odd tip. (www.golfcoursesireland.blogspot.com)

There are always things in golf books that irritate me. An aerial photograph, for instance. When am I ever going to be playing a shot from up there? The other thing is distances. Books will give you the distances from the back tees where you are never likely (or be allowed) to play from. In this book, the distances are given from the regular visitor tees. I do sometimes recommend that you play from the back sticks to enjoy the course fully, and I say so in the relevant reviews.

And finally, Ireland has never really got its head around yards and metres. Courses can choose whichever they want and that can confuse visitors mightily, especially UK visitors because they work only in yards. So 100 m equals 110 yards approximately, if that helps. (This book gives whatever the course has chosen.) And as if that wasn't bad enough, the fairway markers can be to the front of the green or the middle of the green. It is all a bit confusing. If in doubt, ask when you get to the course.

PARKLAND V. LINKS

'Blondes or brunettes?' It was a question posed to me by Mike Corry, the General Manager at Shannon.

Undeniably I am a links man. These courses 'link' the land to the sea, running across sandy soil that creates a wonderfully springy, uneven terrain. And, invariably, they promise spectacular views. They also tend to be more natural in their design and appearance. There's something wild about them that grabs my attention and you will find that many of my highest-scoring courses are links. It is important to note that this often comes down to the score for Location. For instance, Dooks has the best views in the country while Adare is severely restricted because of its dense parkland surroundings.

But you can't beat a beautiful parkland course when the leaves are out or autumn is changing the colours. Rivers, lakes and wildlife, and the dark brooding of huge trees promise mesmerising surroundings and an entirely different golf experience. In a way, the two cannot be compared. I have met enough golfers on my travels to know that some people loathe links golf. When you read a links review it might help to know on which side of the fence I sit.

NEW COURSES

Between 1990 and 2008, new courses were appearing all the time in Ireland. Names like Ernie Els (Kinsale), Ian Woosnam (Borrmount Manor), Retief Goosen (Carrig Glas) and Nick Faldo (Lough Rynn) have all been linked to various planned projects around the country, and our double British Open Champion, Padraig Harrington, is linked to Marlbrook, near Clonmel. Sadly, not all of these will see the light of day. The current downturn has led to some projects being halted. What happens in the future is anyone's guess.

TEE TIME RESERVATIONS

With the huge explosion of golf in Ireland, it is almost always essential to book tee times in advance. The bigger the course and the closer to high season it is, the more important it is that you book – sometimes a year in advance. Most courses allow limited weekend play but, again, you will need to book early.

There are a number of tee time reservation sites and these all do a good job for you. Golf tour operators will look after absolutely everything if that is what you want. And then there are the golf course websites, many of which now take bookings online.

Please be aware that some of these will require payment up front and may not offer refunds if you have to cancel/postpone.

But sometimes phoning up and talking to the pro shop/office reaps far bigger rewards. They will tell you about special deals, negotiate green fees on the phone and warn you about large society outings going out right in front of you. And you can ask them the relevant Questions to Ask (see page xvii), including good times and bad times to play the course.

THREE TEE TIME RESERVATION SITES:
www.teetimes.ie
www.ebookireland.com/golf.htm
www.golf-booker.com

WEATHER

You could not possibly have an Irish golf book that does not mention the weather. I would sum it up as follows: whatever time of year you come and whatever the weather forecast predicts, you would be foolish not to bring your waterproofs. It is a sad fact that Ireland's warmer months are also the wetter ones, borne out by my own experience: between October and December 2007, I played over forty-five courses and was rained on three times. A two-week trip in July 2008 had me putting on waterproofs every second day. The best time for golf is late spring and early autumn. This is a general observation based on the summers of 2007 and 2008, and in the coming years, who knows what climate change will inflict on Ireland? Some say we will be freezing while others predict we will be basking in Bordeaux-like temperatures. It will always be unpredictable.

Whatever the weather, it all adds to the tall tales you tell when you get home.

TWO WEBSITES THAT MIGHT HELP:
www.met.ie (the Irish meteorological service)
www.weather.com

QUESTIONS TO ASK

There are some questions that might make your visit to a golf club that much easier. Have these answered by the club before you go so you can plan accordingly.

Is there a pro shop?
Are handicap certificates required?
What days of the week are open to visitors?
Are visitors allowed to play on Saturday and Sunday?
When is Ladies' Day?
Do you have buggies?
Is there a specific dress code (on course/in clubhouse)?
Are fairways in play/is there placing?
Are there any temporary greens in play?
Is food served all day?
When does the clubhouse close?
Are towels available and, if so, is there a charge?
What is your spikes policy?
How do I get to the course?

GREEN FEES & VALUE FOR MONEY

Talk to any golfer and they will have an opinion about green fees: they are rarely positive. With many courses now charging over €100 per round it is not surprising that golfers feel aggrieved. And yet this focuses too much attention on the big courses (Portmarnock, Royal County Down, Old Head, K Club, etc.). There are dozens of courses that offer amazing value, although they are scarce around Dublin. The links courses of the northwest are excellent value, and Northern Ireland as a whole is great value. A list of the best value for money courses is given later in this section, but green fees are always changing

But here's the thing: even the exorbitant K Club offers heavily discounted green fees if you just know where and when to look, for example:

EARLY BIRDS/TWILIGHT
There are Early Bird and Twilight rates throughout the year at many clubs, and you might get a breakfast/steak dinner and a pint thrown in for good measure. And it doesn't always mean being on the tee at 7 a.m. Some let you play before 10 a.m.

OPEN COMPETITIONS/SPECIAL DEALS

Most clubs have open competitions, especially on weekdays during the summer months. These are perhaps the best value of all and there is even a chance to win prizes. You will find a list of Open Competitions on the Golfing Union of Ireland website (www.gui.ie). 'Specials' also fall under this category and might include a bar meal or a pint. At Down Royal £17 will get you a meal and a round on a rather special heathland course during the summer.

WINTER DEALS

You will always get good deals during the winter months; you might even be surprised at how benign the weather can be. The Mount Juliet Winter Series is a chance to play one of the best parkland courses in the country for under €100.

HOTEL PACKAGES

A lot of hotels put together packages that bundle accommodation with golf. One example is Heart of Ireland (www.golfintheheartofireland.com), which includes some of my favourite courses.

And several hotels have their own golf courses, resulting in lower green fees for guests, e.g. Knightsbrook, Druid's Heath, Skellig Bay, Roe Park.

GOLF PASSPORTS

With so many golf clubs fighting to attract visitors, some clubs have taken the approach that 'if you can't beat them, join them'. The result is a golfer's passport to play a number of local courses at one overall discounted rate. Of course, it usually means that you have to play all the courses to get full value for money, but that is not always the case.

Dungarvan Golf Triangle allows you to play Gold Coast, Dungarvan and West Waterford for the price of two (www.golftriangle.com).

Meath Golf Passport covers Knightsbrook, Rathcore and County Meath (www.boynegolf.ie).

The Kerry Shamrock covers Dingle, the exceptional Dooks, and Killarney (but not the Killeen course, unfortunately). Contact any of the clubs for further information.

Take 3 includes Skellig Bay, Ring of Kerry and Castleisland (www.wellplayed.com).

And there are many more.

CLASSICS

In terms of value for money, there is one final option: the Classic. Numerous Classics take place around the country and if you are prepared to make the commitment well in advance and put together a team, they can be an absolute blast. At the Dunmore East Classic (www.waterford-dunmore.com) in April, for example, you will play Faithlegg, Waterford Castle, Waterford and Tramore. Accommodation and evening meals are included in the price (approximately

€1,400 pps), but many Classics are golf only. You play three or four days in a row and it has become a very popular and competitive event, with some impressive prizes for those of you who want to prove yourselves. But above all, it is a huge amount of fun and you will meet a lot of other fanatical golfers. A very similar event, the Tramore Golf Classic, covers the same courses in September (www.tramoregolfclassic.com).

Erne Waterway Golf Challenge (June) plays Slieve Russell, Castle Hume and County Cavan (www.cavantourism.com).

The P&O Irish Sea Kingdoms of Down (early May) covers Tandragee, County Armagh and Royal County Down golf clubs (www.postnettgolf.com).

Budweiser International Golf Challenge (May) plays six courses, with the final at The Heritage (www.laoistourism.ie).

Donegal Links Classic has three outstanding courses: Ballyliffin, Rosapenna and Portsalon. Contact Portsalon for more details.

Atlantic Coast Challenge is the best of the bunch, playing over County Sligo, Enniscrone and Carne.

OPEN FAIRWAYS

Special mention needs to be made of Open Fairways, a company that produces an impressively large annual publication, offering discounts at over 200 golf courses (and hotels) around Ireland. The typical offer is two green fees for the price of one, and four for two. You can easily cover the cost of the book in one round of golf. There are many excellent courses included and not many restrictions on the time you play.

Open Fairways also produce books for Scotland, England and as far away as Asia.

TOUR OPERATORS

Tour Operators can offer value for money (but not always) and they promise convenience and organisation. Hand over your cash and they do everything for you, including green fees, meals, accommodation and travel. Sometimes that is exactly what you want when you are coming from abroad.

And the final possibility to get a cheaper green fee is simply to ask when you phone up to reserve a tee time. Enough golf clubs need your money to put you in a strong bartering position. Put it this way: if the green fee is €80 and you can get your fourball on the course for €70 each, you've just got yourself a few free pints.

(*Note*: Sterling green fees have not been given a euro equivalent because the currency has been fluctuating a lot.)

GETTING HERE/TRAVEL

Ireland is an extremely popular golfing destination and there is no shortage of companies that want to bring you here. But if you are driving around Ireland, bring a good map.

BY AIR

Ireland has twelve airports and numerous airlines that fly to them. The smaller airports tend to be catered for by Irish airlines, and routes often extend only to the UK.

Many airlines now charge a fixed fee for taking golf bags on the plane, and on the 'cheap' airlines this can easily double the price of your flight.

IRISH AIRPORTS:

Belfast City Airport (BHD) www.belfastcityairport.com
Belfast International Airport (BFS) www.bial.co.uk
City of Derry Airport (LDY) www.cityofderryairport.com
Cork Airport (ORK) www.corkairport.com
Donegal Airport (CFN) www.donegalairport.ie
Dublin Airport (DUB) www.dublinairport.com
Galway Airport (GWY) www.galwayairport.com
Kerry Airport (KIR) www.kerryairport.ie
Knock International Airport (NOC) www.knockairport.com
Shannon Airport (SNN) www.shannonairport.com
Sligo Airport (SXL) www.sligoairport.com
Waterford Airport (WAT) www.flywaterford.com

AIRLINES THAT FLY TO IRELAND:

From UK & Europe:
www.aerarann.com
www.aerlingus.com
www.ba.com (British Airways)
www.easyjet.com
www.flybmi.com
www.ryanair.com
www.airfrance.com
www.flysas.com
www.lufthansa.com
www.flybe.com

From the USA:
www.aa.com (American Airlines)
www.continental.com

www.aerlingus.com
www.usairways.com
www.delta.com

BY SEA
Ferries link Ireland with the UK and France. Four golfers taking a large car will probably save money travelling by sea, as opposed to flying and hiring a car.

Irish Ferries (www.irishferries.ie) routes:
Pembroke – Rosslare
Holyhead – Dublin Port
Cherbourg – Rosslare
Roscoff – Rosslare

Norfolk Line (www.norfolkline.com) routes:
Liverpool Birkenhead – Belfast
Liverpool Birkenhead – Dublin Port

P&O Irish Sea Ferries (www.poirishsea.com) routes:
Troon – Larne
Cairnryan – Larne
Liverpool – Dublin Port

Stena Line (www.stenaline.com) routes:
Fishguard – Rosslare
Holyhead – Dublin Port
Holyhead – Dun Laoghaire
Fleetwood – Larne
Stranraer – Belfast

Ferry routes that have recently stopped operating but may start up again in the future include:
Swansea to Cork
Campbelltown to Ballycastle

CAR HIRE
You will find the usual car hire operators at the airports. Visit the airport websites to find out more. If there are more than two of you travelling, it is worth paying extra to get a large vehicle that will take clubs and cases comfortably.

GOLF OPERATORS
Many of the people I met on my travels were looked after by golf operators. They take care of everything, if that's what you want, including travel, accommodation,

food, entertainment and green fees. These companies can be very small (a great personal touch) or they can be affiliated to larger groups (hotels, airlines).

I am in no position to recommend one over another but you will always find information in the back of golf magazines. And asking around in your local club will usually provide some recommendations. Or try the Irish Golf Tour Operators Association (www.igtoa.com).

FURTHER INFORMATION

WEBSITES

If you're coming to Ireland to play golf, or you're already here, there are plenty of good sources of information. The most obvious starting point is the golf courses' websites. Some are excellent. They offer information on where to stay, places to visit and how to get to the club. You can book online too.

The Irish and Northern Irish tourist bodies give far broader information on visiting Ireland, including accommodation. Here are some recommended links:
www.discoverireland.ie/golf
www.tourismireland.com
www.failteireland.ie
www.discovernorthernireland.com
www.goireland.com

There are also specific golf websites:
www.gui.ie (Golfing Union of Ireland)
www.igtoa.com (Irish Golf Tour Operators Association)

BOOKS

There are hundreds of golf books, each giving a different angle on the brilliance of Ireland's golf courses. Some are good, some are bad. The best one is *Links of Heaven* by Richard Phinney and Scott Whitley. Although it focuses almost exclusively on links courses, it has been written with a passion and insight that will appeal hugely to Americans and those for whom links golf is a religion.

Visit www.irishgolf.com to find out more.

TELEPHONE NUMBERS

Northern Irish numbers can cause confusion. If dialling from the Republic of Ireland the prefix is 048, e.g. Ardglass is 048 4484 1022. If dialling from the UK, the prefix is 028, e.g. Ardglass is 028 4484 1022. If dialling from anywhere else, it is +44 28, e.g. Ardglass is (+44) 28 4484 1022. In this book, Northern Irish numbers are given as though dialling from outside the British Isles.

NINE-HOLE COURSES

Nine-hole golf courses have been ignored for the most part. To have included them would have added over a hundred courses, which would have made the book unwieldy. Many of these are of poor quality and golfing tourists would be unlikely to play them. However, the likes of Connemara Isles, Borris, Cruit Island and Helen's Bay are excellent courses and are considerably better than some of the eighteen-hole courses I played.

LADY GOLFERS

My apologies to lady golfers because I have made no mention of the difference in length from the men's to the ladies' tees.

DIRECTIONS

Some golf courses are well signposted but most are not, and if you are not approaching from the obvious direction (i.e. the main road), then signs are even more scarce. It is a point that golf courses need to take on board. Ironically, Lee Valley in Cork is signposted extremely well and it was the only club where I was asked if I found the place OK.

If you don't know how to find the course, check the website. If there's nothing there, ask them to email you directions.

FOOD, DRINK AND THE 'CRAIC'

As a visitor, the chances are that you will end up in the bar at the end of your golf game. Food, drink and socialising are therefore very important to the overall golf experience. Sadly, it was not possible for me to eat and drink in every clubhouse. It was not just a matter of expense; there was also the issue of autumn/winter golf when most clubs close between 5 p.m. and 6 p.m.

It would be unfair to talk about the great nights I had in some clubs, while other clubs never had a chance to shine. One final suggestion: if you're playing a course out of season, ask when the bar closes and whether or not food is served during the day.

TOP EIGHTEEN HOLES

Picking the top eighteen holes in Ireland is no easy task. Whichever holes I nominate will lead to disagreement. The goal was to create a list of the best eighteen holes in the correct order and to a par of 72. These are holes that light up a round or simply blow you away. It could be because of their difficulty, their beauty or their surroundings. Or all three. No course is allowed more than one hole in the Top Eighteen, which is why Royal Portrush's famous fourteenth doesn't make it.

Everybody has their favourites and holes one and eighteen may stir people the most. Many believe the first hole at Portstewart is the best opening hole. It is stunning, I agree, but Scrabo's is even better. As for eighteen, Adare is mesmerising but the sheer surprise of Carne gets the nod.

Every hole listed is a beautiful hole, and because there are so many of them, I have listed a few runners-up as well (with the par shown in parentheses).

The par 72 includes four par 3s and four par 5s. As a result, I had to do some switching around to get what I thought was the best combination.

Colour photographs of these eighteen holes are provided.

Golf course photographs are always taken from the unlikeliest of positions. Photographers want to use the light, get the best angles and introduce foreground features to give depth of field, but they often end up in places where a golfer will never find him- or herself. The photograph of Druid's Glen's eighth hole, for example, is taken from well above the green in the flowerbeds. But it does show off the hole beautifully. I have tried to source images that show the hole as you will find it, standing on the tee.

HOLE	COURSE	PAR	ALTERNATIVES (WITH PAR)
1	Scrabo	4	Portstewart (Strand) (4), Ardglass (4), Doonbeg (5)
2	Portsalon	4	Powerscourt (East) (5), Tralee (5), Cairndhu (3), Ballybunion (Old) (4), Portstewart (Strand) (4)
3	Killarney (Killeen)	3	Skellig Bay (3), Tralee (3), Mount Juliet (3), Concra Wood (4)
4	Old Head	4	Mitchelstown (4), Clandeboye (Dufferin) (4) Macreddin (3)
5	Royal Portrush (Dunluce)	4	Cork (5), Roscrea (5), Strandhill (5), Bangor (4), Laytown & Bettystown (4)
6	Portstewart (Strand)	3	Rosapenna (Sandy Hills) (4), Donegal (5), Lahinch (4), Doonbeg (4)
7	Lahinch (Old)	4	Malone (4), Dromoland Castle (3)
8	Druid's Glen	3	Narin & Portnoo (4), Castlecomer (4) Moyola Park (4), The European Club (4)
9	Royal County Down	4	Coollattin (4), Narin & Portnoo (4)

HOLE	COURSE	PAR	ALTERNATIVES (WITH PAR)
10	Mount Juliet	5	County Sligo (4), Headfort (New) (4), Fota Island (5), Enniscrone (4)
11	Ballybunion (Old)	4	Waterville (5), Royal Belfast (3), Carne (4), Ardglass (5)
12	Macreddin	4	Abbeyleix (4), Tralee (4), Tramore (4), Enniscrone (4)
13	Naas	5	Connemara (3), Fermoy (4), Rathsallagh (3), Druid's Glen (4), Strandhill (4), Athlone (4), Gracehill (4), Enniscrone (4)
14	Portarlington	4	Doonbeg (3), Royal Portrush (Dunluce) (3)
15	Westport	5	Carton House (O'Meara) (5), Carne (4), Coollattin (3), Mitchelstown (4), Ballybunion (Cashen) (5), Glasson (3)
16	Tralee	3	Portumna (4), Lough Erne (5), K Club (Palmer) (5)
17	The European Club	4	County Sligo (4), Kilkea Castle (4), Moyola Park (3), Carton House (Montgomerie) (3)
18	Carne	5	Druid's Glen (4), Adare (5), Nuremore (4)

TOP TENS

TOP TEN VALUE FOR MONEY (ALPHABETICALLY)

These are listed alphabetically. Many courses in this book score ten out of ten for Value for Money, but the following are what I consider to be the best, and cover a broad spectrum.

Carne
Clandeboye (Dufferin)
Coollattin
County Sligo
Curragh, The
Portarlington
Portumna
Rathcore
Scrabo
West Waterford

TOP TEN LINKS (ALPHABETICALLY)

Ballybunion (Old)
Carne
County Sligo
Dooks
Enniscrone
European Club, The
Narin & Portnoo
Royal County Down
Tralee
Waterville

TOP TEN PARKLAND/SEASIDE (ALPHABETICALLY)

Adare
Clandeboye (Dufferin)
Concra Wood
Curragh, The
Druid's Glen
Headfort (New)
Malone
Mount Juliet
Old Head
Scrabo

TOP TEN 'MUST PLAY' COURSES (ALPHABETICALLY)

These courses are are so different or unexpected that they deserve a special mention.
Carne
Corballis
Curragh, The
East Clare
Mahon
Moyola Park
Old Head
Royal County Down (Annesley)
Scrabo
Strandhill

SCORING SYSTEM USED IN THIS BOOK

No one ever agrees on rankings, whether it's golf courses, rugby players or the world's most expensive city. I have no doubt that this will be the case here. Certainly if you look at the final scores before reading this section, you might bubble over with disbelief.

I have used a scoring system that rates each course against eight different criteria, but I hasten to add that just because a course scores 84 it does not mean I prefer it to a course that scores 81. The most important of the eight criteria is the last one: *golf experience.*

Each course is ranked out of 100:

Course Design (CD) – 20 points: I am no golf architect, so I'm not looking at the course's specific design pedigree. Rather, the points are based on the appearance of the individual holes and how much I think you will enjoy playing them. It is about how good it makes you feel standing on the tee.

Appeal (A) – 10: Appeal focuses solely on the overall appearance of the course. How pretty is it to look at (trees, paths from greens to tees, hillsides to walk, valleys, bridges, streams and lakes)? Is it an enjoyable walk? Does it add to the experience?

Greens/Fairways (G/F) – 10: The shape, the size, the quality, the slopes, the excitement. Fairways add considerably to the appeal of the course, because they lead your eye towards the green. Greens are the climax to any hole and the better they are, the more pleasure you will have, no matter how many shots it takes you to get there.

Bunkers/Water (B/W) – 10: When you're stuck in a bunker, you want to be playing from sand that feels like silk, not brick, and you want it to be a bunker shape, not a sandpit. Bunkers should also be located where they will punish errant shots and where they challenge you off the tee and from the fairway. Water comes in all shapes and sizes and when you play the likes of Druid's Glen or Palmerstown you will appreciate how much it adds to your day (and to your score).

Location (L) – 10: This focuses solely on the surroundings beyond the course. Naturally, links and coastline courses will score well, with sea, beach, island and cliff views. Royal Portrush and Bearna are perfect examples, but there are plenty of parkland courses that offer wonderful views of the Irish countryside (Lee Valley, for example). Unfortunately, some courses are being swamped by houses, roads and industrial estates, and scores reflect this.

Facilities (F) – 10: When you get to a golf club, you expect certain things: bar, restaurant, pro shop, buggies/trolleys, locker room, showers, putting green and driving range. This score indicates how good these are.

Value for Money (V) – 10: Speaks for itself. Is it worth paying €350 when you can play a course that's half as good for €35? You do the arithmetic. For most of us, such price differences can greatly affect the enjoyment we get from the round. Please also refer to the section on *Value for Money.*

I have tried to take into account the relative 'value' of being close to Dublin and the major centres (Cork, Belfast . . .). It should also be noted that in Northern Ireland I have compared the green fees with the entire island, which is why so many get 10 out of 10.

Golf Experience (G Ex) – 20: Ultimately, this is the most important part of your day. When you leave the golf club, what are the memories you will take with you? Were you blown away or were you regretting four hours of your life you'll never get back?

POINTS								
CD	A	G/F	B/W	L	F	V	G Ex	Total
17	9	10	10	6	10	8	20	90

A NOTE ABOUT THE MAPS

There are seven maps in this book, 1–7, with the golf courses indicated by numbered flags. A map reference is given for each course in the Course Reviews, so, for example, Greenore's reference is Map4/B1/164: you will find it on Map 4, in the quadrant B1, flag number 164.

Flag numbers correlate with map codes in the top right-hand corner of each course review; these are *mostly* consecutive.

MAP 1

Flag numbers correlate with map codes in the top right-hand corner of each course review; these are *mostly* consecutive.

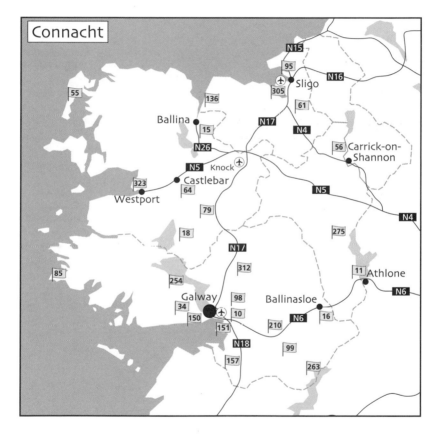

MAP 2

Flag numbers correlate with map codes in the top right-hand corner of each course review; these are *mostly* consecutive.

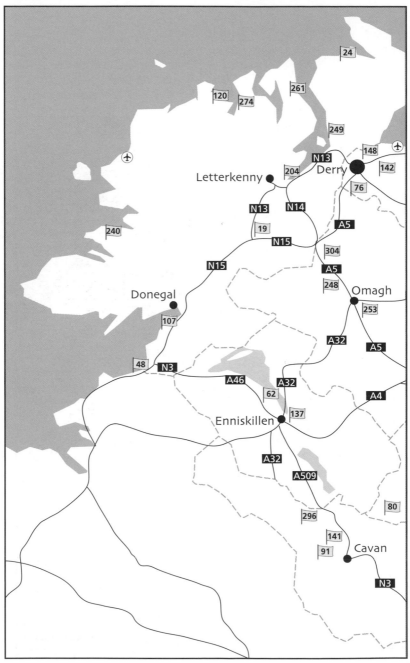

MAP 3

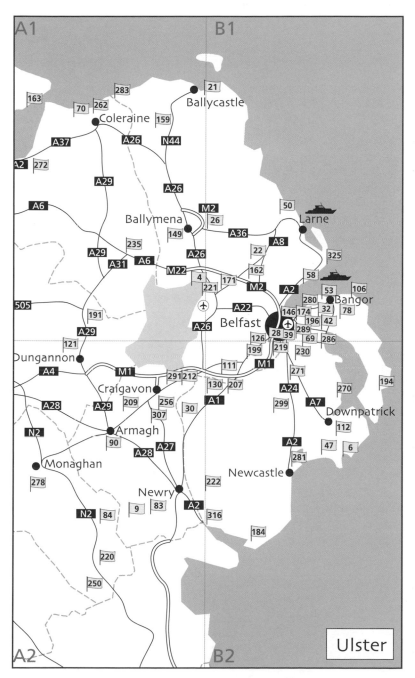

MAP 4

Flag numbers correlate with map codes in the top right-hand corner of each course review; these are *mostly* consecutive.

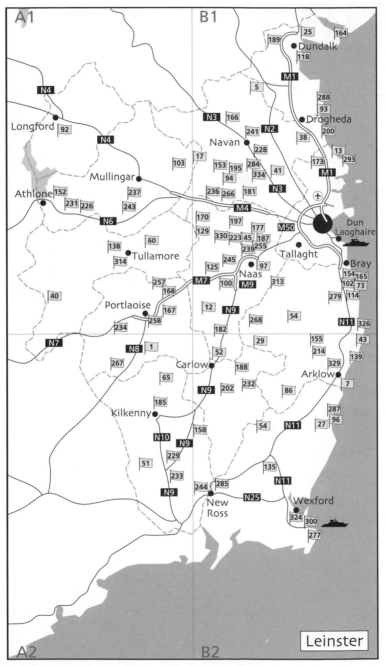

MAP 5

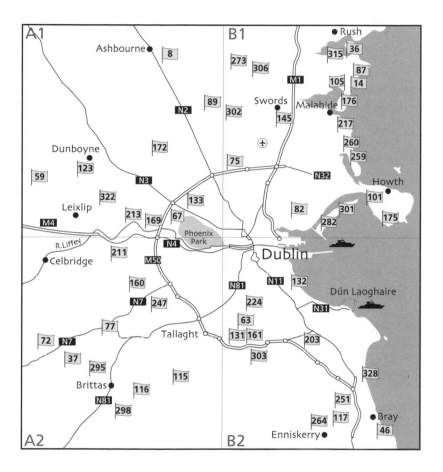

MAP 6

Flag numbers correlate with map codes in the top right-hand corner of each course review; these are *mostly* consecutive.

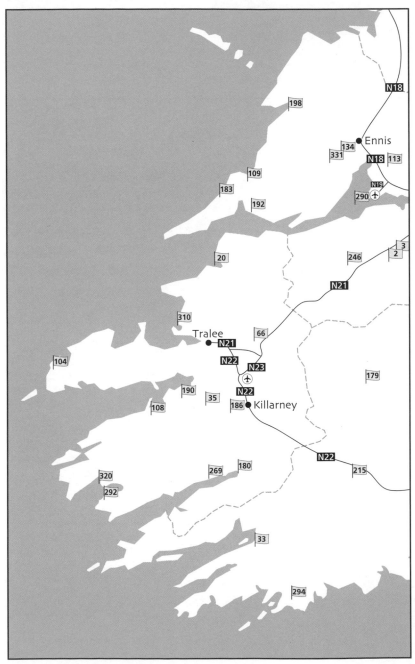

MAP 7

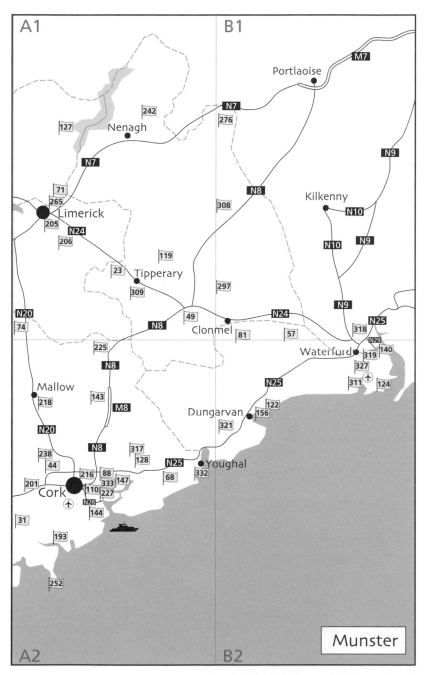

COURSE REVIEWS

ABBEYLEIX   Established 1895

AN EVOLVING COUNTRY PARKLAND

Locals I spoke to were not complimentary about Abbeyleix: what was once a fine, richly tree-covered parkland, nine-hole course had lost its way as an eighteen (added in 2000). I see their point: there is a definite shift in hole variety, and not always for the better. But you know what? It almost works in its favour. For one thing it makes the best holes really stand out.

This is a tumbling landscape where most holes have significant rises and/or hollows, and large beech trees oversee proceedings. The hilltop that dominates the 2nd, 3rd, 8th, 12th and 13th holes is the highlight of the round with trees touching the sky and the opportunity to enjoy wonderful shots.

Sitting on the edge of town, the course mixes in everything, including ponds (on the 4th and 5th) and lots of streams. Yes, there are uninteresting holes too, not to mention the quirky 7th, but the good holes keep you invigorated.

It is short for a par 72 but it offers plenty of challenges. It's not the sort of dynamic setting or beautiful design that grabs the headlines, but it does give you a full golf workout in a pleasant, country setting. It is excellent value, too. Now, if they could only do something about the pokey clubhouse . . .

FAVOURITE HOLE
Par 4 12th. 268 yards. The hole climbs straight up the hill with two big sentry trees on either side of the fairway near the top. The green is set into the wood. Beautiful. And short.

TOUGHEST HOLE
Par 4 7th. 256 yards. Index 7 should tell you something. It is a sharp, late dog-leg. You hit down to what looks like a simple landing area, but there is a stream in front of and behind it. To open up the green you have to land in a space of about 15 yards.

POINTS								
CD	A	G/F	B/W	L	F	V	G Ex	Total
14	8	7	8	7	5	9	15	73

THE COURSE
- Par 72
- Length: 6,059 yards
- Abbeyleix Golf Club, Rathmoyle, Abbeyleix, Co. Laois
- Tel: +353 (0) 57 873 1450
- www.abbeyleixgolfclub.ie
- Green Fees: €25–€30

COURSES NEARBY
Castlecomer
Mountrath
Portlaoise
Rathdowney

ADARE   Established 1995

BIG AND GLORIOUS

I imagine that the beautiful flow of this course might be seen as too American – it was designed by Robert Trent Jones – but the lush environment is 100 per cent Irish. In terms of the 'wow' factor, it is easily in the top three parkland courses in the country and the elegant walk to the first tee will only add to the excitement. The remarkable trees, the big lakes, the River Maigue and Adare Manor create a majestic setting, and the holes simply float through it all – every one as individual as the next. There are no climbs, no long walks, just perfect, manicured parkland golf.

The course is seriously tough. Unlike Fota Island and Mount Juliet – two other big parkland courses – you are not treated with kid gloves. The rough clings viciously and the heavily shaped bunkers are everywhere. They have been placed to interrupt the eye as it looks to the green, and they can create no end of problems, especially as the sand seems rather hard. And they squeeze approaches to greens. You have to find the fairways on this long course to give yourself any sort of chance, and the big greens have sweeping

surfaces so don't expect an easy ride, if and when you find them.

Adare has hosted the Irish Open (2007–2008) and the clubhouse is everything you would expect from such a prestigious course. I imagine the professionals find it a serious challenge, and you will certainly be overawed by it all. Big, colourful, vibrant and beautiful.

FAVOURITE HOLE
Par 4 13th. 407 yards. Another perfectly tree-enclosed hole, with one lone tree on the right adding drama as the fairway tips over the crest and then down to the green. Two good shots needed, but both are gorgeous. The 16th will make your knees buckle.

TOUGHEST HOLE
Par 5 18th. 511 yards. An absolute beast that has the wide river all along the left as you head for Adare Manor. You cross the river to reach the green, or try to swim it, as the 2008 Irish Open winner (Richard Finch) attempted. Play it as a three-shotter.

POINTS								
CD	A	G/F	B/W	L	F	V	G Ex	Total
19	10	10	8	7	10	8	20	92

THE COURSE
- Par 72
- Length: 6,590 yards
- Adare Golf Club, Adare, Co. Limerick
- Tel: +353 (0) 61 605274
- www.adaregolfclub.com
- Green Fees: €80–€125

COURSES NEARBY
Adare Manor
Limerick
Limerick County
Rathbane

ADARE MANOR   Established 1900

AROUND THE RUINS

First off, this is not the Irish Open course. Adare is next door. The names cause confusion, but they are side by side and tee boxes almost merge early on, at the third.

There can't be many courses that boast an old graveyard and the ruins of a large abbey. The stunning abbey holds a few tee boxes and greens. There are also the remains of a large castle behind the 1st green and you walk around them to the 2nd tee. It all makes for a dramatic setting, and that's before you consider the huge, mature trees that flood the course with colour. It is a beautiful location and should offer thrilling golf, but what was a nine-hole course has been squeezed to create a short eighteen (six par 3s). There are also two 'quirks' that a visitor must be aware of for safety reasons: dangerous walks take you from green to tee (to reach the 13th, you cross the 5th and 10th, and you walk back down the 11th to reach the 12th); and combined tee boxes hold the 5th and 18th, and the 4th, 14th and 17th.

And yet, if you ignore these complaints, there are some lovely holes. The 7th is blissful (see below), the 8th is a long par 3 and is the best of the one-shotters and the par 3 14th hits straight into the abbey (see photo on inside back cover). Even on the average holes some majestic tee box and green settings make them appealing.

It is an interesting mix of a beautiful setting and holes that interrupt each other. Odd, but worth a visit.

FAVOURITE HOLE

Par 4 7th. 366 yards. This glorious dog-leg drops down towards a stand of enormous cedars, with a dark, airy wood along the left. It then heads left to a green that could be made far more dramatic.

TOUGHEST HOLE

Par 4 4th. 330 yards. The drive is through a very narrow gap in the trees to a blind-ish fairway, but it is the dog-leg that awaits you that causes the problems because the scorecard diagram does not do it justice.

POINTS

CD	A	G/F	B/W	L	F	V	G Ex	Total
13	9	6	7	7	6	7	14	69

THE COURSE

- Par 69
- Length: 5,764 yards (blue/white tees)
- Adare Manor Golf Club, Adare, Co. Limerick
- Tel: +353 (0) 61 396 204
- www.adaremanorgolfclub.com
- Green Fees: €30

COURSES NEARBY
Adare
Limerick
Limerick County
Rathbane

ALLEN PARK   Established 1997

GOOD, PLAIN FUN

Municipal courses vary dramatically in quality and there is a sense of pot luck when you arrive at one. Allen Park doesn't look like much but you'll be surprised at what you find. The landscape is flat, and mature trees are few and far between (many young trees have been planted), but you have lots of space – both between holes and on fairways. It makes driving inviting and it is always comfortable off the tee. And yet your eye will be drawn to the bunkers that protrude rudely into fairways. They look good, they're well positioned, and this is repeated around and in front of greens. It gives the holes much-needed character. On such flat land this is the main defence and you will find several flags tucked right behind the traps. The greens look good too, and many have sharp slopes dropping from the back. There is plenty of room around them, despite the bunkering, so you can get away with poor approaches.

Three lakes on the formulaic and straight front nine are countered by a more entertaining routing and dog-legs on the back nine. Some deep rough adds vibrancy and lots of gorse has been planted, which will add nice dashes of colour in the future.

On each nine, the two par 5s are back to back, and they include Index 1 and 2. The 11th and 17th holes are two par 3s that sit side by side and they are exactly the same length.

For a par 72 it is extremely relaxing golf and the quality is unexpected.

FAVOURITE HOLE
Par 4 4th. 304 yards. Nice and short, and named 'Oak' for the lone tree on the left of the fairway. More of a kink than a dog-leg, it begs for a big tee shot.

TOUGHEST HOLE
Par 5 6th. 547 yards. Index 1 is a straight hole with water on the right. The narrow approach between a big line of beeches make this the trickiest proposition on the course.

POINTS								
CD	A	G/F	B/W	L	F	V	G Ex	Total
13	7	7	8	5	6	9	14	69

THE COURSE
- Par 72
- Length: 6,343 yards
- Allen Park Golf Club, 45 Castle Road, Antrim, Co. Antrim, BT41 4NA
- Tel: +44 (0) 28 9442 9001 (048 from Rep. of Ire.)
- www.antrim.gov.uk/allenpark
- Green Fees: £17.50–£19.50

COURSES NEARBY
Ballyclare
Galgorm Castle
Greenacres
Hilton Templepatrick
Massereene

ARDEE   Established 1911

TICKS THE BOXES

If you plotted excitement in graph form, Ardee would cruise along at 70 per cent, with strong spikes at the 3rd, 8th, 9th, 11th, 13th and then the 16th to 18th. It is a course that does everything well without quite taking your breath away, although some of the beech trees are astounding. Ardee looks like a flat, open, parkland course from the 1st tee. This is not the case. There are great rolls to some fairways which make for entertaining driving, even hiding greens on the 14th to 16th. Elsewhere the mature tree-lined fairways lead you beautifully in to the greens, and provide several glorious tee box settings. A wide water-filled ditch also slides across four holes. On two of these, the water will trouble big hitters and, generally, you will find that hazards, like fairway bunkers, have been placed with length in mind. For most of the round you have room off the tee but length can prove more troublesome.

Ardee would probably push the par 3 13th as their signature hole: a 200-yard shot over a pretty duck-laden lake that stretches from tee to green. As a visitor, this is not your tee box, but it is worth hitting from the back tees to appreciate it fully. The most stunning green setting is the 16th, where a wood on three sides also makes this the toughest approach of the day.

The only inconsistency that niggled was the D-shaped water in front of the 11th. It looks wrong, especially as it is one of the prettiest holes.

FAVOURITE HOLE
Par 4 11th. 336 yards. The maturity of the trees makes this hole. There are some huge beeches along the right (17th tee) and a lone birch in the fairway which is your line. The green is visible but slightly down to your left. Ignore the ugly pond.

TOUGHEST HOLE
Par 4 18th. 404 yards. The toughest drive. Trees squeeze the tee box on the right, and more trees on the left force you towards a landing area you cannot see. If you get it right the green is in view above you.

POINTS									
CD	A	G/F	B/W	L	F	V	G Ex		Total
14	7	7	7	5	9	7	15		71

THE COURSE
- Par 71
- Length: 6,289 yards
- Ardee Golf Club, Townparks, Ardee, Co. Louth
- Tel: +353 (0) 41 685 3227 www.ardeegolfclub.com
- Green Fees: €30–€40

COURSES NEARBY
Headfort
Mannan Castle
Nuremore

ARDGLASS   Established 1896

FRESH AND BEAUTIFUL

Since I was on my own on the timesheet, Ardglass's pro (Philip Farrell) took pity on me, and I got to play in the presence of real talent. It didn't hurt that he could tell me what line to take and where to land the ball. Ardglass may be short but it demands excellent positioning, so Phil's help made a big difference.

Ardglass does not always feel like a links, with its clifftops, minimal dunes and stretch of flatter holes. But it has sea views, masterful tee shots at every turn and cunning approaches to greens. The 1st (play off the whites) asks you to hit over rock that quickly becomes cliffs, and starts a stunning opening run. The cannons in front of the remarkable fourteenth-century clubhouse (formerly Ardglass Castle) point you in the right direction.

The course is often discussed in terms of the excellent holes and then the rest, but that is unfair. The opening (the 1st to 5th) along the rugged clifftops is mesmerising, with the 1st rising to what resembles a rocky fort entrance, and then the 2nd to 5th taking you as close to the edge as possible, between rocky knolls, around a yawning chasm and down through the rugged landscape. Magnificent. The 10th, 11th and 12th are also superb: the par 5 11th sweeps you around the water's edge with a huge sand bank to the left. It is sandwiched delightfully between two inspiring par 3s (see below). The 18th is a tantalising finish that hits onto a severely tilted fairway below.

So, are the other holes weak? Perhaps they are a little too open – as you come down the 4th, players are spread out and look like ants – but great holes nonetheless. You won't leave disappointed.

FAVOURITE HOLES
Par 3s 10th and 12th. Two stunning tee shots of about 200 yards, both to low greens and both needing less club than you think. Each offers a beautiful backdrop: one of Coney Island, the other of St John's Lighthouse across the bay.

TOUGHEST HOLE
Par 4 13th. 333 yards. One of only two blind drives, the fairway falls away right, with bunkers left. After that, the land drops sneakily to the green so go down a club and punch it in.

POINTS

CD	A	G/F	B/W	L	F	V	G Ex	Total
17	8	9	9	10	7	10	18	88

THE COURSE
- Par 70
- Length: 5,791 yards
- Ardglass Golf Club, Castle Place, Ardglass, Co. Down
- Tel: +44 (0) 28 4484 1219 (048 from Rep. of Ire.)
- www.ardglassgolfclub.com
- Green Fees: £43–£62

COURSES NEARBY
Ardglass
Bright Castle
Kirkistown Castle
Ringdufferin

ARKLOW Established 1927

A TIDY LITTLE LINKS

There is always that sense of anticipation as you roll in through the front gates of a golf club, wherever it is. And when you see the course laid out below you in the morning sunshine, there is a real motivation to get to the 1st tee.

Arklow is a sweet little links. True, it's not in the premier league, but it has the undulating fairways, the low-lying dunes, some narrow brooks, and bunkering and greens to die for. Most flags are within view and there are no blind shots. Fairways are wide enough not to hurt and there are some nice feel-good elements around the place.

A par of 69 with five par 3s (four in the space of seven holes) and five short par 4s under 360 yards will still challenge all your shot-making skills, especially around the greens. Yes indeed, the greens with their sublime slopes simply melt into the landscape and can leave you with some monster putts.

There are a couple of things that frustrate: the 2nd and 6th cross dangerously, and the course is cursed by warehouses bordering the north boundary and a huge, noisy manufacturing plant to the south. Please note that the 2nd is a dog-leg right, so don't aim at the 4th green where the fairway seems to lead you.

Starting at the 13th, the course gently switches to a slightly parkland feel, with several water features between the 13th and 17th. The closing four holes are long and tough with the sneakiest of bunkers waiting out of sight for your second on the 18th.

Arklow is not altogether easy to find and there is no pro shop.

FAVOURITE HOLE

Par 4 4th. 345 yards. A beautiful, straight links hole with two flanking pairs of bunkers on the fairway. Makes for a nerve-wracking drive. The short second is to a long green and you will be caught in two minds how to play it. Good par 3s too.

TOUGHEST HOLE

Par 4 6th. 385 yards. A difficult dog-leg that sweeps right over the 2nd fairway, making distance and line very hard to judge. The green slopes down from the left.

POINTS								
CD	A	G/F	B/W	L	F	V	G Ex	Total
15	8	9	10	6	6	9	16	79

THE COURSE
- Par 69
- Length: 5,969 yards
- Arklow Golf Club, Abbeylands, Arklow, Co. Wicklow
- Tel: +353 (0) 402 32492
- www.arklowgolflinks.com
- Green Fees: €30–€40

COURSES NEARBY
Ballymoney
Courtown
European Club, The
Macreddin
Woodenbridge

ASHBOURNE   Established 1991

A LITTLE MORE LIFE PLEASE

Ashbourne is in the commuter belt for Dublin, so a golf course here is ideal for the weekend wind-down. It certainly has a good membership, but the course only comes to life occasionally – the 11th to 15th most notably. If you want to stand over a ball and be intrigued, challenged and entertained by the shot you have to play, it doesn't happen often enough. It is a relaxing and straightforward 'vanilla' course that doesn't set the blood boiling. Some mint chip would be nice.

You are in open, undulating countryside and there are not many natural features to get your teeth into. As a result there is a lot of mounding that defines fairways and greens, well-placed young trees and a heavy reliance on Broadmeadow River, which runs along the bottom of the course, appearing at the 2nd, 3rd, 11th, 12th, 13th and 14th – the most vibrant holes. The river is well used and appears at just the right moments.

Hole 2 is a short, downhill par 3 with a good pond to the right; the par 4 3rd is tricky with a blind drive over a sloping fairway that runs into a bunker – your second is to a green that sits just over the river: the 11th to 15th is a fine stretch with more depth to the design and far more thrilling shots.

It is a course that will attract many societies, but travelling golfers will find more appeal elsewhere.

FAVOURITE HOLE
Par 5 14th. 471 m. The stream slips along the right-hand side of the hole, pushing you towards a bunker. It continues to the right as the hole moves upwards to a well-bunkered green.

TOUGHEST HOLE
Par 4 12th. 358 m. Even with a good drive your second is scary. Water is everywhere and if you don't stick to the green, your ball will go into water or the bunker – if you're lucky.

POINTS								
CD	A	G/F	B/W	L	F	V	G Ex	Total
13	6	6	7	5	8	6	12	63

THE COURSE

- Par 71
- Length: 6,289 yards
- Ashbourne Golf Club, Archerstown, Ashbourne, Co. Meath
- Tel: +353 (0) 1 835 2005
  www.ashbournegolfclub.ie
- Green Fees: €25–€30

COURSES NEARBY
Corrstown
Roganstown
St Margaret's
Swords Open

ASHFIELD   Established 1990

PYLONS PILE IT ON

This is farmland, with some entertaining slopes that roller-coast their way around the course. You are not going to come here for quality golf (the greens are poor), or stunning vistas (it's gentle countryside), or clever design (the holes go back and forth with single lines of trees dividing holes), or length (par 69), but this is a peaceful spot at the end of a long, narrow lane that offers golf at its simplest. The clubhouse is better than you would expect and a couple were planning their wedding when I was at the bar, so it's a popular venue.

Pylons come into play on several holes and you are quite likely to hit the power lines with your opening drive. Elsewhere, the huge metal legs form part of the fairway, although you get relief if you are directly underneath. The course's only character comes from the sweeping and gentle hillside. You go down, you go up, you go down. Simple, but it maintains your interest because the downhill drives are fun. But hitting in to greens offers too little reward since surfaces are often hidden and there is no finesse to grab your attention. The par 3 6th is the most colourful, hitting over trees and water, while the rise up to the 18th is an intimidating finish.

Easy for societies, kids and beginners.

FAVOURITE HOLE
Par 4 10th. 344 yards. A downhill drive hitting at countryside. It is one of the more difficult tee shots, but the approach is over a dip that rises sharply to a green with fall-offs all around.

TOUGHEST HOLE
Par 4 17th. 444 yards. Index 1 and not surprising at that length. The hole is completely flat and curves gently around to the left. Two big shots. The 5th is called Wishing Well and needs a smart tee shot if you want to attack the uphill green.

POINTS

CD	A	G/F	B/W	L	F	V	G Ex	Total
11	5	4	5	6	7	7	11	56

THE COURSE
- Par 69
- Length: 5,606 yards
- Ashfield Golf Course, 44 Cregganduff Road, Newry, Co. Down, BT35 0NA
- Tel: +44 (0) 28 3086 8180 (048 from Rep. of Ire.)
- www.ashfieldgolfcourse.com
- Green Fees: £10–£22

COURSES NEARBY
Carnbeg
Cloverhill
Killin Park
Mannan Castle

ATHENRY Established 1902

REASSURINGLY GOOD

Take a good, average parkland course, sprinkle in a few flourishes, place in the oven for a few years and you'll discover a perfect, uncomplicated golfing experience. Welcome to Athenry.

I'm not talking about glamour, dramatic oak groves or sweeping rivers – I'm talking about pine- and evergreen-lined fairways that lead you back and forth to appealing green sites, shots that are tempting and rewarding, and fairways that move easily without any climbs. Then, for the extras, there are good tee box settings, some wild spots (a fairy ring on the 1st), some woody dells and hollows (the 4th), a desolate and broken wood (the 12th) and a pine forest that ensures that the closing stretch is the most exciting on the course. And then there is the revamped, plush clubhouse.

Off the tee the trouble comes from the trees; this is particularly so on those holes where the fairways gently curve around them, making the drives seem even tighter than they already are. But you still have space.

You shouldn't lose a ball and I suggest you play off the white back tees for maximum enjoyment. The green tees make it too short.

There are no views, and nothing to make you say 'wow', but you won't be disappointed. The food in the clubhouse makes it an enticing place to end your day.

FAVOURITE HOLES
Par 3s 3rd and 12th. Two par 3s that sit side by side in the prettiest corner of the course. It's woody and vibrant and the two tee shots – one up, one down – are delicious. The 16th is a beautiful, straight Index 1 par 4 into the pine wood.

TOUGHEST HOLE
Par 4 4th. 266 m. Index 18 for regulars, but as a new visitor you have a tough decision to make off the tee. Go for it, or play left and short? Your second shot is to a putting surface you can't see, which makes it very tough to judge.

POINTS								
CD	A	G/F	B/W	L	F	V	G Ex	Total
14	7	8	9	6	9	9	15	77

THE COURSE
- Par 70
- Length: 5,801 m
- Athenry Golf Club, Palmerstown, Oranmore, Co. Galway
- Tel: +353 (0) 91 794 466
- www.athenrygolfclub.net
- Green Fees: €25

COURSES NEARBY
Cregmore Park
Galway
Galway Bay
Gort

ATHLONE   Established 1892

EVERYTHING YOU COULD HOPE FOR

When asked about golf in Athlone, most golfers think of Glasson. But don't dare forget about Athlone. This is a super course that will entertain all day long. Great maturity, great shapes to the landscape, great lake views (Lough Ree is prominent on both sides of the course) and stunning challenges.

The drive down the 1st is a beautiful way to start. From a high tee, you smash your ball down onto a flat fairway below, which then curves and rises to a hidden putting surface. A big beech wood runs along the right and trees divide you from the 18th on the left. And so it continues. The course rolls magnificently and on many occasions you can't see the green's putting surface for your approach. The 9th (Index 1) is a classic example where, the farther you drive on this uphill dog-leg, the less you'll see. And then there's the 13th (see below).

What I like about Athlone is that every shot is enticing, every hole is attractive. Mature trees provide a certain panache that is often lacking on other courses, and the fairways twist to highlight the feeling. Driving is the real fun because you are invited to give it a good lash, even on the many dog-legs. But remember that this is a challenging course – and long for a par 71. One side of almost every hole is crammed with serious danger and approaches are tricky, with bunkers, fall-offs and water too. Yet you cannot fail to have fun. The 11th, 12th and 16th bring you right down to the lake.

The par 3s (the 2nd and 6th) are beauties, while the 15th is an enchanting short par 4 that curves around the trees (and hidden pond).

Simply thrilling.

FAVOURITE HOLE
Par 4 16th. 407 m. Index 2. You are separated from the lake by a lovely wood. The fairway curves over the land, all the way to the green with two great shots needed. The 1st, 3rd and 15th are also excellent.

TOUGHEST HOLE
Par 4 13th. 396 m. A stunning hole that takes you over huge rolling mounds (eskers) in a massive dog-leg. It promises a blind drive (aim over the highest point of the hill) and blind second. Too unfair really, but you won't believe its shape until you see it.

POINTS

CD	A	G/F	B/W	L	F	V	G Ex	Total
16	8	9	8	8	8	10	18	85

THE COURSE

- Par 71
- Length: 5,893 m
- Athlone Golf Club, Hodson Bay, Athlone, Co. Roscommon
- Tel: +353 (0) 90 649 2073
- www.athlonegolfclub.ie
- Green Fees: €25–€40

COURSES NEARBY
Glasson
Moate
Mount Temple
Roscommon

ATHY   Established 1906

NOTHING BUT GOOD VIBES

It doesn't take long for Athy to come to life. This wonderfully natural and moving landscape is quite open, but so nicely shaped that holes ooze individuality, squeezing between shoulders of bunkers, between stands of trees, yet always displaying the open countryside around you. It works wonderfully. Some mounding has been introduced but it is subtle enough to add to the whole experience, rather than detract from it. You will find there is room off the tee, even if it looks otherwise.

It is a short course: the longest of the par 5s measures 501 yards and, with several short par 4s, it is a driver's heaven. In fact, every shot is a pleasure and you have plenty of opportunities to attack the comfortably defended greens. It is the kind of course where you want to go for your shots. You'll take on the bunkers, the gentle dog-legs and the blind shots because the course is set up to entice you. Several greens have difficult tiers and steep slopes but hitting them is fun. Bunkers on fairways and greens are well placed, and certainly give the greens good structure.

The par 3 3rd and 11th are particularly strong, hitting over hollows to tight greens, and the 5th is a strong downhill par 5 that has a pond pressed against the green on the left and a stream running across the front. It presents a dilemma for your second shot.

Not too difficult, but very rewarding and enjoyable.

FAVOURITE HOLE
Par 5 18th. 501 yards. A high tee box drives you into a tilting dog-leg – bunkers flank the left; trees the right. Begs for a big drive that then hits flat and straight to the clubhouse. Big birdie opportunity.

TOUGHEST HOLE
Par 4 16th. 413 yards. Index 1, and with two blind shots it is no surprise. You drive up a gentle slope, that dips into a hollow, before rising to an upturned saucer of a green which sits beside an old graveyard.

POINTS								
CD	A	G/F	B/W	L	F	V	G Ex	Total
15	7	8	8	7	8	10	17	80

THE COURSE
- Par 72
- Length: 6,202 yards
- Athy Golf Club, Geraldine, Athy, Co. Kildare
- Tel: +353 (0) 59 863 1729
- www.athygolfclub.com
- Green Fees: €15–€20

COURSES NEARBY
Carlow
Heath, The
Kilkea Castle
Rathsallagh

BALBRIGGAN Established 1945

AN UNEXPECTED LANDSCAPE

The clubhouse sits right beside a busy road, which does not make for a thrilling start. But when you arrive on the 1st tee, you have to reconsider: the landscape tumbles away ahead of you, curving down, right and up to the green. It is a cracking opening drive, and the approach to the green has to be perfect as the slopes are severe. Index 3. This is the start of a remarkably undulating course.

From the 13th to 18th you have great drives off high tee boxes, some raised greens and a variety of features to make the golf thoroughly entertaining. It's the same throughout, but very noticeable towards the end. And the maturity of the many pine trees lifts the course an extra notch. For me, hole 12, with no elevation, is the only dull hole. I won't deny that certain features have been squeezed in to make holes more difficult (trees, most obviously) but that should not detract from what is an enticing golfing experience.

There is good variety to hole shapes, lengths and perspectives, and the trees can cause problems if you venture too close. Take the short par 4 13th, which offers the best drive of the day. From high up to a flat fairway, the trees seem to stay well back, but it won't take much to find them.

The greens are mostly tame although some short, steep banking will be a curse if you miss the putting surface.

Consistently good.

FAVOURITE HOLE
Par 4 3rd. Probably has the most character as there is an old wall along the left with a wood behind. The fairway curves delightfully between bunkers as it trickles upwards to a picturesque green.

TOUGHEST HOLE
Par 4 9th. 353 m. The water in front of Index 1 makes the 15th the hardest approach, but the 9th is a looping hole, over a hill, around some trees and across a severe slope that just gets more severe the farther you drive. Expect your second to be on a sloping lie.

POINTS								
CD	A	G/F	B/W	L	F	V	G Ex	Total
14	7	7	7	6	7	9	16	73

THE COURSE
- Par 70
- Length: 5,681 m
- Balbriggan Golf Club, Blackhall, Balbriggan, Co. Dublin
- Tel: +353 (0) 1 841 2229
- www.balbriggangolfclub.com
- Green Fees: €35–€45

COURSES NEARBY
Beaverstown
Hollywood Lakes
Laytown & Bettystown
Skerries
Turvey

BALCARRICK   Established 1992

ON VIEW

Balcarrick is not what you expect. With the densely tree-lined Donabate clearly visible next door and both Corballis Links and The Island half a mile away, Balcarrick is an inland, open and exposed course. From the 1st you can see almost the entire course as it drifts away from you. Large windswept trees around the 1st are not continued elsewhere but they show you how wind-battered you can be.

The flat, curving landscape has been heavily mounded (in 2007) which certainly lends individuality to holes even though many are close together ('fore' will be heard). Young trees, carefully positioned, have yet to make their mark, but don't think that you are in for an easy round of golf. Sure, balls often stray onto nearby fairways, but water appears on fourteen holes: attractive ponds on eight holes, and also streams that cross fairways or run parallel to them. Dense with reeds, they are a lethal addition to an already tough course.

Rather than a thing of beauty – it's too bare and there are few views – this is a real test of your skill. You are challenged the whole way round, wind or not. Fairways weave before you, with the mounds, punishing bunkers and water jutting into your line, time and again. The fairways are not exactly generous either. And it is long (under its new guise), so hope to play from the yellow tees.

Highlights are the walk to the 2nd tee when you see lots of the course, the 3rd and 8th (par 3s), and the 12th and 17th (both with water on the right). In places, it is a touch repetitive.

FAVOURITE HOLE
Par 3 3rd. 167 m. Water runs from tee to green and slightly right to left, in a series of pretty reed-laced ponds. It is a very attractive shot, but not an easy one.

TOUGHEST HOLE
Par 3 8th. 197 m. A big hit with water in front of the green.

POINTS								
CD	A	G/F	B/W	L	F	V	G Ex	Total
14	6	7	8	5	6	8	15	69

THE COURSE
- Par 72 (white tees)
- Length: 5,883 m
- Balcarrick Golf Club, Corballis, Donabate, Co. Dublin
- Tel: +353 (0) 1 843 6957
- www.balcarrickgolfclub.com
- Green Fees: €20–€30

COURSES NEARBY
Beaverstown
Corballis
Donabate
Island, The
Turvey

BALLINA   Established 1910

NOT ENOUGH DRAMA

I played here over fifteen years ago and things have certainly changed. Back then I bladed a wedge clean over the clubhouse at the 18th. Today, with the new two-storey building, there would be a smashed window or two.

Yes, things have changed for the better, but not enough. Ballina sits on the edge of town, on a gentle hillside that drops down from the clubhouse. Your views down the 1st and 18th are really promising, with great curves to the lush-looking fairways and some nice tees. Sadly it doesn't last. There is not much room, so holes are a bit close in places and twice tee boxes hit over the previous green. There is not much to keep you interested either, as the holes don't grab your attention. And the quality of the course could be better – fairways particularly. The 1st, 6th, 10th and 16th are the best holes, as they look good off the tee box and use the changes in elevation to their full advantage. It is not a course to go out of your way for and the only other golf course nearby is Enniscrone.

FAVOURITE HOLE
Par 4 1st. 360 yards. A tempting downhill hole with deep trees along the course's perimeter. A great opening drive that you can really hit.

POINTS								
CD	A	G/F	B/W	L	F	V	G Ex	Total
11	4	5	5	3	6	5	8	47

THE COURSE
- Par 71
- Length: 5,778 yards
- Ballina Golf Club, Mossgrove, Shanaghy, Ballina, Co. Mayo
- Tel: +353 (0) 96 21050
- www.ballina-golf.com
- Green Fees: €30–€40

COURSES NEARBY
Enniscrone

BALLINASLOE   Established 1894

CUTTING PEAT

Down behind the pretty 11th green, and visible off the 12th tee box, is a peat bog that shows how peat is cut. It is a quirky highlight. I strongly suggest that you do not try to play Ballinasloe by cutting corners on the many dog-legs. The 5th hole is 290 m and is Index 4, and it is followed by Index 2 at 321 m, so you have been warned. Look at the hole layout on tee box boards.

This is a good, country parkland that offers many tempting shots. It is attractive and inviting. And it is dangerous. You are not about to lose a handful of balls, but the dog-legs and the swift greens demand a healthy respect that will make you stop and think before every shot.

The course falls into two types: the top half has shape and rhythm, and gently sloping fairways that move between the trees. In that regard it is a typical parkland, but then you slip down to the lower and flat half (the 8th to 14th) which was built on a bog. It works, and it has a wilder appeal with ferns and gorse bringing several holes to life.

Ballinasloe is a fine day out – although changing facilities could do with a makeover. And while the par 3s are a bit too tame, the variety elsewhere compensates. The four par 5s are the same length – around 450 m – and as long as you keep your head and drive sensibly, you will have good opportunities to score well on these and the many short par 4s.

FAVOURITE HOLE
Par 5 11th. 449 m. The bunkers look stretched across the fairway, but they show you where the fairway dog-legs right through a narrow gap. A perfect pond rests quietly on the front right of the green, making this a real risk-v.-reward hole.

TOUGHEST HOLE
Par 4 5th. 290 m. Lethal if you have not played before. It curves around the hillside, heading downhill, before it dog-legs up to the left where the green is precariously perched.

POINTS								
CD	A	G/F	B/W	L	F	V	G Ex	Total
14	7	8	7	6	7	9	14	72

THE COURSE
- Par 72
- Length: 5,677 m
- Ballinasloe Golf Club, Rosgloss, Ballinasloe, Co. Galway
- Tel: +353 (0) 9096 42126
- www.ballinasloegolfclub.ie
- Green Fees: €20–€30

COURSES NEARBY
Athlone
Birr
Glasson
Loughrea
Portumna

BALLINLOUGH CASTLE   Established 1998

A (PAT) RUDDY MARVEL

There are some things you rarely see as a golfer, namely the love and devotion required to bring a course to life. I was lucky enough to see a canvas, partially painted, that may well become a masterpiece of the future.

Ballinlough Castle is a beautiful stretch of parkland estate that provides one individual hole after another. The front nine are locked constantly in huge trees, with holes arching gracefully along naturally rolling fairways. If you drive from the back tees you will find that many of these trees wreak havoc. One hole dog-legs left around trees but you have to fade it off the tee and then draw it for your second. It is thinking golf that will hurt hackers and tempt big hitters into big mistakes. Nowhere more so than the tree-lined 476-yard par 4 2nd.

The course sits in front of a castle, not dissimilar to Delvin Castle down the road, but this course is far more majestic, more individual and even more inviting. It is still a work in progress and is a bit hand-to-mouth in terms of finances – it is scrappy around tee boxes, bunkers are grotty and greens are too lifeless in places – but much will be done in the future, including lengthening several holes (tees and greens will be pushed back into the woods, which will add significantly to some of the slightly open and stranded holes on the back nine), building a proper clubhouse and adding a practice area. As the course evolves so the hole order discussed here will change. Points are therefore temporary.

Love it for its aesthetic beauty and its potential.

FAVOURITE HOLE
Par 5 6th. 528 yards. This is a three-shotter. The fairway is not that visible from the tee so be sensible. It runs to a large, natural pond fronting a small, testing green. Go long and you will have to play downhill from a bunker towards the water.

TOUGHEST HOLE
Par 4 2nd. 476 yards. Index 1. Long, straight hole with great movement on the fairway and deep rough on either side. Huge.

POINTS

CD	A	G/F	B/W	L	F	V	G Ex	Total
16	9	7	6	7	4	10	17	76

THE COURSE
- Par 69
- Length: 6,025 yards
- Ballinlough Castle Golf Club, Clonmellon, Co. Westmeath
- Tel: +353 (0) 46 943 3760
- www.ballinloughcastle.com
- Green Fees: €20–€30

COURSES NEARBY
Delvin Castle
Glebe
Knightsbrook

BALLINROBE   Established 1895

A SUPERB MIX

When you enjoy a course as much as this, the round goes very quickly. And it was completely unexpected. I'd like them to lose the sculpted standing stones by the entrance, so you can focus on the thirteenth-century medieval tower by the 10th tee instead.

Not too many slopes/hills, but what is there has been used effectively (the 2nd, 13th and 15th). Fairways tumble along and twist themselves into several dog-legs: some severe, others less so. They all work, none better that the 2nd (see below) and you need to consider where you land the ball as the rough can hold you far too tightly.

Apart from the elegant par 3 13th, there is not anything truly dramatic. But every hole bristles with confidence, which makes for a highly enjoyable challenge. Shane and Billy, my playing partners, muttered over the huge hump on the 15th green, and muttered some more – and I along with them – at the weeping ash which, bizarrely, entirely blocks the par 5 18th green. But these are small gripes.

The course looks appetising with great shape to the land and greens, and colour that changes with every hole. Bunkers are well placed and well defined, and water comes into play on many occasions. It is often just out of sight. And then there are the stone walls and beautiful trees that add a certain old-charm elegance in this open countryside.

It is a great clubhouse, reached via a refurbished farmyard and converted outbuildings. It's a nice touch to a great day out.

FAVOURITE HOLE

Par 3 13th. 155 m. Oak trees, stone wall, pond resplendent with reeds, inviting but sloping green: you get the picture. Add a club.

TOUGHEST HOLE

Par 4 2nd. 394 m. (Probably my favourite, too.) A dog-leg that curls sharply left between drystone walls. Very difficult to judge the line so use the fairway. A long shot to a green that climbs sharply with two threatening bunkers at the entrance.

POINTS								
CD	A	G/F	B/W	L	F	V	G Ex	Total
16	8	9	8	6	10	10	17	84

THE COURSE

- Par 73
- Length: 6,119 m
- Ballinrobe Golf Club, Clooncastle, Ballinrobe, Co. Mayo
- Tel: +353 (0) 94 954 1118
- www.ballinrobegolfclub.com
- Green Fees: €25–€50

COURSES NEARBY
Castlebar
Claremorris

BALLYBOFEY & STRANORLAR   Established 1957

TAKE ME TO THE GRAVEYARD

This is a good parkland course offering pleasant golf. It combines space off the tee with some tight fairways and heavy pine trees at the start. But it is the subtle and not-so-subtle hills that bring much of the course to life. The 1st hole is a perfect example. You stand on a high tee looking across the countryside and the fairway falls away steeply. A blind drive to start is never easy and this is Index 6 at 387 m. At least the rough is wide. B & S rarely ignites into fascinating golf but, by the same token, rarely becomes dull. The best holes are well spread out: the 1st, 3rd, 5th, 7th, 8th, 11th, and the last four holes (excluding the 17th) ensure an excellent finish. The fairways have more shape and vitality at the end and you have to play smarter golf to reach unseen greens.

A lake makes a big impact at the 7th hole, the only par 5. The fairway swings around the water's edge with swans and ducks in attendance. It is a three-shotter as the green sits on the water, separated by only a bunker. The 8th tee box, also on the water, makes these the two prettiest holes. The 16th comes close when the usual tree-lined fairways suddenly introduce a huge beech. Only the 3rd and 7th can be described as dog-legs.

In terms of something different, you play around a graveyard that appears on the 12th, 13th, 14th and 15th. It is empty bar one headstone.

All in all, it is a nice, untaxing day out on a short course.

FAVOURITE HOLE
Par 4 5th. 327 m. Straight up through a swinging fairway and tall pines, the hole tilts this way and that. It looks good and your second is a tricky shot with a large, deep bunker curling around the green. Index 4.

TOUGHEST HOLE
Par 4 16th. 411 m. A viewing post by the tee box gives you your first hint. This is a blind drive over a gentle hill, but your second is also blind. An old, stone, farm building adds interest, as do the mature beeches on the left, but the green is a tame finish.

POINTS								
CD	A	G/F	B/W	L	F	V	G Ex	Total
13	7	6	7	7	7	7	14	68

THE COURSE
- Par 68
- Length: 5,225 m
- Ballybofey & Stranorlar Golf Club, Stranorlar, Co. Donegal
- Tel: +353 (0) 74 913 1093
- www.ballybofeyandstranorlar golfclub.com
- Green Fees: €20–€25

COURSES NEARBY
Letterkenny
Newtownstewart
Strabane

BALLYBUNION (CASHEN) Established 1984

AN IMPRESSIVE YOUNGER BROTHER

I played Cashen immediately after the Old Course, and I expected the excitement levels to drop. For the first two holes they did, but only because the fairways were wider and bump-and-run was out of the question. It is a matter of adapting to what Trent Jones did with this amazing piece of land. It is more mountainous and even more inspiring than the Old, and by virtue of the greens being perched up high, you get to play target golf. And that calls for entirely new skills – and balls! The rough and the bunkers are still lethal but it is quite a different golf experience – and one that links purists undoubtedly frown upon.

With greens set above violent rises, you'll have explosive shots that look both tempting and terrifying. Have you made it, or are you down the bottom? The 17th will kill many a card, with the green above a deep hollow and only a sharp drop to the beach behind. The 15th is truly stunning: your second shot faces a huge canyon far below, with a sliver of fairway winding towards the green perched on a vertical dune. Drop a ball at the edge and watch it soar. The 13th (Index 1) has similar traits, if much reduced, while the 14th has an enthralling green, wedged in the dunes, that may be impossible to hold.

Cashen is quirky but it is wonderful and terrifying, too. It does not pretend to be the Old Course, but it does pay homage to it by having back-to-back par 5s on the front nine and par 3s on the back. Short for a 72, as if that matters in the wind.

Play it after the Old.

FAVOURITE HOLE
Par 4 5th. 303 yards. Do or die. The fairway goes straight up, with the green sitting on a ledge to the right. Yes, you can go for it, but getting caught under the ledge spells the end of a birdie or even par chance. The 14th to 17th are brilliant.

TOUGHEST HOLE
Par 5 8th. 585 yards. A monster. Play short onto the plateau or try for the out-of-sight hill that will take your ball miles down to the bottom. Then you have to go all the way up again. Course management.

POINTS								
CD	A	G/F	B/W	L	F	V	G Ex	Total
17	8	10	10	9	10	10	18	92

THE COURSE
- Par 72
- Length: 5,997 yards
- Ballybunion Golf Club, Ballybunion, Co. Kerry
- Tel: +353 (0) 68 27146
- www.ballybuniongolfclub.ie
- Green Fees: €65

COURSES NEARBY
Tralee

BALLYBUNION (OLD)   Established 1893

SUPERLATIVE

Sometimes superlatives are never enough. Perhaps the word 'Ballybunion' should be a superlative itself, for I cannot do it justice here. The name Tom Watson looms large and the Irish Open was won here by Sjoland in 2000. The big dunes that hold tees and greens, the fairways that curve carelessly and beautifully between them, the views of the sea, the simple but lethal bunkering: for me, this *is* the golf experience on this island. You want for nothing. It is glorious and yet it is a true challenge that tests you to the core. You may leave broken, but you will feel sated. For golfers, this is Mecca, like Royal County Down and St Andrew's.

There is not one weak hole and, like nearby Tralee, the back nine are astoundingly good. The choices you must make are tantalising, and you will swear that you should have used the other club you were contemplating – for you will be contemplating at least one.

There are no easy shots although holes 1, 4 and 5 promise lazier drives to help you find a rhythm. The back nine are not so generous, and some holes have ledges

and fall-offs that are chasm-like, never mind huge slopes off the sides of greens.

The club boasts that its 11th is one of the best holes in the world. It probably is. But so are the 2nd, 12th and 17th.

There is an obvious upside and downside to the town's proximity: the 1st hits at a caravan park, and the 4th and 5th run alongside the road; but accommodation is plentiful and a short trip from a great clubhouse.

The 18th is a true 'love it or hate it' hole.

FAVOURITE HOLE
Par 4 11th. 400 yards (see photo). Simply superb with a huge drop to a second fairway and narrow chute into the green. The par 3 afterwards is a lethal beauty too.

TOUGHEST HOLE
Par 3 15th. 197 yards. As one-shotters go, this is a peach. A wind from any direction will increase the danger and the green sits down in the dunes, with hidden dangers all about. You could go anywhere.

POINTS								
CD	A	G/F	B/W	L	F	V	G Ex	Total
19	9	10	10	8	10	9	20	95

THE COURSE
- Par 71
- Length: 6,200 yards
- Ballybunion Golf Club, Ballybunion, Co. Kerry
- Tel: +353 (0) 68 27146
- www.ballybuniongolfclub.ie
- Green Fees: €180

COURSES NEARBY
Tralee

BALLYCASTLE   Established 1890

AN ERUPTION OF SEASIDE GOLF

Ballycastle certainly raises an eyebrow or two. From a towering clubhouse you cross the road and play five flat, average, parkland holes. The river runs alongside the 1st, and the rest surround a ruined thirteenth-century friary and graveyard. Mildly entertaining with sneaky bunkering, but nothing more.

The fun really begins on the 6th (directly in front of the clubhouse). The four best holes are explosive in shape, with the 6th called Hog's Back for obvious reasons. There is little else on the landscape but the violent hummocks and dips, and it makes your shots absolutely thrilling. The 9th is a different matter (see below), as it leads up high to another style of hole. Up here you play six holes that curve across the hilltop. Direction posts abound on the crests of hills, and while fake mounds try to add some shape, they are uninteresting holes. Except for the awesome par 3 13th, which hits out at the ocean. It is the wonderful views that make these holes. The Mull of Kintyre across the water, the Glens of Antrim and the rugged coastline all add to the experience, so take your time on the 10th and 11th. The 17th is a towering par 3 that brings you back down again.

The challenges vary considerably with the shifting styles of hole but it is not a difficult course. At times it feels more holiday-like, but you will find something to entertain you. Be sure to go to the top of the clubhouse.

FAVOURITE HOLE
Par 4 6th. 301 yards. The shape of the fairway is mesmerising, and the flag sits at the end of it all, up high and tempting. Your drive could be thrown anywhere.

TOUGHEST HOLE
Par 4 9th. 341 yards. The best hole on the course and it is Index 5. A flat fairway simply ends before a huge bank of rough rises up to a higher plain. From the tee box you can't believe it is the green you see high up there, beyond gorse and banks and rough. Brilliant.

POINTS								
CD	A	G/F	B/W	L	F	V	G Ex	Total
13	6	6	7	9	8	7	14	70

THE COURSE
- Par 71
- Length: 5,744 yards
- Ballycastle Golf Club, 2 Cushendall Road, Ballycastle, Co. Antrim, BT54 6QP
- Tel: +44 (0) 28 2076 2536 (048 from Rep. of Ire.)
- www.ballycastlegolfclub.com
- Green Fees: £25–£35

COURSES NEARBY
Ballycastle
Gracehill
Portstewart
Royal Portrush

BALLYCLARE   Established 1923

FRESH COUNTRY AIR

Well tucked away in the countryside, Ballyclare is a fresh, mature and colourful parkland course that lulls you into a relaxed pace. I'm not suggesting it is easy but it mixes up the holes to good effect. The best stretch is the 2nd to 11th with some great movement and thrills to every shot. The remaining holes go back and forth across a gentle hillside, working their way up to the clubhouse with some tricky slopes. It sounds dull but it's not. These are still good holes with solid trees, nice shapes and testing lengths (the 12th, 13th, 14th and 16th are par 4s over 400 yards from the recommended back sticks). The drive on the 18th threatens players on the 1st and 17th.

Ballyclare is a good, testing parkland with tough placement off the tee. The undulating landscape has a lot to do with it because the changes in elevation present deceptions and make you work for your par.

But here's the thing about any good course: when you walk up to the ball, you want to hit it at the inviting vista ahead of you. Ballyclare, like Cairndhu, Galgorm Castle and Gracehill, offers this in abundance. It is not about premier design – it is about getting a warm, fuzzy feeling.

The river that appears on a number of holes, the ponds on the 3rd, 7th and 11th, the big trees and the ease with which the course moves make Ballyclare a fun and rewarding round of golf. When you hit the big, shapely greens (bar the quirky par 3 16th), well defended by deep bunkers, there is a real sense of enjoyment and achievement.

The three short par 5s will help your cause.

FAVOURITE HOLE
Par 4 3rd. 431 yards. Index 1 is seriously tough, but it's a beauty. A high tee hits well down to a fairway that swings around ponds and trees. The drive must be perfect to open up the green and it is a narrow approach with the small river alongside.

TOUGHEST HOLE
Par 3 9th. 191 yards. Some long holes on the back nine will punish stray drives, but the green on the 9th gives you very little room to play with: tight bunkers, good slopes and an angled putting surface. The 10th challenges newcomers because the approach is so narrow.

POINTS

CD	A	G/F	B/W	L	F	V	G Ex	Total
14	8	8	8	6	9	10	15	78

THE COURSE
- Par 71
- Length: 6,063 yards
- Ballyclare Golf Club, 25 Springvale Road, Ballyclare, Co. Antrim, BT39 9JW
- Tel: +44 (0) 28 9332 2696 (048 from Rep. of Ire.)
- www.ballyclaregolfclub.net
- Green Fees: £22–£28

COURSES NEARBY
Carrickfergus
Greenacres
Hilton Templepatrick
Massereene

BALLYKISTEEN Established 1995

WATER BABY

Ballykisteen has a little maturing to do before it becomes a smart course, but all the essentials are here. There is good variety in terms of shape and length, and the layout moves you around constantly. It all adds enjoyment to the round. Of course, what Ballykisteen is known for is its water. Ten holes present real water hazards. Ponds are big and they threaten drives and second shots alike – and even overzealous putts (hole 8). Keep your scorecard map close. Ballykisteen describes itself as rolling parkland, which is a fair description and it explains why some hazards and greens remain out of view.

Undulating fairways, gentle dog-legs and smart greens are well protected by bunkers, but if you took the water out of the equation you could probably call this an easy course, so it should be a joy for everyone. There is plenty of room to drive (the 4th and 10th being the exceptions), and a few drives hit straight at the Galty Mountains.

The trees have yet to make a statement at Ballykisteen and they shouldn't trouble you. The same cannot be said of the rough which is 8 inches deep in places. Pat, my playing partner, duffed his drive 20 yards and we never saw it again.

Unfortunately, of the par 3s, only the 15th excites, with a drop to a green heavily protected by water. The other three are lifeless, which is a shame as there are many other good holes. The 18th is a great finish with three lots of water to overcome and a flurry of bunkers around the green.

It is tied up with a hotel, an unattractive building but with good facilities.

FAVOURITE HOLE
Par 4 11th. 395 yards. Index 1. A slightly blind drive which is best to keep left. Come over the hill and the green is in a stunning setting with a pond to the right and behind. The best second shot you will hit.

TOUGHEST HOLE
Par 4 8th. 314 yards. A blind dog-leg, of sorts. When you reach the 7th tee, look at the pond around the 8th green on your right. This makes driving at the green impossible, so hit an easy 3 iron. The green slopes sharply towards the water, so avoid the bunkers behind.

POINTS

CD	A	G/F	B/W	L	F	V	G Ex	Total
14	7	7	9	7	8	8	14	74

THE COURSE

- Par 72
- Length: 6,334 yards
- Ballykisteen Golf Club, Monard, Co. Tipperary
- Tel: +353 (0) 62 32117
- www.ballykisteengolfclub.com
- Green Fees: €25–€40

COURSES NEARBY
Cahir
County Tipperary/Dundrum
Mitchelstown
Tipperary

BALLYLIFFIN (GLASHEDY)   Established 1995

PLAY IT TWICE . . .

Two courses intertwine at Ballyliffin. Both beauties, one thundering through the high dunes, one through the low. On Glashedy, look right on the 2nd and 4th at the army of dunes, restless and menacing. They are rough, scruffy, claustrophobic and perfect, and the holes weave between them, almost of their own accord. The dunes are not as big as those at courses like Carne or Enniscrone, but they will still steal your ball.

Ballyliffin is a wonderful and famous destination tucked away at the top of Ireland – famed owing to Nick Faldo's renowned (and unsuccessful) attempt to buy the club – and the modern clubhouse is visible from a long way off. You will feel a shudder of excitement and fear on every tee box, with or without wind. You will find no more imposing or beautiful spot than the 7th tee box, the course's highest point. Glashedy Rock is a striking sight in the bay and the brutally shorn mountains reach far beyond the myriad of holes you can see below you. Then, like a roller coaster, you dive down again.

Greens are big and undulating. They welcome low and running approaches, but beware the steep fall-offs, often into the softest of pothole bunkers.

There are times when you feel lost in the dunes and, by seeing so little fairway on the curling and relatively flat dog-legs, I found some holes repetitive. There are nine holes that drift right, so a fade is an advantage. Hookers will find solace on only two holes. Off the tee a driver is not always the answer, even on the 400-yard longer back nine where the fairways widen. I hit a 3 iron on six holes. For some, that approach might feel restrictive.

FAVOURITE HOLE
Par 4 18th. 367 yards. A great finish. A dog-leg right that offers a large fairway landing before it sneaks through a gate of big dunes. Positioning is everything. Other great holes are the 4th and 13th – two par 5s – and the par 3s.

TOUGHEST HOLE
Par 3 7th. 127 yards. Index 18 apparently. Put some wind in the equation and this is nerve-wracking. The tee is sky-high with the dune descending sharply to a lake and two pot bunkers. The green is big but you will be looking at the lake.

POINTS								
CD	A	G/F	B/W	L	F	V	G Ex	Total
17	8	9	10	9	10	9	18	90

THE COURSE
- Par 72
- Length: 6,464 yards
- Ballyliffin Golf Club, Ballyliffin, Inishowen, Co. Donegal
- Tel: +353 (0) 74 9376 119
- www.ballyliffingolfclub.com
- Green Fees: €70

COURSES NEARBY
Greencastle
North West

BALLYLIFFIN (OLD) Established 1973

... YES, TWICE

The whole attraction of Ballyliffin, aside from its obvious quality and wild coastal location, is the myriad of dunes through which the courses run. Glashedy certainly puts you in the heart of the larger dunes, but you won't find the same drama on the Old. Instead, you will discover fairways more easily described as oversized bubble-wrap. Hit a good drive down the middle and watch that ball dance. Try bump-and-run to the green and be prepared for some angst. These fairways are scintillating and only as nature intended. Several greens follow suit, albeit in a gentler tone.

It is less difficult than Glashedy, with more room to play and the opportunity to try one of a number of shots. One thing in common with Glashedy is the demands off the tee. Once again you have holes that dog-leg slightly around dunes and past bunkers to a green you can see, but choosing the club and the direction in which to hit your ball will prove vexing. Why not hit a driver and a 3 iron off one tee – say the 8th – and see how you end up? Obviously, in the wind, it can still prove a monster but it is accessible to

golfers of all abilities, and is all the friendlier for it.

The Old Links finishes with a flourish as you finally get to see the waves as well as hear them. The 14th tee sits above the beach and starts a vicious homeward run into the wind. The 15th and 16th, at 407 and 389 yards respectively, can destroy any golf card. And Nick Faldo's bunkers have certainly made things harder.

Thrilling, from start to finish. And superb facilities.

FAVOURITE HOLE
Par 5 18th. 547 yards. Like Glashedy, the par 3s are beauties, but the 18th pips it. After four holes into the wind, you should enjoy it at your back. As long as you stay well right of the fairway bunkers, you'll be surprised how close you can get in two.

TOUGHEST HOLE
Par 4 15th. 407 yards. Brutal. Look at the green off to the right, over the low, dense dunes and realise they want you to get there in two shots. Two meticulously placed bunkers threaten your drive and finding the fairway is reward in itself.

POINTS								
CD	A	G/F	B/W	L	F	V	G Ex	Total
18	8	9	10	9	10	10	18	92

THE COURSE

- Par 72
- Length: 6,464 yards
- Ballyliffin Golf Club, Ballyliffin, Inishowen, Co. Donegal
- Tel: +353 (0) 74 9376 119
- www.ballyliffingolfclub.com
- Green Fees: €60

COURSES NEARBY
Greencastle
North West

BALLYMASCANLON   Established 1980s

SHORT AND COLOURFUL

A par 68 with only one par 5 might not appeal to some people, but Ballymascanlon is highly entertaining. I'm not talking about superior quality but this mature parkland setting has plenty to offer. Massive trees abound here – the cedars by the hotel/clubhouse are monstrous and there are beeches towering over several tee boxes – and holes like the 8th, 10th, 17th and 18th are in perfect tree-lined settings. The variety is quite startling and adds blazes of colour. You can understand why there is a path winding through the old estate for people to visit the Proleek Dolmen, a megalithic portal tomb behind the 5th green.

I am sure many people would call this a hotel golf course (it's not GUI-affiliated) but there are some seriously good holes here, and the run from the 7th to 12th will test you severely. Trees get very close and several water features appear – the 7th has a pond and then a wide stream you can barely see. They are all relatively short holes, which means you could leave your driver in the bag all day – even on the short par 5 – and play a smart round

of golf. Greens are not difficult to attack (the 7th, 12th and 18th excepted) and they are tame.

Without being insulting, it is a basic course (tee boxes, bunkers) but with a huge amount going for it. With another thirty acres and a serious designer's eye, Ballymascanlon could be great.

At par 68, crammed with colour, variety and value, I imagine this is society heaven.

FAVOURITE HOLE
Par 4 10th. 311 yards. Play from the whites (363) for the full pleasure. Two stretches of water have to be crossed, a tree pushes in from the left, and it is a narrow fairway that requires your best drive. Hit it and you'll be smiling for the next few holes.

TOUGHEST HOLE
Par 4 7th. 374 yards. Another tempting drive as this heads down towards a pond, before the fairway rises into the green and a huge old wall behind. Your second shot is the tougher shot – crossing a wide stream and negotiating tight bunkers around the green.

POINTS

CD	A	G/F	B/W	L	F	V	G Ex	Total
14	8	6	7	7	8	9	15	74

THE COURSE
- Par 68
- Length: 5,456 yards
- Ballymascanlon Golf Club, Dundalk, Co. Louth
- Tel: +353 (0) 42 935 8210
- www.ballymascanlon.com
- Green Fees: €30–€36

COURSES NEARBY
Dundalk
Greenore
Killin Park

BALLYMENA   Established 1903

THE EARTH IS FLAT

Ballymena is a short par 68 and one of the flattest courses you'll play. It sits just off a busy road and has done well to squeeze in eighteen holes – there are some cross-overs and shared tee boxes. Its trick is to throw narrow fairways at you, and you'll encounter enough subtle dog-legs to add to this difficulty. But it is not an exciting course. There is nothing to jump out and grab you. The course boasts a heathland flair, but this is only obvious around the 6th, 7th, 8th and 18th, and if this could spread across the course more – or even just put some gorse around greens – it would add some badly needed vibrancy.

Holes 1, 2 and 13 (which you cross to reach the 3rd) are simply uninteresting. The dark conifers are scattered about but don't add much. In fact, from the 18th fairway you can see all the way across to the 11th on the other side of the course. It does get better, with the heathland touches providing colour and danger, as well as more interestingly shaped fairways. And the conifers get denser. Still, you are unlikely to lose a ball and even with the narrow fairways and conifers you will find room to play. There is good bunkering, with some high faces, and this is the only defence to very accessible, small, flat greens. Driving on holes 5, 6, 8, 9, 15 and 17 are the best shots of the day.

Slemish Mountain may dominate, but even that won't set the pulse racing. Then again, if all you want to do is knock a ball about, the value at Ballymena is hard to beat.

FAVOURITE HOLE
Par 4 18th. 290 m. One of the heathland holes with gorse flanking the tee left and right as you head back to the clubhouse directly behind the green. A good scoring opportunity.

TOUGHEST HOLE
Par 4 6th. 323 m. With heavy gorse and rough heather on the left, this is one of the harder drives. It is a gentle dog-leg left with bunkers on the fairway and a quirky conifer bending over at 45 degrees.

POINTS

CD	A	G/F	B/W	L	F	V	G Ex	Total
11	5	5	7	6	7	6	11	58

THE COURSE

- Par 68
- Length: 5,054 m
- Ballymena Golf Club, 128 Raceview Road, Broughshane, Ballymena, Co. Antrim, BT42 4HY
- Tel: +44 (0) 28 2586 1487 (048 from Rep. of Ire.)
- www.ballymenagolfclub.com
- Green Fees: £23–£27

COURSES NEARBY
Antrim
Cairndhu
Galgorm Castle
Massereene
Moyola Park

BALLYMONEY   Established 1993

CONCAVE AND CONVEX

This family-owned course has a lot going for it. I'm not saying it is fancy or dramatic, but it knows what it is doing when it comes to the basics. Good lines of young trees separate fairways, greens are generous and have good backdrops of trees or Tara Hill (the 2nd, 4th, 5th, 10th, 13th and 16th specifically) as well as some tricky tiers, and holes have used the flow of the land very well indeed. The two nines are divided by a small country road, but they are also divided by the shape of their holes. The fairways on the front nine have a tendency to fall down to a small stream in a gentle depression before rising to a green that is at eye level. Holes 2, 3, 4, 6, 7 and 9 all do this in some shape or other, offering great tee shots and attractive approaches to heavily bunker-fronted greens. The second nine do the reverse, with holes 11, 12, 13, 14 and 17 all requiring you to breach the crest of a gentle hill. Most of these then tumble down the other side, but the 17th sits up proudly, defended by a lone and distinctly irksome tree. Only the 10th and 16th revert to the style of the opening holes.

For the most part (excluding the 13th and 17th) trees divide fairways and rarely feature on the holes themselves, while water appears from time to time – on the 1st, 10th and 18th particularly. The facilities are basic, with a driving range next door, but for these green fees you can't complain. Not for connoisseurs but good, simple golf.

FAVOURITE HOLE
Par 4 16th. 330 yards. The prettiest-looking hole with Tara Hill as a backdrop. It drops down into a hollow and then rises quickly before stretching out towards the green. Chances are you will have a blind second out of the dip.

TOUGHEST HOLE
Par 4 17th. 355 yards. It is a long drive up the hill with fairway bunkers, but this all comes down to the tree sitting in your way, 50 yards short of the green. Over it or around it?

POINTS								
CD	A	G/F	B/W	L	F	V	G Ex	Total
12	7	6	7	6	5	8	13	64

THE COURSE
- Par 71
- Length: 5,987 yards
- Ballymoney Golf Club, Ballymoney, Co. Wexford
- Tel: +353 (0) 53 942 1976
- www.ballymoneygolfclub.com
- Green Fees: €20–€25

COURSES NEARBY
Courtown
Seafield

BALMORAL Established 1914

FLAT AS YOU LIKE

Balmoral sits just off the main road. It has plenty of houses around it, but fortunately not to the point of distraction. And it is flat. Little hints of movement appear here and there, giving a bit of character to the front nine's fairways, but the only excitement appears on the back nine when a watery ditch drops out of sight on a few holes (the 15th most notably) and a remarkably unexpected drop appears in front of the 18th green (see below).

You are looking at a par 69 with two par 5s under 500 yards. Mind you, the shortest par 4 is 341 yards. Essentially it is a tree-lined but open parkland course, and shots into greens will be the biggest challenge as some well-placed bunkers and mounding will keep you guessing. Even so, you can score here as there are few dangers off the tee and what you see is what you get. It is not punishing by any means.

The design offers a straightforward and calm round of golf. A few woods are dotted about – again, the back nine have more to offer – and these serve to separate some stretches of holes.

Elsewhere, several holes are on display at any one time, and balls will get sprayed around dangerously (I had two on the 1st fairway from the 9th). And the 1st and 17th share a green – and a rather small green at that.

I'm not giving Balmoral a hard time – it serves up a gentle experience – and squeezed between the sublime Malone and Belvoir Park, it is a perfectly different experience.

FAVOURITE HOLE
Par 4 15th. 359 yards. A straight drive on a hole that dog-legs late and right. The second must come over trees (if you're not long enough) and a good deep dip that holds water, before rising smartly to the green.

TOUGHEST HOLE
Par 4 18th. 439 yards. Only Index 4, but this is long and has the hardest second shot of the day – there are 10-foot trees right across the fairway, hiding a substantial dip behind. It holds bunkers and a rise to the green, meaning your second has to be inch-perfect.

POINTS								
CD	A	G/F	B/W	L	F	V	G Ex	Total
12	6	6	7	6	7	7	13	64

THE COURSE
- Par 69
- Length: 6,034 yards
- Balmoral Golf Club, 518 Lisburn Road, Belfast, BT9 6GX
- Tel: +44 (0) 28 9066 7747 (048 from Rep. of Ire.)
- www.balmoralgolf.com
- Green Fees: £22–£27

COURSES NEARBY
Belvoir Park
Dunmurry
Lambeg
Malone

BALTINGLASS   Established 1928

DIFFERENT NINES, DIFFERENT GOLF

The 1st at Baltinglass is cruel. This is a peaceful, country parkland course and to send you straight uphill for 359 m may not be your idea of a gentle introduction. It is a good hole, with lots of interest (trees, stream, hidden green) but it knocks the wind out of your sails.

A second nine were added in 2002, starting at the pretty par 3 2nd, and these add a new and exciting dimension to the course. Accuracy is called for as they slide across the hillside, taking you ever higher, between tall pines and ash. The spartan trunks give the holes a dramatic air and they feel almost oppressive. Stray off-line and you're in real trouble. The fairways tilt dangerously, becoming flat for only brief moments, so this is no time to be brash. There is something rather majestic about the whole thing and there are strong green settings, with countryside and sky backdrops.

The 11th takes you back down parallel to the 1st and it is the best drive of the day, hitting over trees. The 12th to 18th do not have the drama of the hillside holes, but you will have far more room and variety. From that perspective you will have more fun down here. The fairways flow easily, with good shapes, and they are very inviting off the tee. The claustrophobic trees are gone, giving way to mature parkland specimens that sit well back. Greens are always on show from the tee (there are three gentle dog-legs up above), which adds flavour to the holes but, with hidden putting surfaces and effective bunkering, there are plenty of challenges to overcome.

The clubhouse is Tardis-like: small from the outside, big inside.

FAVOURITE HOLE

Par 5 3rd. 444 m. Your first introduction to the hillside woods. A superb-looking parkland hole off a high tee. Not too narrow, but trees squeeze you at 220 m. The flag hides behind a steep shoulder and a tall stand of more trees to the left.

TOUGHEST HOLE

Par 4 7th. 400 m. Long, uphill, tight, sloping fairway, trees, hidden putting surface. Need I say more?

| POINTS | | | | | | | | |
CD	A	G/F	B/W	L	F	V	G Ex	Total
15	8	7	7	8	7	8	15	75

THE COURSE

- Par 71
- Length: 5,737 m
- Baltinglass Golf Club, Baltinglass, Co. Wicklow
- Tel: +353 (0) 59 648 1350
- www.baltinglassgolfclub.ie
- Green Fees: €20–€30

COURSES NEARBY

Carlow
Kilkea Castle
Killerig Castle
Rathsallagh

BANBRIDGE   Established 1911

THE HILLS ARE ALIVE

Banbridge may have been here for a long time, but as you rise and fall through the troughs you can easily see the course's evolution – farmland butts up to the course for much of the round. It does a good job taking you in different directions and giving you different feels as you cross over small lanes and through rows of hedges to reach the different sections. It adds to the diversity and interest on what is essentially a short, lively parkland course. There's no fuss, but there is plenty of scope for fun.

From the clubhouse you can't believe that you are playing a seriously hilly course. The tempting 1st offers plenty of movement but it does not look too severe. You won't think that when you stand on the 5th, Index 1, facing the best drive of the day. Be careful not to confuse the tee with the 10th (the second best tee shot of the day) alongside. Both offer soaring tee shots. The 5th is the start of the six really hilly holes, ending on the 11th, but the changes in elevation are everywhere. There are many inviting shots, but it also means that plenty of greens are hidden

around corners and over crests. On a short course (eight par 4s under 340 yards) that can be very dangerous for big hitters and neighbouring golfers.

The quality is of the straightforward type and greens are OK, being quite small and perched in places. It is entertainingly shaped and will please everyone, especially higher handicappers and societies.

FAVOURITE HOLE
Par 4 5th. 358 yards. The hole drops sharply from the tee to a white cottage, then rises almost as fast to a green that is visible from the tee, but not for your approach. On the 6th you have a great approach shot with a pond and trees creating the green setting.

TOUGHEST HOLE
Par 3 10th. 220 yards. Downhill, your tee shot will run from right to left if you land short – and a very sharp ledge on the green's left edge will throw you into the trees. If you go long you will run straight into the perimeter hedge. Play for the front.

POINTS								
CD	A	G/F	B/W	L	F	V	G Ex	Total
13	7	6	6	6	7	8	14	67

THE COURSE
- Par 69
- Length: 5,395 yards
- Banbridge Golf Club, 116 Huntly Road, Banbridge, Co. Down, BT32 3UR
- Tel: +44 (0) 28 4066 2211 (048 from Rep. of Ire.)
- www.banbridgegolfclub.net
- Green Fees: £17–£22

COURSES NEARBY
Edenmore
Lurgan
Portadown
Tandragee

BANDON   Established 1909

CONSISTENTLY DIFFERENT PARKLAND

The variety at Bandon is like a five-course dinner, although it doesn't look particularly appetising from the clubhouse. The four holes on show are the least interesting, with straight lines of pine/evergreen. But much better is to come: to whet the appetite, holes 2 to 4 improve the tone, with the 4th being a little beauty (look for the green as you come off the 3rd), before a pretty walk takes you down to the 'castle' holes. Castle Bernard stands sadly neglected, overlooking three very young-looking holes, including the tough par 3 7th (182 yards) where the castle provides an impressive backdrop. You then cross the road for a couple of tough driving holes – the 11th has steep banks left and right – before the dainty, downhill 'filler' par 3 of 115 yards. Then comes the super stretch where big trees (oak mainly) dominate the holes. Hole 12 dog-legs down into a mature tree setting, and offers the drive of the day, before the 13th, 14th and 15th run alongside a deep wood – all OB – with the 13th and 14th proving exceptionally tough off the tee (Index 5 and 1). You

finish back at the duller holes near the clubhouse, and the 18th is a downhill par 3, where the water feature looks out of place.

So, with all that variety, you are going to find something that appeals to you. Obviously, with all the different types of hole and some sloping fairways and greens, the challenges vary considerably, but with its good length and shapes, it is entertaining. On some courses such variety does not work. Here it does.

FAVOURITE HOLE
Par 4 13th. 412 yards. Only your best drive will make it through the tough flanks of majestic trees. The ones on the right are up high on the bank and dominate your vision completely. The green is lethal, so be below the hole.

TOUGHEST HOLE
Par 4 14th. 415 yards. Index 1, and while the drive is more straightforward than the 13th (both OB on the left) the approach is very tough as the OB almost comes to the greenside.

POINTS								
CD	A	G/F	B/W	L	F	V	G Ex	Total
14	8	7	6	7	9	7	16	74

THE COURSE
- Par 71
- Length: 6,323 yards
- Bandon Golf Club, Castle Bernard, Bandon, Co. Cork
- Tel: +353 (0) 23 8841111
- www.bandongolfclub.com
- Green Fees: €35–€40

COURSES NEARBY
Kinsale
Lee Valley
Macroom
Old Head

BANGOR Established 1903

BRILLIANCE INTERRUPTED

I love parkland golf so it is not often that I complain about trees. Usually I can't get enough of them, but the trees at the suburban Bangor look muddled. Worse, they interrupt each other as well as the holes. Yes, I know you think I'm mad for highlighting such an odd thing and, on a lesser course, I'd agree. The trouble is, if you don't mind some climbing (the 2nd, 4th, 10th), Bangor has enough brilliant holes, thrilling drives and great approaches to make it a must-visit course.

The routing is clever, highlighted by the junction at the top of the course where the 5th, 8th and 16th interchange. There are numerous changes in elevation (offering views over Bangor and out to sea), which promise many inviting shots, both downhill and into curving fairways, and holes have bucket-loads of intrigue. They are smart but uncomplicated in terms of design. In fact, every hole is good, so why does it feel as if the eighteen don't work as a set? There is no rhythm and it comes back to the trees. I'm serious. They are planted erratically in terms of type and quantity and it leads to a stop-start feeling. Compare the flowing

holes near the pine wood (the 6th, 7th, 12th) to the brilliant 10th, where the lone tree looks astonishingly out of place between lines of evergreen. Come and see what I mean because apart from that, you can't go wrong here. And like nearby Donaghadee, this is great value for money.

One other thing: Bangor does not favour a natural draw. Stand on the 1st, 2nd, 4th and tell me you're not nervous of the attentive trees. And the 5th and 12th are tough left-to-right dog-legs.

FAVOURITE HOLE
Par 4 10th. 417 yards. A high tee box hits onto a steep, rising fairway, dead straight at the green high above. Intimidating and beautiful. Your second to a green cut into the hillside above you is so hard to judge. The 8th to 12th is a great run.

TOUGHEST HOLE
Par 4 5th. 455 yards. What a hole. A brilliant drive onto a rising slope, and unless you hit 300 yards you won't beat the dog-leg. The small hedge in front of the tee is repeated in front of the green. A par 5 in all but name.

POINTS

CD	A	G/F	B/W	L	F	V	G Ex	Total
15	7	8	5	6	9	10	16	76

THE COURSE

- Par 71
- Length: 6,169 yards
- Bangor Golf Club, Broadway, Bangor, Co. Down, BT20 4RH
- Tel: +44 (0) 28 9127 0922 (048 from Rep. of Ire.)
- www.bangorgolfclubni.co.uk
- Green Fees: £25–£33

COURSES NEARBY
Blackwood
Carnalea
Clandeboye
Donaghadee
Royal Belfast

BANTRY BAY   Established 1975

BE BY THE BAY

There are a few things you need to know about Bantry Bay: one, expect amazing views of sea and mountains (too many to list) and true Irish beauty – the 2nd, 9th and 10th are the pick; two, expect big greens that will overwhelm you with their massive and, perhaps, over-the-top contours/slopes; three, expect blind drives over/up/down the heavily rolling terrain, often marked with white stakes – yes, it does frustrate after a while, but some of the views that greet you on the other side make it worthwhile; and four, expect a tough test of golf the whole way around. There are no easy shots. On a good length course you have to think hard which club to play because you will be punished for errant shots – you simply cannot attack greens if you are off the fairway.

Without belittling the course, the experience here is about the fantastic views. The fact that there is a well set-up and lush golf course is just a bonus. There is lots of space for the holes to express themselves and, in this stunning setting, that seems appropriate. And yet there is a feeling that it is a bit overdone, that Bantry Bay is trying very hard to be a 'big' course. The truth of the matter is that it is a big course already and some of the mounding is surplus to requirement. As for some of the greens, my partner, Ronan, escaped with a 4 putt on the 14th, while the club's Captain 5-putted.

It is a course where you need your driver, a lot of care and a camera.

FAVOURITE HOLE

Par 4 8th. 362 m. One of two par 4s where the flag is visible, the fairway roller-coasters (left as well as up and down) to a very high green set in the hill. A difficult approach with a big bunker tucked underneath.

TOUGHEST HOLE

Par 4 10th. 371 m. You will be put off by the views, never mind the huge bank falling from the right and the sea on your left. The hole dog-legs right for another tough, sloping approach. Study the legends on all tee boxes.

POINTS

CD	A	G/F	B/W	L	F	V	G Ex	Total
16	8	8	9	10	8	8	18	85

THE COURSE

- Par 71
- Length: 5,910 m
- Bantry Bay Golf Club, Bantry Bay, Co. Cork
- Tel: +353 (0) 27 50579/53773
- www.bantrygolf.com
- Green Fees: €35–€40

COURSES NEARBY

Kenmare
Ring of Kerry
Skibbereen

BEARNA   Established 1996

PURE PLEASURE ON A BOG

There's parkland and there's heathland, and now there's bogland. Bearna sits beautifully on top of a bog, with glorious views out to the Aran Islands and across to the Clare mountains and the Burren. And the golf is an experience you are unlikely to forget either. Basically, there are three choices for where your ball lands: on the vast swathes of rugged fairway that can stretch continuously across holes and around trees; in impenetrable 'don't bother looking for it' rough (gorse, reeds, grasses); or water that's golden brown with the richness of the bog itself – you can see it in the banks of the ditches and ponds all around you, as water appears on almost every hole. A botanist's dream.

Several long walks to tees emphasise the spacious layout and add to the experience. In fact they demonstrate the course's remarkable evolution – check out the 'rough' on your left as you walk to the 5th tee. It is no surprise that drainage is a key challenge. Not on the superb greens though, which are big and creatively sloped, with several thrown up high to offer tough targets. Great driving holes abound (the 4th, 6th, 7th, 9th, 11th, 13th

and 16th) – some requiring long carries – and you will have to use all your skills to conquer the course. The most memorable holes are the 6th (Index 1), 10th (across Lough Inch), and the final four holes which are up high.

There are four men's tees and this may cause confusion at the busy 1st and 3rd tees. I played off the second longest and the difference between this and the daily yellow tees can be as much as 70 m. Everything is well marked (in yards and metres) and signposts are in seven languages. Play it.

FAVOURITE HOLE

Par 4 16th. 336 m. The 10th, over the lough, is regarded as the feature hole, but the 16th has a very high tee to a high green, and a sweeping dog-leg of gorse, grass and water in between. Hit the fairway or say goodbye to your ball.

TOUGHEST HOLE

Par 4 15th. 338 m. A dangerous uphill dog-leg left. There is no way to tell how much you can attack as gorse blocks all but a small bit of fairway. Your approach to the uphill green is marginally easier.

POINTS								
CD	A	G/F	B/W	L	F	V	G Ex	Total
16	9	8	9	10	7	9	17	85

THE COURSE

- Par 72
- Length: 5,746 m
- Bearna Golf Club, Corboley, Bearna, Co. Galway
- Tel: +353 (0) 91 592 677
- www.bearnagolfclub.com
- Green Fees: €20–€35

COURSES NEARBY
Cregmore Park
Galway
Galway Bay
Oughterard

BEAUFORT   Established 1995

THE GENTLE BEAUTY OF BEAUFORT

As parkland golf courses go, Beaufort is in a beautiful setting. Indeed, the stunning Gap of Dunloe is on this same road just a mile away.

Yes, it is a shame about the big, unfinished hotel and apartment block (started in 2008) which will be at the centre of the course and will overshadow some holes, but that seems to be the way it is these days. Fortunately the very pretty front nine will remain relatively secluded and untouched under the gaze of the MacGillycuddy's Reeks. The holes amble between mature, native trees, around gorse and heavy tree plantings (that will mature brilliantly) and over gently undulating and wide fairways.

On the back nine, early on, there is still a sense of maturity and peace. That, for me, was what I noticed most about Beaufort: it is so peaceful. And that includes the golf. It is pleasant and relaxing and, dare I say, easy. There are no great dangers off the tee and the holes are short enough to give you opportunities to attack very visible flags. With bunkers generally staying well back, you'll find the big greens tilted towards

you to make them all the more inviting. Without even realising it, you will find your swing moving more gracefully, and the ball sailing sweetly towards the target.

It is a flat course so you won't expend too much energy, but the back nine definitely get trickier as bunkers move closer and become steeper, and water starts to threaten. Not too much, but enough to make for a thought-provoking finish. The remains of the twelfth-century Castle Core also make a dramatic appearance to add some spice to the back nine.

FAVOURITE HOLE
Par 5 8th. 500 yards. The hole dog-legs left between two big trees and then down a gentle slope. There is plenty of difficulty if you go too close to the trees, but it offers a good birdie opportunity.

TOUGHEST HOLE
Par 4 1st. 419 yards. Not hugely long, but a tough opening hole (Index 1) that demands you avoid fairway bunkers and find a sloping green. The 17th is the hardest drive with lots of water to avoid.

POINTS

CD	A	G/F	B/W	L	F	V	G Ex	Total
15	8	8	8	8	8	7	17	79

THE COURSE
- Par 71
- Length: 6,227 yards (white tees)
- Beaufort Golf Club, Beaufort, Killarney, Co. Kerry
- Tel: +353 (0) 64 6644440
- www.beaufortgolfclub.com
- Green Fees: €50

COURSES NEARBY
Castleisland
Dooks
Killarney (x 3)
Killorglin

BEAVERSTOWN   Established 1985

PICKING PARTY

Beaverstown is known for its vast orchard. Hundreds of apple trees stretch across the course and add an appealing element you won't find anywhere else. They form the framework on this undulating parkland course which sits on the estuary. On my visit, thousands of apples hung from the branches and lay on the ground. The club should organise a picking party when locals can come and take what they want.

Also of great appeal are the greens. Many are raised up and make attractive targets, and the shapes are wonderful with great swings and curls. You will 3 putt here, that's for sure, so adhere to the flag position chart on your scorecard. The greens on the 12th and 14th sit within an orchard setting, over a dropped stream. They are almost identical.

The back nine are a bit flat, but the stream that winds its way down to the estuary and the ponds (the 15th, 16th and 17th) give it some character. The front nine have more interesting shape and some entertaining holes. There are dog-legs, trees in fairways, tall conifers,

a blue conifer wood and plenty of variety to keep you moving. At par 72 it is not long: the longest par 5 is 441 m and par 3s are short too. Nor is it difficult with only a handful of tough shots – mostly drives – so everyone has a chance to score well.

A lot more fun than Donabate down the road. There are several other courses very near, making this a good golf destination.

FAVOURITE HOLE

Par 4 4th. 336 m. A gentle sweep right towards the green. From the tee the sea appears to your right and you hit over a stream between trees to reach a flat fairway. The orchard runs all along the left as you approach the green. Index 2.

TOUGHEST HOLE

Par 4 14th. 354 m. A dog-leg left. A large ash sits in the fairway, at the elbow, with three bunkers just beyond it. A good drive will leave you with a shot that has to carry the deeply set stream into the orchard itself.

POINTS

CD	A	G/F	B/W	L	F	V	G Ex	Total
14	8	8	7	6	7	8	15	73

THE COURSE

- Par 72
- Length: 5,670 m
- Beaverstown Golf Club, Beaverstown, Donabate, Co. Dublin
- Tel: +353 (0) 1 843 6439
- www.beaverstown.com
- Green Fees: €20–€45

COURSES NEARBY
Balcarrick
Corballis
Donabate
Island, The
Turvey

BEECH PARK   Established 1983

FRINGE BENEFITS

Take a lovely, quietly undulating parkland setting surrounded by mature trees, slip a green carpet across the top, mix in some more beautiful trees, add water and you get Beech Park. It is the kind of course that feels perfectly natural when you drive in. And that doesn't change when you start playing.

Sitting just on the edge of Dublin, it is very attractive to a huge number of golfers and this must be society heaven. One of the reasons it works so well is that it starts off gently with the tame and generous holes. You really are eased into the round and, apart from the 5th and 9th, the front nine are open and easy to handle.

Then it gets interesting. Until you reach the 10th, the big trees stay well back, but as you stand on the tee you are enveloped. And so starts a run of six holes that hugs the perimeter, bringing more character, shape and colour to your round. A river and two fountains add some extra oomph, while the 13th dog-legs around a long stretch of water and reeds. There may be no stunning design elements, or anything too fancy, but these are classy parkland holes with real excitement.

Beech Park sets a wonderful rhythm and it is a delight to play. A quiet start builds to an impressive crescendo and you could not ask for more. It is a little tight in places but this is the sort of course everyone will enjoy. And the clubhouse is modern, with good showers. Please note that the card is in metres, the fairway markers are in yards.

FAVOURITE HOLE
Par 4 11th. 269 m. A serious risk-v.-reward tee shot. It is downhill with a river at the bottom, so you can play an easy iron or a big drive. But the easy iron may then be blocked by trees, while the big drive may find bunkers.

TOUGHEST HOLE
Par 5 13th. 458 m. The club calls this section 'Amen Corner'. You drive out of a dense nest of trees with a reed-laced pond arcing all the way to the green. Pressure on the drive and on the second.

POINTS								
CD	A	G/F	B/W	L	F	V	G Ex	Total
14	8	7	8	5	9	9	17	77

THE COURSE
- Par 72
- Length: 5,538 m
- Beech Park Golf Club, Johnstown, Rathcoole, Co. Dublin
- Tel: +353 (0) 1 458 0522
- www.beechpark.ie
- Green Fees: €40

COURSES NEARBY
Castlewarden
Citywest
Slade Valley
South County

BELLEWSTOWN   Established 2004

MOUNTAINS OF FUN

When you come to Bellewstown you need to bring two things with you: some climbing gear and a gang of mates, because this is an absolute riot of golfing fun. Now I'm not talking outstanding quality, but the course sits on the side of a steep hill and when you drive down the club's bumpy road, a couple of the greens above you look as if they are on precipices.

Holes 1 and 2 head straight down. Then there is a bit of messing about on the very bottom of the course before the 9th, 10th and 11th take you to the very top. And just when you thought the steeply angled fairways of holes 12 to 16 meant you were heading back down to earth, the 17th takes you straight down and 18th brings you back up. Feeling seasick yet?

I loved this course. It is more fun than you can imagine reading this, but it is hard work on the legs. And it is hard work on some of the holes, too. Take the 10th that curls up the hill: you have a 100-yard shot, up a 45-degree incline – what do you hit? The 3rd is the only flat hole and it is Index 1.

The holes on the perimeter provide plenty of difficulty off the tee, but there are acres of space inside the course (and dangerously so in places) – at least until the trees grow. There are water features, with the pond on the 224-yard, par 3 17th the most dangerous of all. You get the impression that the course was done for fun, but the 10th and 18th are superior golf holes so it has more backbone than you would expect. Basic wooden clubhouse.

FAVOURITE HOLE
Par 4 18th. 373 yards. Dense lines of mature trees arc up the hill (and all the way to the top), defining a superb finishing hole. The big tree to the right of the tee box adds just that extra bit of drama.

TOUGHEST HOLE
Par 4 13th. 390 yards. Two difficulties here: keeping the ball on the fairway when it tilts at 30 degrees, and staying balanced as you hit your second towards the green. The 14th is the same in reverse.

POINTS								
CD	A	G/F	B/W	L	F	V	G Ex	Total
13	7	6	7	8	6	10	16	73

THE COURSE

- Par 72
- Length: 6,503 yards
- Bellewstown Golf Club, Bellewstown, Co. Meath
- Tel: +353 (0) 41 988 2757
- www.bellewstowngolf.com
- Green Fees: €15–€25

COURSES NEARBY
Balbriggan
County Louth
Hollywood Lakes
Laytown & Bettystown

BELVOIR PARK   Established 1927

MORE PARKLAND BLISS

Malone one day; Belvoir (pronounced 'beaver') Park the next. A feast of golf on two excellent and mature parkland courses. How do you separate them? Three things stand out: here the big trees give you more space – especially after the 4th when there is more breathing room; the fairways are flatter than Malone's, despite the water-filled hollow that stretches across the back nine; and third, the atmosphere around the clubhouses is noticeably different. At Malone's old and grand clubhouse there is a sense that the headmistress will chastise you for bad behaviour. At Belvoir Park it is more relaxing – the very modern, impressive clubhouse towers high above a large portion of the course, with views across Belfast to the Belfast Hills. It is certainly worth walking out onto the balcony before you play to get a taste of the course below.

While Malone has more drama and a bigger presence (the lake plays a major role in this), Belvoir Park has that sedate pace, showing off more of the hole (the 277-yard 1st is a perfect example) and inviting you to swing hard. And despite the mini-chasm across the back nine, it is

friendlier, in golfing terms. You warm to the shots more.

Belvoir Park is an oasis in a sea of houses. There are big trees and woods, a couple of nice walks, and lots of colour. It is in beautiful condition, looks superb (visit that balcony), flows easily and challenges frequently. Everyone will love it.

I'm going against the grain, but I think the much lauded bunkering in front of some holes (4th and 8th particularly) detracts from the beauty.

FAVOURITE HOLE

Par 4 3rd. 427 yards. Index 2 is a so-so drive at big trees, but when you get to the dog-leg the fairway slumps right down and then rises quickly to the green, trees all around. The 10th is a great drive from a height, hitting straight at the hills.

TOUGHEST HOLE

Par 4 17th. 440 yards. The 12th is a longer dog-leg but positioning is even more important on the 17th. The hole swings left and down into the big dip. The sharp rise up to the green will send anything short back down the hill.

POINTS								
CD	A	G/F	B/W	L	F	V	G Ex	Total
16	8	8	8	7	8	7	17	79

THE COURSE

- Par 71
- Length: 6,597 yards
- Belvoir Park Golf Club, 73 Church Road, Newtownbreda, Belfast, BT8 7AN
- Tel: +44 (0) 28 9049 1693 (048 from Rep. of Ire.)
- www.belvoirparkgolfclub.com
- Green Fees: £65–£75

COURSES NEARBY
Balmoral
Dunmurry
Lambeg
Malone
Rockmount

BIRR   Established 1893

AN ESKER EVENT

Revised layout opened in 2009.

Four new holes (4 to 7) have alleviated the pressure on this tight course. It is a beauty and, while two cross-overs remain, the new holes have opened up the heart of Birr and given the centre more space.

Whether or not you like Birr as a golfing experience is a different matter entirely. Look up 'esker' in your dictionary and this will give you a taste of this bright little course. The fairways lift and drop like the ocean, hiding fairways and greens. It is a riveting experience because the landscape is all over the place. I know it can be frustrating to be knocking drives straight over hills, only to find another white directional stone awaiting your second, but that makes it so much more challenging – and rewarding when you do well. Greens sit in a variety of positions, which just compounds matters.

The perimeter holes are the best, with fairway borders rising into woods of mature trees and gorse. The 10th, 11th and 12th are outstanding in their beauty and challenges, and they have to be seen to be believed.

The tight space can still be dangerous and this is emphasised by the 14th and 15th, two par 3s, which are then followed by a very short par 4. Both par 3s are crossed.

FAVOURITE HOLE

Par 4 11th. 380 m. A beautiful tee shot across a double-dipping fairway that then swings left and down into a hollow. A tricky drive, a trickier second, and trees all around.

TOUGHEST HOLE

Par 3 15th. 221 m. A big hit of a par 3. From a high vantage point you can see some of the green but the fairway is hidden by a mound ahead of you (the ladies' tee). It is not wise to go left or right.

POINTS								
CD	A	G/F	B/W	L	F	V	G Ex	Total
15	7	8	8	7	7	9	16	77

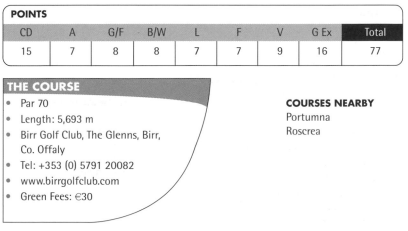

THE COURSE

- Par 70
- Length: 5,693 m
- Birr Golf Club, The Glenns, Birr, Co. Offaly
- Tel: +353 (0) 5791 20082
- www.birrgolfclub.com
- Green Fees: €30

COURSES NEARBY
Portumna
Roscrea

BLACK BUSH Established 1987

A VERY TIDY, GENTLE PARKLAND

With Royal Tara up the road, Black Bush offers a different, but just as welcome, parkland experience. This fairly flat 27-hole parkland course is generous off the tee and promises attractive approaches. The main course is A9 and B9 (I did not play C) and while it fits quite closely together, you will often be surprised at where you are. After the 5th, almost every hole is straight and visible. And while it sounds repetitive and formulaic, it is always nice to see the entire hole and all the trouble ahead of you.

It is deceptively spacious and the tree-lined fairways don't feel like it. Throw in the mature trees and it is hard to believe the club started only as recently as 1987. The truth is that I prefer Royal Tara, but only because the trees there are far more threatening and there is more shape to the landscape. Black Bush is more relaxing, a pleasant stroll that requires you to hit a ball from time to time – or three times in a row off A7 because you have a nasty snap hook. Mustn't grumble.

And mind the well-placed fairway bunkers.

It works easily and the occasional flourish can make all the difference: Black Bush has a superb pond that fronts B9, and then slides through dense trees to cup the tee on A1. It is quite a tee shot too, firing out of the trees. Another pond has trickling water that cascades down from rocks on A8. Pretty and dangerous as it protects half of the green.

Relatively easy and very relaxing.

FAVOURITE HOLE
Par 4 A8. 313 yards. A short, straight hole that has the water feature mentioned above. Like all the greens, this one is tipped invitingly towards you with gentle mounds on the rim.

TOUGHEST HOLE
Par 4 A5. 370 yards. Index 1. The first par 4 and it needs a very good drive on a gentle dog-leg. Nail the drive down the left, avoiding the two fairway bunkers, and the green opens up nicely.

POINTS								
CD	A	G/F	B/W	L	F	V	G Ex	Total
13	6	8	7	6	10	7	13	70

THE COURSE

- Par 73
- Length: 6,410 yards
- Black Bush Golf Club, Thomastown, Dunshaughlin, Co. Meath
- Tel: +353 (0) 1 825 0021
- www.blackbushgolfclub.ie
- Green Fees: €20–€40

COURSES NEARBY
Ashbourne
Killeen Castle
Moor Park
Roganstown
Royal Tara

BLACKWOOD   Established 1994

PARKLAND ADVENTURE

Blackwood Golf Centre. An eighteen-hole course, a par 3 (very good by all accounts), a driving range and a restaurant. Some other important things have been forgotten about. In a way that applies to the course too. The design and quality just seem to lack that killer punch – good, but not great. But here's the thing: Blackwood is the kind of adventure you should not ignore. It is parkland bliss in terms of its location, rolling landscape, water and the maturity around it. Holes sit comfortably in their own space and there are pretty walks through woods to reach some tee boxes. Several drives take you close to deep woods and you will find that they get very, very friendly around some greens. It is wonderfully vibrant.

Yet something is missing – or perhaps it is just that a few holes are weaker and interrupt the momentum. The 6th to 10th holes really get you going, and while the 11th is a good hole, it feels field-like, as do the 13th and 14th.

Off the tee you can be fairly adventurous – wide swathes of rough mean you have plenty of room if you are misfiring and even on tighter holes (the 10th and 11th) you'll usually find room on one side.

Considering the green fees, it is definitely worth a visit. A serious designer's touch would make Blackwood magical.

Directions to the 1st would help – it's a long walk.

Home of Dream On's John Richardson.

FAVOURITE HOLE
Par 3 16th. 164 yards. The back nine are tamer, so this well-tunnelled hole stands out with the green sitting neatly in the gorse. There is very little room around the green which sits just above you.

TOUGHEST HOLE
Par 4 8th. 370 yards. A really tempting drive down a tossing fairway to a stream at the bottom. The trees squeeze in – but not too much – before it dog-legs left around big trees to the green.

POINTS								
CD	A	G/F	B/W	L	F	V	G Ex	Total
15	8	7	7	6	7	10	16	76

THE COURSE
- Par 71
- Length: 6,148 yards
- Blackwood Golf Centre, Crawfordsburn Road, Bangor, Co. Down, BT19 1GB
- Tel: +44 (0) 28 9185 2706 (048 from Rep. of Ire.)
- www.blackwoodgolfcentre.com
- Green Fees: £23–£29

COURSES NEARBY
Bangor
Carnalea
Clandeboye
Donaghadee
Royal Belfast

BLAINROE   Established 1978

SEA SIDE PARKLAND THAT IS A PLEASURE TO PLAY

Standing on the 7th tee, sun in your face, looking down on the golf course and the ocean stretched out before you, is a great feeling. Blainroe's location is certainly one of its key selling-points: there are great views of sea and countryside from much of the higher front nine, while the tough par 5 18th runs along the sea cliffs and the 14th demands that you hit over the crashing sea itself.

The design is solid, rather than inspirational, with several very good holes. For many, what lies on either side of the road is what makes this course so enjoyable: on the sea side, the holes are open and flat, with generous fairways and wide swathes of playable rough, where the trees rarely come into play; on the other side, the holes are hillier, tighter, trickier and more interesting. Even so, for most of the round you will get away with loose shots – the 14th and 18th being two big exceptions – which makes it very appealing for the majority of golfers. The hardest part of your day will be negotiating the ever-present, treacherous

bunkers which are heavy and decidedly unfriendly; the course is long enough that you're sure to find a few of them, either off the tee or around the greens.

Two of the three par 3s deserve a mention: the 8th is downhill all the way and you might want to consider using a putter – it has been done before – while the 15th is long and over water.

FAVOURITE HOLE
Par 4 14th. 296 m. Any shot that hits over cliffs and sea is high on my list (see Tralee and Old Head). Add to that a green that is out of sight, but reachable with the wind behind, and you have to wind up the driver.

TOUGHEST HOLE
Par 5 5th. 440 m. The tree-lined bank and bunkers at the dog-leg mean you will definitely need three shots to reach the green. Once past the trees, the fairway slopes and will push your ball towards the bunkers short of the green. Stay left and lay up.

POINTS								
CD	A	G/F	B/W	L	F	V	G Ex	Total
14	7	7	8	8	8	7	15	74

THE COURSE
- Par 72
- Length: 6,056 m
- Blainroe Golf Club, Blainroe, Co. Wicklow
- Tel: +353 (0) 404 68168
- www.blainroe.com
- Green Fees: €25–€55

COURSES NEARBY
Arklow
Druid's Glen/Druid's Heath
European Club, The
Wicklow

BLARNEY Established 2006

GRIP IT AND RIP IT

John Daly's Irish creation is quite divisive: you have those who like the 'big course' mentality with its big driving platform, eel-like fairways and championship ambitions; and then there are golfers who find it uninspiring and lacking elegance. To be honest, I agree with both parties.

Fairways certainly seem to embrace big hitters (there are glorious 200-yard carries on the 7th and 8th). The many bunkers are absolutely seductive with their soft white sand, superb shapes and perfect placement. On the other hand, the course's hillside location is stark and open. It lacks character because the routing is not that interesting and hillside fairways are often separated by huge banks. Still, they have successfully employed the original trees, gorse and hedgerows – look at the valley on your right as you play the 6th to chart the course's evolution.

And despite Daly's 'grip and rip it' philosophy, you still need finesse around the amazing greens with their bunkers and hollows. Their quality is comparable with Carton House (Montgomerie), the best in the country, and there is severe danger off the back.

Personally, I'd lose the water features but there's that 'big' mentality again. Of the fourteen long holes, you can see the flag on only two – dog-legs and elevation being the culprits. I imagine some people won't like this.

So where do I sit? Having played Muskerry two miles down the road in the morning, the courses can't be compared (despite the scores being so close). Muskerry has substance, maturity and intrigue; Blarney has the trappings of something bigger, but how big remains to be seen. It is part of a hotel resort.

ODDEST HOLE
Par 4 10th. 375 yards. The oddest creation. More of a hairpin than a dog-leg, emphasising that this is a course you need to play twice. You can drive onto the fairway you see, or turn to two o'clock and smash a 3 iron over the trees, leaving a short wedge.

TOUGHEST HOLE
Par 5 8th. 598 yards. How often do you play a hole this long? And they don't even let you see the fairway. The hole just keeps rising.

POINTS

CD	A	G/F	B/W	L	F	V	G Ex	Total
16	7	10	9	7	9	8	16	82

THE COURSE

- Par 72
- Length: 6,518 yards
- Blarney Golf Resort, Blarney, Co. Cork
- Tel: +353 (0) 21 451 6472
- www.blarneygolfclub.ie
- Green Fees: €39–€49

COURSES NEARBY
Cork
Fota Island
Lee Valley
Mahon
Muskerry

BODENSTOWN (BODENSTOWN)   Established 1973

INTRIGUING . . .

. . . and sadly I don't mean it in a good way. Here is a course that has matured very well in terms of its trees and its design (it is clever and tough in places), but the greens and bunkers have been ignored. Let's be brutal: they're atrocious. Even the eight brand new greens (constructed in 2008) which sit up high on mounds are no better. The bunkers, of which there are mercifully few, seem to be turned inside out. Yet all around are smart little touches: alleys of evergreen trees flank tee boxes, shrubbery cascades from other tees and the use of dark stone to define yet more tee boxes looks great. So why have the most important elements been ignored? Also, drainage is clearly a problem.

Back to the design: conifers dominate but they are not too dense and are well mixed with other varieties. As with most parkland tracks they direct you down fairways and are often the main hazard. The 1st is a prime example where your tee shot has to avoid intrusive trees and your approach also has to be carefully threaded.

For a course with such a low green fee it requires more strategy than you would expect. Good dog-legs and very occasional water demand smart placement. For those of you worried about going astray, there are plenty of wide fairways too.

There are some views up where the 6th and 14th meet – the par 3 14th hits over a deep quarry and is the shot of the day.

FAVOURITE HOLE
Par 4 5th. 360 m. Good shape as you drive over a gentle hill onto an unseen fairway. But from the tee you can see the green perched above you in a good setting of evergreens. It looks good. The 13th is quite similar.

TOUGHEST HOLE
Par 4 12th. 343 m. Your tee shot has to reach, but not exceed, the sharp dog-leg if you want to get at the green. There is a slope at the turn which will pull your second towards the trees, tight to the green.

POINTS								
CD	A	G/F	B/W	L	F	V	G Ex	Total
13	6	3	4	6	5	7	13	57

THE COURSE
- Par 71
- Length: 5,856 m
- Bodenstown Golf Club, Sallins, Co. Kildare
- Tel: +353 (0) 45 897 096
- www.bodenstown.com
- Green Fees: €16–€18

COURSES NEARBY
Bodenstown (Ladyhill)
K Club
Killeen
Millicent
Naas

BODENSTOWN (LADYHILL)   Established 1973

A GOLDEN CORNER

My comments about the greens, bunkers and general condition of the course are as true here as they are for the main Bodenstown course.

Ladyhill is a public course and will appeal to an audience who simply want to get out and have fun or want to improve their skills. But don't think the course is easy. It starts and finishes on the flat, with straightforward, lacklustre holes that give you room to play but it becomes trickier after the 3rd and you can't just lash it about. Nice stone-sculpted ponds appear on the 4th and 5th, and the 7th offers the first hint of real shape, with two blind shots to reach the par 5 green tucked below in the trees. The major surprise arrives on the 11th, a par 5 that leads you up into the top corner where a sharp hilltop holds the 14th green. Here are five stunning holes that would sit comfortably with any of the big boys (if only there was better maintenance). Fairways rise, fall and twist; trees squeeze your drives; and gorse rises above you in turrets. They're good touches that create some thrilling shots. The 11th green rises from a deep hollow while the par 4s on the 14th and the 15th are 289 m and 274 m respectively. A big hitter's dream. The drive on the 13th is the best of the day.

The rest of the course doesn't match up, but on a public course that costs €20 to play, it's a great stretch of holes.

FAVOURITE HOLE
Par 5 11th. 432 m. Not dissimilar to the 7th. A slightly blind drive over a rolling hill, and then another blind shot for your second. A dense wood (and OB) along the left needs caution and, to enjoy the hole properly, give yourself a wedge shot over the hollow.

TOUGHEST HOLE
Par 4 15th. 274 m. Index 18. Obviously this is an 'easy' hole if played strategically, but for anyone hoping to drive the green, there is a tree directly in front of the tee (which, I'm sure, has taken a battering), and the green is small with fall-offs.

POINTS								
CD	A	G/F	B/W	L	F	V	G Ex	Total
12	5	3	4	5	5	7	13	54

THE COURSE
- Par 72
- Length: 5,618 m
- Bodenstown Golf Club, Sallins, Co. Kildare
- Tel: +353 (0) 45 897 096
- www.bodenstown.com
- Green Fees: €15–€17

COURSES NEARBY
Bodenstown (Bodenstown)
K Club
Killeen
Millicent
Naas

BRAY   Established 1897

AN ELEVATING BACK NINE

For a new and relocated course that has been slapped on the side of a mountain beside the sea, above a smattering of housing and industrial estates, Bray has a surprising amount going for it. The back nine deliver many inspiring shots and the big, tiered greens almost feel like links – they're a pleasure to play on. The steep hillside has meant carved and well-shaped fairways threaded across the landscape, and this is particularly noticeable on the front nine.

The first eight holes go back and forth up the hillside, while the remainder use the change in elevation far more inventively: the sparkling downhill par 3 9th kicks off a great run of holes. Relish your drive on holes 11, 12 and 14 – the 11th is an imposing shot over a valley and bunkers galore, and this is where you will get the best sea and mountain views. Mature trees play a bigger part after the 9th, particularly on the dog-legs at the 14th and 17th, and nowhere more so than the vicious dog-leg 18th, a strong, almost unfair, par 5 that requires a brave second shot towards (or over, if you dare) a very narrow gap in the trees.

There are five par 3s, of which the 4th, 9th and 13th offer the best tee shots; the par 3 16th is side by side with the 17th, so save some energy and leave your bag on the tee.

If you don't mind climbing, Bray certainly entertains and is well worth a visit. The clubhouse is a glorious wooden structure and a very welcoming sight when you turn the corner at the 18th.

The practice putting green has some amusing slopes.

FAVOURITE HOLE
Par 4 14th. 360 m. A big downhill drive leads to a sharp dog-leg right, and a big green backed by trees below. Two great shots that would be magical but for the road/industrial estate.

TOUGHEST HOLE
Par 3 2nd. 152 m. It is difficult to judge what club to play because it is uphill. But the serious trouble is on the sloping green, where a missed 2-foot putt could leave you with a 30-footer back.

POINTS								
CD	A	G/F	B/W	L	F	V	G Ex	Total
14	7	8	7	7	8	8	15	74

THE COURSE
- Par 71
- Length: 5,700 m
- Bray Golf Club, Greystones Road, Bray, Co. Wicklow
- Tel: +353 (0) 1 276 3200
- www.braygolfclub.com
- Green Fees: €25–€40

COURSES NEARBY
Druid's Glen/Heath
Dun Laoghaire
Glen of the Downs
Greystones
Powerscourt
Woodbrook

BRIGHT CASTLE   Established 1969

GOOD GOLF, PLAIN AND SIMPLE

Bright Castle is tucked away up a country road and you drive past the one remaining castle wall. The course could be improved considerably with decent tee boxes, but there is a lot to recommend this interesting, self-styled short course. It is quirky and has a variety that many seriously designed courses lack. It adds fun. You'll find that bunkers vary with some devilish ones late in the round and greens that lie simply on the land with some hefty slopes and a few creative shapes (the 4th is a giant 'C' around a bunker and the 14th is like a runway). And those are not the quirky features. A hedge runs directly in front of the 6th, the par 3 7th demands a lofted club straight over 50-foot trees and the 18th has a sharply perched green above sand to provide an amusing finish.

Bright Castle is a parkland course that is not as classy as nearby Downpatrick but has more adventure. You start with two par 5s (Index 3 and 6), one straight at a nearby church spire and the next straight at the Mourne Mountains. On neither can you see the putting surface until it is too late to allow for the slopes. From the 5th to 10th (see below) you need to be very straight as evergreen-lined fairways really squeeze you in, and then you hit the only two dog-legs, both sharp left-handers.

The fairways have good undulations with several mildly blind drives (look for the white stones), but take care on the 16th as you cross two holes to reach the green. This is a great society golf course with enough vibrancy to keep you amused constantly.

FAVOURITE HOLE
Par 5 2nd. 490 yards. Play from the higher, white tees. You can just see the flag sitting against the gorse, with Slieve Donard behind. A great lilting fairway the whole way with a nasty, blind fall away to the left of the green. Probably the most natural hole.

TOUGHEST HOLE
Par 4 10th. 390 yards. Play from the back tee (440 yards) to appreciate the tightest driving hole – maybe 8 yards across and 40 yards off the tee. Then it dog-legs gently, rises between links-like bunkers and drops 2 feet sharply onto the green. No room behind.

POINTS								
CD	A	G/F	B/W	L	F	V	G Ex	Total
14	7	7	7	7	6	10	15	73

THE COURSE
- Par 73
- Length: 6,105 yards
- Bright Castle Golf Club, 14 Coniamstown Road, Bright, Downpatrick, Co. Down, BT30 8LU
- Tel: +44 (0) 28 4484 1319 (048 from Rep. of Ire.)
- Green Fees: £12–£15

COURSES NEARBY
Ardglass
Downpatrick
Kirkistown Castle
Ringdufferin

BUNCLODY   Established 2008

AN UPLIFTING GOLF EXPERIENCE

Yes, the golf course with the lift. That's what people call Bunclody. They don't say: 'hey, have you played Bunclody with its brilliant finishing stretch down through the woods and along the river?' No, the lift gets top billing, which is a shame.

It may be new but Bunclody has settled in perfectly. Take the mile-long driveway through a perfect avenue of dark, aged trees and the magnificent clubhouse with its thatched roof. It's a thrilling introduction and you can rely on Jeff Howes to throw a great golfing experience in your path as well.

There are two lots of holes: nine of them play within an open, undulating landscape, bordered by dense trees. These are populated by water features and hundreds of surprisingly mature plantings. This space will age well but it feels a bit open for now. The other nine look and feel like they've been here for years and are far more dramatic. And tougher. They run alongside the River Slaney, and the mature trees of the old Hall-Dare Estate form an impressive defence against errant shots. Holes 6 to 8 are on a plateau by the river, a stretch of holes resembling Woodenbridge, only better.

The approach to the 13th green is the start of Bunclody's brilliant, tight and dangerous finish. The walk down to the 15th tee gets the heart racing as a steep hillside comes down from your left, and a lone tree stands in the fairway, while holes 16 and 17 play alongside the river before the lift takes you up to the tight par five finish. Rich, deep and long, Bunclody changes pace often enough that it promises a thrilling round of golf.

FAVOURITE HOLE
Par 3 14th. 180 yards. It's a downhill hole in deep woodland and it just looks delicious. There's no escape to the right. 15 is a brilliant follow-up.

TOUGHEST HOLE
Par 3 5th. 208 yards. Also downhill but with big water, tight and right, and woods to the left. There is room to bail out (short and left), but a threatening hole and tough in any kind of wind.

POINTS

CD	A	G/F	B/W	L	F	V	G Ex	Total
17	8	9	8	7	10	9	18	86

THE COURSE

- Par 72
- Length: 6,728 yards
- Bunclody Golf Club, Carrigduff, Bunclody, Co. Wexford
- Tel: +353 (0) 53 937 4444
- www.bunclodygfc.ie
- Green Fees: €35–€65

COURSES NEARBY
Coollattin
Enniscorthy
Leinster Hills
Mount Wolseley

BUNDORAN   Established 1894

OPEN SKIES

Bundoran is an open links course right on the edge of town. From the clubhouse it looks gentle. It doesn't pack the same drama (or length) as nearby Donegal or Sligo, nor the intrigue of Strandhill. But you need to play links golf at its best as there are no hiding places here.

The course, despite being a bit squeezed in, is a good test. A number of drives are blind-type shots hitting straight up at the sky and over the hill (the 8th, 9th and 10th are particularly tricky), and the 14th swings left when it gets over the hill. Greens are accessible to the low-running shots and if the wind picks up it is the only way to play. As with any good links, you need to avoid the defences around the greens.

New greens have been introduced and these are considerably tougher. There are also some new tee boxes but it is not really a course that can be fiddled with too much without taking away the natural feel. Bundoran sits on the coast with a backdrop of mountains, a distant, giant sand dune behind the 11th, and views of peninsulas and more hills across

the sea. The town detracts from this setting, unfortunately.

As links courses go, it is not that dynamic and so suits many club golfers who would find other links courses intimidating, even on a good day. In mild weather it is short and without much peril off the tee. The biggest challenge is how to attack the flag. Distance markers are hard to spot on some good lilting fairways.

FAVOURITE HOLE
Par 4 11th. 374 m. Sitting alongside the beach, with the waves curling in, the hole hits straight at a glorious giant dune. The fairway is a very inviting target, dropping right down from the tee before rising to a tantalisingly out-of-sight putting surface.

TOUGHEST HOLE
Par 4 14th. 355 m. Only Index 7, but, to a newcomer, this hole promises a tough tee shot. Aim at the very left-hand corner of the fairway on the hill as this is the shortest line. The green is placid and lies flat, making length hard to gauge.

POINTS								
CD	A	G/F	B/W	L	F	V	G Ex	Total
14	6	7	7	8	6	7	15	70

THE COURSE

- Par 70
- Length: 5,338 m
- Bundoran Golf Club, Bundoran, Co. Donegal
- Tel: +353 (0) 71 9841 302
- www.bundorangolfclub.com
- Green Fees: €35–€45

COURSES NEARBY
County Sligo
Donegal
Strandhill

CAHIR PARK Established 1968

DIVIDED BY THE RIVER

A laid-back parkland course that eases its way through mature trees for nine holes, and around and over water for the other nine (added in 1995).

The original nine start from the clubhouse. These undulate nicely, taking in some wonderfully mature trees that define holes and offer some great backdrops to greens. The 1st is a perfect example, where you have to find a sloping fairway between the trees before a rise takes you to a hidden green surface. The wood that holds the 3rd and 5th tees is charming, and both these par 3s promise great tee shots. These nine are more enclosed and there is less room to err on your drive – I certainly heard plenty of trees being clattered.

But when you get to the newer nine, where trees are scarcer, you will be misled. The driving is just as difficult, but the danger now comes from the water that embraces several holes, and fronts a few greens. In fact, it is probably far more dangerous because it is so flat – you might be tempted to relax. It could ruin a scorecard and, in several cases, you won't get your ball back. It all starts at the 8th (see below) when you drive over the wide River Suir, and it continues until the far-too-short par 3 16th that hits back over the river. It is an impressive walk over the bridge, but if they could just lengthen this it would be a great hole.

The areas around the 5th, 7th and 16th greens and the tee boxes on the 6th, 8th and 17th are dangerous and off-putting, particularly from the 5th tee. Greens look simple and flat, but are deceptive on a good country course.

FAVOURITE HOLE
Par 3 3rd. 184 yards. A pretty tee box setting; a green below, surrounded by huge trees, and 184 yards of flight in between.

TOUGHEST HOLE
Par 4 8th. 354 yards. One thing to remember: you drive over the river, but there is a second water hazard you can't see – a big pond. Look for the red stakes on a tight dog-leg.

POINTS

CD	A	G/F	B/W	L	F	V	G Ex	Total
13	7	7	8	7	8	9	15	74

THE COURSE
- Par 71
- Length: 6,186 yards
- Cahir Park Golf Club, Kilcommon, Cahir, Co. Tipperary
- Tel: +353 (0) 52 7441474
- www.cahirparkgolfclub.com
- Green Fees: €20–€25

COURSES NEARBY
Ballykisteen
Clonmel
Slievenamon
Tipperary

CAIRNDHU   Established 1928

PICTURE THIS

If you are coming from Larne, the Cairndhu experience begins as you drive along the ocean's edge towards the club. When Ballygally Head appears, you see a golf course that rises straight to the top. It looks impossible. And for a few holes, it almost is. Holes 1 to 5 cover the headland in a brilliant blanket of thrills and spectacular views. The 1st and 4th go straight up to the tip. Along with the 5th they are stunning drives. The 2nd is the par 3 everyone raves about, with 360-degree views that take in the glories of Antrim, Ailsa Craig (the 18th is called Ailsa) and the Scottish coast over the water. Hole 3 is almost unfair: a long, blind carry that flies over heather and rock before disappearing down the hill (hint: aim just left of the gap). This is the stretch you will remember and talk about with glee, but more is to come: lovely parkland holes that move quite substantially, with blind shots over crests and around trees, and views that won't leave you alone.

The two par 5s appear late, using the same long dip to offer tempting drives – of which there are many. From the 17th you can see the headland through the trees and the golfers look like ants.

There is a great mix of holes: short par 4s are countered by tough ones (the 10th, 12th and 15th are notable beauties), and the 11th is a 202-yard, par 3 terror. Accuracy is more important than length, but there are plenty of big driving opportunities if you want them.

The greens are very small and that means target golf.

Cairndhu promises fantastic views, superb entertainment and great value for money. Don't drive into Carnfunnock Country Park by mistake.

FAVOURITE HOLE

Par 3 2nd. 147 yards. One of the most beautiful golfing spots in Ireland. Right here, on the tee. Take your time and look around, then figure out whether it's a wedge or a 3 wood. The 10th is a perfect drive, and the 6th a lovely downhill par 3.

TOUGHEST HOLE

Par 4 15th. 417 yards. A blind drive, but manageable. Positioning is everything as the fairway runs left and drops sharply to a small, hidden green. It perches menacingly and you need to be 100 per cent accurate.

POINTS								
CD	A	G/F	B/W	L	F	V	G Ex	Total
16	7	6	6	10	10	10	18	83

THE COURSE

- Par 70
- Length: 5,945 yards
- Cairndhu Golf Club, 192 Coast Road, Ballygally, Larne, Co. Antrim, BT40 2QG
- Tel: +44 (0) 28 2858 3324 (048 from Rep. of Ire.)
- www.cairndhugolfclub.co.uk
- Green Fees: £23–£28

COURSES NEARBY
Ballymena
Carrickfergus
Greenacres
Whitehead

CALLAN   Established 1929

PAINTING BY NUMBERS

Callan is flat, like the countryside around it. Only three holes display any interesting change in elevation so there isn't much soul. Holes 3 to 8 have plenty of mature trees, but elsewhere there is no rhythm to the more recent plantings. As a result, the course is open and relatively easy. Please note the 1st hole is in danger from players on the 2nd tee box.

The course design is straightforward, with fairway bunkers, water features and dog-legs appearing in all the right places. The dog-legs are particularly good, with the elbow ranging from 200 to 250 yards to give you some testing tee shots. There is also a ditch running across some holes that has the same effect. The big boys will feel constrained and frustrated, while average hitters will reap the rewards of playing their usual game. It makes things a bit more equal. The well-positioned water hazards look artificial – that's my way of saying 'get rid of the fountains'.

From the 7th to 13th is the best run of holes with some inventive features, more appealing lines and a greater degree of difficulty (the 8th to 11th are the four lowest indices).

The 15th to 17th are on the other side of a road. The greens are big beauties with lots of shape. Tiers and banks will be hard to handle and second shots into greens have to be carefully considered. Combined with the driving challenges, it adds considerably to what is an average, short course.

Unfortunate to have a sign for Mount Juliet right by the entrance.

FAVOURITE HOLE
Par 4 7th. 300 yards. A good, flat, straight hole you can really swing at. A tall hedge of trees (all OB) runs along the left and behind the green. Poplar trees press in from the left and the green is, in a word, wide.

TOUGHEST HOLE
Par 4 8th. 415 yards. Dog-leg left. From the tee you see bunkers on the corner. They don't look far but behind them is a pond. It is a 250-yard carry to get over it, and the fairway is tight. Hit an iron straight down the fairway and leave a great iron shot over a pair of oaks.

POINTS

CD	A	G/F	B/W	L	F	V	G Ex	Total
12	6	8	7	4	8	6	11	62

THE COURSE
- Par 71
- Length: 6,099 yards
- Callan Golf Club, Geraldine, Callan, Co. Kilkenny
- Tel: +353 (0) 56 772 5136
- www.callangolfclub.com
- Green Fees: €20–€30

COURSES NEARBY
Carrick-on-Suir
Gowran Park
Kilkenny
Mountain View
Mount Juliet

CARLOW   Established 1899

A PARKLAND CLASSIC

Carlow doesn't try to be great, because it *is* great. There are those who say it is outdated, but I find that a refreshing change from those courses which insist on endless upgrades. Courses like the nearby and newer Mount Juliet and Mount Wolseley are the new generation of golf design, but that does not make them better. Rather, it emphasises the brilliant design subtleties that can be found everywhere at Carlow – which was last redesigned in 1937. This is a wide, natural and beautiful landscape where the holes are well spaced out and beautifully routed through woods and hills. The start may be flat, but you quickly realise the dangers you face when you hit up the 4th to a heavily sloped green. There are plenty of changes in elevation thereafter, many from raised tees, and nowhere is this more inspiring than on the 8th, probably Carlow's most famed hole (see below). Steep banking also adds drama to many holes – particularly holes 7 and 14 (Indices 1 and 5) – but every hole is packed with variety. Put another way, when you find yourself in the bar afterwards, you'll remember every hole with affection. Certainly, you will never leave here disappointed and the course is playable all year round.

Use your head to reap the most rewards. Take the short and driveable par 4 10th (271 m) with water all along the right: fools will rush for their driver; others will take a more restrained approach. And such an approach will pay dividends all day as there is plenty of opportunity to get into trouble off the tee.

Carlow offers a perfect mix of parkland holes, and while it is regarded as difficult it is incredibly satisfying golf.

FAVOURITE HOLE
Par 4 8th. 390 m. The open scenery is wonderful from here and the drive dramatic. The hole drops down a steep slope, etched between tall beech trees. It is a threatening shot. The second is rarely easier as it is played off the same slope to a distant green.

TOUGHEST HOLE
Par 4 16th. 377 m. From an elevated tee, the hole rises between gentle hillocks to a tricky green; to reach it you have to negotiate a valley and tiered fairway. Two very accurate shots are needed.

POINTS

CD	A	G/F	B/W	L	F	V	G Ex	Total
17	9	9	8	7	9	10	19	88

THE COURSE
- Par 70
- Length: 5,722 m
- Carlow Golf Club, Deerpark, Carlow, Co. Carlow
- Tel: +353 (0) 59 913 1695
- www.carlowgolfclub.com
- Green Fees: €45–€50

COURSES NEARBY
Kilkea Castle
Killerig Castle
Leinster Hills
Mount Juliet
Mount Wolseley

CARNALEA   Established 1927

SEASIDE BLINDNESS

Two distinct nines, one common feature: blind tee shots. On nine holes you hit over a blind crest at sky. In fact, only the 1st offers a flag, and that is despite three other holes being under 300 yards (including the 266-yard 14th, Index 2). It is not everyone's cup of tea and it can be frustrating. On the plus side, it does often reveal tempting shots into sweet greens. The excellent five par 3s are the highlight of the day: they are so inviting from the tee.

So what is Carnalea? It starts out as seaside golf on a gentle hillside. Dark pines are grouped together to border holes. Their starkness is attractive and you can always see the sea. There is a small headland just beyond the 6th green and you are separated from the water only by a fence on the 7th – a blind and dramatic drive over a rise that looks like a wall. The fairways have a corrugated-roof effect so they are very bumpy. And greens often have sharp fall-offs and are protected by good, treacherous bunkering. On a windy day (most days I expect) you should bump-and-run.

To reach the second nine you walk under the railway line. This is hilltop parkland so there are blind shots and some moderate climbs. Trees are more diverse, the fairways settle down, and you play more regular, basic parkland golf. The par 3s are towering shots and the two sharp dog-legs (the 10th and 12th) are cute and difficult.

Carnalea is a short course. Its condition is good and it is not that punishing, but the drama that should exist is reduced by the blind tee shots.

Changing rooms could do with a makeover.

FAVOURITE HOLES
Par 3s. Whether up or down, the five par 3s are tempting shots indeed. The 9th hits across a dip and the green is buried into the side of a huge bank under the clubhouse. The 13th and 15th are towering downhill shots, with the 13th hitting towards the sea.

TOUGHEST HOLE
Par 4 6th. 334 yards. Index 17 is madness. A blind drive needs to keep right (not all holes have direction posts). The fairway ends suddenly at bunkers, dropping sharply left and down onto the green immediately below.

POINTS								
CD	A	G/F	B/W	L	F	V	G Ex	Total
13	6	6	6	7	6	8	12	64

THE COURSE
- Par 69
- Length: 5,411 yards
- Carnalea Golf Club, Station Road, Bangor, Co. Down, BT19 1EZ
- Tel: +44 (0) 28 9127 0368 (048 from Rep. of Ire.)
- www.carnaleagolfclub.co.uk
- Green Fees: £17.50–£22

COURSES NEARBY
Bangor
Blackwood
Clandeboye
Donaghadee
Royal Belfast

CARNE   Established 1995

THE PLAYGROUND OF GIANTS

The raw energy that comes from standing on the dune-top, battered by the wind, staring at a distant flag across yawning chasms – this is the natural beauty of Carne, one of Ireland's truly remote destinations. Dunes so high and hollows so deep this must have been the playground of giants.

Someone said that Carne was a bit rough at the edges. It's true, but it illustrates how perfect a golf course can be without endless manicuring. The car park, the clubhouse and tee boxes do not instil confidence. Even the first hole, with its troughs and looping dog-leg, is an odd beast.

I have never seen so many bumps, so many sloping lies, so many intriguing shots that flow with the land; you could be in the middle of a fairway with a 10-foot mound in front of you (the 9th), or hitting up a 60-degree hill (the 12th), or watching your ball disappear far below (the 15th and 18th – see photo). Who needs bunkers? For a links course, Carne has everything and at 5,823 m it is a good length for everyone. But there are some serious climbs, and riding in a buggy doesn't do the course justice; it is also dangerous.

The back nine are mesmerising, with greens tucked under and around mountainous dunes, and tees set astride them, offering great views out to sea and serious changes in elevation. Not that the front nine aren't illuminating – the 5th, 6th, 8th and 9th are superb – it is simply a slow start.

Play it twice so you know where you're going (there are dog-legs you won't believe).

While many older links are recognised as royalty, the energy and vibrancy that you'll feel at this remote corner of the world is something you may never feel again.

FAVOURITE HOLE
Par 4 11th. 302 m. A tee box that pierces the sky and giant dunes to drive between. A dog-leg far below turns right and then up a tiered fairway to the green above. There is one lonely, tiny bunker to catch you at the elbow. Magnificent.

TOUGHEST HOLE
It all depends on the wind! The par 4 17th, Index 1, is 392 m with dunes and drops all around. Your second shot is treacherous, to a narrow green that falls away sharply to the right. There is no room for error.

POINTS								
CD	A	G/F	B/W	L	F	V	G Ex	Total
19	10	10	9	9	6	10	20	93

THE COURSE
- Par 72
- Length: 5,823 m
- Carne Golf Course, Belmullet, Co. Mayo
- Tel: +353 (0) 97 82292
  Fax: +353 (0) 97 81477
- www.carnegolflinks.com
- Green Fees: €25–€65

COURSES NEARBY
Ballina
Enniscrone
Westport

CARRICKFERGUS Established 1926

TIGHT AND STRAIGHT

Short, straight, cramped, tree-lined, up-and-down and greens that seem to lie simply on the land. Doesn't sound that enticing, does it? But it is. This is about testing your accuracy and your golfing brain, because trees are far too close for wild driving and the fairways are often tight. It is not a quality design – there are no airs and graces or fussy touches – but play it well and it feels very rewarding.

Basically, it should be no more than your average parkland course, but it promises more. Perhaps it's the 1st hole, which hits over a big pond, and trees that swoop below the tee box (take the opportunity to check out the 6th green over to the right). Perhaps it's the comfortable rhythm of the trees and the land itself. Or perhaps it's just the breezy, relaxed feel.

Accuracy is far more important than length so shorter hitters might even have the advantage. Big hitters should be restricted by common sense and even on the 17th – the only par 5 at 485 yards – you simply don't want to go wild. Yes, there's room, but it is often on another fairway, so caution is needed. A ridge at one end of the course is used to maximum effect, rising into greens or creating blind-ish drives. It is the only change in elevation, affecting several greens and tees.

It is not a course to go out of your way for, but you'll find it an amusing test when you come – and it is superior to Fortwilliam. There's a fair bit of water running across holes, and there are two strong water features on the 7th (a double pond) and 16th.

FAVOURITE HOLE
Par 4 6th. 423 yards. A straight hole that rises very slowly before a sharper rise hides the green. The drop down into a small dell is totally unexpected and will fool any visitor. There is also a hidden pond on the right. Index 2.

TOUGHEST HOLE
Par 4 10th. 436 yards. Index 1 is the longest par 4 and hits straight at the flag. It is tight enough, but the channel that you play through for your second makes it difficult to judge length to a hidden putting surface.

POINTS								
CD	A	G/F	B/W	L	F	V	G Ex	Total
13	6	7	7	5	7	8	14	67

THE COURSE
- Par 68
- Length: 5,657 yards
- Carrickfergus Golf Club, 35 North Road, Carrickfergus, Co. Antrim, BT38 8LP
- Tel: +44 (0) 28 9335 1803 (048 from Rep. of Ire.)
- www.carrickfergusgolfclub.co.uk
- Green Fees: £19–£25

COURSES NEARBY
Fortwilliam
Greenacres
Hilton Templepatrick
Whitehead

CARRICK-ON-SHANNON   Established 1910

A MIDDLE RUN OF SPARKLING QUALITY

The enjoyment here comes from eight spectacular holes, the 7th through 14th. Along with the 6th this new nine opened in 2003. Just be sure to look right as you climb towards the 5th green to fully appreciate what is to come. And if that doesn't convince you, wait till you approach the 6th green, which falls away to a stunning vista of quality holes, water and gentle landscape.

You start off with nothing special – the clubhouse is small and basic and the 1st teebox and 18th green sit on top of the busy N4 road. The first five are good holes that let you know the contoured fairways are well maintained and the greens are firm and slick. They show the care lavished on the course. The 5th tee box hits over the 4th green – a risky business anywhere.

Each of the eight holes above deserves a mention, but I'll focus on the 7th, a par 5 that hits down from a great height, the 8th and 13th (see below), and the 14th, a well-designed drifting dog-leg where short hitters will struggle to see the green that falls away left from the crest of the fairway.

A short course with a great mix of cleverly designed lakeland holes (new nine), and simple parkland holes (old nine) where you have tree-lined fairways and you can putt from 40 yards out. There's plenty of difficulty reading shots as some greens are perched high, or just out of sight.

The paths are nicely done and give a professional touch. There are also very few houses to be seen. With Knock Airport so close, this is easily accessible and worth a detour.

FAVOURITE HOLE
Par 3 8th. 159 m. An idyllic par 3 that crosses a corner of Lough Drumharlow, complete with reeds and cruising boats.

TOUGHEST HOLE
Par 3 13th. 168 m. A tiny, narrow green set in the side of the hill. It is farther than it looks and three bunkers will drag away anything short. Aim left and the bank should bring you back.

POINTS								
CD	A	G/F	B/W	L	F	V	G Ex	Total
15	8	8	7	7	6	9	17	77

THE COURSE
- Par 70
- Length: 5,482 m
- Carrick-on-Shannon Golf Club, Woodbrook, Carrick-on-Shannon, Co. Roscommon
- Tel: +353 (0) 71 966 7015
- www.carrickgolfclub.ie
- Green Fees: €20–€35

COURSES NEARBY
County Longford

CARRICK-ON-SUIR   Established 1939

HILLTOP HAPPINESS

The first thing to applaud on this high course is the airy beauty of the location. Mountains surround you throughout, valleys drift into the distance and the walk through trees to the 11th offers the best opportunity to admire this glorious spot. Second, this is a really fun and pretty golf course. It offers great variety, tempting shots and some nice bursts of character. There is always lots of move- ment to the holes which makes them all the more inviting – especially off the tee. And while some holes may look flat (the 11th, 12th and 17th), they most certainly are not. The same applies to the greens: they look simple, with no great mounds or shapes around them, but there are plenty of slopes that are difficult to read. Expect to be fooled.

There are three distinct sets of holes, all blending seamlessly, and this variety adds considerably to the golf experience. Holes 1 to 4 have the greatest change in elevation and have that heathland flair with rocky mounds interrupting fairways and plenty of gorse splashed about. The 5th to 10th, in front of the clubhouse, are the most open holes with plenty of big trees standing back and giving you room.

These are the easier holes, but the 9th is a bit of a mess and dangerous – it drives over the 8th green and it is a vicious dog-leg that may threaten the 5th. Holes 11 to 17 sit comfortably on a separate hillside overlooking the town. These are the best holes and have the finest views of the Comeragh Mountains.

Long hitters will feel constrained on maybe six holes so it is a perfect spot to demonstrate your course-management skills. Clearly they take great pride in the course's condition.

FAVOURITE HOLE
Par 4 3rd. 286 m. A great-looking, bumpy fairway rises and veers right behind the the trees where a perched green waits up high. Be sensible off the tee and don't be short on the approach.

TOUGHEST HOLE
Par 4 13th. 316 m. When you leave your bag by the 12th green be sure to take at least two clubs to the tee. A drive might be suicide as the fairway drifts through a lazy 'S' shape under trees. A bunker fronts the entire green.

POINTS

CD	A	G/F	B/W	L	F	V	G Ex	Total
15	8	8	7	8	7	10	17	80

THE COURSE

- Par 72
- Length: 5,807 m
- Carrick-on-Suir Golf Club, Garravoone, Carrick-on-Suir, Co. Waterford
- Tel: +353 (0) 51 640 047
- www.carrickgolfclub.com
- Green Fees: €30–€35

COURSES NEARBY
Callan
Clonmel
Mountain View
Waterford

Hole 1 'Giant's Chair'
Scrabo Golf Club
Par 4, 404 yards, Index 1
Play off the back tee to enjoy the views and to appreciate fully this exhilarating gorse-drenched hole. (© Kevin Markham)

Hole 2 'Strand'
Portsalon Golf Club
Par 4, 361 m, Index 3
From an elevated tee, the hole dog-legs around the beach and over the river. Wonderful views of Lough Swilly. (© Kevin Markham)

Hole 3
Killarney Golf Club (Killeen)
Par 3, 166 m, Index 9
The rich textures of the lake, mountains and trees make this a picture-perfect hole over water. (Courtesy of Killarney Golf & Fishing Club)

Hole 4 'The Razor's Edge'
Old Head of Kinsale Golf Club
Par 4, 415 yards, Index 4
The cliffs, the lighthouse, the ocean – it's drama everywhere. Nerve-wracking too. (Courtesy Old Head Golf Links)

Hole 5 'White Rocks'
Royal Portrush Golf Club (Dunluce)
Par 4, 379 yards, Index 9
Welcome to the ocean and a sharp dog-leg that takes you over gentle dunes and out to the water. (© Kevin Markham)

CARTON HOUSE (MONTGOMERIE) Established 2002

AN INSPIRING AND TOUGH LINKS, NOWHERE NEAR THE SEA

'Your eye and senses are struck by the mix of delicate cunning and overpowering drama'. I always enjoy reading the blurb about a course, either on the website or in the course guide. The embellishment is entertaining. On this occasion it is accurate enough: delicate cunning comes from tantalising greens and bountiful pothole bunkers that have been lovingly shaped and perfectly positioned, especially in the crook of the many dog-legs; overpowering drama is a bit of a stretch, but this artfully, lightly tossed landscape hosted the Irish Open in 2005 and 2006. It received *Golf World*'s 'Best New Design of the Year 2004'.

The majestic Carton Estate is an hour inland, yet Montgomerie wanted to design a links-like course. He got his wish. Almost everything about it screams links golf, yet you're surrounded by a park of beautiful trees that frequently stray onto the course. The curving, fast greens are the best I have played, and expect steep fall-offs into bunkers. The tight fairways are also superb with vicious contours and semi-blind drives (the 9th, 10th and 13th really stand out). Believe me when I say

that the Course Guide is an absolute must. Every hole hides an adventure and accuracy is essential.

There is no better feeling than figuring out exactly what you have to hit and then doing it. That is especially true on a links and you'll feel it here too. The good news is you won't suffer ripping winds. The bad news is there's no sea to inspire, which makes it a bit bare.

Some golfers complain that it is too tough. It is, but why not rise to the challenge?

FAVOURITE HOLE
Par 3 17th. 162 yards. Undoubtedly the prettiest hole on the course, with the River Rye slipping into view behind the green and Carton House visible in the distance. You are well above the green which ensures a stunning tee shot.

TOUGHEST HOLE
Par 4 16th. 430 yards. You have to decide how much of this right-hand dog-leg you can cut off. And if you do take it on, there are seven bunkers to negotiate. The uphill green doesn't help either.

POINTS								
CD	A	G/F	B/W	L	F	V	G Ex	Total
17	8	10	10	6	10	10	19	90

THE COURSE
- Par 72
- Length: 6,821 yards
- Carton House Golf Club, Carton, Maynooth, Co. Kildare
- Tel: +353 (0) 1 651 7720 www.cartonhousegolf.ie
- Green Fees: €60–€85

COURSES NEARBY
Carton House (O'Meara)
Kilcock
Westmanstown

CARTON HOUSE (O'MEARA) Established 2002

WHAT A DOUBLE ACT

Carton House is a true golf experience. The stunning Carton House (now a hotel) dates back to 1739, the food is delicious, the facilities are excellent and there are two superb golf courses. You are also very close to Dublin. And to whet the appetite still further the entrance weaves through the Montgomerie course.

Designed as a links course, the Montgomerie feels barren inside a perimeter of huge trees, but it is beautifully crafted. The O'Meara has far more shape, colour and space. It rises and falls between nests of woodland and – for the best stretch – embraces the River Rye. The trees stay well back and rarely come into play, but they add a dramatic feature to events and are home to several foxes (sometimes glimpsed racing around the greens early in the morning).

Houses behind the 1st green are tucked into the woods but are still disappointing on such a lovely old estate. Be aware that you need a lift to the 1st tee and from the 18th green, or take the car.

The course has all the trimmings, as you would expect, with great rolls to the fairways, bunkers cascading their way to and around the greens, and putting surfaces that flow like velvet. Off the tee there are few serious difficulties – only bunkered dog-legs will cause you to pause, so it is a more rewarding and relaxing round than Monty's creation.

Views of the Dublin Mountains come at the top of the course but there's plenty around you to keep you enthralled. A few quiet holes (the 2nd and 4th) make for a tame start, but the 13th to 15th are superb, while the steep 18th and its rocky turret green could just finish you off.

FAVOURITE HOLE
Par 5 15th. 528 yards. Similar to the famous 7th at the K Club. Your drive (from whites) crosses the river. The green sits in a dell of trees, again across the river, with an angry weir spilling down from your right. A perfect setting.

TOUGHEST HOLE
Par 4 11th. 409 yards. Deserving of Index 1. Like several dog-legs, the green is clearly visible, with bunkers restricting your line. This one rises sharply up the hill, leaving you with a sloping lie to a well-protected green.

POINTS								
CD	A	G/F	B/W	L	F	V	G Ex	Total
17	8	10	10	7	10	8	17	87

THE COURSE

- Par 72
- Length: 6,608 yards
- Carton House Golf Club, The O'Meara, Maynooth, Co. Kildare
- Tel: +353 (0) 1 651 7720
- www.cartonhousegolf.ie
- Green Fees: €60–€85

COURSES NEARBY
Carton House (Montgomerie)
Kilcock
Westmanstown

CASTLE   Established 1913

THE BEST OF DUBLIN'S CITY PARKLANDS

With Milltown so close by, and charging a similar green fee, I suspect that Castle is swamped by the demand. It is a far superior suburban course. In fact, it is an excellent parkland, full stop. Grange, also nearby, is probably regarded more highly, with trees playing a significant and colourful role, but it has a few weak holes. Castle has no such problems. Every shot on every hole entertains and challenges. The design of the course has much to do with it. A gently, curving landscape and heavy, green pines create beautifully individual fairways. It is not a long course but you need to use your head to stay on the narrow fairways, avoid the many bunkers and master the gentle dog-legs. In other words, there is plenty of trouble off the tee, even on the wonderfully straight 11th and 12th. And approaches are usually between bunkers that squeeze the entrance to the green.

A stream runs through a hollow that winds across the course and adds variety and slopes to several holes. The steep shot down to the 6th, Index 1, is the best approach of the day. The 10th is a pretty and long par 3 that crosses the hollow,

and the 13th is a shorter version in reverse. In fact, all five par 3s are good.

Enough holes sweep left or right to make someone who knows the course a valuable addition to your group. And it's a tough par 5, 5, 4 finish too.

There's a feeling of relaxation about the place, a quiet refinement that extends all the way into the clubhouse and no one will be disappointed with a round of golf here.

FAVOURITE HOLE
Par 4 6th. 401 yards. Index 1. A good dog-leg left, that disappears over the hill. Aim at the big white house if you want to open up the green. The hole then drops quickly to the green with water on the right. Shot of the day.

TOUGHEST HOLE
Par 4 18th. 403 yards. Certainly the hardest drive with heavy trees pushing in from the left and, seemingly, only a bunker straight ahead. A fade here will ruin a scorecard. Only the perfect drive will give you a shot at the green.

POINTS								
CD	A	G/F	B/W	L	F	V	G Ex	Total
15	7	8	8	6	9	7	17	77

THE COURSE
- Par 72
- Length: 6,003 yards
- Castle Golf Club, Woodside Drive, Rathfarnham, Dublin 14
- Tel: +353 (0) 1 490 4207 www.castlegc.ie
- Green Fees: €50–€75

COURSES NEARBY
Edmondstown
Grange
Milltown
Stackstown

CASTLEBAR   Established 1910

PARKLAND ON THE EDGE OF TOWN

Having played Westport in the morning, the most telling thing I found at Castlebar was the complexity of the greens. Mounds are thrown all around and the greens have some great valleys, fall-offs and slopes – the 4th and 7th shared green is a perfect example. These are at the heart of Castlebar's challenges, yet they leave the approaches open, inviting you to fire at the pins. It's cunning and rewarding too.

I'll get two gripes off my chest straight away: firstly, pitch marks need to be repaired; secondly, I don't believe Castlebar's fairway marker yardage (or metres, in this case). Holes 3, 5, 9 and 13 certainly play shorter, so go with your instinct.

Castlebar is a leafy, uncomplicated parkland course. Holes are mixed up well: sometimes several holes are visible at once; at other times it's quite solitary (the 5th, 6th, 12th, 13th and 14th). It gives you an added focus, particularly the pretty par 3 12th with its backdrop of trees.

Driving is straightforward and, with little change in elevation, most of the greens are clearly visible. The best run of holes is the 11th to 14th, and also the 18th. No doubt it's all to do with how the eye takes in the hole: tree-lined fairways lead you to the green, which adds just enough punch.

There aren't quite enough great holes to make this a 'must play' course, but it is charming if you're nearby.

FAVOURITE HOLE
Par 5 11th. 432 m. The fairway narrows as trees sneak onto the fairway from the left. Hit long or short, they present a hazard either way. There is water to the right of the green and a nest of bunkers to the left. Certainly reachable in two but it is high risk.

TOUGHEST HOLE
Par 4 9th. 405 m. It all comes down to judging your shot to the green. With a long approach, the entrance to the green will push you right, and it is just a touch farther than it looks.

POINTS

CD	A	G/F	B/W	L	F	V	G Ex	Total
14	7	8	6	4	8	8	15	70

THE COURSE
- Par 71
- Length: 5,555 m
- Castlebar Golf Club, Rocklands, Castlebar, Co. Mayo
- Tel: +353 (0) 94 902 1649
- www.castlebargolfclub.ie
- Green Fees: €25–€35

COURSES NEARBY
Ballina
Claremorris
Westport

CASTLE BARNA   Established 1992

AWASH WITH ASH

As someone said to me: 'Every county should have a Castle Barna.' It's true. Castle Barna promises that uncomplicated, fun, country golf. There is no great design, elegance or fuss, but it is in good condition. Greens are smart and trim, bunkers are tidy and gently rolling fairways are lush. On that front there are no complaints. Mature ash trees are scattered about and they add a heap of character as they sit up on mounds of earth – the 1st is a case in point, where you have to drive between two of them. Thereafter they appear time and again, often just on the edges of greens, and they enhance the shape of the holes and the course. They are often used to turn holes into dog-legs.

Greens, good as they are, lie very simply at the end of the fairways and, while bunkers protect them, it's easy to run the ball in. It is not a difficult course (very short) with huge swathes of space off the tee – except on the perimeter – and, to that extent, it can be dangerous in places.

Put it this way: balls fly freely when you have all that space to drive into.

Water appears in places, as ponds, and it demands good carries on the 2nd, 3rd and 12th. You also arrive along the Grand Canal, which only comes in to play on one of the 9th holes. Yes, there are two.

It may not attract heaps of quality golfers, but sometimes a round at Castle Barna is exactly what you need. And you can buy home-made brown bread too.

FAVOURITE HOLE
Par 4 2nd. 306 m. A good high tee offers an excellent view of the hole. There are ash trees on the fairway and a long stretch of water, bordered by boulders, leading to the only raised green.

TOUGHEST HOLE
Par 4 18th. 379 m. Getting your drive into the right place on this gentle dog-leg is the biggest challenge as a line of trees crosses the fairway 200 m off the tee. The green then rises up a slope, and is quite steep.

POINTS								
CD	A	G/F	B/W	L	F	V	G Ex	Total
13	7	6	7	6	6	8	15	68

THE COURSE
- Par 72
- Length: 5,536 m
- Castle Barna Golf Club, Daingean, Co. Offaly
- Tel: +353 (0) 57 935 3384
- www.castlebarna.ie
- Green Fees: €20–€30

COURSES NEARBY
Edenderry
Esker Hills
New Forest
Portarlington
Tullamore

CASTLECOMER   Established 1935

THE BIGGEST UP AND DOWN

In 2003, Pat Ruddy added a new nine to his existing nine. It is now an intriguing beauty. The new nine sit on a hilltop above the clubhouse and the steep walk up to the 1st might fill you with dread, but it is relatively flat up here. Holes 1 to 7 take you through woods of pine and birch, with solitary oaks giving real character to tee boxes and fairways. You will face tricky drives with limited room, and the trees will confuse you on the 2nd and 4th. And when you do see space, there is a bunker lurking expectantly. Driving is made all the more difficult because, until the 13th, greens are never on view from tee boxes. It can be frustrating, especially for new visitors. The 13th, 14th and 16th are stunning, dead straight holes and they are a welcome respite.

The 8th joins the two nines, and you are unlikely to face such a long drop to a fairway ever again. Hit driver. You are high above the trees and it is a spectacular shot that adds hugely to the occasion. When you reach the bottom down a winding path you are on the 'flat' part of the course, but you can still expect good shapes to fairways and steep approaches to greens (the 8th, 9th, 10th and 18th). These are often accompanied by tidy evergreens that would not look out of place in a garden. It's all very pretty, while still offering tremendous challenges.

Castlecomer has lots to offer: variety combined with tough driving and tricky enough greens (the 6th and 12th are almost unfair). There is one very steep climb, to the 11th, but it's worth it as you drive between blasted walls of rock.

FAVOURITE HOLE
Par 4 13th. 297 m. Drive from the top tee, just below the 12th green. It's another great drive, down onto a flat, straight fairway. It is the first green you will have seen from the tee box and it is tucked under massive pines.

TOUGHEST HOLE
Par 5 6th. 469 m. The 4th is Index 1, and requires your best drive, but the downhill 6th is more demanding overall: a stream runs along the right, to the green, demanding accuracy and common sense on your opening shots, while the green is lethal.

POINTS								
CD	A	G/F	B/W	L	F	V	G Ex	**Total**
15	8	8	6	7	6	9	16	75

THE COURSE

- Par 72
- Length: 5,893 m
- Castlecomer Golf Club, Drumgoole, Castlecomer, Co. Kilkenny
- Tel: +353 (0) 56 444 1139
- www.castlecomergolf.com
- Green Fees: €25–€30

COURSES NEARBY
Abbeyleix
Carlow
Kilkenny
Leinster Hills

CASTLE DARGAN   Established 2006

ROLLING AND OPEN

When you consider the vision it must have taken to see a golf course on this desolate, rugged Wuthering Heights-like landscape, you will appreciate its design. The surroundings show you the shape of the land, and this has been enhanced considerably. There are times when the mounding is excessive and interrupts the eye, but this is what Darren Clarke chose to separate fairways and define holes; lines of trees would have been wrong. Yet, because it is so barren, the clusters of mature trees (beech, chestnut, ash) are the feature that stands out most, as well as the old stone walls and the castle ruins in one corner.

There is a professional air to the place and even though the greens are young they are remarkably good – big and sloping. Elsewhere the course still needs to settle in. So, when it matures, will it be a great course?

It is probably too short and not challenging enough to be labelled 'great'. There are also some weak holes: the 4th and 5th are lacklustre, and the 7th and 13th are uninteresting par 3s. The par of 72 includes two par 3s under 130 yards and three very short par 5s. And that means golfers of all levels will be able to score.

The best holes are the 1st to 3rd and the 16th to 18th which employ the ancient castle ruins as a focal point. The whole package includes a hotel and spa.

FAVOURITE HOLE
Par 3 3rd. 117 yards. The tee is high up, beside the old ruin, and you hit down to a wide but shallow green, with a great Irish field behind. A beech leans across you about halfway down. A stunning little shot.

TOUGHEST HOLES
Par 4s 16th to 18th. Three par 4s, all over 400 yards, is a tough finish. The 16th is straight at the castle before the 17th and 18th head back to the clubhouse with particularly attractive and challenging drives. The 18th has a winding stream and a bunker to bisect before it tilts right.

POINTS								
CD	A	G/F	B/W	L	F	V	G Ex	Total
14	6	9	8	8	9	8	15	77

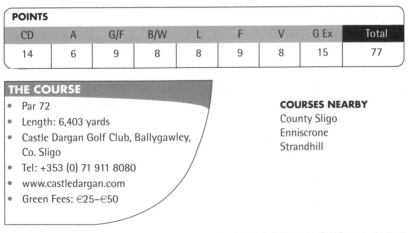

THE COURSE
- Par 72
- Length: 6,403 yards
- Castle Dargan Golf Club, Ballygawley, Co. Sligo
- Tel: +353 (0) 71 911 8080
- www.castledargan.com
- Green Fees: €25–€50

COURSES NEARBY
County Sligo
Enniscrone
Strandhill

CASTLE HUME   Established 1991

DANGER LURKS

When you erect a pedestal and then proclaim that you deserve to be on it, you're playing a dangerous game. Castle Hume boasts a championship golf course that is 'manicured to the highest standards'. If you arrive expecting something along these lines you will be disappointed. There are a few good holes (the 6th to 10th, 15th and 16th) but it is a very lacklustre affair, with shapeless fairways and lifeless greens. I found very little to take pleasure in, including the water and the red bridges, and not nearly enough is made of the mature trees which line the perimeter – nowhere more so than at the 6th and 15th.

The course is predominantly flat and greens have been tilted towards you to make more inviting targets. The trees in the centre of the course are growing well but don't give quite enough character to holes.

All this and then an excellent club-house. I'm not sure what's going on. Nick Faldo's course, Lough Erne, opened in 2009 on the same estate, and it is interesting to see how the two courses sit side by side.

This is not a course for a real challenge or a real thrill, but it will appeal to plenty of societies and casual golfers as a gentle day out.

FAVOURITE HOLE

Par 5 15th. 498 yards. One of the few great drives – you hit straight at a huge beech wood, which then follows the fairway as it dog-legs sharply all the way to the green. You can cut the corner because anything over 240 yards will reach the wood.

TOUGHEST HOLE

Par 4 18th. 314 yards. For first-time visitors this is completely out of context with the rest of the course, with two ponds between you and the green. Landing areas look small and intimidating and you are not sure where to aim. Go for the green – why not?

POINTS

CD	A	G/F	B/W	L	F	V	G Ex	Total
11	6	6	6	5	9	6	10	59

THE COURSE

- Par 72
- Length: 6,339 yards
- Castle Hume Golf Club, Belleek Road, Enniskillen, Co. Fermanagh, BT94 7ED
- Tel: +44 (0) 28 6632 7077 (048 from Rep. of Ire.)
- www.castlehumegolf.com
- Green Fees: £25–£35

COURSES NEARBY
Clones
Enniskillen
Slieve Russell

CASTLEISLAND   Established 2000

WILD ON THE HILLSIDE

What was once a wild hillside has now made way for a golf course. It doesn't look imposing as you drive in and neither does the clubhouse – although a new one will be built elsewhere soon. The opening holes look open and barren, with young tree copses planted well apart on unimpressive, heavily stepped banks. Only the raised and tiered greens have interest.

After the 6th it all changes, when the true wildness of the course comes to life. You are first introduced to a deep gorge that holds a stream and impenetrable trees. You must drive over this on the 7th and 18th, and it adds a touch of character. The 9th is a majestic-looking downhill par 3, with severe slopes falling off the back and endless views behind. The 12th is an even more dangerous par 3 with a big carry to the green or a painful death in the gorse and trees below. Water looks delicious on the 13th to 16th holes, and the 14th and 16th are beautiful drives – both downhill with naturally deep scruff off the tee, water to

beat and views beyond. This wildness shows itself on much of the back nine and it is the heart of the course.

It is a big challenge. Several blind holes and narrow fairways will test your accuracy at the top of the course, and hitting at greens from the rough is lethal.

I didn't find it overly inspiring or of great quality, but it is only a couple of years old.

FAVOURITE HOLE
Par 4 14th. 332 m. A lazy dog-leg around water that many will want to try and drive over. The green sits temptingly below and it is truly a wind-up-the-driver hole, with views behind.

TOUGHEST HOLE
Par 4 7th. 397 m. Index 1 and not hard to see why. A blind dog-leg over a valley of trees, which then sweeps blindly right to a green that sits over a deep ditch. Two of your very best required. Don't mistake it for the 1st.

POINTS								
CD	A	G/F	B/W	L	F	V	G Ex	Total
13	7	7	8	7	6	7	14	69

THE COURSE
- Par 71
- Length: 5,622 m (white tees)
- Castleisland Golf Club, Dooneen, Castleisland, Co. Kerry
- Tel: +353 (0) 66 714 1709
- www.castleislandgolfclub.com
- Green Fees: €25–€30

COURSES NEARBY
Beaufort
Killarney (x 3)
Killorglin
Tralee

CASTLEKNOCK   Established 2006

OVER-ELABORATE

This new course is still finding its feet. Castleknock is part of a hotel resort and it is professionally designed and heavily manufactured. There is tremendous mounding, acres of lakes and crater-like, starfish-shaped bunkers. It is a complicated combination and I found it a bit overwhelming at times, especially on the 6th and 8th (par 5s), where you don't know where to aim off the tee. There are no inclines to speak of, but the rolling fairways stretch all around and ensure there are plenty of hidden greens.

The course may be on the short side but it is not easy. Castleknock is designed to be difficult: fairway bunkers put a premium on accuracy and several greens are raised and tucked just out of sight behind deep bunkers. And with the vast, firm and creatively shaped putting surfaces it is very difficult to put the ball close, even from 100 yards.

There are five par 5s and five par 3s (three exceeding 180 yards), and the latter are the highlight of the round, all featuring swathes of water (see below).

Tarmac buggy paths snake unattractively across your line far too often and there's a feeling that style trumps substance (paths, helicopter pad, fancy tee boxes) to give Castleknock more kudos. It doesn't work. I have little doubt that the course will come of age and that the quality of the fairways will improve, but the green fee is too dear.

My favourite part of the round was the impressive clubhouse.

FAVOURITE HOLES

Par 3 9th, 11th and 18th. Three beauties. The green on the 11th is surrounded by lake on three sides, while the 9th and 18th (182 yards) sit side by side and hit over another huge lake to a shared green in front of the clubhouse.

TOUGHEST HOLE

Par 5 6th. 469 yards. A dog-leg left with water all down the left for your drive. It is a stupid drive as you have no idea where to hit (I landed on the path and shot for miles). It is Index 14, but much tougher on your first visit.

POINTS

CD	A	G/F	B/W	L	F	V	G Ex	Total
14	7	8	8	4	8	6	13	68

THE COURSE

- Par 72
- Length: 6,379 yards
- Castleknock Golf and Country Club, Porterstown Road, Dublin 15
- Tel: +353 (0) 1 640 8736 www.castleknockgolfclub.ie
- Green Fees: €30–€60

COURSES NEARBY
Elmgreen
Hermitage
Luttrellstown
Westmanstown

CASTLEMARTYR   Established 2007

PLUSH AND FAST

As part of a large estate, with hotel and grandeur all around, Castlemartyr has a lot going for it. They promote themselves as an inland links-style course, and it is wrapped up in a boundary of trees. Those in the know will think of the Montgomerie course at Carton House, which claims the same thing. There are some interesting differences between the two. Castlemartyr is far more generous with its fairways and its length, so you can score more easily; bunkers are less interesting and less punitive (Monty's are deep brutes); and the most productive approach when firing at greens is to run the ball in. But please note that the fronts of greens are often hidden with steep banks running up the back. You will need guile.

The course is very open, but the continuous mounding gives holes their individuality and their character. This makes it a manufactured course and one that is not hugely dramatic. Even so, it is in superb condition, with wonderful greens and fairways, and rolling mounds all around you. You won't be disappointed because you can score comfortably (particularly on the short front nine) and

on a course as smart as this, that's a real bonus for everyone.

There are no climbs of note and no lengthy walks to tees. Trees on the course are sparse, so it feels roomy off the tee. If you veer off-line, you will find the many mounds covered in serious rough. There is also a small creek that runs across several holes, notably in front of the green on the very short 9th.

A remarkable clubhouse will greet you after you pass the hotel.

FAVOURITE HOLE
Par 4 16th. 382 yards. The best vista, with the flag just in sight and the tip of the ruined castle over the left-hand bunkers. The hole has great shape, sliding between sentry trees to a putting surface not visible on your second.

TOUGHEST HOLE
Par 5 11th. 523 yards. Index 10 it may be, but bunkers in the middle of the fairway threaten both your first and second shots. The green hides behind mounded shoulders that angle across your approach. Three sensible shots will serve you well.

POINTS									
CD	A	G/F	B/W	L	F	V	G Ex		Total
15	7	10	8	6	8	8	15		77

THE COURSE

- Par 72
- Length: 6,262 yards
- Castlemartyr Golf Club, Castlemartyr, Co. Cork
- Tel: +353 (0) 21 421 9001
- www.castlemartyrresort.ie
- Green Fees: €35–€50

COURSES NEARBY
East Cork
Fota Island
Water Rock
Youghal

CASTLEREAGH HILLS Established 1983

TOPSY TURVY

A very short municipal course that sits up in the hills above Belfast. It's not that hilly, despite the name, and it has a smart clubhouse. If you're lucky enough to be welcomed by Edel or Elaine, then your day is off to a good start. The golf is classic municipal – there's good, there's bad and there's entertaining.

Holes 2 to 8 are just over the road and, as you walk across, you can see the holes laid out below. Behind them are fields that show what the land used to be like. There are lots of mounds running along fairways like frightened rabbits, and young trees scattered about. A stream flows through the middle (ending in a pond in front of the 7th) to add a wild feel to the proceedings. These holes are very straight, using the hill's camber to give shape and interest. There is not much danger off the tee, despite some tight fairways, and driving is fun. A good par 3 appears at either end of this section – one goes up, one comes down.

The other holes have more natural shape as they edge up another hillside – the 10th is excellent and the towering 18th will make you very nervous. They offer far more room, with trees still making only fleeting appearances. Several greens are tiered and/or perched with decent fall-offs adding extra danger.

The quality is about right – better than some other municipals – but there is nothing particularly captivating. Yet, like any good municipal course, it looks after its target audience perfectly, and a little more besides. No par 5s.

FAVOURITE HOLE

Par 4 10th. 396 yards. Index 2 offers the second best drive as you need a smart shot aimed slightly right to use the shoulder across the fairway. The lone tree is your line, and the green then sits comfortably in a bay of poplars.

TOUGHEST HOLE

Par 4 18th. 387 yards. What a drive! Downhill for the first 300 yards. You're not exactly sure what is going on – it's slightly blind – so aim at, but avoid, the big ash dead centre. The green sits up a bit and is protected by two trees on the right.

POINTS

CD	A	G/F	B/W	L	F	V	G Ex	Total
12	5	6	6	6	6	8	14	63

THE COURSE

- Par 67
- Length: 5,177 yards
- Castlereagh Hills Golf Club, Upper Braniel Road, Castlereagh, Belfast, BT5 7TX
- Tel: +44 (0) 28 9044 8477 (048 from Rep. of Ire.)
- Green Fees: £17–£22.50

COURSES NEARBY

Balmoral
Belvoir Park
Dunmurry
Malone
Rockmount
Shandon Park

CASTLEROCK   Established 1901

ROCKING BACK AND FORTH

Three superb links courses squeeze together along this coastline (Castlerock, Portstewart, Royal Portrush). Castlerock is the most open and has a good variety of styles, from dune infested to flat and exposed. Even though it's a short par 73, with lots of opportunities to score, your links skills will be sorely tested. It adds hugely to the enjoyment – even in a battering wind.

It all feels right when you stand on the 1st tee. Erratic dunes roll along the left and there is good shape to the fairway. But know this: your ball will not always run true and avoid the colourful rough. Castlerock buzzes with dark runs of gorse and shifts in elevation. It all promises exciting shots and views (the 17th tee box is the most impressive spot and the water alongside the 6th, 7th and 8th sparkles). Yes, there are holes which are very straightforward (the 3rd and 5th – dead straight par 5s – and the 13th and 14th), but they are inland and well integrated with the better holes. The change of pace works well but, of the three big courses, it is the most erratic in terms of style. You rarely settle into a rhythm.

Without the guidance of my playing partners I would have been in trouble time and again. Restraint and guile are needed off the tee (the 6th has a burn short of the green, the fairway pulls balls into bunkers on the right of the 7th, the 10th has a wicked slope and the 12th has a blue whale buried in the middle of it) and approaches to greens have to respect some unseen steep slopes and fall-offs.

Great clubhouse atmosphere.

FAVOURITE HOLE

Par 4 10th. 386 yards. So tough for a newcomer, this is a convex fairway with the green out of sight. You want to rip it, but you have to hit high and right or the ball sweeps down into trouble. The run into the green is beautifully bumpy.

TOUGHEST HOLE

Par 4 8th. 400 yards. From a high tee you hit into a left-to-right dog-leg. You can't go over the dunes as more lie hidden behind. A good drive opens up a green with a dune backdrop and a big fall-off left. The 16th is Index 18, allegedly.

POINTS

CD	A	G/F	B/W	L	F	V	G Ex	Total
17	8	9	9	9	9	8	17	86

THE COURSE

- Par 73
- Length: 6,506 yards
- Castlerock Golf Club, Circular Road, Castlerock, Co. Derry, BT51 4TJ
- Tel: +44 (0) 28 7084 8314 (048 from Rep. of Ire.)
- www.castlerockgc.co.uk
- Green Fees: £65–£80

COURSES NEARBY

Portstewart
Roe Park
Royal Portrush

CASTLETROY Established 1937

BIG MAKEOVER, BIG SUCCESS

New tee boxes, new greens and a whole new style will meet you at Castletroy. The tee boxes are big and several of them are raised to show off the beautifully curved and perfect tree-lined fairways. It all looks very inviting. Fast and slinky putting surfaces are often hidden – either by the elevation or by smartly placed bunkers. It adds a lot of difficulty to what is an already tight and tricky course. It throws a bit of everything at you, including water, good dog-legs and length. Matching your handicap is an achievement. It doesn't look like it should be difficult, which lulls you into mistakes. The first three holes are between 315 m and 330 m so they should be easy, right? Wrong. If anything, use them to get to grips with what is expected of you and the sort of design characteristics you will encounter.

The back nine are better, with more shape and space, and the downhill tee shots on the 14th and 17th are superb. There is a lot of water too, around the two long and excellent par 3s, the 11th and 14th, making it more vibrant and entertaining.

Considering this is a suburban course, you feel surprisingly away from it all. And despite being a bit squeezed in (front nine), the golf is thrilling enough that you rarely notice. Unless you play with Kevin, Rory and Donal, three youngsters who have perfected their shouts of 'fore'. They wanted a mention, so there it is.

Now, if only it had a little more space.

FAVOURITE HOLE
Par 3 14th. 175 m. A huge downhill shot to a green surrounded on three sides by water. Simply a magnificent tee shot that will have you over-swinging.

TOUGHEST HOLE
Par 4 13th. 301 m. Short it may be, but it is Index 3 for a reason. A big dog-leg that rises up the hill then turns sharply right. It's all about your tee shot finding the fairway, because the trees on the right and the bunkers behind make this lethal.

POINTS								
CD	A	G/F	B/W	L	F	V	G Ex	Total
16	8	9	9	7	8	10	17	84

THE COURSE

- Par 72
- Length: 6,046 m
- Castletroy Golf Club, Limerick, Co. Limerick
- Tel: +353 (0) 61 335 753
- www.castletroygolfclub.ie
- Green Fees: €30–€50

COURSES NEARBY
Limerick
Limerick County
Rathbane
Shannon

CASTLEWARDEN   Established 1990

GENTLE

Golf can be about many things, from exhilarating links to mountain heathland. The most common of all is the gentle parkland, and Castlewarden fits the description perfectly. It is never going to knock your socks off with excitement, but it is perfectly entertaining stuff. It's the usual mish-mash of young trees planted around their older brethren. These define fairways and lead you around several dog-legs, some of which are a bit hard to gauge so it's 'hit and hope'. The 4th is a perfect example where you might want to cut over the trees, but there is a big pond that will catch most drives – my playing partners (Dave, Noel and Paddy) forgot to mention it. Water appears again at the short par 4 10th, one of the best holes on the course, and the par 3 13th, where there is also a fairy ring to the right.

Castlewarden is flat, yet rolling, with good movement on fairways and dynamic slopes on some greens. Surfaces are fast, and the 7th is not the green to be above the hole.

It is an open enough course that gets a bit too cosy where the 6th, 7th and 15th combine. Bunkers are on fairways for a reason, but shouldn't cause the shorter hitter too much trouble. It is a good length, too, and offers golfers of all abilities some great challenges.

It is a touch ironic that the most mature trees are on your drive in, which coasts beside the good dog-leg finishing hole. And, as you walk off the 18th, you can ponder over the plaque dedicated to our Olympc swimming champion, Michelle Smith.

FAVOURITE HOLE
Par 4 10th. 254 yards. Fancy a go? You pass an old walled garden to reach the tee and it's a great straight hole with water right in front of the green. With today's drivers it is just a long par 3.

TOUGHEST HOLE
Par 4 3rd. 436 yards. A strong dog-leg (not the most interesting drive) that heads left towards the good clubhouse. There's water left and right. Look to your right at the turn to assess the 4th hole/green.

POINTS								
CD	A	G/F	B/W	L	F	V	G Ex	Total
14	7	7	7	6	8	8	15	72

THE COURSE
- Par 71
- Length: 6,513 yards
- Castlewarden Golf Club, Castlewarden, Co. Kildare
- Tel: +353 (0) 1 458 9254
  www.castlewardengolfclub.com
- Green Fees: €25–€35

COURSES NEARBY
Beech Park
Killeen
Palmerstown
Slade Valley

CHARLESLAND   Established 1992

SEASIDE PARKLAND

I played here before in 2000, and didn't like it. You start the round playing beside the sea, which is almost always in view. As you progress you head farther inland, and starting at the 11th, you begin climbing a gentle hill that hosts the club's 'signature' hole (a huge downhill par 3 of 218 m). There are good undulations on the holes, nice bursts of gorse, superb bunkering, small and difficult greens and inviting drives – it all sounds promising, but Charlesland is an anomaly. Somehow it lacks definition, as if an artist has drawn it and smudged the edges. It is almost soulless, an odd feeling on a course that has much going for it. However, I liked it a lot better than on my previous trip.

At the start the lack of trees makes it very open, but that's not surprising as you are next to the sea. The holes have strong undulations and wide fairways so you can drive freely, but the greens have difficult little rises coming in to them and they are smaller than average. This is true of most holes and finding greens is the biggest challenge you'll face. They are also well tiered.

The course picks up from the 9th on with far more trees, the hillside, water features and interesting shapes. These are good holes that reward strategic golf. The 11th and 12th are classic 'better safe than sorry' dog-legs, before a tough finishing stretch: the 14th and 16th are the two toughest holes as they skirt the hill and the 18th is a long par 5 double dog-leg. Three of the par 3s are short – evidently to make up for the monster 13th. Score early because the back nine are longer.

FAVOURITE HOLE
Par 5 9th. 462 m. After the easy drives before, the 9th comes as a shock. Pond on the left, trees nesting on the right. The hole dog-legs around two lots of water and calls for three positive shots to get to the green.

TOUGHEST HOLE
Par 4 16th. 409 m. The 14th is Index 1, with its severely sloped fairway, but the 16th calls for a perfect drive (cut off as much dog-leg as you dare) before the approach fires you up through a narrow gap on the hillside. Small, hidden green surface.

POINTS

CD	A	G/F	B/W	L	F	V	G Ex	Total
14	6	7	8	7	9	7	13	71

THE COURSE
- Par 72
- Length: 5,963 m
- Charlesland Golf Club, Greystones, Co. Wicklow
- Tel: +353 (0) 1 287 4350
- www.charlesland.com
- Green Fees: €20–€45

COURSES NEARBY
Delgany
Druid's Glen/Heath
Glen of the Downs
Greystones
Powerscourt

CHARLEVILLE   Established 1941

A DASH OF GREEN, A LANDSCAPE OF TREES

Charleville has a gentle shade of green that clings to every hole. Trees greet you on the first tee and refuse to let you go anywhere alone, getting ever more friendly as the round progresses. They provide the backbone, the beauty and the danger on this shortish course. Dog-legs are littered about, and with gentle elevations your greatest challenge is judging how to beat the turn. For a better game I suggest you play off the back blue tees – it gives you fuller shots off tees and makes the dog-legs more thrilling. With eight holes falling between 360 and 380 yards, you can see how important the dog-legs are, and you can end up crocked by a tree with only a slight misjudgement. This is particularly true on the tougher back nine, where course management is the key to bringing in any kind of score. Positioning is crucial if you're to attack the flat but tricky greens. The 10th, 11th, 14th and 15th are perfect examples, all being of a similar length but the different lengths and angles at the turn give them their individuality. And the 18th is a cut above the rest (see below).

I have not played a more relaxing round of golf in a good while. There aren't any views on this eighteen, but you'll find these if you play the third nine or go up to the driving range. And check out the Waterville scorecard (and photos) over the entrance to the comfortable bar. Signed by Payne Stewart, he and Tiger played a two-ball better ball in 16 under, shortly before the great man died. It was donated by my playing partner, Geoff, when he joined the club.

FAVOURITE HOLE
Par 3 2nd. 163 yards. The hole is flat so you can't see the putting surface (like several others), but it is a beautiful iron shot through tall trees that will scare many.

TOUGHEST HOLE
Par 4 10th. 442 yards. A brute and a beauty that needs a perfect drive. There are two trees along the left that look like goalposts. Anything right of them leaves you completely blocked.

POINTS								
CD	A	G/F	B/W	L	F	V	G Ex	Total
15	9	8	8	4	10	10	17	81

THE COURSE

- Par 71
- Length: 6,467 yards (back markers)
- Charleville Golf Club, Smiths Road, Charleville, Co. Cork
- Tel: +353 (0) 63 81257
- www.charlevillegolf.com
- Green Fees: €20–€35

COURSES NEARBY
Adare
Adare Manor
Kanturk
Mallow

CHRISTY O'CONNOR Established 1996

PUBLIC, LIKE THE AIRPORT

For a public golf course (also known as Silloge Park) this is surprisingly tough. There are narrow fairways, OB on eight holes, trees that get very close and personal (particularly on the left), and small greens. It's a par 71 right next to the airport. If you were any closer, you'd be on the runway. On the 12th you drive straight at the control tower – for fun, count the number of tail fins you see passing behind the green as you play the hole. Apart from one dip (the 2nd, 8th, 10th and 11th) the course is flat. As a result it is not that interesting and the quality is just a little better than you would expect of a public course – you know, that 'rough around the edges' feel. That said, holes 8 and 10 (Index 1 and 2) are good, tough holes and there are plenty of other decent holes throughout the round. The trees certainly add enough to stop you being too rash off the tee. There are also tricky enough dog-legs from the 13th to 16th.

It's never going to set your heart alight, nor is it going to be a destination of choice, but it is the lowest green fee you'll pay on this side of the country.

FAVOURITE HOLE
Par 4 6th. 298 m. A short dog-leg that begs you to go for it, but has plenty of danger left (OB) and a large bank and trees straight ahead.

TOUGHEST HOLE
Par 4 8th. 416 m. How tough is this? You drive over a small valley, avoiding OB left. You have to get far enough to beat the 90-degree dog-leg, which still has OB left.

POINTS

CD	A	G/F	B/W	L	F	V	G Ex	Total
10	5	5	4	4	4	8	12	52

THE COURSE
- Par 71
- Length: 5,924 m
- Silloge Park Golf Club, Ballymun Road, Swords, Co. Dublin
- Tel: +353 (0) 1 842 9956
- www.sillogeparkgolfclub.com
- Green Fees: €15–€26

COURSES NEARBY
Castleknock
Elm Green
Forrest Little
St Margaret's

CITY OF DERRY   Established 1912

CHARMING PARKLAND

A sunny, dew-drenched morning. What better place to be than on a golf course like City of Derry? Not too tough, not too long, and charming. The arrival up a steep hill might set the heart racing but there are no climbs to trouble you. Set on the side of a hill, it overlooks the River Foyle (the best views are from the third nine), and from the 1st you can see holes above and below. Your initial impression that the course lacks excitement will disappear from the 3rd on, and the holes on the other side of a path that divides the course are really good, with some great woodland settings and a pretty stream to cause havoc on the 5th and 7th. Fairways and rough are wide while trees add considerably to the character. Beech mostly, but oak, alder and conifers too, and there is plenty of maturity. They are colourful and remain at a respectful distance – most of the time – inviting you to play at full tilt. Every hole is welcoming, even the tough ones, and you can't help but smile when you arrive on tee boxes often set in the trees.

This is about wonderful, relaxing golf that everyone will enjoy. How could you not? You will score well, especially with placid, receptive greens. A few tough holes will handicap golfers with a draw: holes 4, 6, 11 and 16 are squeezed by trees along the right, and the 18th demands your best drive. At 328 m, driving between two big trees, it is the only occasion when you need a good carry.

The course includes an extra par 3 3rd hole in the winter, when the 8th is out of play.

FAVOURITE HOLE
Par 5 7th. 448 m. A lovely setting for the tee box and the green. It will take two good blows to carry the stream which remains out of sight in a hollow and the wedge from there is delicious. Then it's a beautiful wooded walk to the 8th tee.

TOUGHEST HOLE
Par 4 14th. 393 m. It looks like a tough drive but there is more room than you think. The problem is on the second shot as you will be able to see only the flag tip. The fairway rises and jiggles its way to a sloping green.

POINTS								
CD	A	G/F	B/W	L	F	V	G Ex	Total
14	8	7	7	7	7	9	17	76

THE COURSE
- Par 71
- Length: 5,658 m
- City of Derry Golf Club, 49 Victoria Road, Prehen, Co. Derry, BT47 2PU
- Tel: +48 (0) 28 7134 6369
- www.cityofderrygolfclub.com
- Green Fees: £20–£40

COURSES NEARBY
Foyle
Letterkenny
North West
Strabane

CITYWEST (CHAMPIONSHIP) Established 1994

SHORT, TRICKY AND SUBURBAN

Using your head will reap its rewards on this short course. Longer hitters especially will need to show restraint on the opening holes, as dog-legs wreak havoc. The 1st is a case in point: Index 1 and just 371 yards. It's a nice-looking starter but big drives may find water left or right where the fairway narrows. Then dog-legs on the 2nd, 4th, 5th, 9th and 11th call for similar calculation. Remember this: a 220-yard shot on any of these will leave a second of roughly 150 yards. And good luck on the 246-yard par 4 7th. After the 11th the course improves dramatically with more obvious parkland traits: holes are longer and straighter, and you have more opportunities to go for your shots between avenues of mature trees.

Despite its location, beside one of Ireland's busiest roads, Citywest is a pretty course that is maturing well. Water has been used extensively on the opening nine holes and on the last four. Two of the par 3s (the 3rd and 8th) require strong shots over water. Like the Lakes course, the ponds are attractive and the greens sit well behind them. On such a flat course these features make all the difference – although I have never been a fan of fountains.

There's a two-minute walk from the 9th to the 10th, across the car park and past the Citywest Golf Hotel. It tells you everything you need to know, and you can drop in by helicopter if that takes your fancy. There are numerous, excellent, big golf courses nearby (Carton House and the Dublin links courses), so this is the perfect base.

FAVOURITE HOLE
Par 4 16th. 385 yards. The tee box is only 20 yards from the motorway, but this is one of the best driving holes. It needs to be long and straight as water sits to your right. A good drive opens up the green which is set in trees and promises a tempting second.

TOUGHEST HOLE
Par 4 18th. 416 yards. The longest par 4 and you get that feeling as you walk back to the tee. You are aiming straight at the hotel and a good drive is essential if you want to attack with your second. A small lake lies in wait and the green is no push-over.

POINTS

CD	A	G/F	B/W	L	F	V	G Ex	Total
14	8	7	9	4	7	8	15	72

THE COURSE
- Par 68
- Length: 5,603 yards
- Citywest Hotel & Golf Club, 16 Jigginstown Park, Saggart, Co. Dublin
- Tel: +353 (0) 1 401 0878/0501
- www.citywesthotel.com
- Green Fees: €35–€50

COURSES NEARBY
Beech Park
Grange Castle
Newlands
Slade Valley

CLANDEBOYE (AVA)   Established 1933

BLISSFULLY QUIRKY

Clandeboye has thirty-six beauties, but Ava's eighteen are quite different from Dufferin's. If you plan to play both in a day it makes sense to play Dufferin first as it requires more energy. But if you want to have the perfect warm-up, play Ava first. The course is seriously tight in places, it is wickedly short and greens are small. The landscape also moves more. You will find plenty of blind shots – like big brother – and some decent carries are required over gorse. Several holes are 'hit and hope', but that makes them no less exhilarating. The 9th is a par 4 of 309 yards and all you see off the tee is a flag above gorse. And it's downhill! Hells Bells is the 312-yard 7th (Index 3), and it's a 5 iron off the tee if you have any sense. And so it continues for much of the day.

It really is the kind of golf that demands common sense because you see so little of the holes. They can bend around corners, banks and trees, over gorse or uphill – or all three. You have the violent fairways that can flick your ball away without you seeing it, so a flashing driver can wreak havoc – there are seven holes under 330 yards. You could easily leave your driver behind.

It's the quirkiness that makes this a fun course to play. It looks every bit as beautifully maintained as the Dufferin, but if you called it 'trick' golf, I wouldn't disagree.

The 15th is a dull par 3 and lets the side down badly, while the 17th is crazily blind off the tee.

Play from the whites (300 yards longer) as you are less likely to make silly mistakes.

FAVOURITE HOLES
The 4th hits 319 yards around trees up a hill, leaving you to hit blindly at a deep wood; the 7th is not dissimilar, but from a high tee, while the 14th curls gloriously up the hill beside deep woods.

TOUGHEST HOLE
Par 4 7th. 305 yards. A thrilling hole that hits down into a hollow of trees, making the fairway tight. Then up past the quarry on the left to a completely hidden 'hit-and-hope' green. Adventurous, frustrating and fun.

POINTS								
CD	A	G/F	B/W	L	F	V	G Ex	Total
14	8	8	8	6	10	9	15	78

THE COURSE
- Par 70
- Length: 5,755 yards (whites)
- Clandeboye Golf Club, Tower Road, Conlig, Co. Down, BT23 7PN
- Tel: +44 (0) 28 9127 1767 (048 from Rep. of Ire.)
- www.cgc-ni.com
- Green Fees: £31–£36

COURSES NEARBY
Bangor
Blackwood
Carnalea
Donaghadee
Royal Belfast

CLANDEBOYE (DUFFERIN) Established 1929

BLISSFUL WANDERINGS

So much of what you need to know about the Dufferin course is apparent when you stand on the 1st tee. A wild but perfect fairway rumbles out from under the gorse, throwing up back-kicks of rocky outcrops as it tumbles down to the green. It's all on show and it is like a pint of perfect stout. The rich, creamy, heathland flourishes sink down into a deep, mature parkland. It's heaven all the way.

Trees appear later on and they are beautiful, giving huge presence to holes like the 7th, 8th, 10th . . . It is mesmerising golf and so full of the unexpected that you can't wait to get around the corner or over the crest to see what comes next. That makes a perfect golf experience. You will have no complaints here. Throw in just the right mix of challenges and variety, and you will love it.

As a visitor, you will find some holes are almost unfair: you have no idea how to tackle them (Strokesaver required) and it is long enough that you can't afford to be short off the tee (see below). But when you walk off the 18th, another rambunctious hole that will trip you up

(literally and figuratively), you will want to go straight back to the 1st.

Of course there are plenty of big driving holes on this parkland estate. And even on the blinder holes tee shots are thrilling. The trees rarely crowd you and approaches to greens all look inviting. It's a perfect landscape that changes around you and the holes just glide elegantly through it all. The clubhouse is big and plush – and easy to get lost in.

FAVOURITE HOLE
Par 4 13th. 360 yards. The setting for the green, under a huge stand of trees, straight up the hill, makes this a sweet parkland hole. The par 3s are all good – the 14th is treacherous, with water.

TOUGHEST HOLE
Par 4 4th. 392 yards. Scratching-head time. Between the trees is a sliver of fairway that bends left. Be sensible, because there's too much trouble if you go long. The green sits under trees with an old stone wall, but your second can be totally blind. Beautiful.

POINTS								
CD	A	G/F	B/W	L	F	V	G Ex	Total
17	9	10	8	7	10	10	19	90

THE COURSE
- Par 71
- Length: 6,550 yards
- Clandeboye Golf Club, Tower Road, Conlig, Co. Down, BT23 7PN
- Tel: +44 (0) 28 9127 1767 (048 from Rep. of Ire.)
- www.cgc-ni.com
- Green Fees: £36–£41

COURSES NEARBY
Bangor
Blackwood
Carnalea
Donaghadee
Royal Belfast

CLAREMORRIS   Established 1927

END OF THE ROAD

The narrow laneway to the clubhouse from the N17 is long and dark. It takes you well away from it all and puts you firmly in rolling countryside. It's a good start, which is helped by a beautifully shaped opening hole – there is a terrific curve to the hillside, but you can still see the flag. And the 2nd is a pretty, wooded par 3.

As country parkland courses go this has two distinct sets of holes: the rich and mature hilly holes, and the flat, open and wet holes. Somewhere in there are a new nine (1998) and an old nine (1927). For the most part it comes together very nicely.

Water plays an important part here. Sweet ponds look the part and attractive dykes of water will influence your shots on several of the flatter holes. The line of red wooden bridges is quaint and informative. Local knowledge will help you as you can't always gauge how far you are from trouble.

It is short for a par 73 so scoring opportunities abound: the par 5 3rd is 406 m with only water keeping you in check. Claremorris has been busy planting trees, especially on the new nine, and as these mature they will cause problems. But for now, the two distinct nines require quite different approaches. The best stretch is the 10th to 14th as there is tremendous shape and interest to the holes and it feels like proper parkland golf.

Driving range and chipping green are a long way apart and too far from the clubhouse.

FAVOURITE HOLE
Par 4 1st. 319 m. It's quite an introduction to the course. A severe bank runs down from the right about halfway up the fairway, and it is tough to judge where your drive will land and what is over the shoulder. Makes for a tough second.

TOUGHEST HOLE
Par 5 18th. 462 m. This is Index 16. Unless you're very long, you will be playing two shots to get around the dog-leg that stretches up the slope. The green is totally blind and well right with the pond below and left. An unfair finish.

POINTS								
CD	A	G/F	B/W	L	F	V	G Ex	Total
14	7	7	7	6	6	8	15	70

THE COURSE
- Par 70
- Length: 5,835 m
- Claremorris Golf Club, Castlemagarrett, Claremorris, Co. Mayo
- Tel: +353 (0) 94 937 1527
- www.claremorrisgolfclub.com
- Green Fees: €20–€25

COURSES NEARBY
Ballinrobe
Castlebar
Tuam

CLONES   Established 1913

AROUND THE HILL

Clones cascades around a spectacular wooded hilltop. You half-expect to see a famous boy wizard striding through the trees. This is a course that has great potential if they could just tidy it up – greens are big with some great tiers but are patchy, fairways are littered with drainage channels, and improving the tees would make a huge difference. It doesn't feel loved. The two openers would need to change too, but there are some super holes elsewhere, although with the rather grotty clubhouse you simply don't expect them.

Since I played Slieve Russell the previous day, in all its pristine brilliance, the rough and basic feel walking to the 1st hole did not instil confidence. But Clones sits in a lovely, open, heavily undulating, and very Irish setting with mature trees all around. The 3rd is the start of things, when fairways begin to twist and turn, rise and fall. Raised tees appear frequently – all offering sensational drives: the 6th is a dog-leg around a tree-lined pond that taunts the big hitters; the 11th requires you to walk under a huge beech and through farmland to a lonely tee box; and the 15th (see below) is the pick of the

bunch. The setting for the 18th tee is superb and it is a strong finishing hole. Bar the 2nd, the par 3s are attractive and very tricky. It's hard to believe that the 4th is Index 18, with its narrow green cut into the hillside.

Purists will complain about the quality, but you can't argue with the thrill or the price.

The 11th and 12th are in a separate field and are the most manufactured. Do not play here if they are using temporary greens: they are atrocious.

FAVOURITE HOLE
Par 4 15th. 370 m. The hole runs across the side of the central hill, with a great shoulder pitching down from the left. From your elevated tee box, it's a great view across to the green, backed by beeches, and there's water on the right of the fairway.

TOUGHEST HOLE
Par 5 16th. 483 m. Index 15 (I think not). A blind drive (one of two) past tight beech trees to a dog-legging fairway that is all bumps and slopes. Pure luck is needed to reach it. It's straightforward after that. The ladies' tee is your line.

POINTS								
CD	A	G/F	B/W	L	F	V	G Ex	Total
14	8	6	7	6	5	8	14	68

THE COURSE
- Par 71
- Length: 5,724 m
- Clones Golf Club, Hilton Park, Clones, Co. Monaghan
- Tel: +353 (0) 47 56017
- www.clonesgolfclub.com
- Green Fees: €25

COURSES NEARBY
County Cavan
Enniskillen
Slieve Russell

CLONMEL   Established 1911

AFTER YOU

How do you like your golf: flat or hilly? Clonmel certainly looks like the latter, but it's not too steep. Only the 8th and the 12th are going to hurt, but you will find steep slopes on four fairways so don't expect drives to stay on them. Elsewhere both the climbs and slopes are gentler. And they're worth it. I like hilly courses (see Muskerry) because of views and driving opportunities. Changes in elevation add to the challenge and open up a variety of shots into greens. Clonmel does not disappoint. The greens look flat; in fact, they are anything but. You will learn quickly to stay below the hole and you will want someone else to putt first because there are huge swings you simply cannot see.

It is a short and spacious par 72, but not easy, so sensible driving will be well rewarded. Seriously, do not try to cut dog-legs (the 5th, 6th, 8th, 10th and 12th). The holes are short enough and the trouble bad enough that it's not worth it. Open up the green and decide what to do from there. I suppose that is why there are so few bunkers: there's enough trouble to contend with already.

Hills, mountains and valleys surround you. The 14th (see below) hits straight into the heart of one and is the shot of the day. On the 4th, the ground behind the green disappears as you approach and plumes of velvet, white smoke rise from the factory below. Beautiful in a perverse way. And if you don't have views, you have the woods and quiet walks. The routing is excellent (apart from the 18th which hits over the 2nd).

The course map on the scorecard is tiny, so bring your glasses.

FAVOURITE HOLE
Par 3 14th. 178 yards. A beautiful long drop into a perfect bowl setting. A mountain stream runs along the right, arcing its way across, and a lone oak leans over the green to inspect your shot. It's a charming walk down to the green too, continuing up the 15th.

TOUGHEST HOLE
Par 4 13th. 405 yards. Index 1 and one of two holes over 400 yards. You can see the flag but the very narrow and bumpy fairway loops its way left and then back. It is cut into a steep slope so there is no respite above or below. If you stay on the fairway, be happy.

POINTS

CD	A	G/F	B/W	L	F	V	G Ex	Total
14	8	8	7	8	8	9	17	79

THE COURSE
- Par 72
- Length: 6,068 yards
- Clonmel Golf Club, Clonmel, Co. Tipperary
- Tel: +353 (0) 52 6124050
- www.clonmelgolfclub.com
- Green Fees: €25–€30

COURSES NEARBY
Cahir
Carrick-on-Suir
Slievenamon

CLONTARF   Established 1912

NICELY COMPACT

Clontarf is one of the courses closest to Dublin city centre – competing with Elm Park on the southside. It is lush and green and very tight. Eighteen short holes (the 18th is the only par 5 at 442 m) have been squeezed in and disciples of the big dog are going to be severely restricted if they are to do well here. Clontarf is about course management and using your head off the tee. And a lot safer, too, as fairways squeeze together with only single lines of beautiful trees dividing them. It must get dangerous at busy times.

There are fifteen very straightforward holes and, apart from one nice dip that affects three holes (on the 6th and 7th the greens sit nicely at the top of the rise), these all play on the level. Greens are very accessible (the occasional bunker appears short of the green to challenge your judgement), and the course is perfect for the canny golfer who knows a thing or two about hitting the ball dead straight and doesn't worry about length.

Holes 12 to 14 are a different matter entirely. Stunningly difficult and short holes that have considerable movement. The 12th is Index 1 and worthy of it. The 14th is a taunting dog-leg and only a perfect tee shot over an enormous, fake hump will open up the green.

The only club in Ireland to have fairway distance markers of 125 m. Time for the calculator.

A good clubhouse, and bowls too – if you're in the mood.

FAVOURITE HOLE
Par 4 1st. 297 m. Not dramatic, but it introduces you immediately to the difficulties of the course. A precision tee shot is needed to avoid the trees on the right (a draw won't work at Clontarf), and stay short of the bunker on this short, quirky dog-leg.

TOUGHEST HOLE
Par 4 12th. 326 m. You won't believe that this hole is dead straight. Not possible, you might think, but a tee shot of 200 m is needed to find the plateau that overlooks the drop, green and pond below. Very tough.

POINTS

CD	A	G/F	B/W	L	F	V	G Ex	Total
13	7	7	6	4	9	7	14	67

THE COURSE
- Par 69
- Length: 5,193 m
- Clontarf Golf Club, Donnycarney House, Malahide Road, Dublin 3
- Tel: +353 (0) 1 833 1892
- www.clontarfgolfclub.ie
- Green Fees: €30–€50

COURSES NEARBY
Elm Green
Howth
Royal Dublin
St Anne's

CLOVERHILL   Established 1999

WAIT FOR EIGHT

It is not often that you will find so many of the 'B' quality courses this close together: Ballymascanlon, Killin Park, Ashfield, Carnbeg and Cloverhill. Killin Park is the most entertaining but Cloverhill offers something unique. There are thirteen basic, open holes on gentle slopes, and then five tough beauties (the 8th to 12th). How that tickles you says a lot about your golf. Do you want easy golf or do you want the thrill of playing holes that might lighten your bag by a few balls?

It makes Cloverhill difficult to enjoy completely. What are you coming for? For me, the basic holes are open and danger-ous. There's no focus for your shots (drives and approaches) so you are invited to be wild. And while Colin, the young man who is the club's driving force, has put in strong bunkering, he doesn't have the resources to give the course some proper class (e.g. the greens). The five strong holes hug the side of a wild and rocky hill and work their way around a small lake that hosts two greens: the 9th (see below) and 11th, a sweet dog-leg that drifts around the lake.

Stronger golfers should play from the whites: it's 650 yards longer and makes the stream that runs across the 1st, 5th and 6th a real hazard.

In terms of quirky, the 16th and 17th share the same tee box, yet they go in opposite directions. If the opportunity presents itself, tee off the 9th twice: once for the 9th and once for the 10th. It shortens the walk and it is a brilliant second drive.

You have good views (the Ring of Guillion) all day and the basic clubhouse is seriously hospitable.

FAVOURITE HOLE
Par 3 9th. 107 yards. From a lovely rocky perch you hit straight down into the lake: if you don't hit the green, it's gorse or water. The par 3 12th hits over water into the mountainside.

TOUGHEST HOLE
Par 4 10th. 301 yards. Only Index 9 but this is a beautifully wild hole that slides under the mountain, down through ferns and rock. Two paces left, right or behind the green and your ball is gone. A great setting.

POINTS								
CD	A	G/F	B/W	L	F	V	G Ex	Total
12	6	5	8	8	4	7	13	63

THE COURSE
- Par 69
- Length: 5,417 yards (whites)
- Cloverhill Golf Club, Lough Road, Mullaghbawn, Newry, Co. Armagh, BT35 9XP
- Tel: +44 (0) 28 3088 9374 (048 from Rep. of Ire.)
- www.cloverhillgolfclub.co.uk
- Green Fees: £15–£20

COURSES NEARBY
Ashfield
Killin Park
Mannan Castle

COBH   Established 2009

HILLSIDE AND HARBOUR

Cobh is Ireland's newest golf club, stretching across a hillside that overlooks Cork Harbour, the River Lee and beyond. A long drive takes you up through the middle of the course, giving you a taste of what's to come. You will see immediately that it has been heavily shaped to give life to the holes.

Not surprisingly, the course has a large amount of maturing to do. It feels wide open and stark, and the few tree plantings look forlorn and lost. Time will change this, but it will always be an open course where the mounding dictates much of the design.

Cobh is divided by the driveway, with the lower holes (1 to 5, 16 and 17) having slightly more intrigue and shape. There are, however, two elements that are common throughout and these make Cobh a good test: firstly, your sightline from the tee to the fairway is often obscured by bunkers, mounding and dips, which makes drives that much more challenging; secondly, greens are well protected by fall-offs as well as bunkering that can encroach across half of the green. The sensible shot is to aim at the open part of the green, which might leave you with a long putt over swinging, double-breaking, perfect surfaces.

It may be a short course (with four of the five par 5s under 500 yards), but it is rarely good to miss the green and do not go long.

With its barren feel and pylons striding across the landscape it is a difficult course to love, but the five par 3s are good (two with water features) and you will be tested on a course that has definite signs of quality – the greens specifically.

New clubhouse due.

FAVOURITE HOLE
Par 3 10th. 149 yards. The island green, surrounded by water, the backdrop of views and the soaring tee shot make this a terrifying but wonderful hole. Little room for error.

TOUGHEST HOLE
Par 4 5th. 428 yards. Index 1 is a brute, driving uphill over a bunker to an unseen fairway that then sweeps left. A tough drive to gauge and a long second.

POINTS								
CD	A	G/F	B/W	L	F	V	G Ex	Total
14	6	8	7	8	6	7	14	70

THE COURSE
- Par 72
- Length: 6,250 yards
- Cobh Golf Club, Marino, Carraigaloe, Cobh, Co. Cork
- Tel: +353 (0) 21 481 2399
- www.cobhgolfclub.ie
- Green Fees: €25–€35

COURSES NEARBY
Cork
East Cork
Fota Island
Monkstown (as the crow flies)
Water Rock

CONCRA WOOD Established 2008

LOVE CONCRAS ALL

Lake Muckno is an achingly pretty lake, with tree-filled islands floating effortlessly on a canvas straight from an artist's imagination. Into this stretches a small finger-like peninsula that is home to two of Concra Wood's many remarkable holes – both requiring big drives over water. There is no doubt that the location is a key selling point, the land tumbling down from a gentle hilltop and revealing the lake's beauty from every hole, but that would detract from some stunning design. Holes 3, 8 and 12 are blissfully perfect, and shots on several other holes will stop you in your tracks. The Christy O'Connors have taken the 240 acres and used them brilliantly to create a course that constantly impresses. The routing ensures that you only see the full shape of the hole once you arrive on the tee – it adds to the drama and only disappoints on the 9th and 18th – and gives you so much space. So much space that the generous fairways evaporate quickly into wild, impossible rough and woods. On a course this long and intimidating, it delivers a surprisingly relaxed pace.

Changes in elevation are well dispersed, slotting in with flat holes that hug the lake – far too tightly for some, I imagine. Mounding twists along fairways with the result that you don't always see your ball finish, or see the base of the flag. It all complements the countryside's rolling drumlins and is mirrored around big, beautiful and fast green complexes – the 9th has a 50-yard, three-tiered green.

Brawn off the tee (bar 10), endless confidence and finesse around the greens are the only way you will conquer Concra. But you'll love trying.

FAVOURITE HOLE

Par 4 3rd. 339 m. A big, sweet drive down into a curving hole that takes you down to the lake's edge. It's all on show from the tee and looks perfect. The 8th is another beauty.

TOUGHEST HOLE

Par 4 10th. 407 m. Played once, the hole is relatively easy, so take this advice: hit to the end of the fairway you can see, about 200 m. Any more and you'll find trouble. The hole then drops like a stone to the green, for the best shot of the day.

POINTS								
CD	A	G/F	B/W	L	F	V	G Ex	Total
17	9	10	9	10	10	10	20	95

THE COURSE

- Par 72
- Length: 6,299 yards (gold)
- Concra Wood Golf Club, Castleblayney, Co. Monaghan
- Tel: +353 (0) 42 974 9485
- www.concrawood.ie
- Green Fees: €30–€50

COURSES NEARBY
Ashfield
Mannan Castle
Nuremore
Rossmore

CONNEMARA   Established 1973

BRUTALLY AND BEAUTIFULLY EXPOSED

Connemara (Ballyconneely) is a long way from another course, so consider Bearna, Oughterard or Connemara Isles (nine holes and amazing scenery) on your way here.

I played in benign conditions and I dread to think what it's like in the wind – perhaps that is why the fairways are so wide. On arrival, walk around the excellent new clubhouse and you will see just what's in store. It really builds a sense of anticipation. You start with a sharp dog-leg, steeply banked beyond the turn. Then it changes completely, with huge wide expanses of flat fairway stretching all around you. Bump-and-run heaven. You can watch the ball scamper for miles from elevated tee boxes. Rocks are littered about as if someone dropped a bag of marbles, but they rarely present a hazard, and only the steeply banked greenside bunkers cause problems.

Starting at the 12th you will sense that the land is about to change shape. Now the real fun starts. The 13th is a superb, daunting and solitary par 3 (see below); the 14th takes you higher still, and you get to absorb fully the perfect scenery of Slyne Head and the Twelve Pins. A soaring tee shot to the wide fairway below will challenge the short hitter, and from here on you need to consider every shot. There's more danger and a lot more excitement. The 17th and 18th are excellent par 5s – again with very high tee boxes – that run in opposite directions, so the wind will love you and kill you, one way or another. The approach to the 18th is almost vertical and makes for a superb finish.

Then you can play the third nine – hilly, nearer to the sea, and just as good.

FAVOURITE HOLE
Par 5 14th. 498 yards. A beautifully high tee box and a beautiful drive. Then, ahead, the fairway partially splits: taking the right line is fraught with danger; taking the left offers more room but no view of the putting surface as a bank rises steeply before you.

TOUGHEST HOLE
Par 3 13th. 200 glorious yards. It feels solitary here, perhaps in deference to the difficulty of your tee shot. You cross a gentle chasm to a sloping green that gives nothing away. Even if you hit it, the putt is a slider. And if you don't, the bunkers will catch you.

POINTS								
CD	A	G/F	B/W	L	F	V	G Ex	Total
17	8	9	10	10	10	9	18	91

THE COURSE
- Par 72
- Length: 6,666 yards
- Connemara Golf Club, Ballyconneely, Clifden, Co. Galway
- Tel: +353 (0) 95 23502/23602
- www.connemaragolflinks.com
- Green Fees: €35–€70

COURSES NEARBY
Oughterard
Westport

COOLLATTIN   Established 1930

ARBORETUM GOLF AT ITS VERY BEST

If you like trees – and I mean lots of trees – then Coollattin has more than enough for everyone. This is woodland, not parkland. The course wraps around an old estate house (not the clubhouse) and boasts mature trees of every description, from oak to monkey puzzle, and still they've planted more to separate the tamer fairways. If you can go eighteen holes without hitting or being blocked by a tree, then be thankful.

There are two things that stand out: the fast and difficult greens are tough to stay on and tougher to read, and eleven greens can't be seen from the tee box – either because of slopes or trees. For visitors, that can be hard work. Frustrating too, particularly on dog-legs where positioning is crucial if you want access to the green. There is no course map on the back of the card to help you either.

But Coollattin is well worth your time. The setting is quite imperious, with the huge trees watching over you every step of the way, and golf that is serious fun. There is a superb run in the middle, where the 12th is a short par 3 that is Index 9 and the renowned 15th is the shortest par 3, completely enclosed in a walled garden. The green is daintily perched above a ring of bunkers. The back nine are stronger and more colourful.

The pro shop is at the far end of the car park, and keep an eye out for golfers teeing off when you first enter the course. The three new holes are superb.

FAVOURITE HOLE
Par 4 9th. 383 yards. A downhill dog-leg that needs a perfect drive if you want to attack the green. Trees all along the left make that a tall order, and the only water on the course is to the right of the green.

TOUGHEST HOLE
Par 4 11th. 308 yards. You drive at the old, grey house but all the trouble is on your second. The fairway drops away to your right and the green is down in the corner. Anything short or off target will charge off the green, leaving a very tough uphill chip.

POINTS								
CD	A	G/F	B/W	L	F	V	G Ex	Total
15	10	7	7	6	7	10	18	80

THE COURSE

- Par 72
- Length: 6,337 yards
- Coollattin Golf Club, Shillelagh, Co. Wicklow
- Tel: +353 (0) 5394 29125
- www.coollattingolfclub.com
- Green Fees: €35–€45

COURSES NEARBY
Bunclody
Courtown
Macreddin
Mount Wolseley
Woodenbridge

CORBALLIS   Established 2003

SHORT, DYNAMIC LINKS

A public links course – there can't be many of those. And a punchy little links course it is too. Fingal County Council deserves a big thank-you for a par 66 that has some charismatic dunes, rumbling fairways and really wonderful holes. It could so easily be a housing estate. The four new holes, opened in 2009, are superb, with fairways and greens that twist through some remarkable seaside dunes. They are also extremely difficult, despite being short. Deep pot bunkers litter the greens, and it is simply not something you expect for such generous green fees.

There are some dangerous crossovers and some fairways are too tight together, so get out early to enjoy this popular course properly – you won't regret it. Several par 3s promise great tee shots, while par 4s have blind drives that are even more knee-trembling than usual because the holes are so short. The 2nd is a perfect example: you drive over a gentle uphill slope on the dunes, which hides a plateau on the left and a severe drop on the right. At 231 m you want to go for it, but common sense should prevail. On the 3rd, the tee shot down into a valley between invading dunes is as good a links tee shot as you will face.

The condition of the course is good, and the greens are over 30 m long in places, with lilting slopes. You also get to see the beach and some impressive seashore views – Lambay Island, Ireland's Eye and Howth. Poor facilities, but let's not quibble.

FAVOURITE HOLE
Par 4 5th. 295 m. New. A beautiful tee box in dunes. You drive alongside the beach onto a tossing fairway between impressive dunes. Your short shot to the green faces a tight setting with perfectly lethal pot bunkers.

TOUGHEST HOLE
Par 4 7th. 295 m. New. Totally blind, with a fairway that drops 100 yards in front of you, down on to another violent fairway. A good drive will mean you have no chance of an even lie for your approach.

POINTS								
CD	A	G/F	B/W	L	F	V	G Ex	Total
14	7	8	8	8	3	10	16	74

THE COURSE
- Par 66
- Length: 4,649 m
- Corballis Golf Links, Corballis Road, Donabate, Co. Dublin
- Tel: +353 (0) 1 843 6583
- www.corballislinks.com
- Green Fees: €20–€25

COURSES NEARBY
Balcarrick
Beaverstown
Donabate
Island, The

Hole 6 'Five Penny Piece'
Portstewart Golf Club (Strand)
Par 3, 135 yards, Index 17
The green falls away sharply on all sides on this short, treacherous beauty. (© Bernard Findlay)

Hole 7
Lahinch Golf Club (Old)
Par 4, 366 yards, Index 6
A gentle dog-leg that starts and ends above the sea and slides inland between the dunes. (Courtesy Lahinch Golf Club)

Hole 8
Druid's Glen Golf Club
Par 3, 140 yards, Index 11
One of the most colourful holes around. The green is in the prettiest setting, over water. (Courtesy Druid's Glen Golf Club)

Hole 9
Royal County Down Golf Club
Par 4, 428 yards, Index 5
World famous, this is a blind drive straight at Slieve Donard in the Mourne Mountains. What awaits beyond is as dramatic as it gets. (Courtesy Royal County Down Golf Club)

CORK Established 1888

INTO THE QUARRY

After Fota Island I thought it unlikely that Cork would inspire me in the same way and it didn't: it inspired me in a completely different way. Fota Island is a beautiful course for the whole round, designed to appease and reward golfers. Cork ignores such considerations and lays on some terrific drama and challenges as you play along the water of Cork Harbour and then turn into a lime quarry for the most mesmerising, gorse-drenched holes.

Yet Cork throws in a few tame holes that contrast sharply with the thrills elsewhere. For instance, when you stand on the 1st tee, the three holes within view look dull. They are uninteresting parkland holes. 'What's all the fuss?' you'll think, because Cork has a big reputation. The drive on the 2nd is majestic, but when you reach the 4th, Index 1, *boom*: you've arrived at the stunning stretch of holes. You hit over the water of Cork Harbour and straight up. Brilliant. But it gets better. The 5th takes you to the water's edge for a drive over an old stone kiln and oceans of gorse and scruff. Terrifying, and the green sits perilously close to the water's edge. Brilliant again. But it still

gets better. Holes 6 to 9 are on the floor of the quarry, and it is heaven (or hell, as walls of rough rise up the sides). The beautiful shapes and individuality are impossible to describe here.

After that, the temperature cools, although it is still enjoyable, until you reach the excellent 16th and 17th.

There is a wide variety of holes, different landscapes and different levels of difficulty. But it is a thrilling adventure with those quarry holes living long in the memory.

FAVOURITE HOLE
Par 5 5th. 505 m. All the holes in the quarry are magnificent, and I love the 17th, but the 5th stands out as a seriously brilliant hole. Please play from the white tees to appreciate fully the beauty and the difficulty as you play along the sea.

TOUGHEST HOLES
Par 3 7th and 9th. The 8th squeezes between the two and is a knee-trembler off the tee, but the two par 3s in the quarry need excellent precision, and the green on the 9th is a riot of fun. Both are difficult to par.

POINTS								
CD	A	G/F	B/W	L	F	V	G Ex	Total
16	9	9	9	7	10	7	17	84

THE COURSE
- Par 72
- Length: 5,956 m (white)
- Cork Golf Club, Little Island, Cork, Co. Cork
- Tel: +353 (0) 21 435 3451
- www.corkgolfclub.ie
- Green Fees: €50–€95

COURSES NEARBY
Cobh
Douglas
Fota Island
Mahon
Water Rock

CORRSTOWN   Established 1991

DOG-LEG DAY

The outskirts of Dublin offer a huge selection of golfing opportunities. Corrstown is one and it has some nice touches. There are twenty-seven holes, lots of water, an island fairway and an island green finish. And a fantastic clubhouse (gorgeous showers). There are five par 5s (three in the opening five holes) and five par 3s.

The land is flat, but mounds have been employed effectively to separate fairways and surround greens. It makes a big difference as this farming landscape offers little else. You'll also find dog-legs galore, including some doubles on the par 5s.

The course is not exactly thrilling but it does challenge you constantly. Because it is so flat the dog-legs are all hard to gauge, so calculating where to land drives on narrow fairways is tough. Especially as copses of semi-mature trees are well placed – they will cause mayhem in years ahead. There are fairway bunkers and, on several occasions, tricky bunkers appear very tight to the greens. The water on the 'River Course' (nine holes) adds interest and difficulty, notably on the 2nd (see below) and on the short par 5 5th, where

a stone-walled ditch lies hidden in front of the green. The pond and fountain around the 11th and 13th greens deliver an extra flourish.

Perhaps there are too many dog-legs with bland drives. Hitting straight at a distant green feels more rewarding, as emphasised by the straight 5th hole. But on this landscape the dog-legs are a strong defence and, while Corrstown feels like it should be easy, it is anything but.

FAVOURITE HOLE

Par 3 9th. 141 m. A wonderful one-shotter. From the tee, the stone-walled stream runs diagonally across you as it runs to the green. Then it turns into a pond that fronts the putting surface and runs around to the left. So keep right.

TOUGHEST HOLE

Par 5 2nd. 504 m. A double dog-leg. It is hard to hit a full drive because it is difficult to judge your line. Then you swing right and the problem reappears. An island fairway beyond the trees means plenty of danger, although you can hit right.

POINTS

CD	A	G/F	B/W	L	F	V	G Ex	Total
13	6	7	8	5	9	7	14	69

THE COURSE

- Par 72
- Length: 6,077 m
- Corrstown Golf Club, Kilsallaghan, Co. Dublin
- Tel: +353 (0) 1 864 0533
- www.corrstowngolfclub.com
- Green Fees: €30–€50

COURSES NEARBY
Roganstown
St Margaret's
Swords

COUNTY ARMAGH   Established 1893

TIGHT, ROLLING PARKLAND

All very tasty. This is the kind of parkland that stands out because of its maturity and its beautifully ambling landscape. It sits right on the edge of town, but feels as if it is well out in the country. There is great shape and routing as you head in various directions, and the run of seven holes, from the 7th to 13th, which alternates between par 3s and par 5s gives that extra character you rarely find. County Armagh is a par 70 and it's not long. But it is very tight, and the subtle dog-legs and changes in elevation make for tough driving. In particular, you will find big trees crowding you on numerous occasions – some very close to the tee. Water makes an occasional appearance – on Index 1 16th, it turns a 438-yard par 4 into a par 5 for most golfers – but Armagh is about the trees and a landscape that moves you in more ways than one.

Bunkers have been added, most notably after the 8th, and more are planned. You will find the greens very difficult: subtle slopes make holing out surprisingly tricky, and there are some much bigger slopes on other holes that make it crucial to be below the hole (the 3rd, 10th and 17th). There are few easy shots here and if you are having a wayward day, then good luck with the trees; but if you're playing well it is hugely rewarding.

The obelisk (the 10th is so named) stands very prominently during the middle holes. And you're in for a thrilling late challenge as the last three holes are dastardly. A great value golf course.

FAVOURITE HOLE
Par 3 11th. 170 yards. A beauty of a downhill par 3 with big trees down the right and the green sitting perfectly. The par 3 13th is also good, hitting directly at the obelisk, slightly uphill and to a hidden putting surface.

TOUGHEST HOLE
Par 4 18th. 401 yards. Index 6 is a nasty dog-leg to finish. A perfect drive is required to avoid OB on the inside of the dog-leg and the steep slopes off the other side. Only then can you see the green, similarly perched. Two tough shots.

POINTS								
CD	A	G/F	B/W	L	F	V	G Ex	Total
15	7	7	7	6	8	10	15	75

THE COURSE
- Par 70
- Length: 6,018 yards
- County Armagh Golf Club, 7 Newry Road, Armagh, Co. Armagh, BT60 1EN
- Tel: +44 (0) 28 3752 5861 (048 from Rep. of Ire.)
- www.golfarmagh.co.uk
- Green Fees: £17–£22

COURSES NEARBY
Banbridge
Dungannon
Loughgall
Tandragee

COUNTY CAVAN   Established 1894

CREATIVE HILLSIDE GOLF

The rolling hills and the ancient beech and oak trees are the features of this quiet, country course. Nowhere more so than when you stand on the 8th and 11th tee boxes, on either side of the entrance road. They sit in the shadow of several oak trees that block out the light. Elsewhere, enormous beeches have crept onto fairways (the 3rd, 8th and 16th) and the last four holes flow between lines of mature trees.

There is plenty of variety to the course design, in terms of hole shapes, bunkers and greens. The start is certainly entertaining with a roller-coaster hole taking you through two huge troughs. By the time you walk off the 4th you will be thinking it's hilly, but it calms down after that. A better description is heavily undulating. Greens are muted and sit flat on the landscape (so watch out for some slopes), before evolving into the more current raised and mounded style with deep bunkers.

Fairways are wide at the start but often have tricky slopes (the 1st, 2nd, 6th and 7th). Still, it is a course you'll want to attack and you can do so with limited trouble off the tee.

Holes 12 to 14 let the course down badly – it feels like they don't belong: the 12th is a silly dog-leg that strays far too close to the driving range; the 13th is a lifeless par 3; and the 14th is dull. Fortunately, when you stand at the back of the green on the 14th, the view down the 15th (see below) is wonderful, and the final holes make for a strong, tight finish.

Signs to get you to the 10th and 12th (beside the 1st) tees would help.

FAVOURITE HOLE
Par 5 7th. 488 m. Not an exciting drive as the fairway drifts out of sight, but when you see where the hole goes, all is forgiven. The fairway tilts sharply as it swings down to the green, which is in a lovely wooded setting.

TOUGHEST HOLE
Par 4 15th. 363 m. A very pretty and dangerous hole. Certainly the toughest drive of the day, hitting over a large pond to a heavily tree-lined and tight fairway. Anything right is gone. A small stream lies in front of the green.

POINTS								
CD	A	G/F	B/W	L	F	V	G Ex	Total
14	7	7	6	6	7	8	15	70

THE COURSE
- Par 70
- Length: 5,627 m
- County Cavan Golf Club, Arnmore House, Drumelis, Co. Cavan
- Tel: +353 (0) 49 433 1541
- www.cavangolf.ie
- Green Fees: €20–€25

COURSES NEARBY
Clones
Farnham Estate
Slieve Russell

COUNTY LONGFORD   Established 1900

HILLTOP VISTAS

First off, this is not easy to find, and you will probably overshoot the horrible potholed lane to the club. Second, Longford town is rarely a destination but if you are on your way to Sligo or Westport, drop in for a round. People have been doing so for over a hundred years.

The course is basic, which is not meant as an insult. The tee boxes are poor, some water features are messy and fairway quality varies, but the greens are really good (perhaps the greensman should have a word with the rest of the crew), varying in size and with some tricky slopes and turns. The first nine holes run around the perimeter, while the back nine run side by side in the middle. The course is set on top of a hill, so there are plenty of climbs (the 9th goes straight up 364 m and is Index 1). Trees and water features mix together to create the hazards (the bunkers are dull), and Longford certainly likes its pairs: trees often flank the tee boxes, giving you a nice line to the fairway (the 4th, 10th and 14th), or else they form sentries on the fairway itself. Water appears at the 4th and runs for a few holes, nowhere more effectively than on the greens of the attractive 6th and 12th, where the same water, reeds and ducks come into play.

For a par 72 it is short, with three holes under 300 m. The course is also very open so there is room to move around. Holes 6, 7 and 8 stand out, while 12 and 14 are the best on the back nine.

Poor changing facilities but powerful showers – always a plus.

FAVOURITE HOLE
Par 4 6th. 337 m. Long hitters shouldn't struggle too much, but the tree in the middle of the fairway and lots of water to the right and trees to the left (OB) make for a very tough approach for everyone else.

TOUGHEST HOLE
Par 3 14th. 185 m. It is long and the raised green is partially hidden behind the bunker. It's tough to read and needs a perfect shot – not easy for a first-time visitor. The green is wide.

POINTS								
CD	A	G/F	B/W	L	F	V	G Ex	Total
12	6	7	6	6	5	7	14	63

THE COURSE
- Par 72
- Length: 5,766 m
- County Longford Golf Club, Glack, Dublin Road, Longford, Co. Longford
- Tel: +353 (0) 43 3346310
- www.countylongfordgolfclub.com
- Green Fees: €20–€35

COURSES NEARBY
Athlone
Carrick-on-Shannon
Glasson
Roscommon

COUNTY LOUTH   Established 1892

TACKLING THE WIND FROM EVERY ANGLE

Let's start with the obvious: this is a quality links that held the Irish Open in 2004 and 2009. It starts off looking a bit flat and open, but it quickly changes gear as you approach the completely hidden 3rd green. Yes, you do come back to the flatter, less interesting holes from time to time, but they are well dispersed with the dramatic holes. For example, the 11th (Index 1) is flat, open and dull but the 12th tips you straight back into the dunes for the five best holes on the course. The dunes really swell up around you giving the holes tremendous movement, on and off the fairway. This is enhanced by the high tee boxes (common to almost every hole) which give you great views over the hole ahead as well as others around you.

Baltray has natural and smart routing that allows the wind to hit you from every side. It has great variety and space. Many of the deceptive putting surfaces are hidden and you'll hold your breath if you hit off-line – with some remarkable fairways and entrances to greens you could end up either 6 feet from the pin, in one of the precisely positioned, velvet bunkers, or in the rough at the bottom of a slope. And then there are the surfaces . . . I putted off one green and that was in March.

The only sea views are from the 14th tee (which backs onto the 16th at Seapoint), which is also one of the best drives.

Brute strength will help you off many tees, but the demand for finesse closer to the greens will prove more potent. And that is what makes Baltray so good.

FAVOURITE HOLE
Par 3 5th. 158 yards. A great par 3 tucked up against a dune that will fill you with despair if you hit short or left. Big slopes and a big bunker. Vicious green too.

TOUGHEST HOLE
Par 4 16th. 401 yards. It depends on whether you're talking about difficulty off the tee (landing area and approach shot on dog-leg 16th) or wind (the 9th, 11th and par 3s particularly).

POINTS								
CD	A	G/F	B/W	L	F	V	G Ex	Total
17	8	9	10	7	10	8	17	86

THE COURSE
- Par 72
- Length: 6,716 yards
- County Louth Golf Club, Baltray, Drogheda, Co. Louth
- Tel: +353 (0) 41 988 1530
- www.countylouthgolfclub.com
- Green Fees: €65–€135

COURSES NEARBY
Balbriggan
Bellewstown
Laytown & Bettystown
Seapoint

COUNTY MEATH   Established 1898

SOLID, MATURE PARKLAND

An old parkland that has mellowed well. There is a sense of permanence that comes from maturity and the trees are the bedrock of this. They give character to the course, as well as providing much of the danger (there's not much water here). Consider all the young courses with their semi-mature trees – this is what they will look like in time. The landscape has good movement without ever becoming hilly, and it all adds up to a relaxing round of golf.

The scorecard reads 5,800 m (par 73) from the green visitor tees, so there are several very short par 4s and this is where you will really notice the trees: the 4th has trees completely blocking your route to the green, the 11th is a dog-leg around a line of evergreens, the 14th has a narrowing neck of trees as you approach the green . . . you get the idea. The sloping fairway on the 14th makes this one of the best holes (despite being beside the road). It calls for restraint but also causes some frustration – big hitters will have little choice but to be sensible and the back nine see this a little too often.

It is a course that comes together well, even though it excites only occasionally. Tee boxes are good, as are the greens which are well guarded by gentle bunkers. With their soft apron of mounding running behind, they make welcome targets too.

There are times when you can see other holes, and the spaghetti junction around the 4th, 5th, 8th, 9th, 16th, 17th and 18th can be busy, emphasising that it is tight in places and perhaps a bit dangerous.

Good facilities and big clubhouse.

FAVOURITE HOLE
Par 4 5th. 356 m. The prettiest hole on the course and Index 2. It is long and straight but the conifers on the left, in a little dell, add real character.

TOUGHEST HOLE
Par 5 2nd. 461 m. It is the drive that makes it difficult as the fairway curls right around a large pond. Then another two good blows to reach the green.

POINTS								
CD	A	G/F	B/W	L	F	V	G Ex	Total
13	7	7	6	5	10	7	13	68

THE COURSE
- Par 73
- Length: 5,800 m
- County Meath Golf Club, Newtownmoynagh, Trim, Co. Meath
- Tel: +353 (0) 46 943 1463
- www.countymeathgolfclubtrim.ie
- Green Fees: €20–€35

COURSES NEARBY
Glebe
Knightsbrook
Rathcore

COUNTY SLIGO   Established 1894

MOVED BY MOUNTAINS

Glorious: a links course and location that lift the spirits. The mighty Benbulbin is ever present, looming ominously as you look up from the clubhouse. Whispering dunes reach out to the Atlantic, where rolling whitecaps roar as they crash against beaches and cliffs. Perfect scenery for a perfect round of links golf. History? The Metal Man and warrior queen are just the start.

There are three courses in one here, but your driver will be flashing all day, searching out generous but often dangerous fairways. Your second shots always demand care even when greens are visible, for trouble lurks out of sight with bunkers, hollows and railway-sleepered streams. This is especially true on the stunning plateau-like floor of the course (the 5th to 8th, the 14th to 16th), which is reached with a soaring drive from the sky-piercing 5th tee. The 9th to 13th take you on a different and breathtaking run, starting and finishing with superb par 3s: the 9th hits straight at Benbulbin, while the 13th hits over the beach and down onto the plateau again. In between, the 10th and 11th are solitary with violently formed fairways and the 12th, The

Lighthouse, goes out almost into the sea. From here it is a tough run in, along Drumcliff Bay, with dunes between you and the beach. Tom Watson favours the 14th but the ferocious 17th works for me, rising up majestically beside the 5th.

The course is predominantly out and back so the low dunes invite the wind to rattle you all the way home. Perhaps what makes this course so brilliant is the variety that you don't find at the other mighty links. The landscape inspired W. B. Yeats, and County Sligo will inspire you too.

FAVOURITE HOLE
Par 4 10th. 348 m. Benbulbin lines your left, beyond a wall of dunes as you hit at a distant valley. The hole curves down and gently right with a heavy slope through the fairway's spine. The flag flutters teasingly over the dunes.

TOUGHEST HOLE
Par 4 17th. 385 m. The only drive that will give you serious pause. It is along the flat but you could run out of room. A good lie is essential if you're to reach the green above you and to your left, set in a lethal hollow of heavy rough under the hillside.

POINTS								
CD	A	G/F	B/W	L	F	V	G Ex	Total
19	10	10	10	10	8	10	20	97

THE COURSE
- Par 71
- Length: 5,852 m
- County Sligo Golf Club, Rosses Point, Co. Sligo
- Tel: +353 (0) 71 917 7134/7186
- www.countysligogolfclub.ie
- Green Fees: €70

COURSES NEARBY
Castle Dargan
Enniscrone
Strandhill

COURTOWN   Established 1936

A COLOURFUL PARKLAND COURSE

Ireland's southeast boasts glorious beaches and sunny climes. Not much is made of the golf courses, which is a shame because Courtown leaves a smile on your face.

There are no pretensions here, despite an interesting design that mixes in pretty much everything a parkland connoisseur could ask for – water, undulations, big trees, gentle and sharp dog-legs, and very tricky par 3s. And no houses. The course certainly favours golfers who have a fade, but it is also short enough that careful course management (most notably navigating the trees off the tee) will reap its rewards. The 7th, 11th and 17th are the long and difficult par 4s.

The hilly terrain and bountiful trees promise excellent shots into greens and two terrific elevated tee shots (the 4th and 15th). Water at the 4th, 12th and 18th certainly presents problems – the 18th is a terrific par 3 with a lot of water to carry. But prepare for some angst on the disastrous, remodelled, double dog-leg par 5 9th.

Definitely a very enjoyable day out and well worth a visit if you are nearby. It is good enough quality and will appeal to everyone. You'll certainly talk about it fondly in the warm clubhouse afterwards. More colourful than nearby Seafield.

FAVOURITE HOLE
Par 4 4th. 288 m. A great downhill driving hole that puts you well above the trees and will tempt you into going for too much. So is it a driver or an iron? Very little room for error on this slight dog-leg, with water beside the green. The 15th is similarly dramatic.

TOUGHEST HOLE
Par 3 14th. 169 m. A long hit over a gentle valley. Slopes all around the green mean that pinpoint accuracy is necessary. Miss the green right and you'll have a nightmare shot in.

POINTS

CD	A	G/F	B/W	L	F	V	G Ex	Total
15	8	8	8	7	8	9	16	79

THE COURSE
- Par 71
- Length: 5,696 m
- Courtown Golf Club, Courtown, Co. Wexford
- Tel: +353 (0) 5394 25166 www.courtowngolfclub.com
- Green Fees: €35–€45

COURSES NEARBY
Ballymoney
Enniscorthy
Seafield
Wexford

CRADDOCKSTOWN   Established 1991

EASILY WET

If you can get around Craddockstown without finding water then you will do very well indeed. When you stand on the 1st tee, you will appreciate what I mean. Between some big and beautiful ponds, which look good but play dirty, and numerous streams that often hide out of sight, fourteen holes introduce you to the wet stuff.

The course is subtly undulating so there is no exertion involved – it is a gentle tree-lined parkland that sits in the middle of farmland on the outskirts of Naas. The design is straightforward and it is left to the water to bring holes to life, and the many curvaceous bunkers to give them shape. It all works very smartly too, and holes like the 10th and 12th show off the course brilliantly with nerve-wracking approaches over big water (and swans and ducks).

The length of holes changes to good effect but it is never long. However, it still requires good course management as trees often come close, fairways narrow sharply, fairway bunkers are well placed and dog-legs abound (even if only the most subtle of drifts around trees).

There is a big pond that plays a major part on holes 1, 2 and 3 (the 3rd tee sits in it), but it is the ponds on the 10th, 11th, 13th and 14th that light up the course. Perhaps the only disappointment is the green settings which are tame. With more time (to let the trees make more impact) and some more oomph around greens, Craddockstown will fulfil its potential.

FAVOURITE HOLE
Par 4 10th. 323 m. Index 2. This slightly downhill hole has a tough drive because you simply can't see enough to gauge where to aim. It needs a perfect shot as the hole dog-legs slowly to a green that sits elegantly behind a large pond.

TOUGHEST HOLE
Par 5 14th. 456 m. A sharp dog-leg with lots of water. It might restrict your drive as there is a stream at the turn. There is another one, hidden, 100 m from the green and a pond all along the left. Two very careful shots required.

POINTS								
CD	A	G/F	B/W	L	F	V	G Ex	Total
13	7	7	8	5	8	9	14	71

THE COURSE

- Par 72
- Length: 5,748 m
- Craddockstown Golf Club, Blessington Road, Naas, Co. Kildare
- Tel: +353 (0) 45 897 610
- www.craddockstown.com
- Green Fees: €20–€30

COURSES NEARBY
Bodenstown
Killeen
Naas
Palmerstown

CREGMORE PARK   Established 2007

WONDERFULLY UNEXPECTED

When you drive up to the club, past the owners' house, you expect a very basic, farmland affair. Well, you're in for a surprise. Cregmore Park has a quality that runs through the whole course. Tee boxes, fairways and bunkering are excellent. And the greens are superb: they are fast and dangerous, and even though they are easily accessible, it is a treacherous campaign if you try to stop the ball by the pin. Running shots work effectively here.

This is an open and flat landscape. It doesn't sound interesting, and it is not dramatic, but you will quickly discover that there is an easy rhythm that makes playing a pleasure. Arthur Spring, the designer, knew exactly how to bring character to the holes, and he uses fairway bunkers extremely effectively to give them structure. This is important because the flat landscape makes driving a touch dull. Flags are on show too. There are only a couple of real dog-legs, but even on these you can see the flag. It ensures that the holes attractive and tempting to play. The Ring Fort by the 4th, 8th and 9th is a highlight, adorned with big trees and old walls.

Despite the fescue grasses that separate holes and the strategic and attractive bunkering, you have lots of room and you can drive to your heart's content. True, the first cut of rough is thick enough, but you'll have a shot and you shouldn't lose a ball.

This is a family affair and it works so easily. The facilities are simple at this stage, but more are planned. Time will bring out the best in this course.

FAVOURITE HOLE
Par 4 14th. 409 yards. Perfectly straight, with trees and OB on your right and plenty of room on your left. It is a gently rising hole but I like it for its simplicity.

TOUGHEST HOLE
Par 4 5th. 398 yards. The only big dog-leg, but the green is visible. Bunkers push you left, but big hitters will be tempted to go for more, making it a tough drive. Risk and reward.

POINTS								
CD	A	G/F	B/W	L	F	V	G Ex	Total
14	7	10	9	6	6	8	15	75

THE COURSE
- Par 72
- Length: 6,574 yards
- Cregmore Park Golf Club, Cregmore, Co. Galway
- Tel: +353 (0) 91 799 799
- www.cregmorepark.com
- Green Fees: €25–€30

COURSES NEARBY
Athenry
Galway Bay
Gort
Loughrea
Tuam

THE CURRAGH   Established 1883

HEATHLAND HEAVEN

The Curragh likes to make a lot of its heritage as the oldest course in Ireland. And why shouldn't it? This is vintage heathland golf. Just stand on the high 1st tee and enjoy the spectacle that stretches out ahead of you. You will be able to see holes running through the gorse on the hillside opposite, as well as through old trees to your right. It is a thrilling opening drive – over sheep possibly – and it starts as it means to go on. Great elevation, great shape to the landscape and every shot is tempting. Seriously, there are few courses where you can say that, but as you walk from one hole to the next, there is a sense of expectation. You are rarely disappointed.

Rambunctious fairways stay true to their heathland origin and you could be standing up, down or sideways. Such things make for a thrilling course. There are views here too, and wonderful old trees that steer you around at a leisurely rhythm. Like a great malt whiskey, it must be enjoyed slowly. You need to ponder over your shots as fairway positioning is critical on many holes (the 3rd, 9th, 12th,

17th and 18th especially) and while greens are accessible, there are protective small, sharp mounds and hollows that can prove awkward.

You will appreciate how age has made this course so special. It feels so settled.

The course slips and slides over a couple of hillsides and several bells need to be rung. With its shape, sheep and deep green colours, this is a course to be loved.

FAVOURITE HOLE

Par 5 12th. 519 yards. Starting from a height, you drive towards a soft bend between pine trees. It's open enough, but the hole then sweeps left and up between gorse to a raised green. The views straight over the hole are enchanting. Don't hit the sheep.

TOUGHEST HOLE

Par 4 17th. 437 yards. Index 1. A tough enough drive over a gentle-looking hill, but you must keep left or your shot will be blocked by large trees near the green. It is a long second and you may be on a downhill lie.

POINTS								
CD	A	G/F	B/W	L	F	V	G Ex	Total
17	10	9	7	8	8	10	19	88

THE COURSE

- Par 72
- Length: 6,416
- The Curragh Golf Club, The Curragh, Co. Kildare
- Tel: +353 (0) 45 441 714
- www.curraghgolf.com
- Green Fees: €20–€35

COURSES NEARBY
Dunmurry Springs
Newbridge
Tulfarris

CURRA WEST   Established 1986

KNOCK ON WOOD

This is a par 67, with seven par 3s. It is a farmland scramble-type affair that wouldn't have the word 'quality' associated with it. 'Quirky' is a better word and, to be honest, if you come here knowing this, you will have a good bit of fun. But beware, as it is squeezed in, which will make it dangerous on a busy day, and you'll hear plenty of woodwork.

It is a tumbling landscape that darts about the place with many healthy trees planted to delineate fairways. Some greens lie flat at the end of the fairway; others are piled up high with severe banks and amusing shapes. There are also a number of holes that head up and down fields lined by drystone walls. It adds interest and they aren't as dull as they sound.

Yes, the course is short, but it is quirky enough and littered with tricky green settings and patchy surfaces so that it is far from easy. You will also find a few tricky drives hampered by trees (see below) and random spot bunkers.

The location is pleasant, with calm and distant countryside fanning out when you come over the top of the 2nd.

This course is about fun and knocking a ball about, but not a lot more.

FAVOURITE HOLE
Par 4 14th. 305 m. This is about the downhill drive into a left-hand dog-leg. An ash to the right of the tee will strike fear into anyone who draws the ball, as a marshy area lies out of sight, front and left of the green.

TOUGHEST HOLE
Par 4 1st. 282 m. A tiny, narrow drive makes your opening shot look impossible. It almost is, and finding fairway is cause for celebration. The green sits perched into a bank and is not easy to find.

POINTS

CD	A	G/F	B/W	L	F	V	G Ex	Total
11	6	5	5	7	4	7	13	58

THE COURSE
- Par 67
- Length: 4,586 m
- Curra West Golf Club, Curra, Kylebrack, Loughrea, Co. Galway
- Tel: +353 (0) 9097 45121
- www.currawest.com
- Green Fees: €15–€20

COURSES NEARBY
Ballinasloe
Gort
Loughrea
Portumna

DEER PARK Established 1973

TOO GOOD, TOO BAD

I can't help it. Deer Park gives you a whopping great start and then just fades away until the closing three holes. You get this great entrance that passes a castle, driving ever higher. The views from the clubhouse/hotel are super (though not as good as Howth next door) and when you walk to the 1st tee, your eyes are drawn to the dipping hillside that stretches off to the coastline, the island and ever northwards. And it's a great opening drive, almost straight at the castle below. The 2nd is wonderfully tucked into mature woods, completely on its own (as is the 16th alongside), but then you get to thirteen holes that are so unexpectedly tame – compared to the start – it's startling. They are all flat, and it is only the pockets of semi-mature trees that provide character. There is an old wall stretching across a couple of holes and one lovely copse of Scots pine (9th and 12th) but it isn't enough. The good-looking 10th gives a quick lift with water to the right.

I probably wouldn't be so harsh if it was all like this, but to give you such a start and then drop the tempo by 75 per cent is a real kick in the pants. There are five good holes and the rest are just docile parkland. There is room to play but if you do stray into the trees, you probably won't see your ball again. Greens are slightly raised but don't have much interest and please be aware of 'fore' on a few holes.

There are another eighteen holes here, which are quirkier and more entertaining. They are presented as two nines.

FAVOURITE HOLE
Par 4 16th. 290 m. A great hole after what comes before. You're tucked into a dense woodland avenue that can be terrifying off the tee, and the hole rises sweetly to the green.

TOUGHEST HOLES
Par 4 8th. 380 m. Only because it's long. The 18th is a tough closing uphill par 5 with no sight of the putting surface.

POINTS								
CD	A	G/F	B/W	L	F	V	G Ex	Total
12	6	5	5	7	6	7	12	60

THE COURSE
- Par 72
- Length: 5,825 m
- Deer Park Golf Club, Deer Park Hotel, Howth Demesne, Howth, Co. Dublin
- Tel: +353 (0) 1 832 2624
- www.deerpark-hotel.ie
- Green Fees: €18–€26

COURSES NEARBY
Howth
Portmarnock
Portmarnock Links
Royal Dublin
St Anne's

DELGANY   Established 1908

SHORT, HILLY AND WELL DEFENDED

I played Delgany a few years ago and thought I could review it from memory. If I had, I would have missed so much, including the sweet drive up to the splendid new clubhouse.

Delgany can be summed up as short, pretty, tree-lined and very hilly. I repeat, very hilly. It has matured gracefully over the years and it will challenge you on two levels: mature trees can hurt your scorecard and your pride from the start with some tight holes (the 5th and 11th are seriously squeezed on the left); and the ascents will wear out the fittest golfer. Of course, the advantage of climbing up is that you are left with spectacular drives down, and Delgany has five such holes hitting out to sea, accompanied by views of Wicklow's hillsides. With several short par 4s, big hitters will want to give it a lash. That would be their mistake, as Delgany demands respect – the 7th, at just 301m, is Index 4. If you drive 220 m plus, then dog-legs on the 3rd, 4th and 6th will rein you in and changes in elevation always confuse. Some of the greens are quite tricky too, with only the tips of flags visible – nowhere more so than the Index 1 12th, where the green is perched high and tucked into the corner.

The 16th and 17th are a quirky combination, where you drive off the 17th before playing the par 3 16th. Both are thrilling tee shots: the 17th hits over a sharp valley to a ski-slope fairway and the par 3 16th is a soaring shot to a green immersed in trees below.

FAVOURITE HOLE

Par 4 13th. 285 m. The shortest downhill par 4 and reachable. The fairway mimics a links with a huge roller-coaster hump in the middle, but bunkers squeeze the green completely and a dense wood runs to the right. Still, worth a lash.

TOUGHEST HOLE

Par 3 5th. 163 m. Your first par 3, uphill, and the putting surface is hidden. Then there are the trees all along the left, and one beauty overhanging the green on the right. A very precise shot required. A friend aced it, allegedly.

POINTS								
CD	A	G/F	B/W	L	F	V	G Ex	Total
14	7	8	7	7	9	7	16	75

THE COURSE

- Par 68
- Length: 5,232 m
- Delgany Golf Club, Delgany, Co. Wicklow
- Tel: +353 (0) 1 287 4536
- www.delganygolfclub.com
- Green Fees: €26–€45

COURSES NEARBY
Charlesland
Druid's Glen/Heath
Glen of the Downs
Greystones
Powerscourt

DELVIN CASTLE   Established 1991

A PARKLAND ARBORETUM

After the rather plush finesse of Knightsbrook in the morning, it was a complete change of gear at Delvin Castle. Colossal trees of every description accompany you almost all the way around. They are majestic, and are not shy about getting in your way. This is an amusing, rolling course that has huge variety in the shape and length of holes – even if fairways/greens are a bit weak. Holes 1, 2 and 12 are the only ones without trees, and are the least exciting as a result. Holes 11 to 15 have some twists and bumps to fairways, while the 13th and 14th both use a hill to hide greens. It's a good mix.

An impressive entrance leads up to a small, pokey clubhouse, but the 1st tee sits next to the dark Clonyn Castle. Sadly it rarely appears after that (it's not on the course), but there is an old, ivy- and tree-infested castle that plays a bigger part at the turn, with the 10th hitting alongside it. It adds that unexpected dash of interest.

The 3rd (see below), 4th and 5th holes are dominated by enormous trees that are terrifying from the tee box. Then the 6th drives over a couple of hawthorns and a hill onto a flat stretch by the castle. There are more trees and some uninteresting water features but still plenty of fun.

It requires some thought to get around, particularly on the front nine. You can wind it up a bit on the back (holes 11 and 15 are the only par 5s), but perimeter OB – mostly on your right – appears on six holes so you need to be smart as well as long.

FAVOURITE HOLE
Par 4 13th. 377 yards. Index 2. When you drive up the tumbling slope, you need to get as close as possible to the large tree on the left. This will open up the green to the right which has the only decent water feature right in front of the green.

TOUGHEST HOLE
Par 4 3rd. 410 yards. Index 1. The longest par 4 and you have no idea where to hit your drive as huge trees are lined up in front of you. If you have any shot to the green I take my hat off to you. Oh, and there's a ditch behind the trees.

POINTS								
CD	A	G/F	B/W	L	F	V	G Ex	Total
14	8	6	6	7	5	8	15	69

THE COURSE
- Par 70
- Length: 5,899 yards
- Delvin Castle Golf Club, Clonyn, Delvin, Co. Westmeath
- Tel: +353 (0) 44 966 4315
- Green Fees: €25–€30

COURSES NEARBY
Ballinlough Castle
Glebe
Knightsbrook

DINGLE/CEANN SIBÉAL   Established 1924

DINGLE DANGER

Dingle, or Ceann Sibéal, is a long way from anywhere, and the golf club is even farther – hence the excellent rates if you play it twice on the same day. There's no doubt that when you first arrive you'll be looking towards the coastline, trying to find the flags, the dunes, the shimmering grasses, only to be disappointed when you see the course farther inland. Despite sitting under the Three Sisters and in an evocative Irish setting it looks like it has been dropped onto a lifeless field.

You have been fooled. Dingle may not have the sex appeal of a Waterville, the drama of a Dooks, or the sheer presence of Ballybunion, but it is a true links test that will challenge you completely. The holes go up and down and you can always see lots of the course, but perhaps that allows each hole to express its individuality in a unique way – a bit like the setting. These are real links fairways that throw balls in any direction, while greens can be approached in any number of ways – but the infamous burn that wanders across eleven holes will prove rather magnetic if you do not follow the simplest of rules: course management and avoid the rough – it grasps your club and hitting 40 yards is a bonus.

In the wind there is nowhere to hide and the course's routing has embraced this with relish: there are four holes on the front nine of 360 yards, all heading in different directions; each will play so differently you will be bamboozled.

Despite the holes being very visible, there are good hidden hazards (the burn especially) and the back nine are more dangerous and have steeper greens.

FAVOURITE HOLE
Par 3 10th. 190 yards. Just above the clubhouse this is all carry. Pretty and dangerous with a bunker front left that will swallow anything weak. Make the green and it is a superb shot.

TOUGHEST HOLE
Par 4 17th. 396 yards. One of the toughest drives onto a blind landing area (but you can see the flag), which includes the burn. The green sits behind a small hump and slopes sharply to front left.

POINTS

CD	A	G/F	B/W	L	F	V	G Ex	Total
16	7	9	10	9	8	9	17	85

THE COURSE

- Par 71
- Length: 6,477 yards
- Ceann Sibéal Golf Club, Ballyferriter, An Daingean, Co. Kerry
- Tel: +353 (0) 66 915 6255
- www.dinglelinks.com
- Green Fees: €30–€65

COURSES NEARBY
Castleisland
Killorglin
Tralee

DONABATE   Established 1925

FLAT AND GREEN

There are twenty-seven holes here. I'm told I didn't play the best nine – the Blue course – but from the impressive clubhouse I could see down the 9th. A pond and fountain in front of the green certainly add drama on a course that is far from dramatic.

You get a good impression of the place on arrival, with lots of trees and holes on show. Unfortunately it doesn't live up to that same buzz. Donabate is flat and lifeless, and the good holes are few and far between (the 6th, 7th and 9th on Red; the 5th, 7th and 9th on Yellow). Evergreens and conifers give holes some individuality, but the fairways are so still and tee boxes so low that tee shots simply don't make an impression. That is left for the raised and heavily mounded greens, which promise enjoyable approaches.

There are some dog-legs, particularly on the more creatively shaped Yellow nine (the 5th, 6th, 7th and 9th), and these offer more interest and good challenges off the tee, particularly the 5th (see below). The 6th and 9th are similarly shaped, dog-leg par 5s up a gentle slope.

There is an interesting disparity to the tree planting, which is the real feature of the course. In some places conifers/evergreens appear in long lines, while in others they're planted in small or large copses. And, with lots of young planting, you'll be caught out by the trees at some stage.

Donabate is straightforward and will appeal to higher handicappers and those not wanting too much of a challenge. Beaverstown is a better and more entertaining bet, and don't forget the intriguing municipal links at Corballis.

FAVOURITE HOLE

Yellow Course – par 4 7th. 271 m. The hole sweeps right, along a line of trees, and an army of bunkers lines the right-hand side to stifle the big hitters. It is a downhill hole with a tempting drive.

TOUGHEST HOLE

Yellow Course – par 4 5th. 404 m. The hole is a sharp dog-leg that requires caution off the tee – it might only be a 4 iron. Some may try to go over the dense conifer wood but there is a pond on the other side. Another pond sits to the right of the green.

POINTS								
CD	A	G/F	B/W	L	F	V	G Ex	Total
13	6	7	7	4	8	6	12	63

THE COURSE

- Par 69 (yellow tees)
- Length: 5,736 m
- Donabate Golf Club, Balcarrick, Donabate, Co. Dublin
- Tel: +353 (0) 1 843 6346
- www.donabategolfclub.com
- Green Fees: €25–€35

COURSES NEARBY
Balcarrick
Beaverstown
Corballis
Island, The
Turvey

DONAGHADEE   Established 1899

STRAIGHT AND TRUE

Donaghadee overlooks the sea. The views are interrupted briefly by a line of houses, but the course rises and falls so you see plenty, including the Scottish coast.

The course is an interesting mix that combines parkland, heathland and links but there is not one flat hole here. For the most part it is open and exposed – almost bare – but the sparse trees that dot the early links-like fairways are countered by bigger trees inland and on the slightly separate, up-and-down 5th to 8th. Add in the gorse (the par 3 9th especially) and the mix is complete. Several seriously high tee boxes hit down onto fairways, and three greens are at the top of long, sharp rises. Holes 2 and 12 combine both elements for some great roller-coaster drama, and a deep ditch/stream runs across these and other holes, threatening tee shots whether you're long or short.

The course is mown throughout so there's lots of room to play and almost every flag is on view. Off the tee, the stream and bunkers present the biggest problems. The green complexes are a different matter: the bunkering is excellent, well shaped and tough. It is often tucked under the putting surface, pinching the entrance. Greens are smallish, smooth and have little rises into them, which can take a short ball and playfully toss it in a bunker – so be aggressive or play bump-and-run brilliantly. It's not a long course, so you can go for your shots.

Some more creative tree planting would enhance character and colour – just look at the trees on the 16th. The clubhouse has a serious entertainment programme, so enjoy.

FAVOURITE HOLE
Par 4 16th. 304 m. A high tee box hits down at a flat fairway. The perimeter and OB are on your left, with trees below nudging in from your right. Add a stream and a bunker, dead centre, and it's pure thrill. The 15th is the 16th in reverse and almost as good.

TOUGHEST HOLE
Par 4 14th. 364 m. Lost Horizon. One of only two holes that aren't straight; the 14th is also blind. You hit up a hill at a marker post that then drops rapidly to a ditch in front of the green. The best approach is to leave your drive on the hilltop.

POINTS								
CD	A	G/F	B/W	L	F	V	G Ex	Total
14	6	8	8	7	8	10	15	76

THE COURSE
- Par 71
- Length: 5,263 m
- Donaghadee Golf Club, 84 Warren Road, Donaghadee, Co. Down, BT21 0PQ
- Tel: +44 (0) 28 9188 3624 (048 from Rep. of Ire.)
- www.donaghadeegolfclub.com
- Green Fees: £23–£30

COURSES NEARBY
Bangor
Blackwood
Carnalea
Clandeboye
Scrabo

DONEGAL Established 1959

PATHS TO ENLIGHTENMENT

Donegal is a links masterpiece. Considering its colossal length (par 73 with five par 5s) there is a sweet serenity to the place. The impressive clubhouse sits isolated on the Murvagh Peninsula at the other end of a pretty wooded drive. It is a calm start with a few flat holes sliding between gentle dunes. It's the perfect warm-up with views that are easy on the eye. Perhaps it lulls you into a false sense of security, because arriving at the par 3 5th is like a smack in the face. No wonder it's named 'Valley of Tears'. It is wedged nastily into the dunes and starts a sensational stretch of holes.

From the 6th you overlook the beach with views across to Killybegs, Benbulbin in the distance and the Blue Stack Mountains. Enjoy it, because playtime is over. The course flexes its muscles and ferocious fairways, traps and hollows lure you into the high dunes towards greens tucked out of sight. Club selection becomes a nightmare.

From the 12th on, the course calms down again as you move away from the bay. Fairways are flatter, wider and more sedate. They are still beautiful, but the strategy is more straightforward and big hitters will find room again. The joy here is the space that course designer, Eddie Hackett, used. It is very open and one of the most beautiful courses to play. The high 8th tee emphasises this as you can see almost the entire course and all the views. Two things stick out though: the fabulous greens are confusingly soft so you can attack them hard, and the streams on the 12th and 14th are too artificial for me. It's not as though the course isn't tough enough.

Be sure to ask about the skeleton found under the 1st green.

FAVOURITE HOLE
Par 5 8th. 498 m. The fairway tilts left as it swings in the same direction. There is a large hollow, a drop, a swathe of rough that runs in front of the green, a beguiling green and dead space you can't see. And a bunker.

TOUGHEST HOLE
Par 4 11th. 345 m. The drive is a 'must' since you will invariably be hitting into the wind. Dunes line the left and the green sits raised and pressed in to a dune. The fairway rises into the green across a hollow that will trap anything weak.

POINTS								
CD	A	G/F	B/W	L	F	V	G Ex	Total
18	9	10	8	10	10	10	19	94

THE COURSE
- Par 73
- Length: 6,344 m
- Donegal Golf Club, Murvagh, Laghey, Co. Donegal
- Tel: +353 (0) 74 973 4054
- www.donegalgolfclub.ie
- Green Fees: €50–€65

COURSES NEARBY
Bundoran
County Sligo
Narin & Portnoo
Strandhill

DOOKS   Established 1889

TRUE ROMANCE

This course is 450 yards shorter than Waterville and yet Dooks is more challenging. Fairways are tighter and more rugged, the rough more lethal (gorse, heather and solid, elephant-sized dunes) and the greens more dangerous. It is a case of an incredibly natural links course that has had dynamic, raised greens added. And they demand serious thought on your approaches because playing the 'up and down' game will break your heart.

But take solace from the most stunning scenery you will see on this island. The Dingle Peninsula is mesmerising while the MacGillycuddy's Reeks are breathtaking. It seems a shame you have to put your head down to hit a ball.

While Waterville has that majestic, relaxed air to it, Dooks calls for more cunning. You simply won't get away with a loose shot, even on the holes that show the flag and look straightforward. Hole 1 is a perfect example where your tee shot must be straight, and your approach to a slightly lower green has to be inch perfect. A 3 iron/wood should be used on several occasions off the tee, because there is too much trouble waiting for the errant shot. These are not enormous

dunes, and they don't have the flowing symmetry of other links, but they are brutal, unforgiving and perfect; with a gently, undulating landscape leading down to the sea, you often get to see them in all their glory.

Some holes are perhaps a little tight – although that probably comes from playing the spacious Waterville the day before – and the 16th and 17th feel weak and away from the action, but this is a stunning golf experience. Take the day-rate green fee and enjoy.

FAVOURITE HOLE
Par 4 2nd. 311 yards. The first full view of your spectacular surroundings. The hole hits up the easy hill to a flag that sits on the skyline. Are you going for the big swing to fly the bunkers or will you be sensible?

TOUGHEST HOLE
Par 4 7th. 452 yards. Never mind the length, this is the hardest drive through a narrow channel of misshapen, punishing dunes. The 18th has similarly claustro-phobic dunes at the entrance to the green so only a straight drive gives you a channel in.

POINTS

CD	A	G/F	B/W	L	F	V	G Ex	Total
18	9	10	10	10	8	10	19	94

THE COURSE

- Par 71
- Length: 6,327 yards (white tees)
- Dooks Golf Links, Glenbeigh, Co. Kerry
- Tel: +353 (0) 66 976 8205
- www.dooks.com
- Green Fees: €55–€70

COURSES NEARBY
Beaufort
Killarney (x 3)
Killorglin
Waterville

DOONBEG   Established 2001

NOTHING IS AS IT SEEMS

The Doonbeg 'experience' is a bit too plush for me, with its Lodge (aka clubhouse) and million-euro houses. But when you stare down the 500-yard, dune-lined 1st, at a green tucked into dunes, you know you're facing a serious golf adventure. And perhaps that's what makes Doonbeg so remarkable: things here are different and so unexpected that you are constantly thrilled by it all.

Doonbeg may lack the cohesive flow and traditional links feel of Ballybunion and Lahinch, but it has tremendous intrigue and spirit – even on the tamer inland holes. Greg Norman's eye-catching and dangerous golf links offers a huge variety of holes and challenges through beautiful and wild dunes. You play a game of chance on every shot: some fairways end unexpectedly, while outrageous bunkers hide in the back of dunes and fall-offs appear out of nowhere. You simply don't know what awaits, so go the extra mile and hire a caddie – it will save balls and shots.

The routing is an odd figure-of-eight because the central and most impressive run of dunes has been designated a Special Area of Conservation. It means you weave out to Doughmore Bay and back again with plenty of ocean views. Approaching the 6th tee is fantastic, while the view back to the Lodge from the 9th green is stunning.

The greens demand a special mention. They are difficult to hit and they are amazing roller coasters created straight from the land, allegedly. I had three 30-yard putts (the 2nd, 10th and 18th) and the saddleback 2nd will make you nervous for the rest of the round.

A dramatic new links course that promises the unexpected.

FAVOURITE HOLE
Par 5 13th. 451 yards. A tough drive to judge between dunes, onto an eruption of a fairway. The green sits up high, towards the sea, above the most vicious nest of bunkers (I played out backwards). A risk-v.-reward shot if ever there was.

TOUGHEST HOLE
Par 3 14th. 106 yards. The par 5s are long and will be a nightmare in wind, but Index 18, the 14th, offers something else entirely: a delicate, high shot that must play with the wind and offers only one landing area: the green. Miss it and it's a bogey at best.

POINTS								
CD	A	G/F	B/W	L	F	V	G Ex	Total
18	9	10	10	8	10	8	19	92

THE COURSE
- Par 72
- Length: 6,361 yards (white tees)
- Doonbeg Golf Club, Doonbeg, Co. Clare
- Tel: +353 (0) 65 905 5600
- www.doonbeggolfclub.com
- Green Fees: €75–€170

COURSES NEARBY
Kilkee
Kilrush
Lahinch

DOUGLAS   Established 1909

CALMLY UP AND DOWN

Douglas sits on the outskirts of Cork city on a gentle hilltop that offers various views (including Mahon Golf Club below) and plenty of drives over crests. The course is old and mature and has more atmosphere than you'd expect as you move up and down. It is traditional-style parkland with tree-lined fairways and an extra flourish or two. An occasional tree makes a significant and dramatic statement, while the back nine have some beautifully shaped holes and strong slopes as they slip sideways down the hill.

You can certainly score here, if you use your head and respect trees that offer a generous amount of space. Big hitters will find a driver more of a curse than a cure as bunkers have been placed exactly where big tee shots will land – keep a close eye on the 150-m posts. The bunkers are a bit obvious but they are effective. Using a 3 wood or iron is the sensible approach and will put you on the same level as shorter hitters. Then it's all about hitting the very accessible greens – the 9th and 14th excepted. Surfaces are smooth and contoured, but there are

some tricky fall-offs that can punish even the best approaches. Some of these are downhill and beg for a running shot. Local knowledge is all, I imagine.

It is the kind of parkland course that offers everything you would expect without truly raising the temperature – but you won't find a bad hole. More importantly the closing stretch, the 13th to 17th, is terrific and every shot is challenging. There are also decent enough views. The clubhouse falls into the 'old school' category.

FAVOURITE HOLE
Par 4 13th. 351 m. Certainly the best drive, down onto an angled fairway that tilts and sweeps down to the green, just visible behind trees. Difficult enough, but a real chance to blast one.

TOUGHEST HOLE
Par 4 14th. 345 m. Index 1. Another tilting fairway that sweeps round to the right. It is narrow and bunkers are well placed. You won't have a flat lie for your approach to a perched green with a bunker along the front.

POINTS

CD	A	G/F	B/W	L	F	V	G Ex	Total
14	7	8	7	7	9	6	14	72

THE COURSE

- Par 72
- Length: 5,771 m
- Douglas Golf Club, Maryborough, Douglas, Co. Cork
- Tel: +353 (0) 21 489 5297
- www.douglasgolfclub.ie
- Green Fees: €40–€45

COURSES NEARBY
Cork
Fota Island
Mahon
Monkstown
Water Rock

DOWNPATRICK   Established 1930

PLEASANTLY AVERAGE

Downpatrick kicks off with a tough opener. The entrance to the rolling fairway is pincered by trees, requiring a very straight drive. You will be glad to hear that this is the most demanding drive of the day. As you walk up the fairway you will see other fairways under the trees – there's no rough, so you should always find your ball – and it gives you a taste of what lies ahead. Downpatrick is a smart, tree-lined, parkland course that ebbs and flows in terms of interest. The run from the 7th to 12th is the best, with far more fun and challenges to the holes. Two of these are par 3s, with the 11th sitting in a beautiful setting of water and a tree leaning over the green to the right. The 5th, a love-it-or-hate-it hole, also deserves a mention. Called Lough View, it is a blind drive over the crest of the hill and then it descends rapidly with small turret-like mounds interrupting the fairway and threatening to deflect your tee shot. It's a great view for a delicious second shot, but your ball could have kicked anywhere.

There are some climbs/falls (holes 5 to 7 and 11), but mostly it's a rolling fairway, tree-lined affair. The added bonus is the great views of the distant Mourne Mountains and Strangford Lough.

Downpatrick, with its views, its short length (five par 3s) and its variety of difficulty, ticks plenty of boxes, and it plays into the hands of golfers who want some drama, but not too much.

FAVOURITE HOLE
Par 4 10th. 326 yards. It is better off the higher back tees, as the fairway and green look so much better. You hit over a diagonal ditch, with trees a good distance from the tee, and it's the most satisfying drive.

TOUGHEST HOLE
Par 4 9th. 325 yards. A gentle dog-leg that looks easy. It drops and turns as it dips, making the drive hard to judge with trees on both sides, and two hidden bunkers. A bunker stretches across the middle of the raised green.

POINTS

CD	A	G/F	B/W	L	F	V	G Ex	Total
14	7	7	7	8	6	7	13	69

THE COURSE
- Par 69
- Length: 5,733 yards
- Downpatrick Golf Club, 43 Saul Road, Downpatrick, Co. Down, BT30 6PA
- Tel: +44 (0) 28 4461 5947 (048 from Rep. of Ire.)
- www.downpatrickgolfclub.org.uk
- Green Fees: £23–£28

COURSES NEARBY
Ardglass
Bright Castle
Kirkistown Castle
Ringdufferin

DOWN ROYAL   Established 1997

BILLY THE KID

Ireland doesn't have enough heathland courses. It's a shame because the few that exist, like Down Royal (alongside The Heath and The Curragh), offer serious fun. Down Royal sits inside a big racetrack with a cornucopia of gorse that sets the place ablaze in spring. It is relatively flat and exposed, so wind is a major factor. Holes 12, 14 and 18 (Indices 3, 1 and 5 respectively) sit in parallel and hit into the prevailing wind. That tells you plenty.

Big, gorse-lined fairways, deep rough and dark water give the course a wildness that embraces the golfing experience. Throw in the unexpected and it has a quirkiness all its own. Of course, there are some barren holes, which by their nature should be uninteresting, but the pleasure of playing here and the course's appeal negate that feeling.

There are only two greenkeepers and two full-time staff, and what a great job they do. Yes, the greens need improvement – they sit loosely on the land, are slow and a bit bumpy – but they fit with the completely natural feel. Any changes would have to be small.

The clubhouse is nice and cosy. It is quite simple, sitting at the highest point alongside three greens and the 1st tee (see below), which sets the tone for the day. Most flags are on show, water appears more frequently than you'd imagine, and fairways are wide enough to welcome you. But go too far off target and you're gorsed.

The par 3s are all very testing and strong holes, and you can decide just how tough to make it: the back tees add 1,000 yards. And there's a small extra nine holes too. Great value, great golf.

FAVOURITE HOLE
Par 4 1st. 351 yards. A high tee box heads down onto a flat fairway that races to the green. A ditch bisects the fairway and a huge swathe of gorse and water line the right. A perfect start.

TOUGHEST HOLE
Par 5 2nd. 523 yards. Water slices across this hole twice (and at right angles). On a long hole it makes the drive very hard to judge, and both ditches feed into a pond on the left. The uphill approach on the 9th is the hardest shot of the day (avoid the right-hand bunker).

POINTS								
CD	A	G/F	B/W	L	F	V	G Ex	Total
14	7	7	8	6	6	10	16	74

THE COURSE

- Par 72
- Length: 6,419 yards (white tees)
- Down Royal Golf Club, Dunygarton Road, Maze, Lisburn, Co. Antrim, BT27 5RT
- Tel: +44 (0) 28 9262 1339 (048 from Rep. of Ire.)
- www.downroyalgolfclub.co.uk
- Green Fees: £17–£22

COURSES NEARBY
Edenmore
Lambeg
Lisburn
Lurgan

DROMOLAND CASTLE   Established 1963

FROM THE CASTLE TO THE LAKE

It's big, expansive, curved and covered with beautiful trees. And it's all wrapped up with the magnificent Dromoland Castle. The grand entrance leads you into the estate and it gives a great flavour of the golf to come as you drive past a few holes. The clubhouse is on the right, before the castle.

At the heart of the course is the magnificent lake that you play around from the 7th on, and you see it often. Add in the deep woods and specimen trees, like the giant in the middle of the 18th fairway, and it gives that parkland estate feel that impresses everyone. Dromoland Castle moves beautifully across the elegant landscape with lots of variety. But it's not easy. The green complexes are impressive and dangerous: finding putting surfaces will leave you with much to do and anything weak slips away. The three very short par 4s are huge risk-v.-reward holes. And you'll need a strokesaver to appreciate fully the difficulties on the 2nd and 16th – where you have no idea what is expected of you (a map on the scorecard would help) – while on the 11th and 18th, two similar and attractive par 5 dog-legs that show off the lake's beauty, you have to gauge just how much of the impossible rough (Special Area of Conservation) you can cut off to reach the fairway.

The course kicks off only as you approach the 6th green, because the dull holes – the 4th, 5th and much of the 6th – overlook the unattractive bypass and the ugly Clare Inn. After that it all works. The 7th and 17th are brilliant par 3s (see below), while the 15th, at 266 yards downhill, will sucker-punch you.

FAVOURITE HOLES
Par 3 7th and 17th. The 7th has a perfect tee box setting in huge trees, that shoots out at the castle and then straight down to the green, with lake behind and a pond around the green. The 17th is all carry, straight over impossible reeds and rough with a perfect tree backdrop.

TOUGHEST HOLE
Par 4 16th. 406 yards. A worthy Index 1 and rather impossible to play first time around. You have little idea that big hitters can go right, between the two trees, in an attempt to open up the high green which is beyond impossible rough. Two brave shots.

POINTS								
CD	A	G/F	B/W	L	F	V	G Ex	Total
16	8	9	9	7	8	8	17	82

THE COURSE
- Par 72
- Length: 6,294 yards
- Dromoland Castle Golf Club, Newmarket-on-Fergus, Co. Clare
- Tel: +353 (0) 61 368 444
- www.dromoland.ie
- Green Fees: €60–€70

COURSES NEARBY
East Clare
Ennis
Shannon
Woodstock

DRUID'S GLEN   Established 1995

MORE THAN LIVES UP TO ITS REPUTATION

This is a thrilling golf course in a beautiful country estate setting. Having won awards, hosted the Irish Open four times, and been described as the Augusta of Europe (a bit far-fetched perhaps), you know you are in for something special. Every hole is packed with imagination, shape and character – more so than other big parkland tracks like Mount Juliet and the K Club – and every shot is mesmerising. Majestic trees, old walls, bridges and swathes of water all play their part. Water appears on six holes on the back nine, and the 17th island green is the scariest shot you'll hit all day. Or perhaps that is reserved for the 13th, one of the most remarkable holes in Irish golf (see below).

Do not rush this course. It is worth your time, right from the moment you come through the entrance, and if you take a few extra moments, you will really appreciate the shots you face. This is especially true at the tree-enshrined par 3 8th, a beautiful hole that stretches over water to a green in dappled shadows (see photo). For the 9th, you drive over a gorge before crossing a suspension bridge to reach the fairway. That is what makes Druid's Glen so special: constant moments of beauty and surprise that keep you inspired the whole way around.

Another surprise is the benign greens. They are smooth, surprisingly straight-forward and so welcoming after the challenges of reaching them. It opens up a tough course for golfers of all abilities. To end, the 18th rises to a dramatic Georgian (club) house – the icing on the cake.

A course not to be missed and a day to be treasured.

MOST EXHILARATING SHOT
Par 3 17th. 178 yards. Can you carry 165 yards? Of course you can. Can you carry 165 yards over menacing water to a green surrounded by yet more water? Now that is a challenge. Don't hit the diver – he's probably waiting for your ball.

TOUGHEST HOLE
Par 4 13th. 461 yards. How often do you hit your drive past a cliff face onto the fairway below, preferably with fade? And that is the easy shot. Your second is another monster over water. A cunningly designed hole is a polite way of putting it. Good luck.

POINTS								
CD	A	G/F	B/W	L	F	V	G Ex	Total
18	10	9	10	6	10	10	19	92

THE COURSE

- Par 71
- Length: 6,547 yards
- Druids Glen Golf Club, Newtownmountkennedy, Co. Wicklow
- Tel: +353 (0) 1 287 3600
- www.druidsglen.ie
- Green Fees: €55–€90

COURSES NEARBY
Bray
Druid's Heath
Glen of the Downs
Greystones
Powerscourt
Roundwood

DRUID'S HEATH   Established 2005

NOT FOR THE FAINT-HEARTED

If you want a relaxed and comfortable game of golf, then steer clear – Druid's Heath could break your heart.

It cannot be easy living in the shadow of the mighty Druid's Glen. To be fair, Druid's Heath didn't try, creating a long, tough track that combines links and parkland. The course's rolling fairways and steep banks are a bit barren and over-designed, and they make a tough task even harder. And when the abundance of gorse blazes yellow, it is more of a warning than an attraction. There are ninety bunkers and water appears on four holes, all adding real interest and danger, as if it wasn't tricky enough. Put another way, there is no such thing as a free shot. And the perfect greens are lethal and difficult to attack. Three of the par 3s are 190 yards (the 11th is 250 yards from the back tee, which made the mighty Darren Clarke pause for thought) and the two shortest par 4s – the 9th and 13th – are cleverly designed, with the latter offering an inspiring second shot over water from a tricky downhill lie. The water at the long par 5 2nd also deserves a mention: you will not reach the green with your second,

but be warned; the water you can see from the fairway is not the closest to you – there is more tucked away under the ridge.

The course's best holes are the 2nd, 3rd, 12th, 13th and 14th, but several others fail to inspire. All the same, they are difficult and you will be too busy to notice the scenery. It's a bit too difficult to be truly enjoyable and expect to be exhausted when you finish.

The on-site Marriott Hotel is a perfect golfing base.

FAVOURITE & TOUGHEST HOLE

Par 4 12th. 473 yards. This is a seriously hard golf hole, with danger everywhere. A long drive takes you to the crest of a gorse-drenched hill that gently dog-legs right and downhill to a big pond in front of the green. There is OB immediately to the right of the green and a steep bank to the left. It is a knee-buckling second shot and I cannot do it justice here. Sensible players will lay up short of the pond and hope to attack the flag from there.

POINTS

CD	A	G/F	B/W	L	F	V	G Ex	Total
15	7	8	9	7	7	6	15	74

THE COURSE

- Par 72
- Length: 6,833 yards
- Druid's Heath, Druids Glen Golf Resort, Newtownmountkennedy, Co. Wicklow
- Tel: +353 (0) 1 281 2278
- www.druidsglen.ie
- Green Fees: €35–€75

COURSES NEARBY

Bray
Druid's Glen
Glen of the Downs
Greystones
Roundwood

DUBLIN CITY   Established 2000

DUBLIN CITY VIEWS AND GREAT GOLF

Dublin City is an unexpectedly good parkland track. I say 'unexpectedly' as I had played Dublin Mountain in the morning and was expecting more of the same. Far from it. There are some terrific holes here, like the par 3 2nd: a downhill shot to reach a small green fronted by a pond and clasped in a feast of trees. On the 324-yard 6th the fairway simply vanishes after 240 yards, leaving a terrifying second over a densely wooded gorge that offers no respite – anywhere but the putting surface. The 7th is tough too – a par 3 hitting straight at Dublin city with huge slopes running away from the green. Scoring well is not easy and despite three holes under 300 yards (and a par of 69) you'll find every hole troublesome from tee to green. Off-line long hitters will be blocked time and again.

What I like about this course is the interest that's packed into the good holes – there are enough to keep you going – and the backdrops to the greens which are set in trees or are left hanging on the edge.

There are some negatives: you have to cross a tricky road four times; follow very odd routes to the 7th and 14th tee boxes; persevere with some lacklustre tees and greens; and endure three dull par 3s. And watch your head on the 9th. But take the rough with the smooth and enjoy good value green fees.

FAVOURITE HOLE
Par 4 11th. 250 yards. As you approach the tee, a hillside of gorse and trees greets you. From the tee the green appears, tucked behind trees down below. A beauty if you enjoy the risk-v.-reward game.

TOUGHEST HOLE
Par 4 9th. 400 yards. Index 1. A tight drive has trees and OB left, a bunker at 230 yards to squeeze the fairway into a narrow channel filled by trees and the green is a little devil.

POINTS

CD	A	G/F	B/W	L	F	V	G Ex	Total
14	7	6	5	7	6	9	16	70

THE COURSE
- Par 69
- Length: 5,329 yards
- Dublin City Golf Club, Ballinascorney, Dublin 24
- Tel: +353 (0) 1 451 6430
- www.dublincitygolf.net
- Green Fees: €18–€30

COURSES NEARBY
Dublin Mountain
South County

DUBLIN MOUNTAIN   Established 1993

UNDERWHELMING

Struggle as I might, I can find nothing positive to say here. The main attraction of the club is the scenery, but with South County half a mile away and visible across the valley, that benefit is snuffed out. You'll pay three times as much at South County and get ten times the experience.

In polite terms this course is an extended par 3 experience. Fairways and rough are one and the same (rough), greens are splatted on the landscape (although surprisingly soft) and bunkers are the preserve of burrowing rabbits.

Courses like this certainly serve a purpose, but not for enthusiastic visiting golfers like you and me. There is a line of mature beeches that stretches across the course, and this has been used on numerous holes.

POINTS								
CD	A	G/F	B/W	L	F	V	G Ex	Total
4	2	2	1	8	3	2	3	25

THE COURSE

- Par 71
- Length: 5,635 m
- Dublin Mountain Golf Club, Gortlum, Brittas, Co. Dublin
- Tel: +353 (0) 1 458 2622
- www.dublinmountaingolf.com
- Green Fees: €18–€20

COURSES NEARBY
Beech Park
Dublin City
Slade Valley
South County

DUNDALK   Established 1905

A RELIABLE CLASSIC

Avenues of trees define Dundalk as a classic parkland track. It has great rhythm which ensures a steady momentum as you play over a rolling landscape. Fairways and greens are often hidden and the routing is such that by the end of your round you are so immersed in trees that you really don't know which hole is beside you. That in itself is entertaining.

With numerous, well-placed bunkers and some variable water features (excellent on the 7th, feeble on the 12th) it promises a fun round of golf on a good length course. It is not of such scintillating design or such perfect quality that it's a 'must play' course, but it delivers the warm glow that comes with friendly old courses like this.

Big trees have narrowed several fairways and it means that every hole keeps you occupied and focused. When the trees stand back you would be foolish to go wild, so Dundalk rewards good shots, offers plenty of inviting drives and punishes you if you don't do the simple

things right. (I lost three balls in the first eight holes so I know what I'm talking about.)

There are views of the Mourne Mountains and the sea from the clubhouse and driving range area, but elsewhere you're surrounded by wood.

There are few surprises, but the 8th certainly jumps out as your second is completely blind. You'll also find an occasional and nice wildness to proceedings.

FAVOURITE HOLE

Par 3 5th. 152 m. Slightly downhill, water sits to the left of the green which has, quite literally, been squeezed between bunkers. It's a tough shot if the pin is near the front. It is a pretty setting.

TOUGHEST HOLE

Par 4 3rd. 363 m. A large ridge runs across the fairway, and if you don't breach it, you are left completely blind. It makes the trees feel a lot closer.

POINTS

CD	A	G/F	B/W	L	F	V	G Ex	Total
14	7	7	8	6	9	7	15	73

THE COURSE

- Par 72
- Length: 6,024 m
- Dundalk Golf Club, Dundalk, Co. Louth
- Tel: +353 (0) 42 932 1731
- www.dundalkgolfclub.ie
- Green Fees: €30–€50

COURSES NEARBY
Ballymascanlon
Cloverhill
Greenore
Killin Park

DUNDRUM   Established 1993

A RIVER RUNS THROUGH IT

I was standing on the bank of the Multeen River, right in front of the 7th green, when a heron skimmed across the water below me. The leisurely rhythm of its flight seemed fitting with this glorious parkland course. There are many stunning holes, the best bringing the wide river into play. There are six in all and the river fronts four greens. It is well worth looking at the hole diagrams on every tee box.

There are no great views, but the river and beautiful trees winding across a rolling landscape make for a riveting day out. The opening holes are a little mundane, but then you slip across the road to the 4th, 5th and 6th. A lot of work was needed to create these lakeland holes, which are quite different from the rest. But it's not until you get to the 7th, one of three devious par 5s (Indices 4, 5 and 7), when things really take off. The course just gets harder and more beautiful. The 9th and 10th (Indices 2 and 3) are ferocious: trees press in, fairway bunkers beckon and the river waits. You have a tiny landing area for your drive and your second is terrifying on both. The 11th and 13th, par 5s both, are the prettiest holes

on the course, stretching up a slope into a magical wood of beech trees and conifers, and then out again.

Drives are always exciting, even when greens are out of sight, and bravery will be richly rewarded or punished on the 17th and 18th. Philip Walton has produced a beauty and you can stay in a wonderful hotel too. If you want magnificent surroundings and a testing game of golf, this is the place.

FAVOURITE HOLE
Par 5 11th. 483 yards. Stretching up and over the hill, it's a big fairway that shrinks rapidly as you hit your difficult second into the corner between alleys of trees. Up by the green one old tree is encircled by a bunker. The 13th is a beauty too.

TOUGHEST HOLE
Par 4 10th. 427 yards. Index 3. Look at the map on the tee. The three huge oaks are in the middle of the fairway, and the right is crowded by the river all the way to the green. It's a dog-leg and by far the hardest hole for newcomers. Your second is a terror.

POINTS

CD	A	G/F	B/W	L	F	V	G Ex	Total
17	9	7	10	6	9	10	18	86

THE COURSE

- Par 72
- Length: 6,447 yards
- Dundrum Golf Club, Dundrum, Co. Tipperary
- Tel: +353 (0) 62 71717
- www.dundrumhousehotel.com
- Green Fees: €25–€35

COURSES NEARBY
Ballykisteen
Cahir
Thurles
Tipperary

DUNFANAGHY Established 1906

TESTING GROUND

If you want to learn the links art of bump-and-run, then Dunfanaghy is the place. You are seriously exposed to the elements on this breezy, flat part of the Donegal coast. The course heads in one of two directions, so you know the wind will hit you with the two extremes. It will be punishing. It is not as sexy as Rosapenna or Portsalon, but this is a different type of links, where every shot has to fight the wind and you want your ball to stay low. Greens are very open, and if that doesn't make it obvious what kind of shot to play, please head elsewhere.

Overall, the flat landscape you play over is not inspiring enough to make this pretty – despite the beach and mountain views. The superb rocky outcrop that hosts holes 6 to 10 is an exception, and it is worth playing the course for these holes alone (along with the 17th and 18th).

The first five holes are flat, as are holes 11 to 15. While they don't boast great appeal, you'll find twisting, bumpy little fairways that are naturally enchanting. There are streams too, tucked out of sight, so look for the yellow stakes when you are preparing to drive.

It is the rocky outcrop that thrills: the 6th rises into it; the 7th hits 205 m down and away; the 8th dog-legs back over rocks (one of only two blind drives); the 9th, another par 3, hits over the beach to a green tucked below the dune; and the 10th is the best of all.

The 16th is the only par 5 on this par 68 course. Don't expect beauty; expect an education.

FAVOURITE HOLE
Par 4 10th. 275 m. Called Killahoey, it should be renamed 'Do or Die'. A big carry over the beach from an elevated tee awaits those foolhardy enough to target the green. If you make it, three deep bunkers await. Or follow the fairway and hit left.

TOUGHEST HOLE
Par 4 18th. 330 m. It may be Index 12, but this is a big blind drive over a rugged hilltop that drops quickly to the green. The wind should be behind you, in which case holes 3 and 14 will be very tough.

POINTS								
CD	A	G/F	B/W	L	F	V	G Ex	Total
14	7	7	9	8	7	8	15	75

THE COURSE
- Par 68
- Length: 5,100 m
- Dunfanaghy Golf Club, Kill, Dunfanaghy, Co. Donegal
- Tel: +353 (0) 74 913 6335
- www.dunfanaghygolfclub.com
- Green Fees: €30–€40

COURSES NEARBY
Portsalon
Rosapenna

DUNGANNON Established 1890

THE BASIC PARKLAND ESSENTIALS

All the parkland basics are here – single tree-lined, good quality fairways, entertaining greens, a dash of water – but Dungannon doesn't pack in much excitement. It is a bit too plain in its design, so when you stand on the tee you don't feel much oomph. The 1st would be an obvious example: straight and true and classic parkland style, but the shots aren't tempting. It does improve as the land starts to undulate, with the drop down to the par 5 3rd green offering the first enticing shot, and the start of three good holes that use a gentle hillside. This is repeated on the back nine where the land has greater changes in elevation.

I didn't warm to this short course, but fairways are tight enough to require accurate driving. This seems to be particularly true on the back nine holes – the 17th especially. Even so, there are not too many dangers as the holes are visible. New greens have improved things and there are some interesting shapes already in existence, but more excitement is needed elsewhere.

Darren Clarke learned his golf here – an attraction in itself.

FAVOURITE & TOUGHEST HOLE
Par 4 8th. 390 yards. Perched on the edge of the car park, you might mistake this for the 1st, and it is the most impressive-looking hole. A big drive down onto a tumbling fairway that continues to drop down to the green, over a watery ditch. The hole is improved by the big line of beeches that separates it from the 17th.

POINTS								
CD	A	G/F	B/W	L	F	V	G Ex	Total
11	5	7	6	6	9	6	11	61

THE COURSE
- Par 72
- Length: 5,861 yards
- Dungannon Golf Club, 34 Springfield Lane, Dungannon, Co. Tyrone, BT71 1QX
- Tel: +44 (0) 28 8772 2098 (048 from Rep. of Ire.)
- www.dungannongolfclub.com
- Green Fees: £20–£25

COURSES NEARBY
County Armagh
Killymoon
Loughall
Moyola Park

DUNGARVAN   Established 1924

10 – 20 – 30

This recently created version of Dungarvan sits next to Dungarvan Bay, and the sea appears provocatively on holes 11 to 14. These are the best holes (alongside the 2nd, 8th and 10th) with strong tee boxes, nice lines to fairways and the water alongside. They're worth waiting for. Some of the other holes are dull by comparison, sweeping blandly up and down, although ponds add excitement. This is the challenge of creating new holes: young trees don't provide the fairway dividers you find on mature courses (Tramore) and it makes Dungarvan feel open. On a flat course this problem is compounded, especially when the fairway mounding is as blatant as it is here. Fortunately, the decent backdrop of a heavily wooded valley that rises to the Comeragh Mountains beyond maintains your interest early on.

Despite three good opening holes (the crafty dog-leg 2nd is so different from the rest of the course it has no right to be here), you must wait until the 8th before things take off. It is a great par 3 with large ponds left and right, and a green backed by a line of small sentry-like conifers (out of place perhaps).

The tree planting feels a bit frenzied but time will correct this. It's the type of course that would be worth revisiting in ten, twenty and thirty years' time, just to see the growth.

Drop by, but only if you play Gold Coast and West Waterford as well. Remember to play off the back tees on the 13th and 15th.

FAVOURITE HOLE
Par 4 11th. 376 yards. Everything about this hole works. The tee box in the trees, the drive over a strong stream, the estuary to the left, the trees that force you right to a rising fairway. Best drive of the day and you finally get to see the real views.

TOUGHEST HOLE
Par 4 17th. 408 yards. Only the second real dog-leg, this needs a good straight drive of 240 yards to open up the green to your right.

POINTS

CD	A	G/F	B/W	L	F	V	G Ex	Total
13	6	7	7	7	8	7	13	68

THE COURSE
- Par 72
- Length: 6,488 yards
- Dungarvan Golf Club, Knocknagranagh, Dungarvan, Co. Waterford
- Tel: +353 (0) 58 41605
- www.dungarvangolfclub.com
- Green Fees: €30–€40

COURSES NEARBY
Gold Coast
Tramore
West Waterford

DUNGRANGE VIEW R & R   Established 1990s

PUBLIC APPEAL

When you arrive at the clubhouse your expectations won't be high. It all looks shabby and even the entrance with its lines of small evergreens feels untidy. The same can be said of this course. As a 'public course' (closely related to Bodenstown nearby) I suppose it's no surprise that bunkers are grotty, greens bumpy and fairways cut to the same level as many courses' first cut of rough. There are odd patches of rough and weeds about too, and the wild walk to the 8th is quirky, to say the least.

You are paying a tiny green fee so you'd expect the course to be of basic quality. But there are good flourishes, particularly the attractive, black, stone-lined ponds. They dot the bottom section of the course (the 2nd to 8th) and are full of wildlife. It makes a big difference, adding character, appeal and danger. The variety and colour of trees also brings a smile, especially the blue-painted trunks of copper beech which indicate the 150-m mark.

Essentially there are two stretches of holes: the 1st and the 9th to 18th go up and down a gentle hillside. They are straightforward in terms of design and a bit close together. The other holes have far more interest, some mature trees and the many water features. These are the holes that will catch your attention and there are several shots that entertain.

Off the green tees it's a healthy par 72, but the quality is simply not good enough to attract the better golfers.

FAVOURITE HOLE

Par 4 3rd. 318 m. A straight, flat hole that has good character off the tee. Trees are scattered about on the right and there's water down by the green.

TOUGHEST HOLE

Par 4 6th. 287 m. Yes, it's short, but it will fool you mightily if you don't tread carefully. The course's perimeter is lined with trees on the left, a large pond awaits the big drive on the right, and the only entrance to the mounded green is from the left.

POINTS

CD	A	G/F	B/W	L	F	V	G Ex	Total
12	8	4	5	6	4	7	12	58

THE COURSE

- Par 72
- Length: 5,872 m
- R & R Dungrange View Golf Club, Dunboyne, Co. Meath
- Tel: +353 (0) 1 825 2981
- Green Fees: €17–€20

COURSES NEARBY
Bodenstown
K Club
Killcen
Millicent
Naas

DUN LAOGHAIRE Established 1910/2007

CRISP, SMART AND A BRAND NEW TWENTY-SEVEN

Dun Laoghaire is slightly larger than life. Fancy entrance, big clubhouse, full facilities (golf academy), three equal nines, excellent quality and exuberant green fees. Clearly it has aspirations. As a member of the new breed of course it is so precise and orchestrated that you flow along the fairway and paths like they're red carpet.

From every tee the Great Sugar Loaf stands high and proud between Bray Head to the east and the Wicklow Mountains to the west. The sea is visible and the views grow ever more spectacular as you traverse the creatively moulded hillside; they make a huge difference to your round, and despite the course's artificial feel it blends surprisingly well into the irregular terrain.

As it is a young course (2007), spread over farmers' fields, it is very open and the thousands of saplings have yet to make their mark. It still looks good, especially from the clubhouse as the Lower and Middle nines drop away to the mountains. The routing is effective, water features are ever-present, greens have some great backdrops, and much love has been lavished on the course. But it lacks something. Despite inviting and

beautifully shaped fairways, holes have yet to find their individuality. For instance, too many holes drive between huge flanks of starfish bunkers before swinging left or right to a green heavily protected by more bunkers. It can get monotonous (and forgettable), especially as there are 157 bunkers. They give the holes their definition and they demand accuracy and persistence all day.

With many paths there are also some long walks. Plenty of room to improve – but at least it has the room.

FAVOURITE HOLE
Par 4 15th (Upper). 309 m. Along with the water-laced 6th (Lower) this is the best driving hole. Both offer you a choice: here you can go directly at the raised green over a hilly nest of bunkers, or play safe and go left past the big tree. A good-looking hole.

TOUGHEST HOLE
Par 5 16th (Upper). 483 m. With so many bunkers threatening your first two shots, you have to be accurate and cautious. Your second is downhill into a sea of sand well short of a slippery and sloping green.

POINTS								
CD	A	G/F	B/W	L	F	V	G Ex	Total
16	7	9	8	9	10	6	14	79

THE COURSE
- Par 72 (Lower & Upper)
- Length: 5,755 m
- Dun Laoghaire Golf Club, Ballyman Road, Bray, Co. Wicklow
- Tel: +353 (0) 1 272 1866
- www.dunlaoghairegolfclub.ie
- Green Fees: €50–€75

COURSES NEARBY
Bray
Delgany
Greystones
Old Conna
Powerscourt

DUNMORE EAST   Established 1993

THREE REMARKABLE HOLES

Remember Hitchcock's movie *The Birds*? The 7th green feels just like that. Gulls have taken up residence and they swoop overhead as you approach. I recommend a hat. The same applies to the 15th fairway and the 17th green. They'll probably be long gone by the time you arrive, but it's a creepy experience at 8 a.m.

Dunmore East is a small village on the coast. The golf club sits high above it on the clifftops, with the clubhouse looking out to sea and over the harbour. And as you walk to the 1st you catch a glimpse of the 14th green far below and right on the cliff edge. Sadly, you head in the opposite direction for a handful of lifeless holes – the 1st to 5th and the 10th to 12th are distinctly dull with flat fairways all running side by side and barely separated by small trees and shrubs. The greens – and this applies throughout – are patchy and uninspiring, although there is some good mounding to complicate approaches – the 15th and 17th stand out.

For me, the course is worth playing for three holes: the 6th, 14th and 15th. There are only a handful of courses that can boast such spectacular-looking holes. The 6th hits straight towards the whitecaps lashing Hook Head lighthouse on the other side of the channel. It's a downhill hole with a large pond on the left and you will hit your second off a 20-degree slope. It is always going to be difficult adding vibrancy to a course lashed so tightly across the clifftops, but it feels a bit desolate and diluted, despite the sounds of waves and birds filling your head.

FAVOURITE HOLE

Par 3 14th. 180 m. You hit straight out to sea, a soaring tee shot that drops and drops to the green on the clifftops far below. A heart-in-the-mouth moment.

TOUGHEST HOLE

Par 4 15th. 390 m. Play this from the back tee to experience a great drive, standing on the cliff edge. You must carry 150 m over a chasm to a sloping fairway. Your second is blind and over the brow where the green and harbour appear at the same time.

POINTS								
CD	A	G/F	B/W	L	F	V	G Ex	Total
11	5	5	5	7	6	7	12	58

THE COURSE

- Par 72
- Length: 6,070 m (back tees)
- Dunmore East Golf Club, Dunmore East, Co. Waterford
- Tel: +353 (0) 51 383 151
- www.dunmoreeastgolfclub.ie
- Green Fees: €20–€30

COURSES NEARBY
Faithlegg
Tramore
Waterford Castle
Williamstown

DUNMURRY   Established 1905

COMPACT YET SPACIOUS

With Lisburn nearby, it is interesting to note the differences with Dunmurry. While Lisburn has a dark, enclosed broodiness to it, Dunmurry has more freedom, more openness and more elevation, making the big trees all the more impressive. Lisburn has a more classic parkland rhythm, but some holes at Dunmurry really stand out. Holes 1, 4 and 6 come to mind, with the 15th and 18th offering the sort of intrigue that you'll either love or hate. Dunmurry is a lot shorter too.

The course falls into two sections: the 1st, 2nd and 15th to 18th holes stretch colourfully around the clubhouse. The rest are over the road. There's a distinct difference between the two, but both are good. Barring the surprisingly tame par 3s, these are holes that create intrigue and catch the eye, whether off the tee or approaching the smartly presented greens.

Yet when you arrive on the outer holes it feels young, busy and uninteresting (the lame par 3 3rd doesn't help) because the layout is up and down and young trees in the centre of the course have yet to make their mark. The high section at the far end, however, promises great shots into greens and the drive on the 6th, Index 1, is the best of the round. It has all been done very well, with strong movement to the fairways, precision bunkering and one big pond (the 8th). Shame about the pylons which interfere with gentle views.

The inside holes have a heavier, denser feel, making them more attractive. The 1st is a beauty, down and around a wood-covered hill, while both the 15th and 18th need short, strategic tee shots to take full advantage of 340-yard holes. Simply good fun.

FAVOURITE HOLE
Par 5 4th. 519 yards. An over-the-crest drive at a big desolate pine. The fairway is sloped as it dog-legs right and up the hill to a green beautifully set in more trees.

TOUGHEST HOLE
Par 4 6th. 410 yards. Index 1 promises a beautiful drive from up high, but it is not easy. The perimeter is on the right, young trees left. And even a 250-yard drive won't reveal the green up the slope and to the right. And there's a big slope left of the green.

POINTS								
CD	A	G/F	B/W	L	F	V	G Ex	Total
14	7	8	8	6	8	8	16	75

THE COURSE
- Par 70
- Length: 5,835 yards
- Dunmurry Golf Club, 91 Dunmurry Lane, Belfast, BT17 9JS
- Tel: +44 (0) 28 9061 0834 (048 from Rep. of Ire.)
- www.dunmurrygolfclub.co.uk
- Green Fees: £27–£30

COURSES NEARBY
Balmoral
Belvoir Park
Lambeg
Lisburn
Malone

DUNMURRY SPRINGS   Established 2005

SEVEN COUNTIES

This is a new course that will survive comfortably. It has all the quality you could ask for. It also has almost 360-degree views over mountains and the midlands. It's stunning from the 6th green. The course can be made easy or difficult, simply by letting the fescue grasses grow – ask when you book, as it can make a serious difference to your day.

From the 1st tee much of the course is visible above you as holes glide up and down the hillside. The smartly planted trees are adding to the shape of the holes already, and this shape promises a sense of expectation when you stand on the tee and look at the perfect fairways. It will play into the hands of strategic thinkers. Water, cleverly placed bunkers and dog-legs can all frustrate: I played both the par 5 6th and 10th with a drive and two wedge shots. Some golfers won't like that – namely the grip-and-rip brigade – but from the white tees this is more brains than brawn. The back blue tees add 700 yards and provide a more searching golf experience, so decide which you'd prefer. Either way, driving is fun.

Greens are fast and beautiful. Finding them is a challenge with surfaces often raised out of sight or blocked by bunkers. Sorry, but you will 3 putt.

The large water features are dramatic – the full carry on the par 3 11th (Index 4) and approaches to the 3rd, 9th and 18th most notably. From the high 15th tee box you can see all the way home and the mountains beyond. A glorious way to finish.

FAVOURITE HOLE

Par 4 8th. 388 yards. Index 1. A high ridge runs along the left and severe OB down the right, just beyond a line of bunkers. The hole tilts dangerously towards the sand and you must try and find the top of the fairway mound to see anything of the green.

TOUGHEST HOLE

Par 5 6th. 472 yards. A sharp dog-leg that has OB on your right and a couple of threatening bunkers on the left. If you're short of the turn then it is a blind second which many will hate. But it calls for tactics. The green is above you with sand on the left.

POINTS								
CD	A	G/F	B/W	L	F	V	G Ex	Total
16	8	9	9	8	8	9	17	84

THE COURSE

- Par 71
- Length: 6,096 yards
- Dunmurry Springs Golf Club, Dunmurry Hill, Kildare, Co. Kildare
- Tel: +353 (0) 45 531 400
- www.dunmurrysprings.ie
- Green Fees: €25–€45

COURSES NEARBY
Curragh, The
Heritage, The
Newbridge

EAST CLARE   Established 1997

FULL OF COUNTRY FLOURISH

Peaceful. The hills that roll all around you are silent and green, and remarkably bare of houses. The course has that lazy space that brings its own sense of relaxation.

The club sits at the end of a wonderful maze of little windy roads and it is a charming country surprise. You will enjoy a leisurely start, but after the 7th it throws up great golf holes. There is excellent routing, which shows off the surrounding hills, and the variety in lengths and shapes of holes demands careful consideration. At the start you can be aggressive, but you will find you are tested more and more as the round progresses. The greens change from relatively tame to steep beasts that are suddenly crowded by bunkers. I love the way it has been done, easing you in slowly then switching gear and asking you to play some real golf. Yet you always have plenty of room off the tee. Believe me, you'll need it.

There is a loose wildness to the place, and the water in the big rustic ponds looks like dark chocolate. On Index 1, the 9th, there are two ponds, and four of the five par 3s slap water right in front of you. The 13th is 197 m and is Index 2.

The course's shape comes into its own on the back nine with some gentle hills enhancing the drama and the fun. It is a great adventure for its inventiveness, its country playfulness and its location. Few other courses feel like this.

Beware the 10th, a sharp dog-leg right. Off the tee the green you see is the 18th.

FAVOURITE HOLES
Any of the four watery par 3s, with the 13th and 17th being the pick. The 17th has a high tee, hitting over scruff and water below to a raised green. Nice views beyond.

TOUGHEST HOLE
Par 4 9th. 410 m. Index 1 hits down towards a big ditch that takes water from the two big ponds on the right. If your drive goes far enough to present a shot at the green, beware the carry over water, the bunkers and the big tree bang in your line.

POINTS								
CD	A	G/F	B/W	L	F	V	G Ex	Total
15	8	8	9	8	8	10	17	83

THE COURSE

- Par 71
- Length: 5,813 m
- East Clare Golf Club, Coolreagh, Bodyke, Co. Clare
- Tel: +353 (0) 61 921 322
- www.eastclare.com
- Green Fees: €30–€35

COURSES NEARBY
Dromoland Castle
Ennis
Gort
Woodstock

EAST CORK Established 1968

FOUR IN ONE

It's rare that you get to play four courses in one round, but that is the adventure of East Cork.

Six of the first nine holes are on the side of a hill with straight and narrow fairways, thick rough and tall conifers. They are not difficult but the rough makes them tough. Hole 2, straight up, is Index 1.

Holes 6 to 8 are farther up and are gentler. Here are the best views (ignoring the pylons).

To reach the second nine on the flat land below, you have a thundering drive down the long par 5 9th. It is the last of the hilly holes. The second nine are more enjoyable. There is more structure and you feel as if good shots are better rewarded – at the 11th and 12th in particular (the only holes with water in front of the green – see below).

Holes 13 to 15 slip across the road to give you the final part of the mix. These too are flat and offer themselves simply, with trees squeezing you more than elsewhere (bar the 12th).

The double level pond on the 11th is the only real flourish on what is a natural

and fairly simple short course. No great mounding or tiered greens, just basic golf. Put it this way, one of the four sections is going to appeal to you. There is a full-scale driving range if you want to wear yourself out.

Finally, don't expect the greens to be easy: they are a variety of sizes and shapes, like the rest of the course, and they're all fast.

FAVOURITE HOLE

Par 4 12th. 375 yards. The toughest drive. Dense trees (OB) are tight left and a stand of trees presses in from the right, 100 yards from the tee. It covers half of the distant green and makes a good drive truly special. A pond fronts the green.

TOUGHEST HOLE

Par 4 11th. 363 yards. With such a flat dog-leg you have no idea where to hit, or how far – you can barely see fairway. The bunker is the spot. A touch unfair perhaps. Then sharp left to the pond-fronted green.

POINTS

CD	A	G/F	B/W	L	F	V	G Ex	Total
13	6	7	7	6	8	7	14	68

THE COURSE

- Par 69
- Length: 5,406 yards
- East Cork Golf Club, Gortacrue, Midleton, Co. Cork
- Tel: +353 (0) 21 463 1687
- www.eastcorkgolfclub.ie
- Green Fees: €25

COURSES NEARBY
Cobh
Cork
Fota Island
Water Rock

EDENDERRY   Established 1910

WELL-DEFINED PARKLAND

What jumps out at you at Edenderry are the rippling fairways, the dark, boggy turf, the white paper bark birch (indicating the 150-m mark) and the evergreen trees that are smartly planted in groups of three. On the course, these evergreens are mingled with lots of birch, while the old heavy beeches make quite an impact behind the 18th green.

Edenderry starts down a slope on a short par 4. You are well marshalled by trees and certainly the dense line down the left makes it hard for those who fade the ball. Holes 9, 10 and 18 also use this slope, but the rest of the holes are on flat ground. Good parkland holes abound but the front nine are definitely stronger with lines of heavy conifers defining the holes. They're set well back and rarely impinge, but they give the holes a sedate setting. There is a vibrancy here that makes all your shots enjoyable, something that the back nine (the 11th to 17th) lack.

This is a good old course that could do with some thought going into the bunkering and greens. The latter are just too lifeless in places and don't excite. There is water but it rarely comes into play.

And perhaps you can tell me why the 9th hole is Index 7 (301 m), while the 18th is Index 12 (316 m). They sit side by side facing up the slope: the 9th dog-legs right and the 18th dog-legs left, with dense evergreens in the middle. They're almost identical.

FAVOURITE HOLE
Par 4 3rd. 399 m. Index 1. A long, flat hole that is dominated by pine down the left as the holes sweeps gently right, around a couple of intrusive trees. This is the first rippling fairway and it adds that extra danger. A colourful approach.

TOUGHEST HOLE
Par 4 18th. 316 m. This is the only drive that requires draw. Dense evergreens crowd the left and if you drift too far right there is one tree with an enormous branch that will force your hand. The farther you drive, the more dangerous it is.

POINTS								
CD	A	G/F	B/W	L	F	V	G Ex	Total
13	6	6	5	5	7	7	13	62

THE COURSE
- Par 72
- Length: 5,815 m
- Edenderry Golf Club, Kishawanny, Edenderry, Co. Offaly
- Tel: +353 (0) 46 973 1072
- www.edenderrygolfclub.com
- Green Fees: €20–€25

COURSES NEARBY
Castle Barna
Highfield
Moyvalley
Woodlands

EDENMORE   Established 1992

NEEDS A LITTLE MORE

I don't often start my review in the bar, but Edenmore's doesn't have that 'golf' feel. It is more functional and laid out for eating, which is not that surprising as this is primarily a large conference centre. The question is, does that mean the course has suffered, as often happens when aligned with a hotel-type environment?

The answer, hedging my bets, is yes and no. Edenmore is very short for a par 71 – play off the back white tees and add over 500 yards – and despite plenty of trees it is a bit too open to be challenging. If you fancy easy scoring on a strongly undulating, country course then this is the place. The trees (young and old) stay well back at the start and only interfere on the 1st, 6th and 9th. I wanted them to come closer and I got my wish on the back nine, when big oak and ash come charging into view. As a result these holes are more vibrant and entertaining. If you have a fade, the 10th is a nightmare and the 18th is a devilish, short dog-leg no matter how you hit the ball.

The hardest challenges will be attacking greens. Most are wide open (and look bland), but surfaces are hard and a bump-and-run approach may serve you best. On the five par 3s I held the surface only once. Bunkers vary from quite flat and easy to steep-faced – but they often encroach across the front of greens.

Edenmore is in a pleasant setting, but it lacks real charisma. And the condition of the course was not good for July, when I played. The two 'ponds' on the 18th should be filled in. Please!

FAVOURITE HOLE
Par 4 12th. 249 yards. Index 4, yet the hole is straight, with pin and green visible. What's the trick? Overambition. Anyone with length will fancy a go, but the green sits up on a sharp ledge and the bunkers are well placed. A tough approach from anywhere.

TOUGHEST HOLE
Par 4 16th. 380 yards. Only the 9th, 10th, 16th and 18th offer tough drives. You need to be in the perfect spot between two big trees on the 16th, and the approach is very tricky as a bunker guards the left, a tree the right and a steep slope falls from the green.

POINTS

CD	A	G/F	B/W	L	F	V	G Ex	Total
13	7	6	7	6	8	7	13	67

THE COURSE
- Par 71
- Length: 5,723 yards
- Edenmore Golf Club, 70 Drumnabreeze Road, Magheralin, Craigavon, Co. Armagh, BT67 0RH
- Tel: +44 (0) 28 9261 9241 (048 from Rep. of Ire.)
- www.edenmore.com
- Green Fees: £22–£26

COURSES NEARBY
Banbridge
Down Royal
Lurgan
Silverwood

EDMONDSTOWN   Established 1944

COLOURFUL VARIETY ON DUBLIN'S HILLSIDES

The drive into Dublin's Edmondstown introduces you to the hillier holes on the course. They run down from your right, away from the M50 motorway which has inflicted changes on the course (so too at Grange nearby). The 10th and 11th are new holes below the clubhouse, which don't yet 'fit'. Yet Edmondstown remains another delightful metropolitan course, with several tempting shots at the mountains. It sits on a gentle hillside that gets progressively steeper without ever proving taxing. It has variety and the different holes work well. It is deceptively tight, which you will quickly discover if you don't place your drives precisely on the many dog-legs (holes 1, 2, 4, 5 and 9 make for a tough front nine). One tip: check the wooden markers on the tee for hole diagrams as the 1st will certainly confuse.

You start in a dense thicket of conifers which gives the place a brooding atmosphere, as does the nice old clubhouse. The trees dissipate gradually, but always remain close and big. There are pines well scattered about, and pleasing dashes of gorse and water. Mention must be made

of the greens and bunkering around them: these have been designed immaculately and are often very tricky to approach. Surfaces sit out of view and bunkers will deceive your eye. It's a smart defence, and the course is long enough to make this a challenging round of golf.

The greens on the 4th and 6th sit over a stream in a a dell of violently tossed mounds and bunkers. It is a touch too dynamic for the nature of this course, but they are thrilling approaches.

FAVOURITE HOLE
Par 3 17th. 166 m. A long uphill strike to a smartly shaped green that will leave nightmare putts outside 10 feet. A bunker covers half of the front; trees sit behind.

TOUGHEST HOLE
Par 5 4th. 494 m. A narrow landing area (bunkers and OB left, and trees right) at the dog-leg makes this very tough off the tee. But the approach to the green drops sharply into a stream and then rises up through bunkers and mounds to a lilting green.

POINTS

CD	A	G/F	B/W	L	F	V	G Ex	Total
15	7	7	8	6	8	7	15	73

THE COURSE

- Par 71
- Length: 5,841 m
- Edmondstown Golf Club, Edmondstown Road, Rathfarnham, Dublin 16
- Tel: +353 (0) 1 493 2461
- www.edmondstowngolfclub.ie
- Green Fees: €45–€65

COURSES NEARBY
Castle
Grange
Milltown
Stackstown

ELMGREEN   Established 1996

SLIPS UP AND DOWN THE HILLSIDE

The course sits tucked up against the M50 motorway, yet the constant drone of traffic quickly fades into the background. Despite your proximity to Dublin city, you see only trees and distant mountains. That in itself is remarkable.

Elmgreen's entrance has impressively odd pillars and the old building that is the clubhouse is all over the place – the changing rooms could do with some attention – but I like the course for its simplicity. It is no powerhouse and it won't attract those who prefer to play the bigger name courses, but being this close to Dublin will keep it very busy. For a pay-and-play course, the green fees are very reasonable.

It is not long for a par 71 and there are four very short par 4s, starting with the 1st. It is downhill, wide and only an arc of bunker in front of the green blocks your way. A tantalising start. Wide holes (even if fairways are tight) are flanked by dense lines of semi-mature trees, which can make it monotonous in places despite the intervention of frequent mature specimens and quirky hawthorn. Still, the fairways move enough and numerous

good-looking approaches make this a fun round of golf. The arrival of holes 10 to 12, separated from the rest, is a timely and welcome interruption.

Greens are big, sweeping and fast. Several have putting surfaces that are just out of sight, making approach shots difficult. With an eighteen-hole pitch & putt course alongside, there is plenty to enjoy here. It will suit many, and big hitters will fancy the par 5s and the short par 4s.

FAVOURITE HOLE
Par 4 11th. 336 m. The three huge trees just after the sweep of the dog-leg give this hole the most character. They are your line as the fairway drops slightly before rising again, swinging left to a perched green. Two very enjoyable shots.

TOUGHEST HOLE
Par 4 12th. 385 m. The only drive that puts any demands on you. This is a vicious dog-leg left and anything too long is in impossible rough. You can cut the corner, but judging how far is impossible. Your second will be to a flag and nothing more.

POINTS

CD	A	G/F	B/W	L	F	V	G Ex	Total
12	6	7	6	6	5	9	14	65

THE COURSE
- Par 71
- Length: 5,495 m
- Elmgreen Golf Club, Castleknock, Dublin 15
- Tel: +353 (0) 1 820 0797
- www.elmgreengolfclub.ie
- Green Fees: €18–€25

COURSES NEARBY
Castleknock
Hermitage
Hollystown
Luttrellstown

ELM PARK Established 1924

AIMLESSLY BACK AND FORTH

Elm Park is close to Dublin city centre, which is its biggest advantage. But it's not much of a golf experience. Adventure and excitement are severely lacking, with only six holes worth a mention (the 1st, 2nd, 10th, 11th, 13th and 16th) and that is in spite of a low stream running through the middle. You go up and down mostly flat fairways, which feel like a conveyor belt at times, with sides formed from uninspiring lines of trees. The greens improved dramatically in 2005, which has made a big difference, but located as it is on the flat landscape there is not a lot more the club can do. The approach to the tree-shrouded green on the 10th, beside a large duck-packed pond, is the best shot of the day. That and the tee shot on the pretty and short par 3 1st, which has a disjointed crowd of trees between you and the green.

Ideal if you want an easy round, and it is probably a great course to do business on because you don't have to concentrate on your shots. I hate to say that the clubhouse is stuffy, but the clubhouse is stuffy; and the green fee is silly.

If you are visiting Ireland to play golf, then give this short, dull course a miss. If you're restricted to courses close by, visit Castle or Grange.

FAVOURITE HOLE
Par 3 1st. A dainty, short par 3 in the trees, the most colouful of the lot.

TOUGHEST HOLE
Par 4 16th. 316 m. It is a tough driving hole with dykes hiding behind trees. The 18th is a stronger hole to finish, with a left-to-right dog-leg that promises a decent second shot.

POINTS								
CD	A	G/F	B/W	L	F	V	G Ex	Total
12	5	8	6	3	7	3	10	54

THE COURSE
- Par 69
- Length: 5,253 m
- Elm Park Golf Club, Nutley House, Nutley Lane, Donnybrook, Dublin 4
- Tel: +353 (0) 1 269 3438
- www.elmparkgolfclub.ie
- Green Fees: €70

COURSES NEARBY
Castle
Grange
Milltown

ENNIS   Established 1907

SUBURBAN GOLF

Perched on the edge of town, Ennis Golf Club is split by a busy road and houses are scattered around the perimeter. The top section is on a gentle slope with downhill curves at both ends, while on the other side there is one significant drop to a flattish plateau. The holes utilising this drop are the most interesting on what is an average parkland course: they offer tempting tee shots and greens wedged into the hill with steep, punishing slopes.

There are some interesting elements to catch the eye. The top half is tree-lined with nice belts of trees and the far corner (the 5th green, the 6th tee box) is over a curve that makes the 5th difficult to approach. On the lower half the trees are far less frequent but they are mature – no young saplings here – and it provides an interesting and quirky feel. This is enhanced by surprisingly bumpy fairways and odd rocky outcrops that pop out of the ground, like around the 9th green.

Howlers have to be mentioned: the water feature/banking on the 3rd is terrible and ruins the hole, while there is dangerous crossing on the lower section. Unavoidable on such a tight course, I know, but it is important that you are aware of this as it is so open. Ennis have done a good job with what they have, but it is never going to set your pulse racing.

The biggest danger you'll encounter (apart from 'fore') is your overenthusiasm to score points.

FAVOURITE HOLE
Par 3 16th. 169 m. A downhill shot, between the trees – actually, very slightly around them – to a flat green.

TOUGHEST HOLE
Par 4 17th. 303 m. One of only a few tricky drives, you hit between trees to a bumpy, narrow fairway that then rises to a well perched green. The 6th, 12th and 14th are over 400 m!

POINTS

CD	A	G/F	B/W	L	F	V	G Ex	Total
12	7	7	7	5	7	5	12	62

THE COURSE
- Par 69
- Length: 5,492 m (green tees)
- Ennis Golf Club, Drumbiggle, Ennis, Co. Clare
- Tel: +353 (0) 65 682 4074
- www.ennisgolfclub.com
- Green Fees: €35–€40

COURSES NEARBY
Dromoland Castle
East Clare
Shannon
Woodstock

ENNISCORTHY   Established 1906

COUNTRY GOLF THAT IS DESIGNED TO PLEASE

Definitely one of those friendly, country golf courses that you find all over Ireland, and always a pleasure to play. Predominantly straight holes that are completely natural, with generous fairways and easy rough – ideal for golfers of all abilities. Holes are well divided as the course starts lazily across a flat landscape (opening five holes). It then shifts to a more entertaining design, with some steep drops/climbs giving holes some thrill. The 7th hits down to a flat fairway and the 8th then comes back up (see below). This is repeated on the tempting par 5 11th, where the fairway drops and swings left just at the point it disappears. If you feel particularly brave you can aim right at the corner (OB left) and hope to catch the steep slope. This will add another 80 yards to your drive and makes the green easily reachable in two. The 16th completes the set and is the prettiest hole on the course: the tee box sits nicely in mature trees with a straight fairway below. Again, OB lines the left with heavy trees right. It is a short hole and one where you'll want to nail your drive. The green, like several here, has some fast slopes.

There is plenty of variety at Enniscorthy, which means an array of challenges. But most of all, the straightforward design ensures plenty of enjoyment. The best holes are the 8th, 9th, 11th, 15th, 16th and 17th, and when you walk off the 18th, you will be pleasantly surprised at how much fun you have had.

Interestingly, the long par 5s run consecutively on both nines (the 4th and 5th; the 10th and 11th) and head in opposite directions. There is no scenery to speak of, but it is a nice relaxing setting. This is what golf is all about, including the lively clubhouse.

FAVOURITE & TOUGHEST HOLE
Par 4 8th. 347 m. An innocuous-looking drive, but keep it to the right for a realistic chance of reaching the green in two. A big uphill draw is required to hit a very well protected green. If you fade the ball, enjoy the enormous bunker.

POINTS								
CD	A	G/F	B/W	L	F	V	G Ex	Total
13	7	7	6	7	7	9	15	71

THE COURSE
- Par 72
- Length: 5,925m
- Enniscorthy Golf Club, Knockmarshall, Enniscorthy, Co. Wexford
- Tel: +353 (0) 53 923 3191
- www.enniscorthygc.ie
- Green Fees: €17–€30

COURSES NEARBY
Bunclody
New Ross
St Helen's Bay
Seafield
Wexford

ENNISCRONE Established 1918

PERFECT DUNES, PERFECT GOLF

When the great Irish links courses are debated, Enniscrone is rarely given enough credit, and that is just wrong. It has everything you could want from a links course, including an extra nine holes. Holes 2, 12 and 13 are just mesmerising, with wonderful dunes and invisible troughs. On the 2nd, you drive straight into a sea of dunes with no view of the fairway: you are guaranteed to wonder if you will ever see your ball again. Talk about using the land to perfection. You are never far from the wonderful dunes that run around the course; you are always in them or on top of them. Even on the stretch of five flatter, more open holes in the middle of the round, the dunes have simply decided to be more accommodating. These holes stand out because they are so different – and the course is all the better for the variety.

There is a true sense of excitement hitting into the endless dips and hollows or emerging from valleys to see distant horizons or Killala Bay. Sometimes no flat lie exists, or the greens are perched so high up that a classic low-running links shot is impossible. It is a shot-maker's dream that requires guts and patience. I promise you that there is not one bad hole and you will love every minute of it, including a great buzz in the clubhouse. No matter how you play, you'll come in and enjoy a pint.

With Carne to the west (where the dunes are even more majestic), and Strandhill and County Sligo to the east, this is a superb golfing destination.

A perfect, embracing links experience and great value for money.

FAVOURITE HOLE
Par 4 13th. 338 yards. It feels almost like a spiral staircase the way it dog-legs down from a high tee, winding its way around the dunes to a pocketed green.

TOUGHEST HOLE
Par 5 7th. 524 yards. A gentle-looking hole that will fool you. The green is a thing of beauty, rising almost vertically from an invisible hollow. It will not be easy to get on, or stay on.

POINTS								
CD	A	G/F	B/W	L	F	V	G Ex	Total
19	10	9	10	9	9	10	20	96

THE COURSE
- Par 73
- Length: 6,814 yards
- Enniscrone Golf Club, Enniscrone, Co. Sligo
- Tel: +353 (0) 96 36297
- www.enniscronegolf.com
- Green Fees: €30–€60

COURSES NEARBY
Ballina
County Sligo
Strandhill

ENNISKILLEN   Established 1896

OAKS AT THE END

Enniskillen was extended to eighteen holes in the 1980s, and while you start with the newer and more challenging nine, it is the flatter back nine and their perfect mature trees that are the more inspiring.

The opening hole is superb. And terrifying. A huge drop falls from the tee before a tight fairway rises sharply to the green, and anything hit remotely right will disappear into heavy trees. Tight, tree-lined fairways predominate as holes roll over and across the hillside. There are a couple of views but nothing exciting. The 4th (see below), 6th and 7th are the best holes and not one of them is flat.

The best run starts on the back nine, at the 12th. There is great maturity and serenity to the holes, and 200- to 300-year-old oak and beech trees pepper the countryside. The 12th tee box and 13th green are surrounded and you'll feel insignificant as they silently watch you approach. This corner (including greens and tee boxes) blends seamlessly with the National Trust's Castlecoole Park alongside, highlighting that this is part of a grand old estate. A definite and

challenging feature on this flatter part of the course is the fondness for creating flat greens (the 15th to 18th) that sit just out of sight at the bottom of slopes. Judging distances is tough, but you'll have plenty of fun trying to figure it out. And watch out for more streams. And the tree in the middle of the 18th.

Enniskillen is not long but it presents many challenges. Reaching the back nine gives you a chance to relax and enjoy yourself after the climbs on the front nine.

FAVOURITE HOLE
Par 4 12th. 359 yards. A slightly raised tee presents a lovely driving hole with mature trees along the right and a stream in the middle. The green, gloriously visible, sits in front of some grand trees.

TOUGHEST HOLE
Par 4 4th. 395 yards. You can see enough fairway slopes to know your drive has only a small landing area if the green is to be reachable. 230 yards to the lone tree. Big hitters can be severely punished and end up on a downslope that then rises to a tough green.

POINTS								
CD	A	G/F	B/W	L	F	V	G Ex	Total
14	7	7	6	6	5	7	14	66

THE COURSE
- Par 71
- Length: 6,145 yards
- Enniskillen Golf Club, Castlecoole Road, Enniskillen Road, Co. Fermanagh, BT74 6HZ
- Tel: +44 (0) 28 6632 5250
  (048 from Rep. of Ire.)
- www.enniskillengolfclub.com
- Green Fees: £20–£25

COURSES NEARBY
Castle Hume
Lough Erne
Slieve Russell

ESKER HILLS Established 1997

FORTY-FIVE BUGGIES

You have been warned: this is hilly stuff. There may be forty-five buggies but be sure to book one in advance as they're the popular way to travel. Yet, if you choose to walk, it's nothing like as severe as you avoid the hillier buggy paths.

If you see the huge excitement that a hilly course offers, then Esker Hills is for you. It is not a single mountainside, it is endless rolling hilltops that dip and swing all around you. Even on good drives you won't always see the green and the holes sit enticingly on their own. Right from the 1st tee you know you're never going to be playing level, and for me that is just a thrill. Awesome tee shots and some stunning approaches to greens make Esker Hills one of those golf rounds that will leave you exhausted or pumped with adrenaline.

Trees, gorse, some splashes of water and bunkers all lend to the experience, and a few walks up to high tee boxes fill you with expectation (the 7th and 15th). It is a quality course, with Christy O'Connor Jnr's name attached, and for a designer who likes mounding, this must have been heaven. He has thrown in a few ponds which make the shorter holes difficult (the 10th is only 298 yards).

One of the beauties of a course like this is that several holes slide between huge shoulders, so even if you hit off-line you can kick down onto the fairway.

The 4th, 7th, 8th, 12th, 14th and 18th are superbly shaped holes and the par 3s have ferocious fall-offs. Love it or hate it.

FAVOURITE HOLE

Par 4 4th. 353 yards. A massive uphill drive between steep shoulders littered with trees. If you are up far enough to see the green on the other side of a big hollow, you're faced with a gem of a shot into a green set into an amphitheatre.

TOUGHEST HOLE

Par 4 17th. 415 yards. Index 2. A touch harder than the 3rd (Index 1), this dog-legs gently uphill, before a long shot takes on a perched green with a steep front and a lethally placed bunker right underneath.

POINTS								
CD	A	G/F	B/W	L	F	V	G Ex	Total
16	8	8	8	7	7	9	18	81

THE COURSE

- Par 71
- Length: 6,166 yards
- Esker Hills Golf Club, Ballykilmurray, Tullamore, Co. Offaly
- Tel: +353 (0) 57 935 5999
- www.eskerhillsgolf.com
- Green Fees: €25–€45

COURSES NEARBY
Castle Barna
Moate
Mount Temple
New Forest
Tullamore

THE EUROPEAN CLUB   Established 1987

REMARKABLE IN SO MANY WAYS

The mystery of a links course is never knowing what lies around the corner or over the hill or down in the hollow. You feel nervous on the tee, knowing that with any shot the course can crush you. And that is what makes links golf so exhilarating.

The European opens your eyes to the excitement and challenge of golf: it is isolated, it has carved dunes, treacherous rough, laser-sharp greens, a tumbling sea that accompanies you on several holes (the beach is in play on the runway-length par 5 13th), and an atmosphere of vitality that can be found only beside the sea. For me, the argument of links golf v. parkland golf is resolved right here. How can you beat the sheer thrill of a magnificent, natural links like this? This is golf at its very best and most beautiful.

If you fight the curse of a snap-hook or vicious slice, then bring a lot of balls because the rough will swallow you whole. But the fairways are generous and true, ensuring that good shots are rewarded – something not common to all links.

For all its brilliance, The European is gloriously unpretentious. The basic club-house emphasises the love lavished on the course by Pat Ruddy. He has created twenty holes (two additional par 3s) packed with adventure and danger. The railway-sleepered bunkers are always terrifying, and getting out at the first attempt will swell you with pride. Holes 7, 13 and 14 have received various 'best' awards, and many are named after golfing greats.

An absolute must. Tiger Woods bogeyed the 14th in 2002, so score a par and celebrate.

FAVOURITE HOLE
Par 4 17th. 389 yards (see photo). While many players would list the 7th, 8th or 12th, I prefer the 17th for its sense of bleakness. It is a beautiful driving hole down into a valley with small wind-battered trees that lull you into a sense of solitude.

TOUGHEST HOLE
Par 4 12th. 438 yards. The sea makes its first real appearance on a tough driving hole. Your landing area is narrower than elsewhere and surrounded by danger (bunkers). The green, undoubtedly the biggest in Ireland, is farther than you think, so add a club.

POINTS								
CD	A	G/F	B/W	L	F	V	G Ex	Total
20	10	10	10	9	8	8	20	95

THE COURSE

- Par 71
- Length: 6,720 yards
- The European Club, Brittas Bay, Co. Wicklow
- Tel: +353 (0) 404 47415
- www.theeuropeanclub.com
- Green Fees: €100–€180

COURSES NEARBY
Arklow
Blainroe
Macreddin
Wicklow
Woodenbridge

FAITHLEGG   Established 1993

AN EASY START, A TOUGH FINISH

Waterford is a great golf location: six courses and excellent accommodation. If you stay at Faithlegg, you'll have golf on tap. The house dates back to 1783; the course 1993. It is an ideal combination and the drive up to the hotel splits the course beautifully.

Faithlegg is a shortish parkland course that is smarter and more elegant than nearby Waterford Castle. It is dominated by oak trees at the start and finish, and views of the River Suir in between. The land flows around you and several holes have good rises and falls that open up the landscape. Three holes incorporate the remains of a walled garden; a line of ponds affects several holes; and you end by hitting straight at Faithlegg House.

It is an easy start with four high Indices. The 1st is a 280-yard, slight dog-leg between magnificent oak trees. The 2nd has large, picturesque ponds all along the right and OB left as it rises to the finish, and the 4th green is immersed in a small wood. Then, as you walk out of the walled garden on the 5th, look to your right: holes 7, 10, 11 and 14 are right there with views of the river beyond. These holes are the weakest on the course, but the 8th, 9th and 13th make up for them. Walking over the crest on the par 5 13th is one of the best moments as the green appears below you, flanked by trees, against the backdrop of the river.

The houses built inside the estate's perimeter irritate me. The 5th is a perfect example where a lovely driving hole is spoiled by houses on the horizon. The same is true on the 2nd, 3rd, 4th and 15th.

FAVOURITE HOLE
Par 4 8th. 356 yards. A dog-leg that hinges on a huge sycamore, which stands like a sentry before you. It is the second most intimidating drive. Shame about the smoking stack beyond the green.

TOUGHEST HOLE
Par 4 17th. 397 yards. The hardest drive on a long dog-leg. The oaks flank the fairway and they are majestic. Then it's an uphill shot to a well-defended green.

POINTS

CD	A	G/F	B/W	L	F	V	G Ex	Total
15	7	8	7	7	8	8	15	75

THE COURSE

- Par 72
- Length: 6,335 yards
- Faithlegg Golf Club, Faithlegg, Co. Waterford
- Tel: +353 (0) 51 380 587
- www.faithlegg.com
- Green Fees: €30–€45

COURSES NEARBY
Dunmore East
Tramore
Waterford
Waterford Castle
Williamstown

FARNHAM ESTATE   Established 2008

OPPOSITES ATTRACT

Two remarkably spacious loops of holes greet you at this Radisson SAS resort. There is so much space that you rarely see another hole, which leaves a couple of long walks.

A brand new course that has two different nines. The quality is of that perfect carpet variety (including circular tee boxes – a Jeff Howes favourite), and the greens are firm, fast and true. No clubhouse or other facilities (plush hotel excluded) are yet available.

The opening nine are an interesting mix of trees, slopes and open spaces. The 1st is wide open, rising up the hill, yet the 2nd has a terrifically tight drive downhill around chestnut trees, with water in front of the green. There is so much land around you that the course almost appears to be floating, the perfect fairways drifting through fields and past trees. In all honesty it feels alien and it is startling to look at. The bunkers are shallow, bizarrely shaped and fringed with impossible fescue grass – you'll be better off in the sand – but they continue that alien feeling.

The back nine are better, rising into dense forest with a number of holes completely trapped by the boles of tall trees. After the open spaces of the first holes, there is no room for error here. The 18th is the signature hole – a par 5 curling around a big pond and then threading between the trees.

As it is a Jeff Howes course you know it's going to be quality. Undoubtedly it will come of age and there is always lots to see.

FAVOURITE HOLE
Par 4 2nd. 393 yards. The drive is tough (see above), but the view of the hole from the tee is glorious. It looks so perfect, with the green far below surrounded by trees and with the stream running across the front.

TOUGHEST HOLE
Par 4 4th. 427 yards. A blind drive (the only one) over a crest, with a fairway that splits around three big oaks. Hit at them and fall left for any chance of hitting the green that has pretty water along the right and behind.

POINTS

CD	A	G/F	B/W	L	F	V	G Ex	Total
16	8	8	7	6	4	7	16	72

THE COURSE

- Par 72
- Length: tbc
- Farnham Estate Golf Club, Farnham Estate, Cavan, Co. Cavan
- Tel: +353 (0) 49 437 7700
- www.farnhamestate.com
- Green Fees: €40–€65

COURSES NEARBY
County Cavan
Clones
Slieve Russell

FAUGHAN VALLEY   Established 2000

BASIC ENTERTAINMENT

To call this a good golf course would be fishing for a compliment it doesn't deserve. It is basic in terms of design, facilities and quality, but this is the course's niche. Holes 1 to 10 are set on a sloping field of young tree-lined fairways. The River Faughan flows along the left and also behind, making a nice feature of the 5th tee box which sits right on top of it. And off the 1st a hooked tee shot might take out any of the fishermen on the river's bank. But the fairways and greens lack substance, bar the 3rd green which is about 50 yards long and surrounded on three sides by a pond.

The 11th is a different matter entirely (see below) and kickstarts the five best holes. The 12th is a short, straight par 4 of 230 yards, through pampas grass and up to a steeply banked green. The 13th is nothing special, the 14th is a quandary (see below), and the 15th offers the only fairway with character, arcing uphill with a gentle, hidden hollow. The 17th and 18th are across the road.

This is a course of average quality, designed for friends and those looking to discover the game and their own abilities.

At 5,452 yards it may seem short but four of the par 3s fall around 190 yards. It is very open, there is some criss-crossing and some tees and greens are a bit close. It's a jeans, t-shirts, trainers and granddad's old clubs kind of course. If that sounds like you, then you'll certainly enjoy it for £9.

Holes are very appropriately named, e.g. Shanks (the 11th). The greens, grotty at the start, improve towards the end.

FAVOURITE HOLE
Par 4 11th. 332 yards. 'Shanks'. You stand beside the clubhouse and hit well down onto a flat, curving fairway. The river slides right alongside, deep and wide, and hugs the fairway so tightly it is a slicer's nightmare.

TOUGHEST HOLE
Par 4 14th. 300 yards. The Bridge is Index 1. It is a pincer-type hole where the generous fairway has water on both sides (making the fairway so much harder to hit) before narrowing on the approach to the green. The bridge behind adds considerable appeal.

POINTS

CD	A	G/F	B/W	L	F	V	G Ex	Total
10	5	4	6	5	4	8	10	52

THE COURSE
- Par 69
- Length: 5,452 yards
- Faughan Valley Golf Club, Carmoney Road, Campsie, Co. Derry
- Tel: +44 (0) 28 7186 0707 (048 from Rep. of Ire.)
- www.faughanvalleygolfclub.co.uk
- Green Fees: £10–£12

COURSES NEARBY
City of Derry
Foyle
North West

FERMOY   Established 1892

A GOOD WORKOUT

Someone told me not to bother playing Fermoy. I have no idea why as this is a strenuous and different test of golf. You get a hint of it on the 1st tee when you look straight over a deep valley to the green. With the positioning of the conifers, with no rough underneath, and some rumbling fairways on the front nine, I was reminded of Portugal. Gorse and heather then add a heathland touch and this stuff is lethal – if a ball goes in, it stays in.

On the par 5 6th, take a moment and sit down on the Captain's bench behind the tee. Listen to the trees creak, the wind hush and admire the views – a moment of contemplation that few of us take – then tee off and play the best hole on this nine. It rockets over a steeply sloping fairway and opens up a green in the corner of the course.

When you leave the 9th and walk over the road, you'll be thinking, 'Glad that's over.' That's what I thought. Drives may be relatively danger-free, but slightly short or inaccurate approaches to greens can dent your enthusiasm. Surely the second

nine will be easier? Not a hope. The holes are hillier and twice as dangerous. They are superior too, with fantastic shapes, great tee shots and a very real sense that par is as good as a birdie. The views are better, stretching across the Avondhu countryside, and these hit you on the 10th and 13th particularly.

Like Muskerry, many will struggle with the climbs and the demands made of your shot-making ability. If that is a red flag to a bull, then you will thrive at Fermoy.

FAVOURITE HOLE
Par 4 1st. 320 m. This is a kick-start if ever there was one. It is like the 13th (below) in miniature. You might dislocate something trying to kill the ball – it's that tempting.

TOUGHEST HOLE
Par 4 13th. 423 m. The fairway just drops away from the tee, out of sight, way down. Then it reappears, rising rapidly to a green that's almost at eye-level. The fairway also slopes right. Index 1.

POINTS								
CD	A	G/F	B/W	L	F	V	G Ex	Total
15	7	7	7	8	7	10	15	76

THE COURSE
- Par 70
- Length: 5,596 m
- Fermoy Golf Club, Corrin, Fermoy, Co. Cork
- Tel: +353 (0) 25 31472
- www.fermoygolfclub.ie
- Green Fees: €23–€33

COURSES NEARBY
East Cork
Mallow
Mitchelstown

FERNHILL   Established 1994

A BIT TOO MUCH OF NOTHING

Fernhill is rather amateurish and rough around the edges. A gentle hill adds some variety to the holes (including the best stretch, which starts at the downhill, 170-yard 8th and runs to the 13th) offering better tee shots and better views of greens. But there certainly isn't much excitement or creativity with holes running up and down flat, semi-mature tree-lined fairways at the start. Fernhill is the kind of place you come to when you're learning the game and you need room to manouevre, or you fancy a knock around with friends. At the same time, it is going to be dangerous if there are lots of golfers about. From a challenge perspective, there is little to trouble you off the tee or as you approach greens, so it's not going to attract golfers who want some testing golf and some drama. The only views are of pylons.

It starts with a dog-leg and you get a pretty good idea from this what you are going to face in terms of the course's appeal. There are plenty of dog-legs and, with the flat ground, it's hard to judge how far you should drive. The best holes are the par 4 7th and 11th which both dog-leg at the last moment.

Despite lots of bunkering, only the raised greens impress with some great shapes, tiers and slopes. They're surprisingly good quality. They tilt towards you to make inviting targets between paired bunkers and they are the best feature of the course.

There is a hotel and a leisure club here too, but the whole set-up is a bit tame.

FAVOURITE HOLE
Par 3 8th. 170 yards. The first dose of interest with a tee shot that hits down between lines of trees to a small well-raised green.

TOUGHEST HOLE
Par 4 3rd. A dog-leg, hitting over a quarry on your left. It's difficult to judge just how far you can go.

POINTS

CD	A	G/F	B/W	L	F	V	G Ex	Total
10	4	6	5	3	5	4	9	46

THE COURSE
- Par 69
- Length: 6,053 yards
- Fernhill Golf & Country Club, Carrigaline, Co. Cork
- Tel: +353 (0) 21 437 2226
- www.fernhillcountryclub.com
- Green Fees: €18–€25

COURSES NEARBY
Douglas
Monkstown

FORREST LITTLE   Established 1940

WONDERFULLY SIMPLE

You can't beat a basic, straightforward course like this. No pretensions, no attempts to glamorise, just a mature and vibrant parkland course that sticks to the simple things and does them exquisitely well. My only complaint was the poor condition of the greens and that may have been owing to the weather.

Forrest Hill is flat, with subtle shapes to the fairways and a straightforward layout that goes back and forth – although you won't know it. Trees are well placed and dense enough to push the fairways apart, and often become a feature of the hole, either off the tee or approaching the green. They add interest and every hole is enjoyable.

There is a good variety of hole length and shape. It is not difficult but you need to be accurate off the tee as there are several narrow fairways, fairway bunkers and a couple of good short dog-legs (the 1st and 12th) which demand respect and caution. If you are a little wild, you'll find some tricky rough and trees blocking you on almost every hole. A couple of stream-filled ditches come in to play on several holes.

No, it won't blow your socks off, but it's the kind of course that everyone will enjoy, especially when you get back to the clubhouse. Take the chance to relax right next to Dublin Airport.

FAVOURITE HOLE
Par 3 7th. 126 m. Better from the back tee (140 m), this is an elevated tee shot to an elevated green surrounded by bunkers with water at the bottom of the slope.

TOUGHEST HOLE
Par 4 8th. 386 m. The only hole with a sloping fairway. You drive down onto it and you will be lucky if you're not partially blocked by the tree that sneaks onto the fairway. The green surface will probably be hidden, presenting a tough approach.

POINTS								
CD	A	G/F	B/W	L	F	V	G Ex	Total
14	7	7	7	5	8	8	15	71

THE COURSE

- Par 71
- Length: 5,632 m
- Forrest Little Golf Club, Cloghran, Co. Dublin
- Tel: +353 (0) 1 840 1763
- www.forrestlittle.ie
- Green Fees: €35–€45

COURSES NEARBY
Corrstown
Malahide
Roganstown
St Margaret's
Swords Open

FORTWILLIAM   Established 1891

PAINTING BY NUMBERS

This is a basic and short par 70 parkland course, sitting on a hillside under the quirky shapes of Cave Hill and overlooking Belfast Lough. Essentially you're hitting up at the hill or down at the water. There is not a huge amount of variety and there is no design flair to grab your attention. What you will find are narrow fairways and trees that get close – particularly on the steeper outside holes (the 2nd to 8th). As a result these are trickier because the elevation makes club selection harder. For anyone with length, this means leaving your driver alone. You could easily get away with a 3 iron/wood, even on the two short par 5s. Shorter hitters will find it easier to compete, but if you're wild off the tee, the chances are you'll be stuffed. And roaring 'fore'.

On the inside holes there is more room (the 18th excluded) but there is still not much in the way of excitement. What you see is what you get, and it doesn't grab you. In fact, it is really only the changes in elevation that bring character to the course, with some over-the-ridge approach shots to greens and some green settings up above you, set against Cave Hill.

The quality is fine, but it's not thrilling and it feels cramped. There are better courses nearby.

FAVOURITE HOLE

Par 4 16th. 331 yards. A straight hole that starts flat and then rises sharply to the green, framed by the hills behind. A very tempting drive. No bunkers and a big tier runs front to back on the green – a quirky touch.

TOUGHEST HOLE

Par 4 13th. 358 yards. Index 2 is a dog-leg that tests your accuracy and length off the tee. The hole then heads left and rises so you can't see the green.

POINTS								
CD	A	G/F	B/W	L	F	V	G Ex	Total
11	6	6	5	7	7	6	11	59

THE COURSE

- Par 70
- Length: 5,692 yards
- Fortwilliam Golf Club, 8a Downview Avenue, Belfast, BT15 4EZ
- Tel: +44 (0) 28 9077 0980 (048 from Rep. of Ire.)
- www.fortwilliam.co.uk
- Green Fees: £22–£29

COURSES NEARBY
Balmoral
Belvoir Park
Carrickfergus
Holywood
Malone

FOTA ISLAND   Established 1993

A BEAUTIFUL, LUXURIOUS OCCASION

Absolute class, from the moment you arrive. Fota Island held the Irish Open in 2001 and 2002. The course is bordered by majestic trees and the estuary, so you are promised a great variety of holes and shots. Plenty of dog-legs curve around bunkers, over gentle crests and between the trees. And yet the course is generous. Fairways are wide, greens are accessible and smooth, and there is no excuse for not scoring. It's a great combination of beautiful golf that encourages you to do well. Put another way: glamour and relaxation.

There is a 'but', and if you are serious enough about golf, I suggest you get the strokesaver. I'm not a fan but there are some hidden hazards you cannot see from the tee or on approaches: water on the 8th and 14th, and a hidden creek on the 12th. It is also useful on the dog-legs elbowed by bunkers.

Water is gloriously dangerous: there are three island-type greens and the 18th is a card maker or breaker, while your approach into the stunning, downhill par 5 10th has water all around the back. It would make you nervous if you knew how close it was.

The 8th and 9th are the least interesting (blind-ish) drives but they are Index 1 and 5 respectively, so your strokesaver will help. Elsewhere, driving is a dream and the only tough one comes on the 18th, where you are squeezed between trees.

There are twenty-seven holes. I played the original eighteen (Deerpark), but the nines are swapped continuously. I have no doubt that you will love whichever eighteen you play. A Sheraton hotel comes with the resort. Spend some quality time in the luxurious clubhouse. Fota Island Wildlife Park is next door.

FAVOURITE HOLE
Par 5 10th. 487 yards. A hole that flows down the hill and curves around the dense wood on the right. A peach of a drive. Then it gets interesting as one huge tree forces you to play right, towards water that also surrounds the green.

TOUGHEST HOLE
Par 4 8th. 450 yards. Dog-leg around a nest of bunkers that pushes you farther from the hole. Then it's a long shot up a gentle slope, which must tackle unseen water on the left of the green. Two very tough shots.

POINTS								
CD	A	G/F	B/W	L	F	V	G Ex	Total
18	10	9	9	7	10	8	19	90

THE COURSE
- Par 71
- Length: 6,488 yards (Deerpark)
- Fota Island Golf Club, Fota Island, Cork, Co. Cork
- Tel: +353 (0) 21 488 3700
- www.fotaisland.ie
- Green Fees: €60–€85

COURSES NEARBY
Castlemartyr
Cobh
Cork
Mahon
Water Rock

FOYLE   Established 1994

A DECENT PACKAGE

Foyle is still young and you will find the evidence on many fairways where young trees are thriving. I take my hat off to a course that prefers deciduous trees to conifers. The long-term result will be more impressive and of far greater appeal. The young oaks and beeches blend with the few mature trees and prove delightful on the 6th and 15th particularly.

There is nothing spectacular to the course in terms of creative design elements, which is 'what you see is what you get'. It has been built across farmland by the local farmer. That might make it sound a bit basic but it is a pleasant enough round of golf for everyone. Holes go all over the place and you cross a quiet laneway four times. The 1st to 5th and the 16th to 18th are near the clubhouse and are the least interesting as they go up and down – the par 3 3rd with its pond being a notable exception. You cross a lane (you'll need a code to get through locked gates) to play the 6th to 8th, and then again for the 13th to 15th. Combined, these holes are the best on the course,

with good parkland character, tighter drives, more maturity, gorse and a hillside that has resulted in the 14th being affectionately known as 'heart-attack hill'. Amelia Earhart landed here on her transatlantic flight in 1932. Holes 9 to 12 are near the clubhouse but lower down where a small lake asks a lot of your drive on the 10th and 11th – two tricky dog-legs.

It's part of an International Golf Centre, with a par 3 course, full-scale driving range, a restaurant and wine bar.

FAVOURITE HOLE
Par 4 10th. 353 yards. A good drive from a high tee into a dog-leg that clings to a small lake. Choosing your landing area is the big moment and the biggest reward.

TOUGHEST HOLE
Par 4 15th. 419 yards. The best driving hole and one that needs a beauty. Big beeches line the boundary on the right which is tight, and you need to find the fairway if you are to reach in two.

POINTS								
CD	A	G/F	B/W	L	F	V	G Ex	Total
13	6	7	6	6	7	7	14	66

THE COURSE
- Par 71
- Length: 6,331 yards
- Foyle International Golf Centre, 12 Alder Road, Londonderry, BT48 8DB
- Tel: +44 (0) 28 7135 2222 (048 from Rep. of Ire.)
- www.foylegolfclub.co.uk
- Green Fees: £12–£20

COURSES NEARBY
City of Derry
Faughan Valley
Greencastle
North West

GALGORM CASTLE   Established 1997

SPACIOUS PARKLAND WONDER

A great find. If you're heading from Dublin to the northern links, you can go east or west of Lough Neagh and play an excellent parkland course along the way: Moyola Park to the west, Galgorm Castle to the east. Both have that maturity, spaciousness and an easy, relaxing rhythm that make it such a pleasure to play golf.

The long drive into the estate shows off one of the best holes (the 10th) – it looks wild, spacious and enthralling. And so it continues for much of your round. The only uninteresting shot is your drive off the 1st. After that it is one playable hole after another. There's lots of interest off the tee, and lots of room to hit at. Big trees and pretty ponds abound, and the rivers Braid and Main merge behind the 13th green and streak around the course in between. You also cross bridges on several occasions – another plus in my book. It undulates gently so it feels like a pleasant walk, which makes golf all the more enjoyable. You are invited to play from the greens tees or, for a better challenge, the 500-yard-longer white tees. Even so, it is not a difficult course as you nearly always have room and the greens are big, inviting and accessible.

What I found so special was the rhythm of it all. There is no brilliant hole but they all fit perfectly to give an extremely rewarding round of golf.

It is well routed, and hole lengths offer good variety. The par 5s are short and give good opportunities to score. More impressive facilities are due soon and, once the younger trees grow, this will be superb. And the castle may be open soon, too.

FAVOURITE HOLE
Par 5 10th. 483 yards. A lovely-looking hole that drifts down from the tee with trees along the left and a pond and more trees on the right. There's plenty of fairway to hit at before the hole dog-legs right. Colourful.

TOUGHEST HOLE
Par 4 11th. 443 yards. Index 1 is flat and it dog-legs right. It is hard to gauge what you can do off the tee but you need to find the fairway to have any chance of reaching the green.

POINTS								
CD	A	G/F	B/W	L	F	V	G Ex	Total
15	9	7	8	6	8	10	18	81

THE COURSE

- Par 72
- Length: 6,230 yards
- Galgorm Castle Golf Club, 200 Galgorm Road, Ballymena, Co. Antrim, BT42 1HL
- Tel: +44 (0) 28 2564 6161 (048 from Rep. of Ire.)
- www.galgormcastle.co.uk
- Green Fees: £40–£55

COURSES NEARBY
Antrim
Ballymena
Cairndhu
Massereene
Moyola Park

GALWAY   Established 1895

HAS MOVED WELL WITH THE TIMES

You have to feel sorry for Galway. Established in 1895, it must have been a glorious location with views over Galway Bay to the Burren and Aran Islands. Now it is surrounded by houses and severed by a busy road. An underpass takes you to the 1st tee and it's an impressive view that greets you as you emerge from the gloom. You play four holes here (three with water) before the tunnel returns you to the 5th.

Despite the heavily tossed fairways, this is a parkland course at heart. The 1st hole makes two things abundantly clear: bunkers could ruin your day and well-shaped, banked and sloping greens demand accuracy if you are to score well. Tree-lined holes give way occasionally to the nightmare that is gorse, but it is easy to see that the course will look its best on a sunny day in spring when the gorse flowers.

The second nine, which stretch up behind the clubhouse, are more interesting with changes in elevation adding a dramatic element to several holes, both in terms of difficulty and the views.

While most greens are clearly visible there are some that are tucked away behind fairway swells or the crest of hills. Fairways are smooth but they are narrow, and the first cut of rough can be thick – it also runs for 80 yards or so in front of some tee boxes. The chipping green and driving range are a long way apart, and the range is little more than a wedge in length.

Galway ticks the right boxes and offers enough to keep you entertained, making it a challenge everyone will enjoy. The clubhouse is new.

FAVOURITE HOLE
Par 4 14th. 352 m. A big downhill drive that you can watch all the way, with the Clare mountains as a great backdrop. The approach to the green, between bunkers, is well presented.

TOUGHEST HOLE
Par 4 15th. 350 m. After the 14th, you turn around and go straight back up the hill, only this time your drive has to carry a dense thicket of gorse.

POINTS

CD	A	G/F	B/W	L	F	V	G Ex	Total
14	7	9	8	8	8	8	15	77

THE COURSE

- Par 70
- Length: 5,716 m
- Galway Golf Club, Blackrock, Salthill, Co. Galway
- Tel: +353 (0) 91 522 033
- www.galwaygolf.com
- Green Fees: €30

COURSES NEARBY
Athenry
Bearna
Cregmore Park
Galway Bay
Oughterard

GALWAY BAY   Established 1993

AROUND THE BAY

This is a silken, manicured parkland that sits on Galway Bay and sweeps over an exposed landscape down to the sea. From the temporary clubhouse you can see over much of the course as it falls towards the water, and some of the best holes sit right above the sea.

Once a barren location, considerable mounding now creates an easy and often dramatic flow to the holes. It works perfectly, producing a links-like track and, given the setting, that seems only fitting. Excellent routing takes you out to the sea on both nines, mixing in views of distant flags with some tricky dog-legs. Holes are separated by deep strips of rough, gorse and wind-bent trees. When you walk to the 1st tee the trees stand as fair warning of the battering you might endure.

There are large, dark ponds, which, like the rest of course, are immaculately presented. Combined with glorious greens and green complexes it confirms that Galway Bay is the full package of quality, design and intrigue. There are 131 bunkers here – many of them vicious – and when

you stand on the 8th tee, you can see eight of them in front of you. That's what I call daunting. It is definitely an enticing course to play but it is long and challenging from start to finish. In particular, your driving will need to be on song to find some fairways, and approaches to greens have to be carefully considered – they look idyllic but the dangers are many.

The back nine should play harder, especially with holes 11 and 12 being two sharp dog-legs, and indices 3 and 1 respectively.

FAVOURITE HOLE
Par 3 7th. 140 yards. A picture-perfect hole with the tee box on the shoreline and the green sitting directly over a pond in a ring of gorse and bunkers.

TOUGHEST HOLE
Par 4 12th. 431 yards. A long, sharp dog-leg that puts a premium on position from the tee, and sheer bravery for your second as you head downhill and over a pond.

POINTS

CD	A	G/F	B/W	L	F	V	G Ex	Total
17	8	10	10	9	6	7	19	86

THE COURSE

- Par 72
- Length: 6,797 yards
- Galway Bay Golf Club, Renville, Oranmore, Co. Galway
- Tel: +353 (0) 91 790 711
- www.galwaybaygolfresort.com
- Green Fees: €45–€65

COURSES NEARBY
Athenry
Bearna
Cregmore Park
Galway

GLASSON   Established 1993

'THE GLASSON EXPERIENCE'

The 'Experience', as the resort promotes itself, focuses on a beautiful piece of parkland landscape that drifts down to Lough Ree for the final holes. It is an impressive finish that starts as early as the 13th. The hotel is excellent, the drive in (look left) is mouth-watering and the test of golf is severe.

The design of the course is uncomplicated, although it doesn't fascinate the way it does at Athlone across the lake. Here you will find straightforward drives and plenty of unassuming approaches. The greatest challenges are the length, several hidden putting surfaces and some steep green contours. Having played here some years ago (atrociously, I might add), I recalled that Glasson starts slowly. You would think a magnificent rolling landscape with such impressive and calming lake views would deliver intrigue from the very start: but apart from the two excellent par 3s (the 3rd and 5th) and the 8th and 9th, it doesn't truly ignite until you cross in front of the hotel and play the 13th. From here on you are really tested. But more than that, the holes are divine. As you climb up to the 14th tee in the beech wood, you'll feel the hairs on the back of your neck rise, while the 15th is the acclaimed par 3 over Lough Ree.

There are some nice walks between the 8th and 9th, and the 9th and 10th, and I think they should make more of this green-to-tee experience on the opening holes. It would make a huge difference.

Glasson has a great reputation and it is very popular. It is a very friendly hotel and, as golfing packages go, you'll find it hard to beat. Visit Athlone Golf Club too.

FAVOURITE HOLE
Par 4 13th. 369 yards. Index 3. The hole immediately below the driveway. It curves uphill with good bunkers on the left, and a stunning wood behind the green. A super driving hole with a nightmare green – stay right of the flag.

TOUGHEST HOLE
Par 4 16th. 417 yards. Index 1 and long. The drive has to deal with a pond on the right and bunkers left. You have room, but it's a long way up to a well-defended putting surface which, again, you can't see.

POINTS								
CD	A	G/F	B/W	L	F	V	G Ex	Total
15	8	8	8	8	10	7	16	80

THE COURSE
- Par 73
- Length: 6,836 yards (white tees)
- Glasson Golf Club, Glasson, Athlone, Co. Westmeath
- Tel: +353 (0) 90 648 5120
- www.glassongolfhotel.ie
- Green Fees: €45–€55

COURSES NEARBY
Athlone
Moate
Mount Temple
Roscommon

GLEBE   Established 1993

TYPICAL FARMLAND FARE

I know we have 'parkland' courses, but can we have a new descriptor: farmland? Glebe is a classic example where fields have been turned over to a golf course. Holes 1 and 2 sit obviously in fields, clearly defined by the rows of low hedging. The landscape undulates gently and trees are planted sporadically, but you never quite escape that farm feeling.

Serious golfers won't be rushing here – there simply is not enough interest and the greens are just laid flat. They are big and have some serious bumps, but it is just trimmed-up fairway. The 9th to 12th is an interesting stretch of holes but it's not enough.

You've probably gathered that I'm not a fan, but there are elements here that will appeal to plenty of golfers: wide and straight fairways, big greens and few bunkers. The stream in a ditch that crosses several holes is the only serious hazard, so there's plenty of room to have fun. There are lots of trees too, but the big ones rarely affect you. Only on the three par 3s and the quirky 11th will you find them a problem.

FAVOURITE HOLE
Par 4 9th. 310 m. A pleasant tee box under big ash. A flat hole that has more character as you are forced out to the right. A good approach in over water.

TOUGHEST HOLE
Par 4 11th. 306 m. It is Index 14 but it's a right-angled dog-leg that has large ash stretching across the turn. You can go for the green (there is a bell beside it) or else you have to lay up, which means finding a landing area of 20 yards.

POINTS

CD	A	G/F	B/W	L	F	V	G Ex	Total
10	5	5	5	6	6	5	10	52

THE COURSE

- Par 73
- Length: 5,906 m
- Glebe Golf Club, Dunlever, Trim, Co. Meath
- Tel: +353 (0) 46 943 1926
- www.glebegolfclub.com
- Green Fees: €12–€25

COURSES NEARBY
County Meath
Delvin Castle
Knightsbrook
Rathcore

GLENMALURE   Established 1993

'WHY BOTHER?'

At least, that was the response I received when I asked a couple of golfers about whether they had been to Glemalure. And yes, I see their point. In terms of a golf course the quality is poor: greens are little more than small, mown patches of fairway; fairways and tee boxes need some serious TLC; and the design rolls up and down the steep hillside in a fairly uninteresting manner – despite some quirky dog-legs.

But that would detract from a very pretty location in the Wicklow Mountains. Gorse flows everywhere, trees add charm (the 4th especially) and every hole has views. The 12th is entertaining: it sits at the very top of the course and a sign on the tee box actually tells you that the green is straight ahead of you; you look up and all you see is gorse and a white post rising beyond it with an 'X' on the top.

The course is a par 66 and very short. Plenty of par 4s would be reachable for bigger hitters, but the greens are very small and are tricky around the edges. Some of the par 3s, conversely, are quite long so the course does tease you a bit.

It's not worth going out of your way to play the course, and the facilities are poor, but in terms of seeing some of the Wicklow Hills, it might be worth a visit.

FAVOURITE HOLE
Par 5 9th. 488 yards. About the only fairway with real shape. It tumbles down the hill with two trees spaced out down the fairway, and humps of gorse alongside. A bizarrely placed pond sits halfway. The 3rd is a tempting, short, uphill par 4.

TOUGHEST HOLE
Par 4 12th. 307 yards. You simply need to believe the sign that directs you, but because it's a short hole, it is hard to know what to do or how far you have to carry.

POINTS								
CD	A	G/F	B/W	L	F	V	G Ex	Total
8	8	2	3	9	4	5	10	49

THE COURSE
- Par 66
- Length: 5,497 yards
- Glenmalure Golf Club, Greenane, Rathdrum, Co. Wicklow
- Tel: +353 (0) 404 46679
- www.glenmaluregolf.com
- Green Fees: €15–€20

COURSES NEARBY
Arklow
European Club, The
Macreddin
Woodenbridge

GLEN OF THE DOWNS   Established 1998

LINKS ON THE SIDE OF A MOUNTAIN

There is an interesting links-like feel to a hillside course that sits under the Great Sugar Loaf Mountain. Put it this way, it is windy and bare (hardly a tree on the course), wicked rough punishes the wayward, and you can run your shots in to a variety of nicely protected greens.

In fairness, the course doesn't sound that appealing. It was rolling fields until recently (similar to but not nearly as hilly as Bray), and views of the nearby sea and the Great Sugar Loaf are the only consolation. But the topography is entertaining and, once you get stuck in to the golf, the smart design and quality of the course will speak for itself. You can drive like a mad thing, but if you play the sensible running game, you will need to keep it straight. The length of the rough is the course's main defence and if it's long, a wayward drive will disappear. The greens are beautifully created with excellent bunkering and dramatic breaks. If you are a fan of putting, you will love the fast surfaces.

There are some great touches too: you have to walk to the front of the 12th tee box to assess your line and see what awaits your drive far below; the five-tier double green for the 8th and 10th is a masterpiece; and the very driveable 18th could lead to a wet end, but offers a real birdie chance. The modern, tidy clubhouse is stunning and does great grub.

One more thing: contrary to the course designer's claims, only two of the five par 3s are worthy of acclaim: the 7th and 16th both offer soaring tee shots while the 4th is the weakest hole on the course.

Ask for directions for the practice putting green.

FAVOURITE HOLE
Par 4 10th. 361 yards. The hole curves right and up to the green. It's all on show in the great wide open and you have to decide how much to bite off with your drive. You will probably try for too much. Your second is all uphill.

TOUGHEST HOLE
Par 3 16th. 159 yards. Pinpoint accuracy required, with serious banks and slopes wreaking havoc on the wayward. Like the 1st, the green is shallow, but miss it and you might not be able to see the green, let alone the flag.

POINTS								
CD	A	G/F	B/W	L	F	V	G Ex	Total
14	6	9	8	7	8	7	15	74

THE COURSE
- Par 71
- Length: 5,980 yards
- Glen of the Downs Golf Club, Coolnaskeagh, Delgany, Co. Wicklow
- Tel: +353 (0) 1 287 6240
- www.glenofthedowns.com
- Green Fees: €35–€65

COURSES NEARBY
Bray
Charlesland
Greystones
Powerscourt
Woodbrook

GOLD COAST   Established 1939

A WILD ATLANTIC COAST

To reach the club, you drive beside the sea for a mile. And I mean right beside the sea. Then the 1st teebox sits with its back to the water and a host of bobbing boats. Welcome to Gold Coast – a seaside parkland adventure.

In terms of sheer drama, this course beats nearby Dungarvan hands down. The beautiful Dungarvan Bay is always in sight and it gets up close and personal on several holes, three of them requiring shots over water. The mountains are less prominent, but Ballyvoyle and Helvick Heads look like portly walruses dropping into the ocean as the course leads you around the Atlantic coastline, out to the lighthouse and beyond.

Compared with the views the golf is almost secondary, especially as there is a real mish-mash of holes. Some run a bit close together and the original and new nines produce quite different appearances. For example, the 13th is a tight and mature tree-lined hole that requires absolute accuracy, while the 12th is wide open and uninspiring. From that

perspective it offers many different challenges.

There are two excellent runs of holes: the 6th, 7th and 8th are your first direct encounter with the sea; and the 15th to 18th ensure a fine and difficult finish. The wind will make a huge difference to these last holes and, as Brendan (my playing partner) quipped, 'The last time we had a calm day was 1984'. Several of the tee boxes are specifically defended against the wind so you'll appreciate his point.

FAVOURITE HOLE
Par 3 7th. 144 m. You stand beside the lighthouse and hit straight at the sea. The par 3 8th is excellent too and hits over the beach.

TOUGHEST HOLE
Par 4 15th. 344 m. Hitting over water when you're standing on the shore's edge is enough to wrack the nerves of any golfer. It is not a big shot, but you won't want to be laughed at for knocking it into the sink.

POINTS								
CD	A	G/F	B/W	L	F	V	G Ex	Total
13	6	6	7	9	6	9	16	72

THE COURSE
- Par 72
- Length: 5,913 m
- Gold Coast Golf Club, Ballinacourty, Dungarvan, Co. Waterford
- Tel: +353 (0) 58 44055
- www.goldcoastgolfclub.com
- Green Fees: €25–€30

COURSES NEARBY
Dungarvan
Tramore
West Waterford

GORT   Established 1924

ON THE UP

Gort is one of those peaceful parkland courses (constructed in 1996) that sits in a quiet rhythm of hills. The clubhouse is at the highest point and the course ducks and dives its way around some interesting slopes and sharp dog-legs (holes 1 to 3, and 7 most notably). A few climbs, especially in the opening holes, will make you think it's hilly, but really it is just attractively shaped. It offers up some thrilling drives (the 1st, 10th) and plenty of blind ones (marked by white stones), with the 2nd and 3rd providing dreadfully unrewarding tee shots.

The hilliness comes and goes and the flat holes in between are all good. Holes 4 to 6 are thrilling and the wildness here is repeated on numerous occasions. It gives a young course a lovely mature feel. Walls, wild hedging, ponds, ferns and dense hawthorn create this effect, and holes move comfortably between them all. There are no mammoth trees, which gives the course some airiness.

The back nine are prettier and offer better scoring opportunities, but don't ever feel comfortable. There are slopes and bunkers you cannot see, generous fairways followed by tight ones and greens that are inviting and dangerous in equal measure. Fortunately, the bunkers are relatively easy.

Anyone who plays Gort will be tested and thrilled by what it has to offer, and there will be no complaints about the quality. On the tricky dog-legs (the 2nd, 3rd, 6th and 7th) study the tee box map carefully. Nice par 3s too.

FAVOURITE HOLE

Par 4 6th. 271 m. A short dog-leg right. It's a great tee box setting and you can either go for it over the trees or take the sensible approach and hit at the lone tree in the fairway. An embracing line of hawthorn gives the green character.

TOUGHEST HOLE

Par 4 2nd. 397 m. A tough blind drive so early makes this almost unfair. Even a superb drive will be punished as the fairway is steeply sloped, yet you need distance to see a green with fall-offs and a hollow front right. Play the long 7th as a par 5.

POINTS								
CD	A	G/F	B/W	L	F	V	G Ex	Total
15	8	8	7	7	8	10	16	79

THE COURSE

- Par 71
- Length: 5,707 m
- Gort Golf Club, Castlequarter, Gort, Co. Galway
- Tel: +353 (0) 91 632 244
- www.gortgolf.com
- Green Fees: €20–€30

COURSES NEARBY
Athenry
Curra West
Galway Bay
Loughrea

GOWRAN PARK   Established 2001

HORSES FOR COURSES

Here's an idea: build a golf course in an old estate and around a popular horse-racing track. A bit far-fetched? That's what happened at Gowran Park in 2001, courtesy of Jeff Howes. The three-storey clubhouse (bar at the top) is the same building where thousands cheer on the nags. To reach the first tee, you must cross the track itself (and six times in all) – you will be pleased to hear that golf is not allowed on racing days. It wouldn't be a fair contest.

The golf is an adventure, with five holes inside the track and two par 3s that hit across it. The best holes are outside, starting when you disappear into some wonderful old woodland on the way to the 4th tee. Trees push in on you and the fairway shrinks. It's remarkable how it focuses the mind, and you'll encounter it again at the 8th and 15th. Elsewhere you can be looser, but not much. That's what I like about Gowran Park: it mixes the difficulty and the interest, but always entertains. For a new course it has settled in very well and, with few manufactured mounds, it feels very natural. There's plenty of water which threatens on the 4th, 8th and 9th – 8th is a short par 5 through a tight line of trees and it will leave many thinking they can make it in two. There is no room for error so it's a tantalising choice.

The mix of holes promises enjoyment and really adds to the day's excitement. Not one of the five par 3s is easy.

FAVOURITE HOLE

Par 4 15th. 360 m. A beautifully straight hole. It is not long so you'll fancy your chances, but the tall lines of 100-foot trees are closer than you think. Hit this one straight.

TOUGHEST HOLE

Par 4 4th. 403 m. If you're a long hitter, now is the time to show restraint: there's too much trouble off the tee (trees, water, dog-leg). If you drive short, you need a very accurate second to negotiate the various water hazards.

POINTS								
CD	A	G/F	B/W	L	F	V	G Ex	Total
15	8	8	8	7	8	10	17	81

THE COURSE

- Par 71
- Length: 5,788 m
- Gowran Park Golf Club, Gowran, Co. Kilkenny
- Tel: +353 (0) 56 772 6699
- www.gowranpark.ie
- Green Fees: €20–€40

COURSES NEARBY
Castlecomer
Kilkenny
Mountain View
Mount Juliet

GRACEHILL   Established 1995

A TRICKY, WET PARKLAND

The car park at Gracehill puts you in a very relaxed mood (assuming it's not packed). It is ornamental and the walk around the clubhouse is similarly calming.

What starts out looking like a spacious, big-tree parkland course rapidly changes into one where you will get very wet if you're not careful. Three of the four excellent par 3s are swamped by water and from the 5th to the 12th the ponds are beautiful. Rich brown, laced with reeds and wildlife, with smartly routed paths showing them off to maximum effect. The walk around the idyllic pond on the 9th is enchanting and unique in Ireland: trust me. Remarkably, these are not the best holes: the run from the 13th (see below) to 16th is outstanding, with a wildness on the 15th (heather) that is startling. They are also solitary, running around the perimeter.

The challenges at Gracehill come in various sizes. Length is not a problem, but the water and some deep, bowl-like bunkers will cause problems. There is lots of room off the tee on the less interesting 2nd to 4th, but on others (the 8th, 10th, 12th, 13th and 18th) you need laser-like accuracy. Approaches are all exciting shots but they test your nerve. And even though the greens are big, they have numerous slopes to fool you.

The centre of the course feels open but everything else makes it thoroughly enticing – and barely a house in sight. Certainly the changes of hole variety and difficulty make it more alluring and there are enough great holes to make Gracehill stand out. Sadly, changing facilities are basic.

The 1st is Index 10 and a nightmare for newcomers with one of the most lethal approaches you will face. Over water, uphill, between trees. Majestic.

FAVOURITE HOLE
Par 4 18th. 385 yards. Play from the back tee to enjoy this hole fully. On the only big dog-leg, you hit out of beeches, over the perfect pond that runs in front of the 1st and onto a rising fairway. The green sits above between big trees. The 1st, 6th, 13th and 15th come close.

TOUGHEST HOLE
Par 4 13th. 400 yards. Index 1 is a flat hole that drives needle-like between trees. The pines are your line and only a perfect tee shot opens up the green as the fairway pinches you. It's a beauty. Then it's a 200-yard par 3 over water.

POINTS								
CD	A	G/F	B/W	L	F	V	G Ex	Total
15	9	7	9	6	5	10	17	78

THE COURSE

- Par 72
- Length: 6,186 yards
- Gracehill Golf Club, 141 Ballinlea Road, Stranocum, Ballymoney, Co. Antrim, BT53 8PX
- Tel: +44 (0) 28 2075 1209 (048 from Rep. of Ire.)
- www.gracehillgolfclub.co.uk
- Green Fees: £15–£32

COURSES NEARBY
Ballycastle
Portstewart
Royal Portrush

GRANGE   Established 1910

A WOODED AMBLE NEAR DUBLIN

Starting with two par 3s always makes things interesting: the first is a long, uphill hole with a green ensconced in mature trees; the short second then drops quickly to an attractive green fronted by a stream. Believe me when I say it's a start that could ruin your card. And four more par 3s follow.

Grange is close to a hundred years old and has recently added a new clubhouse and six extra holes, which can be mixed in with the old course to increase the original par of 68. The original course is very short and has been well slotted into the limited space available, with the lush maturity you would expect from such an old course. There are plenty of trees defining the course (Marlay Park runs along one side) and there's a nice walk through woodland to reach the 8th tee and then back again to the 17th. It belies its suburban location. The design follows the roll of the land and the best flourishes come from the elevation changes on the front nine.

It is a straightforward course that mixes good holes (the 1st, 4th, 7th, 11th, 17th and 18th) with some weaker holes, particularly on the outside nine, which go up and down with little excitement. But it's a great finish with the par 5 17th sweeping up into the corner and the tough 18th requiring your two best shots.

There's enough to keep you interested, with all the usual graft of a strong parkland.

FAVOURITE HOLE

Par 3 11th. 177 m. You have to carry the whole distance or risk dropping down a steep slope into a vicious bunker, from where a par is impossible.

TOUGHEST HOLE

Par 4 18th. 354 m. Alongside the 10th, the 18th is the only hole that demands two shots of absolute precision. The green is well protected by the Kilmashogue River and trees around which you must fade your ball.

POINTS

CD	A	G/F	B/W	L	F	V	G Ex	Total
14	7	8	7	5	8	6	15	70

THE COURSE

- Par 68
- Length: 5208 m
- Grange Golf Club, Whitechurch Road, Rathfarnham, Dublin 16
- Tel: +353 (0) 1 493 2889
- www.grangegc.com
- Green Fees: €80

COURSES NEARBY

Castle
Edmondstown
Milltown
Stackstown

GRANGE CASTLE   Established 2002

A GOOD, TESTING MUNICIPAL

This municipal course has nice shape, plenty of water and sits just over the M50 motorway. It is surrounded by roads and noise, but the great value green fees and its proximity to Dublin will guarantee its popularity. What jumped out most was the easy flow and how easily the holes are separated. Plenty of subtle mounding is home to long rough and trees.

As a municipal course it's never going to blow you away with brilliance, but it sets about entertaining you with a smart start that rarely lets up. The front nine work better, moving over gentle fields and around a couple of lakes that don't actually threaten but add to the attraction. Hole 1 is Index 1, curving 393 m down the slope between a couple of trees. A lake sits on the right and this also affects the 9th, while a bigger lake affects the 3rd, 4th, 6th and 7th. The back nine are typically relaxed parkland, but don't have the same rhythm (the 12th and 13th are too artificial). It does, however, have a small orchard on either side of the 17th.

There is plenty of room off the tee, which you'd expect on a municipal course that appeals to high-handicap golfers, and greens are similarly generous. It all looks good from the tee.

You also finish with a short, woody par 5 of 408 m, which is fun and promises a final blast of glory. Expect solid quality and a functional clubhouse.

FAVOURITE HOLE
Par 4 4th. 357 m. You drive over the big lake on the course's only serious dog-leg. A drive of 220 m is needed if you want to see the green sharp left, which is fronted by more water. Two very accurate shots needed.

TOUGHEST HOLE
Par 4 16th. 361 m. Like the 4th, this needs a perfect drive up the hill. The green is visible, but at 200 m there is a pond on the left, shrinking your landing area and potentially leaving a long second. Index 2.

POINTS								
CD	A	G/F	B/W	L	F	V	G Ex	Total
13	6	6	7	6	5	9	14	66

THE COURSE

- Par 72
- Length: 5,872 m
- Grange Castle Golf Club, Nangor Road, Clondalkin, Dublin 22
- Tel: +353 (0) 1 464 1043
- www.grangecastlegolfclub.ie
- Green Fees: €23–€32

COURSES NEARBY
Citywest
Hermitage
Lucan
Newlands

GREENACRES   Established 1995

GREEN ACRES

This is a golf centre well out in the countryside, with mini (crazy) golf, a par 3 course and a driving range. A bar and restaurant sit separately. Regardless of what I say below, this is good value for money.

It is not scintillating golf design, but it is in good condition and when the trees grow (mature trees are scarce) it will improve considerably. For now it is open and lacks definition for many of the holes. The barren 1st doesn't help proceedings. Fortunately the landscape starts to change as you progress, and ponds make an appearance, before things really improve from the 8th to 12th. These holes rise and fall over hillocks and troughs to great effect. Greens are blind and there's more adventure. It also restricts any wild driving.

There are some impressive water features – you get up close and personal with the pond on the 18th from the practice putting green – but the greens are what really stand out at Greenacres. The size varies but there are some shapes that are ferociously difficult (the 8th, 11th, 12th). Leave yourself any more than a 15-foot putt and you could easily run off the surface and into bunkers. It adds some fire to proceedings although bunkers are a bit too beach-like for my taste.

Off the forward blue tees Greenacres is short for a par 70. The ponds around the par 3s, the 4th and 6th, add vibrancy, and the 18th is a good par 5 dog-leg of 470 yards. It offers a big risk-v.-reward finish with an attractive pond fronting the green. Gentle 360-degree views from the 12th tee give a peaceful air to proceedings. 'Greenacres' says it all.

FAVOURITE HOLE
Par 4 12th. 396 yards. This is Index 2 and it is a good, late dog-leg around trees. Your drive needs to be 230 yards plus if you want to see a green that sits on the rise of a good hollow. The green is a terror with sharp slopes off all sides.

TOUGHEST HOLE
Par 4 10th. 380 yards. A straightforward enough drive hits at countryside and the tip of the flag. But you will be blind for your approach and the green is heavily defended with steep slopes and a pond left. Hit and hope.

POINTS

CD	A	G/F	B/W	L	F	V	G Ex	Total
12	6	7	6	6	8	9	13	67

THE COURSE
- Par 70
- Length: 5,700 yards
- Greenacres Golf Club, 155 Ballyrobert Road, Ballyclare, Co. Antrim, BT39 9RT
- Tel: +44 (0) 28 9335 4111 (048 from Rep. of Ire.)
- www.greenacresgolfcentre.co.uk
- Green Fees: £16–£24

COURSES NEARBY
Ballyclare
Cairndhu
Hilton Templepatrick
Massareene

GREENCASTLE   Established 1892

DESIGNED TO PLEASE AND APPEASE

Sometimes getting to a club is half the thrill. Ballyliffin, North West and Greencastle all get you going with views long before you get there. The course is pressed up against the sea and several holes play right beside it, putting quaint little beaches only yards away (some in play). It was updated in the 1980s and is all the better for it. While it is a very open space, with some good rocky outcrops covered in gorse and ferns, there is variety to fairway and green shapes. One hole may be flat and tame while the next will be heaving with possibilities, staying loyal to its links roots. Yet there are few occasions when driving presents a challenge. A creek on a few holes and fairway bunkers are all avoidable, and the worst you should find are wide swathes of rough. In fact it is the wind that presents the only real threat.

The views stretch from Inishowen Head to Benbane Head and across the mountains of Derry, and you play from three tee boxes that sit right on the rocks. In terms of wind, Heather Bank, the par 3 11th, could be a wedge or a driver. The 12th, Lighthouse, is the hole of the round,

followed closely by the dastardly par 3 6th.

It's a good and pleasurable challenge that would best be described as seaside golf. On a still day it would be easy because of the lack of danger and the length (six par 3s). There are slight hills but nothing to exercise you and the back nine, while flatter, are slightly better owing to the links landscape. Basic, friendly clubhouse.

FAVOURITE HOLE

Par 4 12th. 298 m. Lighthouse. From an elevated tee above the clubhouse you hit across a beach to a severely tossed fairway. The flag, in view from the tee, then disappears as the fairway hitches up, rolls a bit and falls away to the green.

TOUGHEST HOLE

Par 3 6th. 168 m. What a beauty! Tee box and green are both on the sea edge. Chances are you will hit over rocks and a beach to find the surface, but it is very difficult as there is no bail-out area and the green drops directly onto another beach behind.

POINTS								
CD	A	G/F	B/W	L	F	V	G Ex	Total
14	7	7	6	8	6	8	15	71

THE COURSE
- Par 70
- Length: 5,146 m
- Greencastle Golf Club, Greencastle, Co. Donegal
- Tel: +353 (0) 74 938 1013
- www.greencastlegc.com
- Green Fees: €20–€25

COURSES NEARBY
Ballyliffin
Foyle
North West

GREENORE   Established 1896

GLORIOUSLY OPEN

On the shores of Carlingford Lough, this is an open, flat and glorious course. An old raised railway line sits on a ridge that separates you from the water and also hosts four tee boxes. You will enjoy spectacular mountain views (the Mourne Mountains and Slieve Foye) from here especially, as well as the best tee shots.

As soon as you step out of the car you know you'll be battling the wind all day. The course acknowledges this with open fairways, no blind drives and only gentle dog-legs. If you doubt me, and you happen to arrive on a still day, look at the angles of the skeletal conifers that are a stunning feature of the holes near the clubhouse. Their tall, bare trunks dwarf greens and flags, most noticeably on the long, straight par 4 16th.

There's not much trouble off the tees – gorse and copses of evergreen/conifer trees appear sparingly. That said, holes are a good length, with five holes in the first eight falling around 400 yards, and club selection may need to be reviewed.

Water plays an important and beautiful part. Holes 6, 7 and 8 have lots to contend with, and it is tidal so there is plenty of wildlife. Little bridges cross the streams, islands appear from time to time and you have to hit over water on numerous occasions – most notably on the 6th (see below) and 7th. Where there isn't water, you're back to those remarkable conifers.

The routing is smart and the intersection comes at the 2nd and 10th, when they share a green (shame they didn't do the same on the 11th and 14th). Holes 3 to 9 head straight out and back (think wind), and the three excellent par 3s change the course's direction.

FAVOURITE HOLE
Par 3 6th. 115 yards. Your first walk up to the old railway line and the incredible views. A downhill shot to a green with water front and left. You hit over small trees and gorse. Very pretty.

TOUGHEST HOLE
Par 4 7th. 393 yards. A great follow-up to the 6th. Driving over water – do not go left – judgement off the tee is crucial as the fairway narrows at 240 yards, before swinging left around gorse. A tough tee shot and you may find the green hidden for your second.

POINTS

CD	A	G/F	B/W	L	F	V	G Ex	Total
16	7	8	7	9	9	8	17	81

THE COURSE

- Par 71
- Length: 6,337 yards
- Greenore Golf Club, Greenore, Co. Louth
- Tel: +353 (0) 42 937 3212/3678
- www.greenoregolfclub.com
- Green Fees: €40–€50

COURSES NEARBY
Ballymascanlon
Killin Park
Warrenpoint

GREYSTONES   Established 1895

ONE UP, ONE DOWN

The first thing you might notice is that there are no scores for Greystones. I have been playing here since the age of five and whatever score I give will not go down well at the club: score it too high and people won't take my other scores seriously; score it too low and I won't be welcome back.

I love Greystones. It is a short par 69 with two par 5s and five par 3s and like most golf books claim it divides into two distinct nines. The front nine are the more interesting as there is more shape to the land, with Jones's Hill serving as the centrepiece around which six holes move easily. Apart from everybody's least favourite hole – the par 3 5th – these are the most exciting holes on the course. Tee shots thrill and there is plenty of risk v. reward on each of these. Gorse plays an important role and gives added character and danger, especially on the brilliant 6th. The fairways are good and the greens even better.

The walk down to the 10th reveals a flat outer nine, but you can't see the good rise that hosts greens and tees in the opposite corner. This is a typically sedate parkland stretch that runs back and forth with fairways divided by single lines of

trees. It's a touch cramped, and the 15th and 18th cross. As such, you need to be very accurate (although you might hit fairways next door). The 13th and 17th are the best holes here, with great appeal off the tee and very tricky approaches.

Greystones is a tidy course that needs common sense on the front nine (a driver is not always necessary), and good straight hitting on the back.

Friendliest clubhouse in the country – obviously.

FAVOURITE HOLE
Par 4 6th. 328 m. Index 3 is a beauty. A high tee hits down between two banks of gorse that run to the green. It's all downhill, so the bunker on the right is easily within reach. The green sits below enticingly under a backdrop of big trees.

TOUGHEST HOLE
Par 4 17th. 349 m. Don't believe the Index 6 because this is horrible for visitors. The drive takes you to the bottom of a hillock from where you can barely see the sideways green, which sits just over a stream and bunkers immediately behind. Lethal.

THE COURSE

- Par 69
- Length: 5,144 m
- Greystones Golf Club, Whitshed Road, Greystones, Co. Wicklow
- Tel: +353 (0) 1 287 4136
- www.greystonesgc.com
- Green Fees: €25–€30

COURSES NEARBY
Bray
Charlesland
Delgany
Glen of the Downs

HEADFORT (NEW)   Established 2000

MAGNIFICENT (1 OF 2)

The beauty of a course like this captures every part of the imagination. It is a stunning example of mature parkland (even though it's young) with water featuring on all but a few holes. And it is genuine water too, with several holes located on a wooded island and others that require tee shots (and long walks over bridges) to cross it.

This is part of the old Headfort Estate, where wonderful woods of every variety flow onto and along fairways, and surround greens to create daunting backdrops. Half a dozen walks take you through the woods. There are several places where a wild shot will never see the light of day again.

The course is mostly flat with good rolls to the fairways, and there are no blind drives so you will see plenty ahead of you. I was delighted to see that Christy O'Connor Jnr refrained from his trademark mounding – apart from the 5th, 6th and 16th – since this would have detracted from the magnificent setting. What a superb job he's done. There are no views (the 15th tee is best) but the mature trees and water are more than enough. The par

3s (three with water, one with Headfort House as the backdrop) are stunning.

The first eleven holes are wonderful in their solitude, adding tremendously to the course appeal. That and the abundance of wildlife. From the 12th it opens up more, but the holes are still gorgeous to play. The 18th is a tame finish.

It is a tough, long track made harder by fairway bunkers, but this will be one of the most enjoyable parkland rounds you will play. The Old Course is a worthy round too.

FAVOURITE HOLE
Par 4 1st. 370 m. What a start. A dog-leg left with tall woods on either side. A strong drive is needed to open up the green, which is slightly below with a bridge over the River Blackwater behind. A great taste of what's to come.

TOUGHEST HOLE
Par 4 13th. 370 m. Deserves its Index 1, leading uphill to the Headfort Estate. The approach is the tough shot, with some dead land in front of the green which fools the eye, and good slopes above and below.

POINTS

CD	A	G/F	B/W	L	F	V	G Ex	Total
18	10	9	10	7	9	10	19	92

THE COURSE
- Par 72
- Length: 6,164 m
- Headfort Golf Club, Navan Road, Kells, Co. Meath
- Tel: +353 (0) 46 924 0146
- www.headfortgolfclub.ie
- Green Fees: €25–€55

COURSES NEARBY
Ballinlough Castle
Delvin Castle
Moor Park
Navan

HEADFORT (OLD)   Established 1928

MAGNIFICENT (2 OF 2)

Shorter, easier and perhaps a bit more fun than its younger sibling alongside, this is a classic, mature parkland track that deserves its reputation. Combined, you couldn't ask for thirty-six better parkland holes.

The course is always in excellent condition and colour (especially in autumn) and there is a superb consistency to the shape of holes. Mature trees are everywhere, stretching along fairways and towering over tee boxes. They rise and fall with the rolling landscape and create great diversity to the holes. Certainly anything off-line might leave some serious trees between you and the pin. And yet the course is not tight.

It is difficult to discuss the course's virtues without comparing it to the New course: bunkers are more subtle here and seem less threatening; greens are much smaller; the course is more compact; and you see a lot more of other holes. It doesn't have the same drama, but it is still exciting. The obvious thing is to play the Old before the New.

The 13th to 15th is a brilliant burst of holes: a beautiful drive down the 13th must tackle a beech tree that creeps across the fairway's edge before you're left with a tricky second; the 14th is a great par 3 that hits out from under a massive oak and over a hollow (that hosts the ladies' tee); and the 15th takes the biscuit – a sharp dog-leg that golfers with a fade will hate.

Anyone who loves golf will find this a truly entertaining experience, and the clubhouse is excellent. The driving range requires a car journey.

FAVOURITE HOLES
The 1st and 18th. The perfect welcome and farewell to this cracking course. They sum up what this course is about, with a dog-leg par 5 opener and a tough par 4 to finish.

TOUGHEST HOLE
Par 4 16th. 352 m. The only blind drive of the day and it needs to be straight and left, preferably. Your second is more straightforward.

POINTS								
CD	A	G/F	B/W	L	F	V	G Ex	Total
16	8	9	8	6	9	10	17	83

THE COURSE
- Par 72
- Length: 5,780 m
- Headfort Golf Club, Navan Road, Kells, Co. Meath
- Tel: +353 (0) 46 924 0146
- www.headfortgolfclub.ie
- Green Fees: €20–€50

COURSES NEARBY
Ballinlough Castle
Delvin Castle
Moor Park
Navan

THE HEATH   Established 1930

SHEEP, GORSE AND GREENS

The Heath, like The Curragh, is just that little bit different. They belong to a special club – one that allows sheep to roam freely over the course, immune to your victories and failures. Both are laced with lethal gorse and some holes at The Heath are drowned by it (the 3rd, 4th and 5th particularly). In spring it is spectacular.

This is open countryside and the course itself feels very open with plenty of views. It can be dangerous with some holes a bit close together, but fairways are separated by trees (evergreen and birch) and the roll of the land is well used to steer you.

The Heath is heathland golf, with the kind of earth that plays perfectly in winter or summer, and runs and runs on a dry day. But beware, for the same applies to the greens. They are slick, steep and thrilling. You can roll off greens and the slope on the 3rd green will tell you all you need to know. With many of them up high, with long rises, you can easily stall short – but that is probably preferable to being 10 feet above the hole.

In terms of design it is straightforward stuff, with holes using the natural landscape. This gives rise to the occasional dog-leg (the 5th, 16th and 18th) but you can still drive freely, and you are never restricted off the tee. But run out of room and it's a gorse grave.

It can play long but it is always pleasantly different.

FAVOURITE HOLE
Par 4 13th. 388 m. Index 1. Straight and long. The difficulty comes from the second shot, which hits up a slope to a green that looks like it has earth walls protecting it. You have to fly it all the way.

TOUGHEST HOLE
Par 5 16th. 482 m. Index 15. Your second and third shots are the big challenge here as the hole curves around gorse and over a shoulder that hides the green. Laying up on your second will allow you to attack the steep, large green.

POINTS								
CD	A	G/F	B/W	L	F	V	G Ex	Total
14	8	8	8	7	8	10	16	79

THE COURSE

- Par 71
- Length: 5,873 m
- The Heath Golf Club, Portlaoise, Co. Laois
- Tel: +353 (0) 57 864 6533
- www.theheathgc.ie
- Green Fees: €25–€35

COURSES NEARBY
Abbeyleix
Heritage, The
Mountrath
Portarlington
Portlaoise

THE HERITAGE   Established 2004

TRULY BUNKERED

I was seven when a ball landed in the rough at my feet during the Carrolls Irish Open in Woodbrook. Up strode Seve Ballesteros with that twinkle of genius in his eye and smacked it casually onto the green. I am a big fan, so I arrived at his Irish course with much excitement.

The complex includes a four-star hotel and health spa. It is plush and modern (amazing clubhouse locker rooms), and with Seve's 'Natural Golf' school, it is a golfer's paradise. The course is impressive too, moulded on top of a flat, slightly raised landscape. The views of open countryside are simple and it is left to the sheer quality of the course to take your breath away. The circular tee boxes are perfect, the wide, chequered fairways are hypnotic, the greens are like ice rinks and the magnificently decorated water features are lethal. With four par 4s over 430 yards, this is a stern and beautiful test of golf, and yet it is an easily paced one. Few trees and open space give it a relaxed air.

But the ninety-eight bunkers are claustrophobic (they overwhelm several greens and are ever-present on fairways) and their continuously angular shape is ugly. For example, a pretty stream runs down the 2nd fairway, yet your eye is drawn instead to the nest of large, angry bunkers beside the green. I won't deny that they are well placed, nor that the sand is soft (you'll want to bring the kids), but they detract from the beauty elsewhere. And there is plenty of it: the 9th and 18th run in parallel on either side of a lake, and every hole looks perfect. Driving is rewarding and your bravery is challenged constantly on approaches to velvet greens.

FAVOURITE & TOUGHEST HOLE

Par 4 12th. 468 yards. A long, gently sloping dog-leg that hinges around a bed of bunkers on the right-hand side. The fairway is easy to find, but that leaves a monstrous second off an uneven lie. The tight green is guarded by water on the right, a bunker to the left. The toughest shot of the day. Every hole works and flows easily, creating a good rhythm for eighteen holes.

POINTS								
CD	A	G/F	B/W	L	F	V	G Ex	Total
17	8	10	8	6	10	9	17	85

THE COURSE

- Par 72
- Length: 6,889 yards
- The Heritage Golf Club, Killenard, Co. Laois
- Tel: +353 (0) 57 864 5500
- www.theheritage.com
- Green Fees: €40–€50

COURSES NEARBY
Dunmurry Springs
Heath, The
Portlaoise
Portarlington

HERMITAGE Established 1905

A SURPISINGLY CALM ROUND, CLOSE TO DUBLIN

You can't help but warm to this old, peaceful parkland course. Lost in the Dublin sprawl, it is an oasis of gorgeous green and tall, mature trees that become companions, hole after hole. It is thoroughly relaxing, with some good challenging holes thrown in.

The course is shorter than many with generous, undulating fairways and enjoyable second shots. Every hole has its interest: the trees can create nightmares for the wayward driver, while several gentle dog-legs, unexpected hills and blind shots provide the intrigue. The only constants are the brand new soft greens and lush fairways.

You will love the stretch from the 9th to 12th: four smashing holes on a demanding run. Hole 10 is a remarkable par 3 that seems to be miles below you. It begs for a soaring tee shot that will come down with snow on it – a spectacular shot we all dream about. Then you hit a beautifully enclosed par 5 (see below). The 18th, with its green tucked into a copse of trees, sums up the course perfectly. The 1st hole is the tamest, while the 16th is just wrong.

It is an unpretentious design that gives plenty of enjoyment to golfers of all abilities. To reach the club from Dublin city you have to drive past it on the dual carriageway and come back over the bridge.

Members only at weekends.

FAVOURITE HOLE
Par 5 11th. 505 m. This is a gorgeous hole, with a tree-lined avenue holding all your attention. Your second and third shots are the real challenge, with bunkers begging for the ball and the River Liffey hidden behind the trees on your right.

TOUGHEST HOLE
Par 4 16th. 362 m. The least rewarding hole on the course. An easy drive uphill leaves a totally blind second shot, so walk to the top to get your bearings. The angled down-slope means that a good second shot can be unfairly punished.

POINTS								
CD	A	G/F	B/W	L	F	V	G Ex	Total
14	8	8	6	5	9	8	16	74

THE COURSE
- Par 71
- Length: 5,801 m
- Hermitage Golf Club, Lucan, Co. Dublin
- Tel: +353 (0) 1 626 8072
- www.hermitagegolf.ie
- Green Fees: €30–€50

COURSES NEARBY
Castleknock
Grange Castle
Lucan
Luttrellstown Castle
Westmanstown

HIGHFIELD   Established 1991

INTRIGUING IN PLACES

Highfield is an odd beast. One of those places where there is more style than substance. And I'm not even talking about the golf course. There are log cabins, a large log clubhouse encircling an open putting green and a leisure club. It all looks good, but the changing rooms are a bit slap-dash. The bar is made from a fallen chestnut tree, which adds a nice touch.

This may be Ireland's most entertaining opening drive. You walk to the roof of the clubhouse where the tee awaits. It is a tantalising opening drive down over the driving range. Sadly, the bunkers and the flat, uninteresting green are poor. This is repeated all day.

It may look flat, but there are subtle shapes to the landscape, with only a small amount of mounding – most of this appears around the double 11th/16th green. Some tee boxes are raised – the 8th is enormous – and trees have been planted in large swathes. Several mature specimens make an enormous impact: the twisted ash on the 3rd, the sycamore on the 9th, the beech on the 11th and the battered chestnut on the 17th. Good, imposing trees all.

It will attract plenty of holiday golfers and societies, but you're not going to come here for a serious game of golf. There simply is not enough to absorb you and it is scruffy around the edges. The best runs are the 4th to 6th and the 9th to 11th, with the 1st, 13th and 18th also lend a hand. Certainly the 4th to 6th have good shape, with water enhancing holes considerably. The 6th is Index 1 at 442 yards but there are several very short par 4s too, which big hitters will love.

FAVOURITE HOLE
Par 4 1st. 319 yards. Walking to a tee on top of the clubhouse is a bizarre experience, and it is a tempting, short par 4 that dog-legs around a hollow of rough and water in front of the green. A 5 iron and a sensible approach.

TOUGHEST HOLE
Par 5 12th. 523 yards. Two good shots are required on a straight open hole. The first has a couple of trees to slip between, and your second has to stay right of another line of trees. Length and accuracy required.

POINTS								
CD	A	G/F	B/W	L	F	V	G Ex	Total
11	6	5	5	5	7	5	12	56

THE COURSE
- Par 70
- Length: 5,744 yards
- Highfield Golf Club, Carbury, Co. Kildare
- Tel: +353 (0) 46 973 1021
- www.highfield-golf.ie
- Green Fees: €20–€25

COURSES NEARBY
Edenderry
Knockanally
Moyvalley
Woodlands

HILTON TEMPLEPATRICK Established 1999

MORE TO COME

One of the more serious courses around these parts, Templepatrick has aspirations. It has length, the hotel, remarkable green complexes and lots of space. The big water features don't hurt either. It is already hosting championships so it is well on its way to something big. But it has some way to go yet and the reason is this: the landscape is a little flat and lacks definition. There's not enough thrill off the tee and while the approaches to the huge, immaculately shaped greens are better, driving feels like a missed opportunity.

As an example, take the 17th: a good tee box setting under mature trees, and a green with a similarly attractive backdrop – but in between there is a flat fairway and spreads of young trees that do nothing for its appeal. I'm not trying to knock it, just emphasising how much better it will be with time. Ten thousand well-positioned young trees promise much for the future – both in terms of appeal and challenge.

Good mounding appears around greens, which deserve a special mention: they are beautiful beasts and they are oh-so inviting. You will need very soft hands to hold their myriad of slopes.

The better back nine have more exciting shape and routing. There are more mature trees and the river lights up the 11th and 13th. The front nine use more ponds and streams (beware the marker boards on the 2nd, 3rd and 5th: they are inaccurate), which threaten golfers of all abilities. The difference between the tees is 800 yards.

FAVOURITE HOLE

Par 4 12th. 431 yards. Index 1 hits past a long, tall line of poplar trees towards a big wood. It's the best-looking hole and the shot into the green is good too, with an inviting surface and a pond to the left.

TOUGHEST HOLE

Par 4 14th. 356 yards. Four par 4s are well over 400 yards and the 14th is the second shortest, but it is the only big dog-leg and it demands a perfect tee shot between bunkers. Even then, the narrow putting surface is hidden behind a mounded bunker.

POINTS

CD	A	G/F	B/W	L	F	V	G Ex	Total
15	7	9	8	6	9	7	15	76

THE COURSE

- Par 71
- Length: 6,718 yards (white tees)
- Hilton Templepatrick Golf Club, Castle Upton Estate, Templepatrick, Co. Antrim, BT39 0DD
- Tel: +44 (0) 28 9443 5500 (048 from Rep. of Ire.)
- www.hiltontemplepatrick golfclub.com
- Green Fees: £40–£58

COURSES NEARBY
Allen Park
Ballyclare
Greenacres
Massereene

HOLLYSTOWN   Established 1992

WATER MAKES THE DIFFERENCE

At the entrance a sign boasts:
'Championship golf at affordable prices'.
This is always a dangerous ploy, as it raises
expectations of something special.
Hollystown is very pleasant, but it's not
special. It's flattish, pretty, short and open.

There are three nines here, of which
Yellow and Blue form the main course.
Yellow boasts more trees and more
maturity, while Blue has more mounding,
creativity and interesting greens. It is a
pleasant mix that moves you around the
course at an easy pace. It doesn't
challenge you too much and you can
score freely on the shorter holes.
Tree-lined fairways have lots of breathing
room and it is left to the water features to
trick you. They are scattered about and
swans have certainly taken a liking to the
ponds near the clubhouse. The large pond
between the 10th and 11th stands out
particularly. Laced with reeds, it is a
definite threat on both holes but also

adds considerable charm.

This close to Dublin it is not surprising
to find a small housing estate glued to the
top of the course. It appears for two of
the best shots of the round: the par 3 6th
and your approach to the 12th. All in all,
a tame round at a very reasonable green
fee.

FAVOURITE HOLE
Par 4 10th. 371 yards. Index 1. There is a
lovely curve to the hole as it swings left
across the face of an attractive pond. Big
hitters could reach it, so beware. The
second must take on a small stream, as
well as a twisted tree before the green.

TOUGHEST HOLE
Par 4 7th. 423 yards. A long, blind drive
over a mound is needed if you are to open
up the green. There is water along the
right and the dog-leg arrives late, with
the green well protected by a pair of trees.

POINTS								
CD	A	G/F	B/W	L	F	V	G Ex	Total
14	7	6	8	4	6	8	14	67

THE COURSE
- Par 71
- Length: 6,295 yards
- Hollystown Golf Club, Hollystown, Dublin 15
- Tel: +353 (0) 1 820 7444
- www.hollystown.com
- Green Fees: €20–€35

COURSES NEARBY
Castleknock
Christy O'Connor
Elmgreen
St Margaret's

HOLLYWOOD LAKES   Established 1992

A HILLSIDE OF TRANQUILLITY

No, I don't know where the 'Hollywood' comes from, but the 'Lakes' bit is easy. On a fairly tranquil and very short parkland course, water is the big and frequent challenge. And a few holes in the middle will leave you with sloping lies that draw your ball magnetically towards the hazards.

A new clubhouse is raising the club's profile substantially as everything on the course is entertaining and of good quality. As a short track everyone can hope to score, but I imagine big hitters will find it troubling – my advice is to keep an eye on the 150- yard posts. Dog-legs, fairway slopes and water will always frustrate you. This is the kind of course for my dad, where straight hitting is at a premium and distance is secondary. Apart from the 583-yard par 5 14th (641 yards from the back), that is.

The best holes are at the start, with the 4th to 8th being the pick. The sloping fairways on the middle holes are a bit monotonous, but that is not meant as a criticism. The course is enjoyable to play and you'll find plenty of room and interesting shapes as you travel the hillside and absorb the gentle views. The greens are very good indeed and look spectacular with the water and wildlife bustling around underneath.

Judging by the different languages I heard, this is a popular destination for golfing tourists.

The 18th is reminiscent of the same mighty hole at Druid's Glen.

FAVOURITE HOLE
Par 3 4th. 129 yards. One of those beautiful one-shotters up the hillside and over a couple of ponds in a picturesque setting. You don't see the putting surface, and, if you're short, you're wet.

TOUGHEST HOLE
Par 5 14th. 583 yards. No surprise that this is Index 1. It may be downhill, but it is still three big blows and there are subtle challenges facing each.

POINTS

CD	A	G/F	B/W	L	F	V	G Ex	Total
14	7	9	8	8	8	10	15	79

THE COURSE
- Par 72
- Length: 6,391 yards (yellow tees)
- Hollywood Lakes, Ballyboughal, Co. Dublin
- Tel: +353 (0) 1 843 3406
- www.hollywoodlakesgolfclub.com
- Green Fees: €10–€20

COURSES NEARBY
Ashbourne
Balbriggan
Beaverstown
Skerries

HOLYWOOD   Established 1991

HILLY ENTERTAINMENT

The home of Rory McIlroy might be reason enough to visit this tight, hillside course with views over Belfast Lough and the hills beyond.

Some of you will see 'hillside' as a big red STOP sign, but the layout is done smartly enough that the only big climb starts at the 8th green and stops at the 11th tee, with two short par 3s in between. It's hard work but worth it.

Holywood starts slowly with the initial holes being open, dangerous (the 3rd tee especially) and a bit tame. But the hillside hides many ridges and hollows to produce blind shots, and the surprisingly small and flat greens are often precariously perched. The par 3 4th and 6th are downhill beauties (6th is called Nuns' Walk and it sits quite alone in the trees). But there's not much excitement here – or at the very end of the round.

The fun run begins on the 10th, a par 3 that sits alone on a mammoth mound high above you. Holes 12 and 14 are the best and toughest long holes – they are brilliant because they're so different – and the 11th and 13th are worthy companions. Alongside the gorse, the shape of the land

simply erupts. It is undoubtedly a disappointment when you come back down to the regular holes which finish off your round with a couple of tricky blind drives (the 15th and 18th).

There is only one par 5 and there are plenty of short non-driver holes. You will get into trouble if you're brash. Several hidden stream-filled ditches also cause difficulty so watch out for yellow posts.

Be sure to check out the Rory 'Wall of Fame' in the bar.

FAVOURITE HOLE

Par 4 14th. 388 yards. The best drive of the day, down through a channel of trees and scruff to a narrow fairway below. A good carry is needed and the hole then swings right, around a steep bank. Glorious.

TOUGHEST HOLE

Par 4 12th. 438 yards. Index 2 is devilishly tricky. It needs length off the tee, but go too far and you run down the hill, leaving you blind. The approach is astounding as the green sits on the most erratic piece of mounding imaginable. Shame about the lone house.

POINTS

CD	A	G/F	B/W	L	F	V	G Ex	Total
13	7	7	6	7	8	9	13	70

THE COURSE

- Par 69
- Length: 6,019 yards (whites)
- Holywood Golf Club, Nuns' Walk, Demesne Road, Holywood, Co. Down, BT18 9LE
- Tel: +44 (0) 28 9042 3135 (048 from Rep. of Ire.)
- www.holywoodgolfclub.co.uk
- Green Fees: £15–£30

COURSES NEARBY

Blackwood
Carnalea
Knock
Royal Belfast

HOWTH   Established 1916

AN EYEFUL

Two things will be very obvious when you arrive at Howth: you will have spectacular views of Dublin, distant mountains and the coastline all day long; and it's very hilly. Getting to the men's locker room is just the start of it, but if you like what hilly courses have to offer, then Howth is a thrill a minute. This is pretty, heathland golf with huge rocky outcrops, swathes of gorse across hillsides and bumbling fairways that go up, down and sideways. You're unlikely to have a flat lie on any fairway but it is fantastic fun that calls for no small amount of skill. Drives soar over the city (the 9th and 18th are awesome), approach shots can go up or down, and on a windy day (nearly always) you'll need bump-and-run. Looking down over St Anne's and Royal Dublin will inspire you, perhaps.

Please note that it is a bit tight in places with tee boxes driving over the preceding greens. There are also some interesting walks to tee boxes (the 9th especially), and the greens are tame.

Still, it is entertaining stuff that demands smart strategy and restraint off the tee – i.e. good placement. Several sharp dog-legs (the 2nd, 5th, 14th and 17th) will ruin a card if not respected and if you find the gorse, which will prove very easy, then your ball is gone. There are several blind holes where you won't know where you are going, so be positive off the tee. With all these hillsides, it's something to embrace for the whole round.

The course is short for a par 71, with few bunkers. Be thankful for both.

FAVOURITE HOLE
Par 4 9th. 245 m. You stand high above the green, in the gorse, and you will be sorely tempted to try and drive the green. A sign by the tee warns you about it. A soaring drive that will disappear if you go long!

TOUGHEST HOLE
Par 4 17th. 345 m. The most testing drive in terms of placement. You hit down, over a hillside of gorse, to a small landing area. The hole moves left and I'm sure some are crazy enough to try and drive it.

POINTS								
CD	A	G/F	B/W	L	F	V	G Ex	Total
16	9	7	7	9	7	8	17	80

THE COURSE
- Par 71
- Length: 5,479 m
- Howth Golf Club, Carrickbrack Road, Sutton, Dublin 13
- Tel: +353 (0) 1 832 3055
- www.howthgolfclub.ie
- Green Fees: €40

COURSES NEARBY
Deer Park
Portmarnock
Portmarnock Links
Royal Dublin
St Anne's

THE ISLAND   Established 1890

PASSION ON THE PENINSULA

The Island and Portmarnock are often compared. One has the class of a master craftsman; the other has the electricity of wild genius. This is a little peninsula of links heaven – it's a great mix of holes and thrills and challenges and fun. And dunes: you arrive at the club and they're just waiting for you. Stand on the 1st tee and they squeeze the fairway into a channel that makes for a tricky opening. And so it continues.

There are flat fairways and tumbling fairways. There are perfect bunkers, but not too many. Greens, with great backdrops, beg to be attacked but will punish you if you make mistakes. There are high tee boxes, treacherous, ball-swallowing swathes of rough, protected wildlife sanctuaries, marinas. You get the idea.

The golf is superb and the opening nine (eight par 4s to start) are short enough that you can score. Once you figure out how to play the greens and keep control of your aggression off the tee (no driver please on the 5th and 8th), you will feel you are playing real golf. Wind can smack you from every side as the routing is smart and holes never go in the same direction. The 4th to 6th holes, the crazy 8th, 12th and 18th are excellent holes, but the stretch from the 13th to 16th is the best of the bunch. I last played here twenty-five years ago, and I remembered well the 190-m tee shot into the wind on the par 3 13th, and then the needle-like drive down the 14th.

Everything you could ask for, but not so difficult that you won't enjoy yourself.

FAVOURITE HOLE
Par 4 14th. 318 m. A low but rough-hewn dune ripples along the left. The marshes beckon on the right. And a narrow fairway streaks down the middle. A short hole that should have the wind behind and begs for a big swing . . .

TOUGHEST HOLE
Par 3 13th. 192 m. Imagine a strong breeze in your face. What do you play when there's little bail-out area and it's all carry? Need I say more?

POINTS								
CD	A	G/F	B/W	L	F	V	G Ex	Total
18	8	9	10	8	10	9	19	91

THE COURSE
- Par 71
- Length: 5,972 m (green)
- The Island Golf Club, Corballis, Donabate, Co. Dublin
- Tel: +353 (0) 1 843 6205
- www.theislandgolfclub.com
- Green Fees: €55–€115

COURSES NEARBY
Beaverstown
Corballis
Donabate
Malahide
Turvey

KANTURK   Established 1974

GREENS OF TERROR

The long and the short of it – and it's mostly short – is that Kanturk is a simple parkland course. The majority of holes are straight up and down on a gentle hillside, looking out to the yellow and green fields that rise to Mount Hillary and the Boggeragh Mountains. Fairways are separated by tall conifers but you are always at risk from wild shots, so listen for the roar of 'fore'.

It is short and that might lead you to believe that, with its straight holes, you will score easily. You won't. The thick rough is one thing, but the greens possess a lethal beauty. I played with Kevin and Mark, mid-teen handicappers, and one of us always ran through the green, typically from inside 40 m. They're little domes with slick fall-offs, and landing on them directly is usually a mistake. Clever bump-and-run is the answer. And with short holes there is plenty of opportunity to master these shots. Four holes are 300 m and under (the 12th at 256 m is straight down) and holes 1 and 15 are par 5s of 432 m and 414 m.

It is not an exciting course, but there are plenty of big drives and, if you can hit them straight, you will have some great scoring opportunities. There are good touches too: the fairways on the 5th and 9th split around trees although if you could see this from the tee box it would be more appealing; the 6th is a sharp dog-leg and, at 285 m, you are welcome to cut the corner over the sheds and trees; and the 18th is a superb finishing hole with huge conifers creating a narrow tunnel of light for your drive and one final wicked green.

FAVOURITE HOLE
Par 4 7th. 377 m. Index 1 and probably the most attractive drive of the day. It's downhill, towards the mountains, and it has to avoid the trees and OB along the right.

TOUGHEST HOLE
Par 4 18th. 300 m. See above. The difficulty of the drives on the back nine grows ever more pronounced and the 18th is the crunch.

POINTS

CD	A	G/F	B/W	L	F	V	G Ex	Total
12	6	8	6	7	6	7	13	65

THE COURSE
- Par 71
- Length: 5,433 m (back markers)
- Kanturk Golf Club, Fairyhill, Kanturk, Co. Cork
- Tel: +353 (0) 29 50534
- www.kanturkgolf.com
- Green Fees: €25–€30

COURSES NEARBY
Charleville
Lee Valley
Macroom
Mallow

THE K CLUB (PALMER)   Established 1991

THE MOST PRETENTIOUS COURSE IN IRELAND?

What can you say about the K Club that has not been said before? This is one of Ireland's biggest parkland experiences, but despite recent green fee reductions, you'll still be paying a wedge of cash. And their attempt at first class customer service still comes across as being superior. Of course, that will not stop people from playing the venue of the 2006 Ryder Cup.

But how good is it? Like Mount Juliet, The K Club has its detractors, who claim the course is too American, and not a particularly good one at that. I have not played in the US, so I don't know, but it is an experience you are unlikely to forget. You won't find the peaceful rhythm of Mount Juliet here – instead you will find some remarkable and superb holes mixed with a few lame ducks. Once you accept that the course is over-manicured and terribly fussy, holes like the 7th, 8th and 17th, and the four outstanding par 5s will last long in the memory. If you can just put the snobbish feel and green fee behind you, you will find plenty to enjoy.

Arnold Palmer designed it to be long and spacious, and the beautifully black River Liffey snakes around four of the thirteen watery holes. Thomas Bjorn drowned his European Open chances in 2004, so have a laugh and drive from the same pro tee on the 17th. It will send shivers down your spine.

After all that, the greens are fairly benign and accessible.

FAVOURITE HOLE
Par 5 18th. 518 yards. 'Hooker's Graveyard'. A tough, blind, driving hole, which then reveals the most tantalising second shot: bunkers and hillocks to the right, a lake to the left and a green that juts out into it. Go for it and finish with style.

TOUGHEST HOLE
Par 4 17th. 364 yards. Even from the regular tees, the Liffey threatens the left-hand side all the way to a tricky green. A torment of a hole.

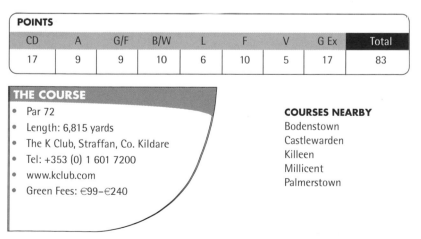

POINTS								
CD	A	G/F	B/W	L	F	V	G Ex	Total
17	9	9	10	6	10	5	17	83

THE COURSE
- Par 72
- Length: 6,815 yards
- The K Club, Straffan, Co. Kildare
- Tel: +353 (0) 1 601 7200
- www.kclub.com
- Green Fees: €99–€240

COURSES NEARBY
Bodenstown
Castlewarden
Killeen
Millicent
Palmerstown

THE K CLUB (SMURFIT)   Established 2003

VERY DISAPPOINTING

The second half of the mighty K Club, and it is weak. If you could play the last six holes three times, you would have a great round of golf; unfortunately the first twelve are dull by comparison. The European Open may have been played here twice, but the green fees remain high for such an average course. The clubhouse and facilities are separate from the Palmer course.

Early on, there is little style or character to get your teeth into. It's very average in appearance, with mounding and shapes adding the interest. The 5th and 6th are the best holes, but the multimillion-euro water feature along the 7th is vanity gone to extremes. The course has some nice ups and downs to create good driving holes, but overall it is too fake and open. Honestly, until you reach the 13th, you'll be kicking yourself for paying to play here. Fortunately, the closing stretch is a complete reversal. Water comes into play and, in an instant, the holes are crammed with interest, where every shot demands your full attention. Even with houses crushing in on the 18th, it is a classy finishing hole. And then you get to spend time in the big, brash and magnificent clubhouse.

There are no steps up to tee boxes, so if it is wet – which it was when I played – be careful. Expect good quality, but not excitement.

FAVOURITE & TOUGHEST HOLE
Par 5 18th. 518 yards. A winding hole that demands you cross water twice. The big water is on your drive and requires some nerve if you go for it. But your approach to the green also has to be perfect, or you will end up wet. The same applies to the excellent par 3 beforehand.

POINTS								
CD	A	G/F	B/W	L	F	V	G Ex	Total
14	6	8	8	5	9	4	12	66

THE COURSE
- Par 72
- Length: 6,815 yards
- The K Club, Straffan, Co. Kildare
- Tel: +353 (0) 1 601 7200
- www.kclub.com
- Green Fees: €75–€190

COURSES NEARBY
Bodenstown
Castlewarden
Killeen
Millicent
Palmerstown

KENMARE   Established 1903

A LOVELY SETTING FOR GOLF

Another of the nine-to-eighteen brigade. The course was upgraded in 1993, and many say that it was better as a nine. That's harsh, but the old nine are certainly more entertaining and vibrant. Lush tree settings for tees and greens and the ever-present water of Kenmare Bay give it a wonderfully rich texture. For example, on the nasty dog-leg 13th, the green sits in the corner right on the water, and the 15th (Index 2), requires you to drive over it. If you duff your drive into the mud do *not* rescue it as you will sink without trace. The water also affects the two excellent par 3s: the 14th and 17th. It is good, fun and tricky.

Over the road (and through a housing cul de sac) sit the other nine (the 3rd to 12th). They fall into the category of new parkland holes where they are closer together (albeit in two different sections) and more obvious. The 4th and 7th are too uphill to match the gentle pace of the original nine, and some of the mounded channels that create fairways are too manufactured, yet there is still plenty of merit. Big oaks flank some holes and the hilly landscape offers some great drives

and strong shapes to fairways. A few holes have great individuality (the 5th and 11th most notably).

Kenmare is a short course on the edge of town, with plenty of flags visible and playable by all. The quality is good enough, and the clubhouse quirky enough to make it worth your time. The Kerry backdrop (mountains, water) is wonderful. When you play the 16th, go to the back tee and picture the tight, tight drive. This used to be the 1st.

FAVOURITE HOLE
Par 4 15th. 402 yards. A lovely-looking drive over the estuary (and over the 17th green), with a large stand of trees above you and to the right. The fairway tilts down sharply to the left, promising a tough second to a green set against more big trees.

TOUGHEST HOLE
Par 5 7th. 519 yards. Index 1 and the most unsatisfying and dangerous hole. It's a dog-leg left that heavily restricts the drive (hitting towards the 4th and 8th) and then heads sharply up the hill to a green high above – reminiscent of the 4th.

POINTS

CD	A	G/F	B/W	L	F	V	G Ex	Total
14	7	7	8	9	7	8	15	75

THE COURSE

- Par 71
- Length: 5,689 yards
- Kenmare Golf Club, Kenmare, Co. Kerry
- Tel: +353 (0) 64 6641291
- www.kenmaregolfclub.com
- Green Fees: €25–€35

COURSES NEARBY
Bantry Bay
Kenmare
Killarney (x 3)
Ring of Kerry

KILCOCK   Established 1984

TIGHT LINES

Another course recently revamped, Kilcock is a standard, undulating parkland course with a few sweet twists. These come in the shape of water, bunkering and greens.

Of the eighteen holes, ten hug each other tightly as they go back and forth across the middle of the course, separated by scatterings of trees. It sounds dull, but the holes look attractive and there are enough challenges to keep you on your toes. Water plays a large part in this, with lakes around six greens and a stream causing problems elsewhere. But perhaps the key to Kilcock is the tight fairways and the trouble you'll face if you miss them. It is not long from the green visitor tees but if you find the rough then the chances are you're also in the trees. It is that tight. Approaches are always inviting, but the bunkering and water ensure that once you're in the rough, you're going to struggle.

The course's bunkering has changed substantially. It has great shape and is tucked into mounds along fairways and under/around greens. They're well positioned, especially when you look from the tee. The new greens are curvy and rather perfect. They are a pleasure to putt on and look good from any angle. These new elements lift Kilcock above the average.

It is worth mentioning that it is a bit dangerous in the middle of the course, where the semi-mature trees give the course an airy feel and, perhaps, not quite enough protection.

FAVOURITE HOLE
Par 5 5th. 482 m. One of the only stretches of mature trees lines the right (separating you from 4th), giving some character to the hole. It's the green that sits in a big dip with a pond on the left that makes it exciting. And worth laying up in two.

TOUGHEST HOLE
Par 4 18th. 306 m. Short, but Index 6 for the nerve-wracking OB tight and right. This hole dips sharply, down to a stream and a lone tree on the left. All uphill for the approach.

POINTS								
CD	A	G/F	B/W	L	F	V	G Ex	Total
13	7	8	8	5	6	8	14	68

THE COURSE
- Par 72
- Length: 6,042 m (proposed)
- Kilcock Golf Club, Gallow, Kilcock, Co. Meath
- Tel: +353 (0) 1 628 7592
- www.kilcockgolfclub.com
- Green Fees: €20–€30

COURSES NEARBY
Carton House
K Club
Knockanally
Rathcore

KILKEA CASTLE Established 1996

FIVE PAR 3 BEAUTIES

I could spend this entire review talking about the par 3s: the 10th, 14th and 16th are so pretty it's worth playing the entire round to get to them, while the 4th and 6th are almost as good. The 17th and 18th are dramatic par 4s; the 18th hits right up to the hotel castle walls and it promises a dramatic and exciting finish that lifts the round entirely.

The golf club is out in the country on a fairly flat, flowing landscape, with holes drifting easily between the trees, over the gentle River Greese and around the castle. It is on the longer side for a par 70, some fairways are surprisingly narrow and greens can be small. It will test your accuracy, that's for sure, but at least the bunkers are not too punishing and you have lots of room to get into the green.

Ideally this should all promise wonderful golf, but there is one 'but': driving is not inspiring enough. You simply don't see enough of the fairways off the tee. Perhaps that does not bother you, but driving is my favourite part of the game and, if I hit a good one, I want to see it

flying high, bouncing and then finishing on the fairway. Too often you hit over a crest on the many gentle dog-legs, unsure exactly where the fairway is. It detracts from the ample beauty elsewhere. The back nine are better on that front.

There are a few walks – the one to the 12th being the longest – and a couple of the bridges, on the 3rd and 8th, come under fire from other holes.

FAVOURITE HOLE

Par 4 17th. 333 m. The second shortest par 4. It is Index 1 and the best hole on the course. You must drive over the river that runs ahead diagonally – so choosing your line is tough. Then you dog-leg sharply right into the trees.

TOUGHEST HOLE

Par 5 2nd. 483 m. A lethal drive that is exceptionally tight and has to cross the river. Will a drive carry it? A 4 iron might be the tee shot. The hole then goes right and up the slope, leaving you blind for your second.

POINTS

CD	A	G/F	B/W	L	F	V	G Ex	Total
13	7	7	7	6	9	7	14	70

THE COURSE

- Par 70
- Length: 5,891 m
- Kilkea Castle Golf Club, Castledermot, Co. Kildare
- Tel: +353 (0) 59 914 5555
- www.kilkeacastlegolfresort.ie
- Green Fees: €25–€40

COURSES NEARBY
Athy
Baltinglass
Carlow
Rathsallagh

KILKEE Established 1896

THE CLIFFS OF KILKEE

Kilkee boasts an impressive location. It sits on the edge of the Atlantic, on a run of cliffs that rise up to impressive proportions for the entire 3rd hole, as well as on the 2nd and 4th. The rest of the course doesn't have such intimate encounters, yet the cliffs, the roar of the sea and the stunning coastal views are always a turn-of-a-head away – even on the inland holes. There's no doubt that this is what makes Kilkee an entertaining round of golf, because the quality of the course is not going to bowl you over. Changes are ongoing, but the holes run up and down across open, curved slopes, so these are minor cosmetic improvements as opposed to wholesale alterations. The greens are small, dangerous and uncomplicated. They are like the greens at Kilrush, and the two courses fall into the bracket of holiday golf. But while Kilrush has the twisting fairways and interesting flow, Kilkee's location will prove more attractive.

There is lots of room for you to play with and driving is rarely a danger. Even the rough stays low. Bunkers change hugely in appearance: on the 1st it is a basic sandpit, but on the 2nd they are pot bunkers, and this difference continues. Greens change too, but the good-sized ponds in front of the 2nd and 6th are the only thing stopping a day of bump-and-run. On a fun, uncomplicated seaside course, battered by the wind, it is a much needed skill. On the later holes you'll encounter a multitude of low bushes that indicate exactly what the wind is capable of.

Beware the distances: in metres on the card and tee but in yards off the fairway.

FAVOURITE HOLE
Par 4 3rd. 292 m. Clifftop golf. Look around you and breathe it in. You hit into an archway of cliffs as well as hitting over a crevasse. And while the hole is flat, it is what's around you that makes this so special. Look over the back of the green – carefully.

TOUGHEST HOLE
Par 5 2nd. 443 m. A blind-ish drive, it is the second and third shots that hold the danger. A large, unseen pond sits beneath a tricky, well-enclosed and well-bunkered green. Be sure to lay up – this is no two-shotter.

POINTS								
CD	A	G/F	B/W	L	F	V	G Ex	Total
13	6	5	6	9	7	7	14	67

THE COURSE
- Par 70
- Length: 5,555 m (white tees)
- Kilkee Golf Club, Eastend, Kilkee, Co. Clare
- Tel: +353 (0) 65 905 6048
- www.kilkeegolfclub.ie
- Green Fees: €30–€40

COURSES NEARBY
Doonbeg
Kilrush
Lahinch
Woodstock

KILKEEL   Established 1924

AROUND THE PARK

This is not just parkland; this is an estate parkland in the Mourne Kilmorey Estate. It's lush and green, covered in oak, beech and conifer that roll across the landscape at the foot of the Mourne Mountains. The trees don't give you an easy time, with three sneakily claustrophobic holes (the 7th, 9th and 14th), and plenty of others where a wayward drive will disappear for good. At times it is hauntingly beautiful.

There are, for me, a few too many dog-legs and blind drives (fairway markers show the way and bells need to be rung), but the upside is tee shots hitting at woods or mountains – particularly in the centre of the course where it rises and falls over a gentle hill – and great shots into greens. It requires intelligent thinking off the tee, nowhere more so than the par 5 1st and 6th (see below), when an iron might be the best option. With these shapes of holes and swaying fairways, it's anything but an easy course because positioning is crucial. I imagine that high handicappers may struggle with the constant threat of trees, but the setting is so enchanting you're sure to enjoy it.

The course can't be described as hilly

but there are excellent changes in elevation to bring out the best in the course. Greens and tee boxes are nestled in beautiful wooded settings and there is a lovely natural flow.

Please forgive (and avoid) the fake water feature in front of the 14th as it detracts from what is already a very tough hole. The 12th is named 'Hackett's', which gives you a hint as to the course's designer – and yet there is considerably more potential.

FAVOURITE HOLE
Par 5 6th. 475 yards. A dog-leg – what else! – where a driver is risky. You come to the turn and the green is in an enchanting setting in the distance, cut high in the slope. The fairway tumbles down, over a stream and then up again towards the mountains.

TOUGHEST HOLE
Par 4 7th. 334 yards. It is Index 4 for a reason. An iron off the tee is a 'must' as dense wood is straight ahead, left and right. Positioning is everything, and even then you're unlikely to see the green as the land rises and then falls sharply to the green.

POINTS

CD	A	G/F	B/W	L	F	V	G Ex	Total
15	8	7	7	7	9	9	16	78

THE COURSE
- Par 72
- Length: 6,268 yards
- Kilkeel Golf Club, Mourne Park, Kilkeel, Co. Down, BT34 4LB
- Tel: +44 (0) 28 4176 5095 (048 from Rep. of Ire.)
- www.kilkeelgolfclub.org
- Green Fees: £25–£30

COURSES NEARBY
Ardglass
Royal County Down (Annesley)
Warrenpoint

KILKENNY Established 1886

SMARTLY SUBURBAN

If I tell you that this is a stunning, mature little parkland course you might feel disappointed when you stand on the 1st tee and glance around. A flat fairway reaches a crest and disappears out of view, and it looks flat everywhere. If I tell you that you need to be smart off the tee, mixing accuracy with length, you'll look at the wide crest ahead of you and say 'Bah, humbug', and reach for your driver. Big mistake. Huge. It's Index 2 for a good reason, and it is the start of a sparkling front nine that shows you how entertaining and how dangerous it can be to play short holes. Holes 2, 4 and 5 stand out, with big changes in elevation and just enough curve to lure you into foolishness. The three tree islands in the beach-like bunker on the 4th are a highlight. Another beach appears on the long par 3 10th, and, in time, this will be equally dramatic.

Kilkenny is a lot of fun if you play it sensibly. I found the trees with a wayward driver on almost every hole, and played out sideways to let any semblance of a score slip away. The mightily colourful trees are everywhere, and vary from attractive stands to deep woods. Considering that this is heavily suburban, you rarely notice the surroundings. In that way, and several others, it is a lot like the Castle in Dublin. Not as densely lined, but more dynamic. Kilkenny's back nine are flatter, but still classic parkland.

Greens are good and not that easy to attack as they have some interesting shapes – the 1st is a perfect example – and they are dangerously bunkered. Excellent tee boxes. Drop in soon.

FAVOURITE HOLE

Par 4 5th. 273 m. A very tempting proposition off the tee. The fairway falls down and then rises to the green, approaching almost out of the trees on the right. It demands a good smack of the driver, but . . .

TOUGHEST HOLE

Par 5 9th. 435 m. A gentle dog-leg to start, that then turns too abruptly left at the top of the rise. Unfair on new visitors. The 1st also falls into this category, but it's your choice to hit over the crest – so don't, or stay on the left.

POINTS								
CD	A	G/F	B/W	L	F	V	G Ex	Total
15	8	8	9	5	8	9	17	79

THE COURSE

- Par 71
- Length: 5,682 m
- Kilkenny Golf Club, Glendine, Kilkenny, Co. Kilkenny
- Tel: +353 (0) 56 776 5400
- www.kilkennygolfclub.com
- Green Fees: €30–€45

COURSES NEARBY
Callan
Castlecomer
Gowran Park
Mount Juliet

KILLARNEY (KILLEEN)   Established 1893/1937

LAKESIDE TRYST

The Killeen and Mahony's Point courses part company at the clubhouse, heading on different journeys over undulating terrain until they are reunited near the club's entrance. Two interesting routes; one glorious location. This is Killarney Golf & Fishing Club, and it leans lazily into Lough Leane, under the MacGillycuddy's Reeks. As parkland courses go, the setting is perfectly matched by Killeen's international reputation (it's popular with Americans). Host to the Irish Open in 2010.

Killeen starts on the lake, demanding a nerveless drive as the hole sweeps around the water (and deer, if you're lucky), before asking you to tackle the lake again at the 3rd (see photo) and 4th. It reappears behind the par 3 10th, but you'll discover streams and ponds too. It adds both beauty and danger to stunning and classic parkland holes that are immersed in colourful flora and fauna. And don't forget those deer. The course weaves through mature trees and dark woods, but often breaks out into a more open setting. It gives the course a variety of shapes and challenges: some drives are extremely tough as they are hampered by trees (the 2nd and 8th) or water (the 4th and 18th);

most dog-legs leave you wondering how far you can hit or how much you can cut off (Index 1 especially); fairways dip and rise beautifully and they are tight enough to cause consternation; and even when you reach the raised and curvaceous greens you will have lots to do.

Golf at Killarney is about natural beauty, quality, classic parkland holes and an air of relaxation that should soothe the soul no matter how you play. Then again, that's before you reach the 17th and the extremely threatening 18th.

FAVOURITE HOLE
Par 4 18th. 372 m. A high tee that shows the entire hole. Water runs all along the left in a series of ponds, right to the green. It makes the bunkers on the right look like the safe option. The green sits under the clubhouse, so you will be watched.

TOUGHEST HOLE
Par 4 8th. 363 m. A high tee promises a beautiful and very hard drive which must avoid a tree directly en route to the fairway. There are bunkers left, if you choose to take the 'safe' line, and the green has some big contours.

POINTS								
CD	A	G/F	B/W	L	F	V	G Ex	Total
17	9	9	9	9	10	9	18	90

THE COURSE

- Par 71
- Length: 6,047 m (white tees)
- Killarney Golf & Fishing Club, Killarney, Co. Kerry
- Tel: +353 (0) 64 6631034
- www.killarney-golf.com
- Green Fees: €60–€90

COURSES NEARBY
Beaufort
Dooks
Killorglin

KILLARNEY (LACKABANE) Established 1999

A DISTANT COUSIN

With Killeen and Mahony's Point sitting so idyllically on Lough Leane, beneath the MacGillycuddy's Reeks, the far more recent Lackabane course was always going to have a hard time of it. No lake is visible, and a rather large factory tends to catch your eye instead of the mountains.

But if you want a tough test of golf, then Lackabane has plenty to offer. It is excellent quality – as you'd expect – and despite it looking wide open there are deceptive shifts in the land and many traps. A stream appears frequently to threaten your drives and it runs across several holes on its way to an impressive pond down by the 11th. The shapely greens are also a force to be reckoned with, most of them well raised with fall-offs into bunkers and swales. Accurate shot-making is a must. And with narrow fairways that need good carries to reach them, the only 'easy' shots are to the rather dull par 3s.

The course horseshoes around a factory, between a road and a hillside (which holds the 4th and 6th tee boxes and offers the best views), so you never really escape the feeling that it's a bit squeezed in. For the time being you'll see plenty of flags and other golfers as you follow the course's interesting routing, but as the course matures, I imagine Lackabane will improve dramatically. The trees between holes are few and far between – and I applaud the club's restraint – choosing instead a dense rough that looks harmless but is anything but. In terms of danger, the short 9th and 12th are terrors.

More challenging than nearby Beaufort, and although it is not as pretty, it is a sterner test than Mahony's Point.

FAVOURITE HOLE
Par 5 11th. 497 m. Almost a double dog-leg that leaves you tackling the perilous pond on both your second and third shots. And the green tilts towards the water too.

TOUGHEST HOLE
Par 4 15th. 356 m. Index 1. It may not be long but this dog-leg is hard to gauge off the tee. How far can you go before you run into trouble? And water to the right of the green makes it a tricky approach if your drive is not perfect.

POINTS								
CD	A	G/F	B/W	L	F	V	G Ex	Total
15	7	8	8	7	9	6	15	75

THE COURSE
- Par 71
- Length: 6,011 m (white tees)
- Killarney Golf & Fishing Club, Killarney, Co. Kerry
- Tel: +353 (0) 64 6631034
- www.killarney-golf.com
- Green Fees: €40–€50

COURSES NEARBY
Beaufort
Dooks
Killorglin

KILLARNEY (MAHONY'S POINT)   Established 1893/1937

A (MAHONY'S) POINT OR TWO BEHIND

The Mahony's Point and Killeen courses part company at the clubhouse, and the former is slow to start. Killeen introduces you to the lake straight away but here, holes 1 and 2 are low-key par 4s. In fact, much of the front nine are open and lack the same vibrancy of Killeen. There are good dips and rises on fairways and tricky approaches to greens, but you don't feel as immersed and it is just not as exciting off the tee. It is well suited to all golfers (Killeen is far more challenging), but that does not mean it's easy, because the rough is still of the grasping variety and the trees arc big enough to cause all kinds of chaos if you stray off-line. The greens, while not as immaculately formed as Killeen, are just as big and just as difficult.

The most colourful stretch comes at the end, starting at the pretty tree-lined 15th. The 16th is a sharp dog-leg par 5 that swings down quickly to the lake and offers the best second and/or third shot as you hit at a chocolate-box painting. The 17th hugs the lake closely as it dog-legs its way to a very tough finish: the well-known par 3 18th with its stunning backdrop of pine trees on the water.

Combined, these two courses (let's exclude Lackabane for the moment) are supposedly the great Kerry parkland experience. You will find it hard to beat the lake and the haunting MacGillycuddy's Reeks, but Killeen is the superior track by far. Mahony's Point needs some revitalisation.

There's a food hut where the two courses meet near the entrance.

FAVOURITE HOLE
Par 5 16th. 435 m. A par 5 that is reachable in two with a good drive at the shoulder of the hill which could help your ball run. Then it's the best shot of either course as you hit down at the green with lake and mountains behind.

TOUGHEST HOLE
Par 4 10th. 336 m. A dog-leg that seemingly hits at a defensive wall of trees. There is a route through, but off the tee it is very hard to judge where that is, so don't be surprised to be in deep rough or stuffed behind a tree. The green has a violent tier.

POINTS

CD	A	G/F	B/W	L	F	V	G Ex	Total
14	7	8	8	9	10	5	13	74

THE COURSE

- Par 70
- Length: 5,826 m (white tees)
- Killarney Golf & Fishing Club, Killarney, Co. Kerry
- Tel: +353 (0) 64 6631034
- www.killarney-golf.com
- Green Fees: €50–€70

COURSES NEARBY
Beaufort
Dooks
Killorglin

KILLEEN   Established 1992

AN INJECTION OF MOUNDING AND WATER

Killeen sits quietly out in the countryside. It is a little too flat to be called exciting, which explains the heavy, sharp mounding along several fairways and around greens. They try to bring shape to the holes, offering you something to aim at. For the most part it works, but it is the water that gives Killeen its drama. Fifteen holes have water, and the stretch from the 12th to 18th brings out the best of the round. And it will bring out the best in you, too, as your concentration is needed to avoid getting wet.

Killeen plugs the par 3 18th over a pond as its signature hole, and certainly this pond by the clubhouse is dramatic (it also hosts greens on the 2nd and 4th). It is not their best hole by any means, but if a course ranger stood here for an hour he'd catch a lot of people who seem incapable of repairing pitch marks. On greens this good, that tease you all day long, this is just wrong.

With no changes in elevation you'll find driving a bit dull – compared with Naas nearby – especially at the start when you are in the open, central part of the course. It is easy off the tee, despite the bunkers and semi-mature trees that lace the fairways together. After the 6th it gets tighter and more vibrant, but everything you need to know about the hole is laid out in front of you. There are no hidden surprises and, if you can avoid the water, it is a comfortable round of golf. The best holes are at the end, which always leaves a sweet taste.

FAVOURITE HOLE
Par 5 16th. 458 yards. A short par 5, all on show, that uses three lots of water to intimidate you. But it is the huge beeches – the only seriously impressive trees on the course – that give the hole its beauty, and they hide the 17th tee.

TOUGHEST HOLE
Par 4 15th. 402 yards. A gentle right-hand dog-leg around a pond, with another up beside the green. The perimeter trees on the left make this a tough drive to judge, and the length makes the approach just as tricky.

POINTS								
CD	A	G/F	B/W	L	F	V	G Ex	Total
13	6	7	7	5	8	6	14	66

THE COURSE

- Par 72
- Length: 6,468 yards
- Killeen Golf Club, Kill, Co. Kildare
- Tel: +353 (0) 45 866 003
- www.killeengc.ie
- Green Fees: €40–€50

COURSES NEARBY
Bodenstown
Castlewarden
Craddockstown
Naas
Palmerstown

KILLEEN CASTLE   Established 2008

ROLL OUT THE CARPET

It's impossible not to be overwhelmed by the Killeen Castle golf experience. It is a magnificent Jack Nicklaus venue with first class service, and there's that air of perfection everywhere. Trees form a dense perimeter around this handsome and vast estate and they make the golf course feel very open. It's a mesmerising place and the opening holes have long walks to emphasise its vastness. You rarely see other golfers.

Not surprisingly, the castle is the centrepiece and on the 18th it forms a stunning backdrop. Everything works here, and I loved the way lush, green fairways streaked through the fields of silver and gold, and the water features could have been painted.

You will learn a lot about the course from the 1st tee. Look down the carpet-like fairway and you will notice the bunkers. They are plentiful, big, deep and treacherous. With so much water around, I am reluctant to say they are the course's main defence, but approaching most greens your eye will always search for the sand. And yet it is the bunkers that push up the pristine greens to give them their beautiful shapes.

There is something almost soporific about Killeen Castle. Perhaps it is the lazy flow or simply that every golf hole is easy on the eye, as generous fairways drift away. No hole truly stands out, but every hole looks good. There is a certain element of style over substance, so it is elegant, relaxing golf rather than the dramatic, dynamic golf that I prefer, but it is accessible to everyone and it is an experience to be savoured. The word 'corporate' springs to mind.

There is also the impressive Dave Pelz Scoring Game School.

FAVOURITE HOLE
Par 5 12th 505 yards (blue tees). The dense trees run down the left and show the way as they then curl right. It is risk v. reward on the second shot as Rock River tumbles in front of the green.

TOUGHTST HOLE
Par 4 17th 428 yards. The lake that gives this hole its shape is as dangerous as it is beautiful. The dog-leg curves around it and you get to choose how much to bite off. A tricky approach too.

POINTS								
CD	A	G/F	B/W	L	F	V	G Ex	Total
18	9	10	10	7	10	8	19	91

THE COURSE

- Par 72
- Length: 6,535 yards
- Killeen Castle Golf Club, Dunsany, Co. Meath
- Tel: +353 (0) 1 689 3000
- www.killeencastle.com
- Green Fees: €75–€125

COURSES NEARBY
Black Bush
Moor Park
Navan
Royal Tara

KILLERIG CASTLE   Established 1993

HOTEL-DRIVEN

This is a Ramada resort and the golf course weaves its way around the large white block. It's young and tree-lined with views stretching off over distant fields, but it remains featureless for now. It was fields itself until recently and so finds definition only occasionally – holes 6, 13 and 14 most noticeably.

Killerig Castle's designer, Des Smyth, has been subtle with the land, keeping the mounding low, adding some gentle rolls to fairways and throwing in several water features. The ponds surrounding the greens are well placed and add considerably to the interest.

There is little danger or thrill off the tee, but that is countered by some strong shots into greens. This is helped greatly by the gentle slope of the land (more severe from the 13th on), and the good mounding around putting surfaces. But it is the bunker settings that catch the eye: they have been carved intricately into the mounds on fairways and around the greens.

There are a few good holes and the 18th is a great straight uphill finish, but there's not enough to keep the excitement going. Time will improve things.

FAVOURITE HOLE

Par 5 13th. 421 m. A sweet drive down to a narrow gap, with OB along the right and a mature copse and stream on the left. The hole then turns right with a green sitting slightly below and defended by five bunkers. The most solitary hole.

TOUGHEST HOLE

Par 4 14th. 359 m. Index 1. It's all down to the drive on a 90-degree dog-leg. Strategy dictates a 200-m drive, but you may want to go over OB and trees to leave a tiny chip in. The green has lots of water around it and it is not worth the risk.

POINTS

CD	A	G/F	B/W	L	F	V	G Ex	Total
13	5	7	7	5	5	6	11	59

THE COURSE

- Par 72
- Length: 5,836 m
- Killerig Castle, Killerig, Co. Carlow
- Tel: +353 (0) 59 916 3000
- www.killerig-golf.ie
- Green Fees: €15–€30

COURSES NEARBY
Baltinglass
Carlow
Kilkea Castle
Leinster Hills
Mount Wolseley

KILLIN PARK   Established 1991

EVERYTHING SLOPES

The great advantage of playing a course that has not been designed by a 'name' is that there is more scope for quirkiness. There aren't many designers who would entertain the dog-leg 10th (across the side of a hill, then down over a river to the green) or the 185-yard par 4 13th, or the stunning uphill par 3 16th where, if you're short, the ball could run almost back to the tee. That's what makes Killin Park so exhilarating.

We are not talking quality, on any level, but some of the holes are simply brilliant and it's all natural. The landscape is a series of small, violent hills, so no hole looks flat – endless shoulders barge down across fairways, hide greens and create ski slopes to drive over – and trees are big and beautiful. I defy you to find a copper beech as impressive as the one beside the 6th green and several tee boxes are tucked beneath more mature beauties.

Killin Park is short (par 69) and is of a quality that will deter many better golfers. But that would be a mistake because you will find many thrilling and challenging shots, and the 12th is as good a parkland hole as you will find – a deep wood lies along the left all the way to the green, impossible rough off the hill to your right, and it is perfectly picturesque with its stone wall.

Facilities are poor (locker rooms are in portakabins), tee boxes and fairways are basic, but it is a riot of fun.

If you want a classy parkland go to Dundalk. If you want thrills, come here or try Ballymascanlon.

FAVOURITE HOLE
Par 3 16th. 173 yards. Index 2, straight uphill, over a splash of water. How you are supposed to stay on the putting surface is anyone's guess because the fall-offs are all around.

TOUGHEST HOLE
Par 4 9th. 358 yards. Index 1 and deservedly so as the drive breaches a steep slope before whipping down and away to a green embraced by water. Your drive must be over 250 yards if you want to see the green. The 1st is a tough start.

POINTS								
CD	A	G/F	B/W	L	F	V	G Ex	Total
14	8	6	7	6	4	10	16	71

THE COURSE
- Par 69
- Length: 5,097 yards
- Killin Park Golf Club, Killin, Dundalk, Co. Louth
- Tel: +353 (0) 42 933 9303
- www.killinparkgolf.com
- Green Fees: €20–€30

COURSES NEARBY
Ashfield
Ballymascanlon
Mannan Castle

KILLORGLIN   Established 1992

TILTING TOWARDS THE MOUNTAINS

When you walk out of the clubhouse and down to the 1st tee, the view of Dingle Bay and the Slieve Mish Mountains is exhilarating. That is the key attraction of this young hillside course, because until it matures there is no drama and no great character. It's all on show and it looks boxed in. Holes simply amble between the plantings of semi-mature trees, with some dog-legs thrown in for good measure. Greens look smooth and straightforward as you approach and there is not much to threaten you.

What I like is that every drive feels rewarding. You can watch your ball soar, land and roll. The lack of a dynamic design means the fairways simply run out ahead of you, waiting for your tee shot. Hole 1 hits straight downhill and is an obvious example, so while it doesn't offer golfing thrills it is a pleasant, young, parkland experience loved by societies.

A surprisingly good length and a very important type of course squeezed between Killarney, Beaufort and Dooks.

FAVOURITE HOLE
Par 3 10th. 179 yards. A lovely tee shot, straight at the mountains, which will hang for an age and then drop down to the green. The tricky uphill, gentle dog-leg 16th around a big chestnut is also worth a mention.

TOUGHEST HOLE
Par 4 2nd. 408 yards. A dog-leg right that has no great features to help you judge the distance to the elbow. Water sits front right of the green with a tree to the left, promising a tricky approach.

POINTS

CD	A	G/F	B/W	L	F	V	G Ex	Total
10	6	6	5	9	7	6	12	61

THE COURSE

- Par 72
- Length: 6,435 yards
- Killorglin Golf Club, Stealroe, Killorglin, Co. Kerry
- Tel: +353 (0) 66 976 1979
- www.killorglingolf.ie
- Green Fees: €25

COURSES NEARBY
Beaufort
Dooks
Killarney (x 3)

KILLYMOON   Established 1989

A WHOLESOME PARKLAND ADVENTURE

I always like courses that know exactly what they have and embrace it wholeheartedly. Killymoon may not play in the major leagues – it's a bit too short and the design is comfortable rather than stunning – but this is a great adventure and the course will appeal to golfers of all abilities. It ducks and dives up and down slopes, weaves in between and around big, colourful trees and has that mature, parkland air that warms the heart.

There are six tempting par 3s, while the remaining holes are dog-legs to some degree. Combined with the many slopes, Killymoon requires a sound golfing head. There are several blind shots (some blinder than others – the 9th, 17th and 18th) and unseen putting surfaces, and it adds to the difficulty as well as the entertainment. The 1st hole is a perfect example – a short par 5 that sweeps right, around trees, and then down to a green where only the tip of the flag is visible, no matter how far you drive. And while you will have plenty of opportunities to swing freely with a driver, holes like the 4th, 5th and 10th need more caution. And one thing you will certainly find is that the course plays longer than the card. Perhaps it's the big greens or some sharp rises up to the putting surfaces, but you will often end up short. And a couple of watery holes make that a real problem.

It is a friendly course with great shape, plenty of thrilling shots and enough challenges to keep it interesting. Well worth a visit.

FAVOURITE HOLES
Par 3 7th and 8th. Back-to-back par 3s. Perfectly individual and complete opposites. The 7th goes 184 yards down into a dell, while the 8th climbs 152 yards out of it. Good tee box settings, a nice feeling of wildness and good trees make these a great couple of holes.

TOUGHEST HOLE
Par 4 10th. 347 yards. The 12th is Index 1 and the longest par 4 by far, but the 10th is a real challenge off the tee. As a newcomer, you won't know what is expected, so hit an easy iron towards the gap and avoid the trees left and the pond at the bottom of the drop.

POINTS								
CD	A	G/F	B/W	L	F	V	G Ex	Total
15	7	7	8	6	8	10	16	77

THE COURSE
- Par 70
- Length: 5,762 yards
- Killymoon Golf Club, 200 Killymoon Road, Cookstown, Co. Tyrone
- Tel: +44 (0) 28 8676 3762 (048 from Rep. of Ire.)
- www.killymoongolfclub.com
- Green Fees: £11–£28

COURSES NEARBY
Dungannon
Gracehill
Loughall
Moyola Park

KILRUSH Established 1938

COUNTRY, HOLIDAY GOLF

A holiday course that rolls over terrific undulating and erratic fairways (just look at the 1st). It is one of those odd courses that has various quirks and surprisingly difficult holes, without ever delivering on the quality aspects – there's no fancy design, the tee boxes are patchy and the basic greens tend to be cut from fairways, making them very hard to hold and read. These are not criticisms, as the course is 'country' in nature and promises a good dose of golf if you come here with realistic expectations. The fact that it is a popular course speaks volumes for the fun to be had. In fact, for less than the price of some Irish green fees, you can become a member.

As a first-timer you will find it very tough because the rolling fairways block views and deceive you time and again on length. Fortunately, there aren't too many bunkers – the first arrives on the 7th – but those that appear thereafter are usually hidden. Deep rough comes in spurts, so beware of the young tree plantings which are fenced in.

In recent years the course has gone from nine to twelve to fifteen to eighteen holes; gradual increments that ensure you move around a lot, and mean you often don't know what way you are facing. That in itself is amusing. Unfortunately, they didn't have enough space on the 6th and 7th which share the same fairway – so be careful.

If you're not interested in too serious a game of golf and the quality of the course, Kilrush will do you fine.

FAVOURITE HOLE
Par 3 9th. 159 yards. A good tee box setting that hits over trees, down on to a large, sloping green. The pond you must cross is the highlight.

TOUGHEST HOLE
Par 4 11th. 416 yards. A blind drive – aim at the yellow house. The hole dog-legs around a pond and up to the green, with hidden bunkers beyond. Index 1.

POINTS								
CD	A	G/F	B/W	L	F	V	G Ex	Total
13	6	6	5	7	7	7	13	64

THE COURSE
- Par 70
- Length: 5,736 (yellow tees)
- Kilrush Golf Club, Parknamoney, Kilrush, Co. Clare
- Tel: +353 (0) 65 905 1138
- www.kilrushgolfclub.com
- Green Fees: €25–€30

COURSES NEARBY
Doonbeg
Kilkee
Lahinch
Woodstock

KINSALE   Established 1912

HILLTOP PARKLAND

Kinsale is a straighforward parkland course that throws in a few testing and satisfying holes. Like Dungarvan, not too far away, it is a young course that needs time to make more of the tree planting.

Gentle dog-legs and a couple of blind tee shots will keep your driving in check – the 3rd is a perfect example where your judgement off the tee is critical if you are to see the green on your second. In essence, the gentle hilltop slopes add to the difficulty and the interest with semi-mature trees and mounding delineating fairways. You really don't need your driver that often and a good 3 iron or wood would be more than sufficient on the first four par 4s, and then sporadically on the back nine. Because you may not be sure exactly where your fairway goes or turns, the safe shot is the best (the excellent back-to-back par 5s on the 8th and 9th are a case in point), especially as there isn't much trouble around the greens.

The best run is the 14th to 17th where the maturity of the perimeter and the shape of the holes give far more oomph to proceedings. The 14th hits down a long hill while the 15th is a pretty par 3 surrounded by trees and hedges. For the 16th and 17th see below.

The 9th and 18th are very similar par 5s running side by side towards the clubhouse up a gentle incline. The shared lake juts out into both fairways and wreaks havoc on second shots. There is a more picturesque nine-hole course a few miles away, which is part of the same club.

FAVOURITE HOLE
Par 4 16th. 361 yards. From the pretty tee box you're faced with a conifer in the middle of the fairway. The obvious line is to go left, but it is a far riskier shot as it needs a good carry to find the fairway. The green is above you.

TOUGHEST HOLE
Par 4 17th. 404 yards. Mature trees along the left just push far enough into the fairway to make this a difficult drive. The hole then sweeps left and the green is surrounded by three small artificial ponds.

| POINTS | | | | | | | | |
CD	A	G/F	B/W	L	F	V	G Ex	Total
13	6	6	7	6	7	6	13	64

THE COURSE
- Par 71
- Length: 6,440
- Kinsale Golf Club, Farrangalway, Kinsale, Co. Cork
- Tel: +353 (0) 21 477 4722
- www.kinsalegolf.com
- Green Fees: €25–€40

COURSES NEARBY
Bandon
Fernhill
Old Head of Kinsale

KIRKISTOWN CASTLE   Established 1902

THE HIGHS AND LOWS

Kirkistown Castle is a high-up or low-down links course, with no in-between. Two small but sharp hilltops have been used to stunning effect: one has an old circular tower and hosts greens for the 2nd, 15th and 16th; the other is gorse-drenched with greens for the 8th, 10th, 11th and 13th. It is a unique feature and worth the green fee alone. The course is barren and scruffy in places, but the real concern is the proximity of several greens and tee boxes – when the wind blows, as it surely does, it must be lethal. On the par 3 8th, I hit two tee shots: one landed on the 9th tee, and one on the 12th. The green is squeezed dangerously between the two.

It is an enjoyable ramble over gentle links fairways laced with beautiful, soft and punishing bunkers. The short par 4 3rd (Quarry) should be renamed 'Lips' for the immense bunker awaiting your drive. The bunkers make approaches to the low-lying greens far more enticing.

When you are not trying to avoid the rough, beat the wind and hold the greens, you'll be admiring the raised holes, but take time to appreciate flat holes that tease and taunt with hard-to-read fairways and approaches. This is bread-and-butter links and it means trouble if you can't master bump-and-run.

Only one distance (medal tees) is given on the card, but the front tees can be well forward.

FAVOURITE HOLE
Par 4 12th. 397 m. The fairway drops slightly but then flattens out into a perfect, wide, links fairway. A great driving hole. Then there is a big lift to the green which requires guile to find. Run it up or land it on?

TOUGHEST HOLE
Par 4 10th. 398 m. A dog-leg with OB left and nasty bunkers right. Only a perfect drive will do, before the fairway simply lurches up in front of the green, almost vertically. It is a tight shot with real trouble – gorse – flanking the green.

POINTS

CD	A	G/F	B/W	L	F	V	G Ex	Total
14	7	8	10	7	7	8	15	76

THE COURSE

- Par 69
- Length: 5,639 m
- Kirkistown Castle Golf Club, 142 Main Road, Cloughey, Newtownards, Co. Down, BT22 1JA
- Tel: +44 (0) 28 4277 1233/1004 (048 from Rep. of Ire.)
- www.linksgolfkirkistown.com
- Green Fees: £25–£30

COURSES NEARBY
Ardglass
Downpatrick
Scrabo

KNIGHTSBROOK   Established 2006

SERIOUS ROLLERS

Knightsbrook is big and modern. It is in great condition and has all the necessary qualities you'd expect of a high-profile Christy O'Connor Jnr course. But it's not for me. First, there is too much mounding on such a gentle landscape – it has rhythm, but it is too heavily manufactured (look around you on the 1st); and second, several tee shots don't excite as you hit onto wide, rather characterless fairways. Shots into open greens are much more enjoyable.

The shortest par 4 is 389 yards, so unless you play from the very front tees, short hitters will find themselves stretched. The many dog-legs demand strong driving to reach the turn, and approach shots can also be long. Add in the good-looking par 3s, which have plenty of water to worry about and it is a serious test of golf.

Mature trees are well spread about. The area around the 7th, 9th, 10th and 17th is the highlight and it adds the character that the mounding doesn't. The impressive water features are also influential, appearing on eleven holes and providing serious threats on most of these – they are big ponds and the one by the 14th green holds dozens of balls. At 444 yards, many golfers will be adding their own.

Since it is part of a big hotel you know there is plenty of glamour about the place – the changing rooms are excellent, the food is good and it is a full-bodied golf experience, but it is soulless in places. Big, open and challenging, but there's too much grind and not enough fun.

FAVOURITE HOLE
Par 4 9th. 396 yards. The hole with the most character drifts around some trees, before opening up a raised green with more big trees behind it. It is the best second shot of the day and the green is raised (as are most of them), making it a difficult approach.

TOUGHEST HOLE
Par 4 2nd. 415 yards. Starting with Index 3 and 5 is hard going. The 2nd requires a great drive to the right to open up the green. A couple of big trees at the turn might play a part, but this is two big accurate shots very early on. Very like the 8th, Index 1.

POINTS

CD	A	G/F	B/W	L	F	V	G Ex	Total
14	6	9	9	5	9	7	14	73

THE COURSE
- Par 72
- Length: 6,891 yards
- Knightsbrook Golf Club, Trim, Co. Meath
- Tel: +353 (0) 46 948 2100
- www.knightsbrook.com
- Green Fees: €25–€50

COURSES NEARBY
Ballinlough Castle
County Meath
Glebe
Rathcore
Royal Tara

KNOCK   Established 1895

KNOCK, KNOCK

Shandon Park and Knock on the same day. Two courses that deliver loads of enjoyment: Shandon Park has a good, deep and smart rhythm; Knock is more dynamic, more energetic, and despite having less panache, it has some thrilling holes. It is a strong, suburban, parkland course that is encircled by roads – and while you can hear traffic, you see it only rarely.

Your initial impression when you drive in is not overly positive. The holes you see don't show off the best of the course and you drive past one of the course's danger spots (two greens flank a tee), but you do get a taste for the big trees. After that, all you have to do is mix in some unexpected curves and landscapes (front nine especially), and you have yourself an adventure. It starts on the 1st which goes up and dog-legs sharply right, followed by the 2nd which goes straight down – driving at a towering apartment block.

I liked Knock. There are plenty of exciting drives and strong shapes to fairways that can easily lure you into mistakes – tight tree-lined fairways are interspersed with more generous holes, and you never know when the next one will appear. Only the 1st and 9th are serious dog-legs, so you can swing easily off the tee at all the flags on show. That in itself makes it more rewarding.

Approach shots are not as exciting. Greens lie a little too flat and are surrounded by blunt banking. It's just disappointing on such a creative course. At least the rocky stream running across several holes adds the final touch.

FAVOURITE HOLE

Par 4 7th. 384 yards. Coming after the brilliant 6th, this one starts flat and then curves, 'S'-like up the hill with a wood of huge trees on the right, and two nasty bunkers left. It's a beauty, and the green is narrow, banked, tiered and long.

TOUGHEST HOLE

Par 4 3rd. 452 yards. Index 3 is the longest par 4 and the toughest drive. It's tight between the trees, and one tree on the left almost blocks the fairway, demanding a perfect draw. A stream lies ahead on the way to a flat green.

POINTS								
CD	A	G/F	B/W	L	F	V	G Ex	Total
14	7	8	7	6	8	9	16	75

THE COURSE

- Par 70
- Length: 6,264 yards
- Knock Golf Club, Summerfield, Dundonald, Belfast, BT16 2QX
- Tel: +44 (0) 28 9048 3825 (048 from Rep. of Ire.)
- www.knockgolfclub.co.uk
- Green Fees: £20–£35

COURSES NEARBY
Belvoir Park
Castlereagh Hills
Holywood
Shandon Park

KNOCKANALLY   Established 1985

AROUND THE HOUSE

Knockanally House is one of the more entertaining clubhouses you'll find. As a nineteenth-century Palladian mansion it has real charm and atmosphere. It would be worth coming for that alone, but there is fine golf too. The house sits up high and the 1st drives down onto the flat below. Index 3 to start is not very friendly, but you will warm to the place immediately. Holes 2 to 6 are flat, with water dominating. The par 4 4th is 243 yards long, but there are five water hazards en route. There is excellent variety to what is demanded of you: some drives are tricky (the 4th and 5th) and some approaches need caution (the 1st and 6th). Its flatness adds to the difficulty because the water can be hidden (look for the yellow posts).

After the 8th the course becomes more vibrant. The hillside offers bigger trees, great downhill drives and hard-to-judge uphill approaches. The corner around the 10th and 13th greens and the par 3 11th is most memorable. A large pond – surrounded by dense, old trees and complete with island and bridges – adds drama and danger. (Unfortunately the resident turtle has moved on.)

The dog-legs on the back nine are gentle but still need smart placement to open up the greens. Bunkers are big and generous so there's little to fear. My only complaint on this perfectly pleasant course is that the greens don't thrill early on: too flat and still. Greens on the 9th, 12th and 16th come as a real shock where the steep incline must be murder in summer.

A golf society's heaven on Saturdays, or any day. Short for a par 72. Showers so good they hurt.

FAVOURITE HOLE
Par 4 12th. 362 yards. A tight uphill hole with the tee box tucked up against the water. The fairway has great shape as it rises to a green that is beautifully blocked by one large tree. The green is vicious and OB along the left adds to the difficulty.

TOUGHEST HOLE
Par 4 14th. 332 yards. Play it sensibly. The tee box sits behind the island with trouble/OB all down the right. A driver might put you in the water; an iron in the bunkers. Water short of the green will also catch weak approaches.

POINTS								
CD	A	G/F	B/W	L	F	V	G Ex	Total
14	7	6	8	6	8	8	16	73

THE COURSE

- Par 72
- Length: 6,127 yards
- Knockanally Golf Club, Donadea, Naas, Co. Kildare
- Tel: +353 (0) 45 869 671
- www.knockanally.com
- Green Fees: €35–€50

COURSES NEARBY
Carton House
Kilcock
Moyvalley
Rathcore
Woodlands

LAHINCH (CASTLE)   Established 1975

ACROSS THE ROAD

Across the road from the Old course and away from the sea, this is a completely different set-up. Here, the Castle has none of the dunes of its mighty sibling. It is much flatter and lacks the same charisma, particularly off the tee. It is very short, with several short par 4s and 5s. And, with its generous fairways, this is a gentle introduction to the beauty of links golf. Without being cruel, it offers an enjoyable, uncomplicated warm-up for the main event next door. But don't think that means the quality is poor, because it is not. It is a leisurely links that welcomes big drives, sets itself up for bump-and-run, and punishes you with long rough and good bunkering. And some of the fairways are perfectly explosive.

The routing is good and varied and its name comes from the old ruin at the top of the course. Holes 6, 7 and 8 use this to maximum advantage, with the short par 3 7th hitting straight at it. The course sits beside a salt marsh and runs towards a mobile home park at the opposite end to the castle, so don't expect any great views.

With its own small clubhouse, this is 'junior' links.

FAVOURITE HOLE
Par 4 8th. 275 yards. This dog-leg starts under the castle and skirts around the edge of the marsh (OB). How much you take on is the big challenge but it is an elevated tee that offers a tempting drive.

TOUGHEST HOLE
Par 4 17th. 386 yards. Played into the wind you are sure to have a restricted view for your second shot. A small dune hides the putting surface, behind a beautiful rugged fairway, and it is easy to fall short or end up in the rough behind.

POINTS								
CD	A	G/F	B/W	L	F	V	G Ex	Total
13	7	8	8	7	6	7	14	70

THE COURSE
- Par 70
- Length: 5,556 yards (white tees)
- Lahinch Golf Club, Lahinch, Co. Clare
- Tel: +353 (0) 65 708 1003
- www.lahinchgolf.com
- Green Fees: €30

COURSES NEARBY
Doonbeg
Ennis
Gort
Kilrush
Woodstock

LAHINCH (OLD)   Established 1892

GOLFING GREATNESS

There will always be the Ballybunion v. Lahinch debate (despite nearby Doonbeg and Tralee). Which is better and why? Neither disappoints on any level, so play both. Lahinch is longer, but Ballybunion feels more muscular. I found the rhythm at Lahinch more sensuous, more embracing. From Mackenzie to Hawtree (with a flutter of Tom Morris), the design is enticing. And lethal. Like any great links, a caddie means fewer shots and fewer lost balls, as well as an appreciation of the nuances and hidden dangers. I had Martin Barret playing with me, a man who knows Lahinch better than anyone. When you're told to go left, you go left. There are serious difficulties falling off greens, and the bunkers are traps that shut you out so play with someone who knows the course to get the full enjoyment.

You will find the big dunes above the sea embracing you from the 3rd to 11th, including two of the original and most famous holes, the 3rd and 4th. The par 3 3rd, 'The Dell', has a hidden green, and a white stone is moved daily to indicate the pin position behind dunes; 'Klondyke', a par 5, fires down a mesmerising channel of dunes, which come to a dead end, and you must hit over another dune to reach the green. They don't make them like that any more. The remaining holes are wrapped up in smaller dunes that still create intriguing shapes. And they're more sheltered from the wind.

With any perfect course you want to know that every shot will thrill you. At Lahinch it does. Drives are exhilarating and approaches to greens give you that same sense of awe: hit a green, stay on it, and try not to smile.

FAVOURITE HOLE
Par 4 6th. 412 yards. A blind-ish drive up onto a fairway that whips left around the dunes. Your second, if you are long enough, is a thing of beauty, hitting at the sea with the green well below. Watch out for the huge hollow at 300 yards.

TOUGHEST HOLE
Par 4 13th. 267 yards. In the wind, clearly the long holes will be nightmares, but this short hole will tempt the brave and/or foolish golfer. Do not stray right, into the dense, blind hollow and remember that anything left just keeps going.

POINTS

CD	A	G/F	B/W	L	F	V	G Ex	Total
19	9	10	10	7	10	8	19	92

THE COURSE

- Par 72
- Length: 6,613 yards (white tees)
- Lahinch Golf Club, Lahinch, Co. Clare
- Tel: +353 (0) 65 708 1003
- www.lahinchgolf.com
- Green Fees: €90–€125

COURSES NEARBY
Doonbeg
Ennis
Gort
Kilrush
Tralee
Woodstock

LAMBEG   Established 1986

SHORT, QUIRKY MUNICIPAL

Municipal courses come in all shapes and sizes. And lengths. Lambeg is a mere par 66. It appeals to a very different audience from nearby Dunmurry and Lisburn. Here, you will find beginners, youngsters and messers, and people who just want to have fun. I've played some excellently maintained municipal courses (Corballis, Mahon) and, while this isn't one of them, there are things to commend it.

Several par 4s are very short indeed (208 m, 218 m, 255 m and 257 m), which has its own attraction and it makes for a quick and friendly round – queues permitting, as it is very popular. There are no bunkers, so getting in to basic greens is easy enough. It's in a nice setting, with good heavy trees, some real wildness, an easy rolling landscape and only a few pylons. It is most certainly not your average back-and-forth layout, with holes 3, 4 and 5 worthy of any parkland, immersed in big, tight lines of trees. The

4th may only be 208 m but the oak in front of the green is a quirky obstacle. The 15th to 17th is another good stretch, heading up into some big cedars and pines.

If you want quality golf, you're not going to come here, but if you want golf that doesn't take itself seriously, then you will find your money well spent.

FAVOURITE HOLE
Par 4 4th. 208 m. It should be easy, and the hole looks lovely from the tee, but it can prove dangerous with the oak short of the green and pretty birch to the right. It is too tempting and that means trouble.

TOUGHEST HOLE
Par 4 3rd. 340 m. Index 1 is an unexpectedly tight drive. You have a 20-yard-wide fairway and big trees squeezing in. Then it dog-legs right where a stream fronts the green and deep rough waits behind.

POINTS
CD	A	G/F	B/W	L	F	V	G Ex	Total
11	7	5	5	5	5	8	13	59

THE COURSE
- Par 66
- Length: 4,139 m
- Lambeg Golf Club, Bell's Lane, Lambeg, Lisburn, Co. Antrim
- Tel: +44 (0) 28 9266 2738 (048 from Rep. of Ire.)
- email.lambeggolfclub@btconnect.com
- Green Fees: £12–£14.50

COURSES NEARBY
Balmoral
Edenmore
Dunmurry
Malone

LAYTOWN & BETTYSTOWN   Established 1909

RUMBLING ALONG

Laytown & Bettystown is rarely mentioned as a big links player but it has used its decent-sized dunes to maximum effect on the opening holes. They duck and dive to confuse line of sight and inspire fairways and greens. Holes go all over the place and they are exhilarating. Strategic, too, as fairways are not fully visible and balls could kick anywhere. There is something unrewarding about that but, from a design perspective, this short course has some really dynamic, early holes that will thrill you. Driving has to be precise, approaches to greens even more so: holes 4 and 6 are nightmares, with the 4th hiding behind a rising slope, and the 6th perfectly perched high. It will test your bump-and-run skills for sure. If you're not on the green then you're in deep bunkers or well below the putting surface. Your short game needs to be rock solid.

After the 10th you are out of the heaving dunes and it is less dramatic – Index 1 looks dull to say the least. You are, however, now heading into the wind back to the clubhouse. The wider, gentler fairways are a welcome sight and you can finally get your driver going at full swing.

The course undoubtedly suffers from a shortage of space and some holes are very tight, which is nerve-wracking and dangerous in the wind. I imagine that this is one reason why Laytown & Bettystown is not in that top tier of links courses. A couple of trees appear in the middle of the round. They're so out of place, it's cute. The views are best from the high tee boxes.

The 18th is a double blind and deserves a page of its own.

FAVOURITE HOLE
Par 3 9th. 152 m. A great par 3. The green sits up a bit, in a nest of dunes, and offers only a tiny entrance on the left. If you don't land it on, your ball could go anywhere – the hidden bunker below the green most likely.

TOUGHEST HOLE
Par 4 10th. 375 m. A small sliver of fairway is visible and you have no idea what or how far to hit. It is a good dog-leg that breaks left and then drops down a steep ledge that you have no idea is there. The green sits below.

POINTS								
CD	A	G/F	B/W	L	F	V	G Ex	Total
16	7	9	8	7	8	8	16	79

THE COURSE

- Par 71
- Length: 5,688 m
- Laytown & Bettystown Golf Club, Bettystown, Co. Meath
- Tel: +353 (0) 41 982 7170
- www.landb.ie
- Green Fees: €50–€60

COURSES NEARBY
Balbriggan
Bellewstown
County Louth
Seapoint

LEE VALLEY Established 1993

SIMPLICITY IN ITS BEAUTY, BUT MATURITY NEEDED

This course is an explosion of scenery across the Lee Valley and distant mountains. It stays with you for eighteen holes, mostly because shot after shot hits straight at it. Nowhere more so than your approach to the 13th where the plateau green sits right on the edge. It's the killer shot of the round. Ireland is blessed with forty shades of green, and most of them are here.

I was asked by a visiting golfer if I had any tips. My response was that you have plenty of room on your drives and approaches to attractive greens. I forgot to mention that while the fairways are wide and the trees set well back, the army of fairway bunkers will ensnare any wild drives. It adds a considerable challenge. I also forgot the dog-legs and the water: the six sharp dog-legs all require control off the tee as the elbows crook between 190 and 240 yards (from the whites), so check the bin lids for diagrams; and the water on the 8th and 13th, par 5s, epitomises the brains-v.-brawn approach to golf.

Despite its hillside setting there is little climbing (the 2nd, 9th and 18th), with most holes having attractive rises/falls to fairways/greens. There is a lot of sky but a ferocious amount of planting – 20,000 trees – will change that in times to come. Elsewhere, several raised flowerbeds add a wonderful touch. There are other touches too, like the halfway house – you order from the 9th tee and collect your grub at the 10th.

It is a strong course design that makes it very playable, but it lacks character at this stage. The 8th, 9th, 12th, 13th and 15th are stunning holes, but its real strength is consistency, wide fairways and big green complexes.

FAVOURITE HOLE
Par 4 9th. 303 yards. Set in a tract of conifers, this uphill hole is a beauty. It oozes class with a bunker splat in the middle at 230 yards. The green is long, narrow and steep. Fred Couples bogeyed it.

TOUGHEST HOLE
Par 5 15th. 525 yards. A blind drive. The green comes into view as you reach the fairway and what a sight it is, tucked in to the left behind a lake that protects it jealously. A sensible second still leaves the lake. Christy O'Connor Jnr's favourite.

POINTS								
CD	A	G/F	B/W	L	F	V	G Ex	Total
15	7	9	9	9	8	8	14	79

THE COURSE
- Par 72
- Length: 6,424 yards
- Lee Valley Golf Club, Ovens, Co. Cork
- Tel: +353 (0) 21 733 1721
- www.leevalleygcc.ie
- Green Fees: €35–€40

COURSES NEARBY
Bandon
Blarney
Macroom
Muskerry

LEINSTER HILLS   Established 2000

HILLY AND QUIRKY

Leinster Hills could not be more appropriately named. It sits on a hillside and stunning views of mountains accompany you all day long (the 10th has the best 360-degree views) and some of the greens are equally as mountainous. They are very fast and several are unfair, so be warned: they will break your heart. A ball that lands in the middle of the green can take a sharp turn and roll 20 yards down steep slopes and into the rough. I suggest you prepare for it, and not get frustrated. After a while, it's actually quite fun and you could spend ten minutes messing around on the double-tiered, ski-slope 8th. It is a perfect example of a course that needs to be played twice.

This is a fun, new course with lots of great shots. Despite some people saying it is too hilly and a bit crazy, it offers lots of entertainment. Don't expect Mount Juliet quality because Leinster Hills is rough around the edges and tee boxes need some care. Time will improve things. No hole is flat and the inclines offer some spectacular tee shots hitting at the mountains (the 3rd, 8th, 11th, 12th, 14th,

15th). Only the 2nd is a poor hole, while the 12th and 18th are creative dog-legs: the 18th is more of a U-leg.

Holes have good individuality and this is despite an open feel to the place. There is one dense wood in the middle of the course and mature ash trees are littered about. Their scarcity adds character and danger, as do the gorse and water in one corner. Many young trees have also been planted.

A 'love it or hate it' course.

FAVOURITE HOLE
Par 4 7th. 362 yards. Index 1. You can see the flag above you and to your right. You need a good drive to fly the pond and gorse, but not find the rough at the elbow of the dog-leg. Then you hit sharply uphill to a hidden and tiered green.

TOUGHEST HOLE
Par 4 8th. 378 yards. Index 2. A long drop to a fairway that then sweeps up the hill. The green is above you for your second and staying on the green is hell. You could take five putts and roll off the green every time.

POINTS								
CD	A	G/F	B/W	L	F	V	G Ex	Total
14	7	8	7	8	6	8	16	74

THE COURSE
- Par 70
- Length: 6,381 yards
- Leinster Hills Golf Club, Nurney. Co. Carlow
- Tel: +353 (0) 59 91 48974
- www.leinsterhillsgolf.com
- Green Fees: €25–€35

COURSES NEARBY
Bunclody
Carlow
Gowran Park
Killerig Castle
Mount Wolseley

LEOPARDSTOWN

INTO THE GREAT WIDE OPEN

This is a straightforward, unexciting golf course slapped in the middle of a race course on the outskirts of Dublin. There is little change in elevation and there is no real design to capture your imagination, with flat, open fairways and greens. Certainly there are a few hazards to interrupt your round, with a smattering of gorse and trees, and some raised greens.

Mind you, you can certainly thrash your driver about – perhaps too dangerously. The par 5 towards the end is a long straight hole that runs parallel to the race track.

There is a full driving range and impressive all-weather chipping and putting green attached to the clubhouse.

Perfect for beginners, but doesn't deliver many thrills for better golfers.

POINTS

CD	A	G/F	B/W	L	F	V	G Ex	Total
8	4	5	4	5	5	5	8	44

THE COURSE

- Par 67
- Length: 4,947 yards
- Leopardstown Golf Club, Leopardstown Racecourse, Leopardstown, Dublin 18
- Tel: +353 (0) 1 289 5341
- www.leopardstown.com
- Green Fees: €15–€20

COURSES NEARBY
Old Conna
Stackstown
Woodbrook

LETTERKENNY   Established 1913

OLD, NEW AND WET

Letterkenny falls into two sections: holes 2 to 10 are down along the Lough Swilly estuary on a flat piece of land, while the 12th to 18th are rolling, mature parkland holes that you drive through to reach the large clubhouse. Two excellent holes, the 1st and 11th, join the two: the 1st is a big drop; the 11th is straight up. The best views of the countryside are on your way to the 1st tee – always a good start – where you'll face a sweet drive between trees and down onto the plateau.

Major work (ongoing) has solved the club's drainage problem, and the first ten holes now all have ponds and/or ditches. The par 5 2nd has a wide ditch of water that splits into a T-junction short of the green. The water brings the flat, generous fairways to life and presents some great challenges. Tee boxes (the 2nd to 5th) sit up on the very edge of the estuary and these are eerily dramatic. It is smart, attractive and strategic, as well as deceptive, so pause before you take your driver. The big, swaying greens (all eighteen) are super, while trees will cause problems with some taking up residence in the

middle of fairways (the 9th to 11th).

Up above, the final seven holes benefit from rolling fairways, dense woods and mature oak and beech. Tee boxes sit in nooks of trees giving Letterkenny a last blast of real charm.

There is some way to go, so the scores below won't reflect what you face when you arrive, but this will be a round that should entertain mightily.

FAVOURITE HOLE
Par 5 11th. 443 yards. You're unlikely to reach in two. The fairway is flat and wide, but a birch stands in the middle at about 200 yards. The hole then rises rapidly, narrowing between the trees all the way to the green. The 18th is a good finish.

TOUGHEST HOLE
Par 4 15th. 412 yards. A new pond sits on the right of this gentle, downhill dog-leg with the fairway steeply sloped in its direction. There is no flat lie for your second (unless you drive 280 yards) and a copse of trees on the left makes it a very difficult approach.

POINTS

CD	A	G/F	B/W	L	F	V	G Ex	Total
15	7	8	8	7	7	9	15	76

THE COURSE

- Par 72
- Length: 6,275 yards
- Letterkenny Golf Club, Barnhill, Letterkenny, Co. Donegal
- Tel: +353 (0) 74 9121 150
- www.letterkennygolfclub.com
- Green Fees: €25–€35

COURSES NEARBY
Ballybofey & Stranorlar
City of Derry
North West
Portsalon

LIMERICK   Established 1891

TIDY AND TIGHT

Course management. I suppose I could leave it at that, because that's what is required at Limerick. It is not long for a par 72, and you will find many gentle dog-legs that float around the big trees lining and separating fairways. Once you put your drive in the right spot, the rest is relatively easy. If you misjudge the distance or stray into the trees you will be hitting out sideways or playing wedges over the top.

Limerick has an excellent new clubhouse which sets up a pleasant and relaxing day's golf. There's no climbing required, no great effort needed and you can leave the driver in the bag on many of the par 4s. As I said: course management.

Limerick is a bit squeezed in and, if it is a busy day, you will see lots of bodies through the trees, and the shout of 'fore' will not be far away.

There is no dynamic design, just a simple rhythm that takes you back and forth, offering good scoring opportunities. Holes 4 to 9 are the pick of the bunch

and, apart from the par 3 7th and straight par 5 8th (see below), they all dog-leg sweetly (or perhaps repetitively) around the trees. You will regard the 14th, 15th and 16th as quirky or daft as they are two short par 3s with one very short par 4 squeezed in between.

Designed for enjoyment, not for difficulty. No views, but you are buried amongst the trees, close to the city. And it's in good condition.

FAVOURITE HOLE
Par 5 8th. 457 m. Flat, spacious and dead straight (and a bit of a relief), you'll find a pretty stream angled across the fairway. It then turns and runs along the right side to the green. A hole that may tempt you to make a mistake.

TOUGHEST HOLE
Par 4 6th. 345 m. Immediately after Index 1, this needs more accurate placement off the tee. The green, like some others, has surprisingly steep slopes. And the bunker front right is perfectly placed.

POINTS								
CD	A	G/F	B/W	L	F	V	G Ex	Total
13	7	7	7	5	9	6	15	69

THE COURSE
- Par 72
- Length: 5,745 m
- Limerick Golf Club, Rosbrien, Ballyclough, Co. Limerick
- Tel: +353 (0) 61 415 146
- www.limerickgolfclub.ie
- Green Fees: €50–€70

COURSES NEARBY
Adare
Adare Manor
Castletroy
Limerick County
Rathbane

LIMERICK COUNTY   Established 1994

SMART, ENTERTAINING PARKLAND

You see nothing of the course as you drive up to the clubhouse, and the car park could do with a makeover. It doesn't impress. Fortunately, the course is an entirely different matter: it shines.

Whoever planted the trees knew how to make an impact. Heavy, young woods and numerous feature trees give character and shape to holes. They complement the mature trees perfectly. Whoever created the bunkers clearly favours the left side of greens, likes elaborate shapes (the 4th and 6th, while the 18th has an 80-yard beach up the right) and believes in making them deep and punishing. Whoever routed the course has found a path that gives every hole individuality and drama, especially with some high tee boxes. And nature has given them all a wonderful canvas that has a hilltop early on (the 4th, 5th, 7th, 8th and 9th offer relaxing vistas) and lots of elegant and threatening ponds on the back nine. It all works beautifully and it is well maintained.

Every hole and shot looks inviting and the variety – shape, length, difficulty – illustrates how pretty a young course can be without being forced. In fact, apart from the drive on the 10th, it feels very spacious.

The curving greens are not easy to attack, especially as the fairway approaches to some greens are reduced to a single run of the lawnmower.

The five short par 3s are beauties and they're all lethal. The three par 5s are short but, again, dangerous. And the short par 4s will destroy the over-adventurous. When Limerick County matures it will be magnificent. Well worth a visit in a very busy golfing region.

FAVOURITE HOLE

Par 4 5th. 392 m. On the hilltop, you drive at a pretty hillside and views beyond, but you need to hit the ball either 180 m or 230 m, as there is a steep hill down to a well-bunkered green. Oh, and it's Index 1.

TOUGHEST HOLE

Par 4 7th. 251 m. A beauty that curves up and around a rocky hillside covered in gorse, with no room right. Judging the tee shot is crucial as the green is well protected and heavily tiered. Short but destructive.

POINTS								
CD	A	G/F	B/W	L	F	V	G Ex	Total
16	8	9	9	7	8	10	17	84

THE COURSE

- Par 71
- Length: 5,417 m
- Limerick County Golf Club, Ballyneety, Co. Limerick
- Tel: +353 (0) 61 351881
- www.limerickcounty.com
- Green Fees: €15–€25

COURSES NEARBY
Adare
Adare Manor
Castletroy
Limerick
Rathbane

LISBURN   Established 1905

TO A TEE

You only have to walk onto the 1st tee to know you're playing a quality course. It is startling what a difference a perfect opening tee box makes to how you feel about a course. Here there are stone walls, shrubs and beds of colour. It helps, of course, that the drive is just as good. Big trees and dark woods follow you around, growing increasingly friendly, and while the start makes occasional demands of your driving, from the 8th on you will be tested frequently. Some drives are beautiful (the 8th, 9th and 14th), others are frustrating (the 11th and 12th). The course is not horribly tight but it will give you a good hiding if you don't properly negotiate the challenges from the tee.

Lisburn has that classic, refined parkland air to it. There are small woods, scatterings of trees and plenty of mature beauties to give that graceful air – the oaks overhanging the 5th green are perfect, with the par 3 6th promising a tree-enshrined shot over water. You might also be fooled into thinking this is a flat course, but hole 7 dispels that notion (a scintillating roller coaster) and holes 14,

17 and 18 have big changes in elevation.

There are two loops of nine, lots of bunkers, three excellent par 3s, variety, quality and excitement. And how can you resist a hole that's called 'Leg of Mutton'? Even though not many greens are on show, shorter hitters may hold the advantage. Only the 7th and 10th are seriously long – both 448 yard par 4s – on a short 72.

FAVOURITE HOLE
Par 4 17th. 382 yards. A lovely straight hole that rises perfectly between big trees to the green. The 14th is a knee-trembling drive and the 5th has the most dramatic tee setting. The long downhill par 3 18th promises a tricky finish.

TOUGHEST HOLE
Par 4 11th. 385 yards. The 10th is 448 yards and Index 1, but the 11th has a tricky drive that hits confusingly at the 16th green. It is disconcerting as you need a fade. Around the corner a tiered green sits behind and beside a pond. Somewhat unfair.

POINTS

CD	A	G/F	B/W	L	F	V	G Ex	Total
15	8	8	8	5	9	8	17	78

THE COURSE
- Par 72
- Length: 6,295 yards
- Lisburn Golf Club, Blaris Lodge, 68 Eglantine Road, Lisburn, Co. Antrim, BT27 5RQ
- Tel: +44 (0) 28 9267 7216 (048 from Rep. of Ire.)
- www.lisburngolfclub.com
- Green Fees: £35–£50

COURSES NEARBY
Down Royal
Dunmurry
Edenmore
Lambeg
Malone

LOUGH ERNE   Established 2008

IMMACULATE RHYTHM

Lough Erne is a major resort at the upper end of the scale. It promises serious pampering and the golf course matches this. It is immaculate, beautiful and enticing, immersing you in the elegance that is Lough Erne. Time and again the lough delivers glorious views and tough challenges, while a long bridge crosses water to reach the 1st tee. No expense has been spared to make this one of the top parkland courses in the country. Does it rival Concra Wood, Adare Manor and Druid's Glen? Absolutely. And yet, like these three great courses, it is incomparable.

The course has different elements that work well together. It starts in deep woods, shifts to a plateau that heads down to the lough and then finds a classic parkland rhythm between tall trees and ponds, where there is an intriguing dichotomy between perfect golf holes and wild, untouched rough. The course returns to the lake for a final flourish – the closing three holes all tied up with water.

Holes vary dramatically in difficulty but fairways are usually generous. It ensures good playability for all standards, and despite some challenges from the tee it has not been designed to intimidate. Approaches are far harder with shoulders of elaborately shaped bunkers stalling short of surprisingly tame and true greens, or water encroaching to put a premium on accuracy.

A large halfway house will prove an irresistible break before you play the 10th, a short and driveable par 4 with the green in the lough. Undoubtedly it will be a bit too manufactured for some, with a couple of weak holes, but it's a thrilling golf experience with amazing hospitality.

FAVOURITE HOLE
Par 5 16th. 590 yards. Play from the inspiring back tee. Up by the woods, lake below right and a tempting fairway below. The ball will soar off the tee for one of the course's many thrilling shots. Shame about the 'lodges' behind.

TOUGHEST HOLE
Par 4 17th. 348 yards. The 14th may be 600 yards long, but the 17th demands accuracy and bravery off the tee as the hole sweeps around the lough, and then again to reach the green.

POINTS								
CD	A	G/F	B/W	L	F	V	G Ex	Total
18	10	9	9	10	8	8	19	91

THE COURSE

- Par 72
- Length: 6,241 yards (white tees)
- Lough Erne Golf Resort, Belleek Road, Enniskillen, Co. Fermanagh, BT93 7ED
- Tel: +44 (0) 28 6632 3230 (048 from Rep. of Ire.)
- www.loughernegolfresort.com
- Green Fees: £60–£105

COURSES NEARBY
Castle Hume
Clones
Enniskillen
Slieve Russell

LOUGHGALL   Established 2000

GLORIOUSLY FLOWING FARMLAND

There are plenty of farmland-style parkland courses – the ones where someone plants trees, throws in a few mounds and calls it a 'golf course'. Loughgall qualifies, but it is a beauty. It is similar to Blackwood (outside Bangor) in the golf-course hierarchy – both are pay-and-play facilities that aren't given nearly enough respect, despite a perfect and spacious parkland landscape. There is no sensational quality or finesse, but on a course this adventurous that is a minor complaint. Here you will have fun with five par 3s and five par 5s.

There are gentle hills to climb and lots of big trees to avoid/enjoy (delete as appropriate) – several of which stand resolutely alone and in your way. The greens are big swinging beasts and water appears occasionally, making the short par 5 6th very tricky indeed. Everything combines creatively to deliver fun holes, and the location's maturity stretches into the distance time and again, going far beyond the course's boundaries. The shapes of the holes promise variety and on nearly all of them you simply want to get up and smack the ball. The best runs of holes are the 1st to 6th and the 13th to 17th.

It is very short for a par 72 and generous enough that you can score comfortably (the back nine especially). But beware the deep and wild rough that, at times, you aren't even allowed to go into.

Loughgall calls itself a 'country park and golf course'. It includes a football pitch, tennis courts, walking/cycling tracks and a campsite, but no pro shop or bar.

FAVOURITE HOLE
Par 4 14th. 250 yards. A hole where you can let rip. The tee box sits under a giant beech and the green implores a big hit, protected by only a few bunkers. Plenty of room, unlike the 2nd which is 258 yards with two very quirky bunkers – one in a pond.

TOUGHEST HOLE
Par 4 17th. 423 yards. The indices are way off (the straight 303-yard 10th is Index 6), and the 17th, at Index 4, is the longest par 4 with heavy woods on your right, a seriously sloping fairway, a dog-leg and a big tree influencing your approach. The putting surface is hidden.

POINTS

CD	A	G/F	B/W	L	F	V	G Ex	Total
15	8	6	7	7	6	10	16	75

THE COURSE
- Par 72
- Length: 5,917 yards
- Loughgall Golf Club, 11–14 Main Street, Loughgall, Co. Armagh, BT61 8HZ
- Tel: +44 (0) 28 3889 2900 (048 from Rep. of Ire.)
- www.loughgallgolfclub.co.uk
- Green Fees: £20

COURSES NEARBY
Banbridge
County Armagh
Dungannon
Portadown
Tandragee

Hole 10
Mount Juliet Golf Club
Par 5, 553 yards, Index 7
Go left? Go right? The stand of majestic trees in the fairway guards a heavily
bunkered green. (© Mount Juliet Golf Club [www.mountjuliet.ie/golf])

Hole 11
Ballybunion Golf Club (Old)
Par 4, 400 yards, Index 2
Stretched above the beach, the world-famous 11th is the toughest hole on a superb
back nine. (© Simon Duffield)

Hole 12
Macreddin Golf Club
Par 4, 364 m, Index 1
A supremely difficult and stunning dog-leg from an elevated tee. You have to cross Ballycreen Brook, possibly twice. (Courtesy Macreddin Golf Club)

Hole 13
Naas Golf Club
Par 5, 502 yards, Index 7
A straight, relaxing hole that is all on show from a high tee. Simplicity wins the day. (Courtesy Denis Mahon)

Hole 14
Portarlington Golf Club
Par 4, 348 m, Index 4
The lone oak is a captivating sight as this peaceful dog-leg leads you into the trees. (© Conor Twomey Photography)

LOUGHREA   Established 1954

CALM AND OPEN

Loughrea is a basic parkland experience that does enough to entertain you for eighteen holes – especially at these green fees. It sits on gently rolling hills that get steeper and more intriguing on the back nine. You will find the best shots here, with some excellent drives (the 12th to 15th) and approaches (the 10th, 11th and 13th to 15th). And, with the late arrival of some good water features, the interest and challenges are ramped up a gear. After a tame start, you are assured of a more enthralling finish. The back nine also flow better so you will warm to the task, especially when you see the impressive and tricky uphill approach to the par 5 10th.

There are no views to speak of, but you are out in open countryside. Flanks of young trees are scattered about but there seems to be no rhythm to the planting. And the topiaried trees on the 10th and 12th seem out of context, considering the setting.

While there are few dangers off the tee, your main challenges will come from some blind shots (notably the par 5s: the 10th, 12th and 16th) and the greens, which can have surprisingly steep slopes. It's always good to see an average parkland like this laced with quality greens.

The 13th to 15th are the highlight and are worth the green fee alone. Average changing rooms could do with a makeover.

FAVOURITE HOLE
Par 4 14th. 337 m. A towering drive that offers up a ditch at the bottom of the slope, a large pond around which the hole dog-legs, and an attractive approach to the green. Index 2.

TOUGHEST HOLE
Par 4 15th. 342 m. A nicely elevated tee shows off the water-filled ditch ahead, but this is only the first water hazard. The second lies after the dog-leg, just short of the green, and hides out of sight. Two careful shots required.

POINTS

CD	A	G/F	B/W	L	F	V	G Ex	Total
13	7	8	6	6	6	8	14	68

THE COURSE
- Par 71
- Length: 5,638 m
- Loughrea Golf Club, Graigue, Loughrea, Co. Galway
- Tel: +353 (0) 91 841 049
- www.loughreagolfclub.com
- Green Fees: €20–€25

COURSES NEARBY
Athenry
Ballinasloe
Cregmore Park
Curra West
Gort

LUCAN   Established 1897

A GOOD TILT

It is amazing how often golf clubs end up with two differing nines, and it is not always because the second nine came later. Some courses see the advantage of the differences, while others simply take what they can get. At Lucan, you start with six holes that curl up a hillside, before playing the last eleven on very level terrain – only an indented stream and occasional mound interrupt the eye.

The 1st tee offers a great drive onto the fairway below. You hit over bushes, a road, a stream and telegraph cables. It gets you off to a flier. The front nine have more shape and character as the long, slow hillside takes you up and down. The short 6th starts flat on the top of the slope and then drops sharply to a nicely set green. And then comes the 7th (see below).

The final eleven holes are on the other side of the clubhouse, divided by long lines of evergreens on fairways – on the 14th they seem to go on forever. These are not dramatic holes by any stretch but

they feel right and fall into an easy rhythm.

The green settings are good, and the 18th may be the pick of the bunch – as you enter the club, you will see a small waterfall in front of you and this sits under the green. The hole is 531 m so it may take some time to get there – especially as the 17th is also a par 5.

FAVOURITE HOLE

Par 3 7th. 139 m. Like the 1st, you hit over stream, road and telegraph lines. The green sits neatly in a dell of trees with a sharp bank rising along the right-hand side. On the left a couple of deep bunkers are the main threat.

TOUGHEST HOLE

Par 4 1st. 377 m. The long holes get the lowest indices here, but the 1st is the most demanding and entertaining drive of the day. Your second looks straight-forward but there is water tight on the left of the green.

POINTS

CD	A	G/F	B/W	L	F	V	G Ex	Total
13	6	7	8	4	8	7	14	67

THE COURSE

- Par 71
- Length: 5,844 m
- Lucan Golf Club, Celbridge Road, Lucan, Co. Dublin
- Tel: +353 (0) 1 628 2106
- www.lucangolfclub.ie
- Green Fees: €40

COURSES NEARBY

Grange Castle
Luttrellstown
The Hermitage

LURGAN   Established 1893

SWEET AND SHARP

A nice laneway past a lake brings you out of Lurgan town and to the golf club. Sadly the lake appears only fleetingly on the 10th and 18th, but water isn't important here. This is a testing, sweeping game of golf between plenty of big, wandering lines of parkland trees. I'd say there is a nice rhythm but there are too many curving dog-legs that interrupt your flow. It makes a short course feel longer and the dog-legs are the key challenge as your positioning is tested off the tee constantly. As a newcomer, you will find it hard to figure out the line, and one of my wildest shots ended up in the perfect spot. It will restrict and frustrate big hitters, so it plays into the hands of the less aggressive golfer. And, during the summer, you are far better off landing the ball short because the accessible greens are hard, making length less important – the longest par 4 is 410 yards.

Despite the presence of the trees, there is room to land your ball, even on the dog-legs. The challenge is all about accuracy. Some raised tees and good undulations (the 9th is a beauty) add a good driving element, but they also highlight the danger of hitting nearby fairways. It gets a bit too cosy from time to time.

The par 3 17th, under oak, and the par 4 12th are perfect holes. The par 4 opening hole of just 240 yards is followed by two par 3s. A quirky start.

FAVOURITE HOLE

Par 4 12th. 379 yards. Index 2 offers a tempting but tricky drive. It's a sharp dog-leg left and only a perfect tee shot opens up the green, which sits up high in a backdrop of trees. Drive too far and you're in the ditch; too short and big trees block you.

TOUGHEST HOLE

Par 4 7th. 410 yards. Index 1 slides down the hill then dog-legs right and up. At the perfect landing spot water waits on both sides. Then it's uphill to a blind putting surface.

POINTS								
CD	A	G/F	B/W	L	F	V	G Ex	Total
14	7	7	6	6	8	9	14	71

THE COURSE

- Par 70
- Length: 5,995 yards
- Lurgan Golf Club, Demesne, Lurgan, Co. Armagh, BT67 9BN
- Tel: +44 (0) 28 3832 2087 (048 from Rep. of Ire.)
- www.lurgangolfclub.com
- Green Fees: £12–£25

COURSES NEARBY
Down Royal
Edenmore
Portadown
Silverwood

LUTTRELLSTOWN   Established 1993

STILL GROWING

All Dublin golfers know the name, and Luttrellstown has proved a popular venue for many outings, events and bigger things. It was remodelled in recent years and is even plusher than before, with a majestic wooden clubhouse. The Luttrellstown estate, on which it sits, and the castle of the same name add tremendous panache.

It is a long, tough and some might say beautiful course. It spends much of its time weaving through large and often contorted beech trees. And the threat of water is never far away: the 3rd green is surrounded on three sides and there are lakes, rivers and a fountain too. There are no easy holes and precious few easy shots – the pothole bunkers have seen to that. Trees are constantly in your line although this really only happens after the 6th, which is when the course comes to life.

The landscape ripples, something amplified on the large greens with their major swings and hillocks that bemuse and frustrate. Fortunately, most putting surfaces are clearly visible so you can judge pin positions. It also ensures more

exciting approach shots. The 3rd, 5th, 7th, 10th, 13th, 14th and 17th are excellent.

With so many trees and so much water you will want to have a good day's golf. And at 6,812 yards (white tees), it is long. Outings will play from green tees, measuring 6,364 yards.

It is worth spending some time in the clubhouse, so bear that in mind when booking your tee time.

FAVOURITE HOLE
Par 4 10th. 398 yards. The huge beech trees arrive with a bang. Water in front of the tee leads to a big gathering of beeches that forces you right on a dog-leg left. The trees are everywhere. For your second, the green has a backdrop of water.

TOUGHEST HOLE
Par 4 17th. 449 yards. Another dog-leg left and one that needs a big drive down the right to open up the green. The fairway dances serenely through the trees and the green sits confidently in their midst. Your second is longer than it looks.

POINTS

CD	A	G/F	B/W	L	F	V	G Ex	Total
15	8	9	9	6	9	10	16	82

THE COURSE

- Par 72
- Length: 6,812 yards
- Luttrellstown Golf Club, Castleknock, Dublin 15
- Tel: +353 (0) 1 860 9600
- www.luttrellstown.ie/golf-resort
- Green Fees: €30–€45

COURSES NEARBY
Castleknock
Hermitage
Lucan
Westmanstown

MACREDDIN   Established 2008

THE FIRST OF MANY

Macreddin Village is always worth a visit with its hotel and superb Strawberry Tree restaurant. But the new golf club will quickly take centre stage. Paul McGinley's course will live long in the memory.

Located in an enchanting Wicklow valley, Macreddin's hillsides, trees and a babbling brook embrace you. Fairways move between tall pine woods, up and over many curves before dog-legging into beautiful and perfect greens. Drives look tempting and approaches promise the perfect combination of backdrop, danger and thrills.

The back nine are hilly, particularly the 12th (see photo) to 17th, and this can be punishing (the 15th particularly). Fortunately, the dog-legs cut across the hillside through the pines to ease the pain somewhat.

There are a number of things to note: there is some walking to get to tees (the 9th to 10th), and you might play the 8th fairway from the 5th tee if you're not careful (head right). A basic and temporary clubhouse is up by the 1st tee, across the road.

McGinley has a flair for design, that much is obvious, and he had an interesting and fun landscape to work with. The more open section (the 3rd to 9th) will soon be dazzled by gorse, adding to the atmosphere. It is long, challenging, pretty and fun. And while there are a few tame holes they are countered by three absolute peaches: the 12th and 13th, which rise and fall dramatically around the brook, and the truly towering par 3 4th.

Will mature beautifully.

FAVOURITE HOLE

Par 4 12th. 364 m. Index 1 is a thriller. A huge driving hole that heads down to the brook, the fairway and the pines below. It's a big shot to get over the water. It then swings right, along the course of the brook to a green tucked in the corner.

TOUGHEST HOLE

Par 4 9th. 377 m. McGinley tricks the eye. The drive is to a curving fairway that just tweaks the nerves. The approach may look straightforward, but the bunkers will easily fool you, being 20 yards short of the green.

POINTS								
CD	A	G/F	B/W	L	F	V	G Ex	Total
17	8	9	9	8	5	10	17	83

THE COURSE

- Par 72
- Length: 5,937 m
- Macreddin Golf Club, Macreddin Village, Co. Wicklow
- Tel: +353 (0) 402 36999
- www.macreddingolfclub.com
- Green Fees: €30–€50

COURSES NEARBY
Arklow
Coollattin
European Club, The
Glenmalure
Woodenbridge

MACROOM   Established 1947

LONG ON TOP, SHORT ON THE SIDES

Macroom has an intriguing character. You wouldn't think it playing the 1st, but from the 2nd you will be seduced by oak and lime trees and steep falls. The 3rd is a beauty that arches up and over the hill to a green pitched up high. Your best views are from here. The 4th and 5th go down and up fairly tamely, and then it's back to the glorious natural setting from the 6th to 9th, the best run on the course. Superb tee shots fire out of trees onto picture-perfect fairways. On the 7th a twisted oak overhangs the tee, and on the 8th you leave the course and walk over farmland to reach an artificial tee. Bizarre and brilliant – almost as brilliant as having to drive through castle gates to get here.

The course is short and easy if you can handle some big slopes and greens, but the back nine are even easier, measuring just 2,626 m. And that includes two par 5s. It's a different nine entirely. It is flatter (but not flat) and introduces you to the River Sullane – at first it runs just behind the trees before arcing right in front of the 12th green and 14th tee. There is no doubt that these holes have been squeezed in to make up the numbers – four par 4s are 300 m and under – but the ponds, the river and a derelict bathing house all provide plenty of enjoyment. Given the space, I would love to see the 13th green become the 12th green. Now that would be some second shot over the river. The 17th and 18th are good finishing holes with the roller-coaster terrain returning.

Very peaceful and charming.

FAVOURITE HOLE

Par 4 9th. 357 m. A tee shot down into a tree-lined valley, over the stream to a humpbacked fairway. The green in the distance is a lovely sight. Don't expect a good drive to be rewarded though, as the fairway slopes sharply.

TOUGHEST HOLE

Par 4 18th. 356 m. You try to hit into another tree-lined valley. A good drive makes it easier, but your steep shot up to the green has to allow for long tumbling slopes (you will see them coming from the 9th) and trees tight right.

POINTS								
CD	A	G/F	B/W	L	F	V	G Ex	Total
14	8	9	8	6	6	9	15	75

THE COURSE

- Par 71
- Length: 5,416 m
- Macroom Golf Club, Macroom, Co. Cork
- Tel: +353 (0) 26 41072
- www.macroomgolfclub.com
- Green Fees: €25–€30

COURSES NEARBY
Bandon
Kanturk
Lee Valley

MAHON   Established 1982

MUNICIPAL MAGIC

When you see the word 'municipal', you might be inclined to dismiss Mahon, but this highly entertaining, well-maintained and surprisingly spacious short course is worth a visit. It is a tumbling affair that runs beside the estuary, and water threatens on six holes. Stand on the joint 5th/11th tee box, which juts into the estuary, and you will see dozens of failed drives littered across the mud at low tide. Rescue them at your peril.

Do not expect easy golf. Enjoyable, yes, but also challenging. There is little room for error on the opening three holes, which go up and down a steep hillock (once known as 'heart-attack hill'). Thereafter your drives need to be carefully positioned to take full advantage of some very short holes – it is par 33 out (four par 3s) and 37 back. You'll find good variety, too, as the course stretches along the estuary. Trees come and go, the terrain flattens in the later stages, but the location is always embracing.

The run of holes from the 4th to 11th is the most creative. It uses the estuary, a big reed bed, trees and good slopes and hollows. The four par 3s are hugely entertaining with the 4th and 6th both hitting down towards the estuary, and the 9th hitting up into dark trees.

The 11th to 14th and the 17th to 18th are of the newer, classic, parkland style, and you walk under the South Ring Road to reach the 15th and 16th, two thrilling little par 4s (220 m and 310 m, respectively) pressed up against the estuary.

It will be too short for many, but it is definitely fun. While not easy to find, the pub alongside is rather convenient.

FAVOURITE HOLE
Par 4 5th. 325 m. Index I drives over the estuary and trees onto a flat fairway that swings right, around more trees, and up to the green. Positioning of your drive is crucial. The 7th offers you some amusing choices.

TOUGHEST HOLE
Par 4 10th. 310 m. You drive over a crest with no idea where you'll end up. Out of sight is a huge sloping fairway that will drag every ball to the bottom, from where you will be blind to the green fronted by a big bunker. Lethal.

POINTS								
CD	A	G/F	B/W	L	F	V	G Ex	Total
15	8	7	8	8	6	10	16	78

THE COURSE
- Par 70
- Length: 5,033 m
- Mahon Golf Club, Cloverhill, Blackrock, Cork, Co. Cork
- Tel: +353 (0) 21 429 2543
- www.mahongolfclub.com
- Green Fees: €15–€29

COURSES NEARBY
Cork
Douglas
Fota Island
Monkstown
Water Rock

MALAHIDE   Established 1892

BLUE, RED AND YELLOW

Malahide is a decent parkland course north of Dublin. There are gentle climbs close to the big clubhouse on what is predominantly a flat course. Some fairways have creative shapes (the Blue and Red 8th stand out), greens are raised and create good targets, and water creates danger and drama – swans on the Red 7th are quite a sight while on the Blue 3rd and 6th, two par 3s, there is a heavy stream running alongside.

There are very few blind shots so you get to enjoy the course for everything it has to offer. It also means the dangers that lie ahead of you are clear to see, and that makes the course more accessible and easier to attack. Holes may go back and forth but they are well separated by strong lines of trees and the fairways tend to sweep lazily around these.

The 6th, 7th, 8th and 9th on the Red course (i.e. the 15th, 16th, 17th and 18th) deliver a strong finish, with the 6th green perched up high, good water in front of the 7th, a challenging and rolling par 5

8th, and the 9th promising a pretty one-shot hole through a densely channelled wood.

The course is exciting enough without ever stunning you. And with three nines (I didn't play the Yellow nine) it will be enjoyed by plenty of golfers looking for an easy-paced and pleasurable round.

Blue and Red form the main eighteen.

FAVOURITE HOLE
Par 4 10th. 290 m. Hole 1 on Red, the tee shot heads downhill to a green fronted by a pond and fountain. It is a great-looking hole with mature trees left and right, and your approach to the green is daunting.

TOUGHEST HOLE
Par 4 5th. 383 m. Blue course. From a slight elevation, the hole sweeps right. Positioning your drive is crucial if you are to reach the green in two. There is water right of the green as well as in front so you can be heavily punished.

POINTS								
CD	A	G/F	B/W	L	F	V	G Ex	Total
14	7	7	8	5	8	6	14	69

THE COURSE
- Par 70
- Length: 5,783 m
- Malahide Golf Club, Beechwood, The Grange, Malahide, Co. Dublin
- Tel: +353 (0) 1 846 1611
- www.malahidegolfclub.ie
- Green Fees: €37–€55

COURSES NEARBY
Howth
Island, The (as the crow flies)
Portmarnock
Portmarnock Links

MALLOW   Established 1947

STRONG PARKLAND WITH ALL THE RIGHT MOVES

The beech is king here, but there are many subjects: oak, eucalyptus, ash, conifer and maple abound and are most impressive on the opening nine holes. Unlike Charleville nearby, the trees are at a more respectful distance, but if you can avoid a woody encounter then you are doing well. Mallow is not as pretty or rhythmic as Charleville, but there is more drama here. It all comes down to the views of the Galty Mountains and a hillside location that leaves many sloping lies and challenging shots. With drives hitting over rises onto unseen fairways you won't see many greens, but when the greens finally appear, they are in lovely settings made by the trees. It gives Mallow a good buzz.

The second nine move to the centre of the course but continue the theme of blind drives and gentle slopes. Without the same density of trees it doesn't hold as much intrigue. The 10th, 15th and 16th are the pick of the bunch. The 10th drives straight at the Galty Mountains.

There are five par 5s and five par 3s, none particularly long. Holes 2, 3, 4 (par 3, 5, 3) are a lovely start. A huge beech stands in your way on the par 5, making it unreachable in two. There are other touches: some tee boxes are faced with a dark limestone rock and a lot of shrubs have been planted to add colour.

There is a small amount of climbing and, if you take a buggy, remember that you can't get to the 2nd tee or green. Like Bandon, the par 3 18th is a great viewing hole from the clubhouse.

FAVOURITE HOLE

Par 5 6th. 440 m. Called Tree Sisters for a reason. One of the tighter drives as you hit towards the green and a swirling fairway. Hole 3 is a close second, also with a tight drive, and a giant beech hides the green.

TOUGHEST HOLE

Par 4 15th. 345 m. Hit at Mount Hillary but don't expect to hold the angled, unseen fairway that runs all the way to the green.

POINTS

CD	A	G/F	B/W	L	F	V	G Ex	Total
14	8	8	7	7	7	8	15	74

THE COURSE

- Par 72
- Length: 5,769 m
- Mallow Golf Club, Ballyellis, Mallow, Co. Cork
- Tel: +353 (0) 22 21145
- www.mallowgolfclub.net
- Green Fees: €35–€40

COURSES NEARBY

Charleville
Fermoy
Kanturk
Mitchelstown

MALONE   Established 1895

MALONE'S MUSCLE

You know how you feel after a really good meal – that deliciously full sensation? That's what it feels like when you walk off the 18th (or the 27th if you fancy the third nine). You will be sated by a lovely, big, heavy, parkland course. The old trees are majestic, running in dense lines along the perimeter or standing in isolation over fairways, tees and greens. But the younger trees have been planted sympathetically and smartly, and not in their thousands as many courses boast. Malone flows easily and dangerously over the undulating terrain, finding a great route and a greater rhythm. Plenty of dog-legs set the tone, challenging you off the tee. It often requires you to be long to beat the turn, but big hitters can find plenty of trouble, too (Index 1 is lethal).

With the great shapes to the landscape and the vibrancy of the trees, there isn't a dull shot. It is all good. Add to this a beautiful lake that runs in front of the clubhouse and affects three holes (the 13th, 15th and 18th hit over water), and it promises a sublime parkland experience.

It's not the kind of place you will come to for a flippant round of golf as it tests you and thrills you in equal measure.

I was warned about the rather superior air around the clubhouse – yes, it'a bit old school, stuffy, jacket-and-tie affair, but go with the flow and love the golf.

FAVOURITE HOLE
Par 4 9th. 365 yards. It curves left ever so gently over a bunker. Then it rises to a high green in front to the impressive, old clubhouse. And it is all through a channel of huge trees. The 18th is a tough and attractive finishing hole, while the 15th is the pick of the par 3s.

TOUGHEST HOLE
Par 4 7th. 460 yards. You would think on a hole this long that a big drive is crucial. It is, but only if you can beat the unbeatable dog-leg: the bunker and steep slopes on the left force you right, on to a tiny plateau which then flicks left to a well-guarded green.

POINTS								
CD	A	G/F	B/W	L	F	V	G Ex	Total
17	9	9	8	6	10	8	18	85

THE COURSE
- Par 71
- Length: 6,438 yards
- Malone Golf Club, 240 Upper Malone Road, Dunmurry, Belfast, BT17 9LB
- Tel: +44 (0) 28 9061 4917 (048 from Rep. of Ire.)
- www.malonegolfclub.co.uk
- Green Fees: £40–£85

COURSES NEARBY
Balmoral
Belvoir Park
Dunmurry
Lambeg
Rockmount

MANNAN CASTLE   Established 1994

TALES OF THE UNEXPECTED

Nuremore in the morning; Mannan Castle in the afternoon. Hardly seems like a fair comparison, does it? And first impressions are not promising. Yet Mannan Castle packs a surprising amount of punch for what is a second-, possibly third-tier, course. It does not have the professional touch or the elegance of Nuremore, but it has intrigue. Some remarkable holes cut across the hillsides and there are enough thrilling shots to keep you upbeat. I wouldn't go so far as to say it is quirky, but there are holes that make you draw breath: the 4th is Index 1 (see below); the 8th has a slope off the tee box that you might fall down; and the short par 4 12th (274 yards) hits between mature trees and over a mound through a tiny gap, before dropping to an unseen green. The 1st, 3rd, 4th, 6th and 8th are all stimulating and testing dog-legs that will thrill any golfer. Hit too far right on the 8th and you could end up in a ravine. These all give Mannan Castle a burst of personality. It is simply not what you expect. There's an old walled garden and the 2nd would undoubtedly be regarded as a signature hole: it hits down just 150 yards to a green fronted by a double stream, with an old mill wheel behind.

Despite all its adventure, this is a tricky course that benefits the smart golfer.

It sits in a wide valley of farmland: stray too far off-line and you might run into a cow. Seriously. The last five holes are beside the clubhouse and are flatter and tamer. They have bridges, lots of water and plenty to think about. A course to be enjoyed and one with plenty of potential.

FAVOURITE HOLE
Par 5 5th. 521 yards. Long and narrow. It is a tight tee box cut into the hillside. From here you must thread your shots down a narrow channel between gorse and conifer that rise menacingly on either side. Daunting and attractive.

TOUGHEST HOLE
Par 4 4th. 400 yards. Long. You hit towards a narrow gap that then dog-legs between laurel and a hillside beech wood. Only perfect positioning makes the green on the other side accessible – threading a needle comes to mind. And the fairway bunker pushes you in the wrong direction.

POINTS								
CD	A	G/F	B/W	L	F	V	G Ex	Total
15	8	7	6	6	6	10	17	75

THE COURSE

- Par 70
- Length: 5,907 yards
- Mannan Castle Golf Club, Donaghmoyne, Carrickmacross, Co. Monaghan
- Tel: +353 (0) 42 966 3308
- www.mannancastlegolfclub.ie
- Green Fees: €25–€35

COURSES NEARBY
Ardee
Ashfield
Concra Wood
Nuremore
Rossmore

MASSEREENE Established 1964

A GOOD, DISTINGUISHED AIR

From the moment you arrive, you get a sense of quality and purpose. Everything screams classic parkland creation, so expect all the challenges that have grown over time. There are two distinct nines, but one common theme: dog-legs. You open on the hillier section and this nine are the more charming. The 1st is a tough opening hole, introducing you to the mature trees, calm pace and decent curves. It drops from the tee, swings right and heads uphill to a tricky, steeply banked green. It's a great introduction.

If you play from the forward green tees a driver is not always necessary, and despite the big trees all around, there's room to play.

The back nine are flat and less exciting – until the 16th at least – and the course likes to claim that these are 'links' holes. Yes, but only in origin. You won't find any links features apart from an erratically bumpy 18th fairway. Holes 10 and 11 are over a small road and while the dog-legs on this nine continue, they are less severe. The 15th and 16th offer the briefest glimpses of Lough Neagh (the clubhouse promises better views) and, while their

ponds are good, they are scant consolation.

The 17th is magnificent. Straight and true between a disorganised rabble of colourful trees. Coincidentally, the other exceptional hole, the 4th, is the only other straight hole.

It is a tidy course that demands a tidy game of golf. The fact that there are so many dog-legs doesn't detract from the score because you get to see so much around you and ahead of you. And the trees give it that easy pace.

FAVOURITE HOLE
Par 4 4th. 354 yards. From the tee, you see the flag and tree-stuffed backdrop, but you have no idea that the land in front of you drops like a precipice onto a beautiful fairway; when you get to the top, it's a thrilling sight.

TOUGHEST HOLE
Par 4 6th. 431 yards. Called Devil's Elbow. You need a perfect fade around big trees if you want to see the green. There is room, but the rough is deep enough to cause problems.

POINTS								
CD	A	G/F	B/W	L	F	V	G Ex	Total
15	8	7	8	6	9	10	16	79

THE COURSE

- Par 72
- Length: 6,391 yards
- Massereene Golf Club, 51 Lough Road, Antrim, Co. Antrim, BT41 4DQ
- Tel: +44 (0) 28 9442 8096 (048 from Rep. of Ire.)
- www.massereene.com
- Green Fees: £15–£30

COURSES NEARBY
Allen Park
Galgorm Castle
Greenacres
Hilton Templepatrick

MAYOBRIDGE   Established 1997

QUIETLY BASIC

The most obvious comment is that this is not a real golf course. It doesn't have finesse, it doesn't have proper greens (upside-down plates), it doesn't have fairways – it's one giant lawn. I could criticise it all day, but that would be missing the point: there is a very specific target audience for this type of rough-and-tumble club and Mayobridge caters to its audience of casual golfers delightfully. As golf experiences go, you are unlikely to come here on a golfing trip, but it is a good laugh and exceptionally forgiving.

It's a great rolling landscape with seven par 4s under 310 yards and only one par 5, but what really stands out are the quaint and ruined cottages in the centre of the course. They brush up against the 6th, 7th, 11th and 18th, and it feels like you're on the derelict set of *The Quiet Man*. It's not a feature you will find on many courses.

Despite the course's overall grottiness there are some entertaining holes and you can have a go off the tee. Several of the greens are raised to make enticing targets – it's just a shame that their quality is similar to the fairways on Royal County Down.

The new clubhouse makes all the difference.

FAVOURITE HOLE
Par 4 10th. 246 yards. Driveable, but the green is a long way above you up a steep slope. It sits on the skyline and beckons. Trees left and right and it is Index 4.

TOUGHEST HOLE
Par 3 13th. 196 yards. Worthy of any course, this is a terror of a hole. Water and OB are tight left of the tiny green, and a severe bank runs along the right all the way to the putting surface – hit it and you'll be deflected into the water.

POINTS								
CD	A	G/F	B/W	L	F	V	G Ex	Total
10	5	3	5	7	5	6	11	52

THE COURSE

- Par 67
- Length: 4,759 yards
- Mayobridge Golf Club, 50 Crossan Road, Mayobridge, Newry, Co. Down, BT34 2HY
- Tel: +44 (0) 28 3085 0295 (048 from Rep. of Ire.)
- www.mayobridgegolf.com
- Green Fees: £12–£16

COURSES NEARBY
Cloverhill
Kilkeel
Royal County Down
Warrenpoint

MILLICENT   Established 2001

LONG AND OPEN

Arriving at Millicent's small and basic clubhouse does not inspire, especially not having played Carton's O'Meara in the morning. But once you reach the 1st tee, it gets rosier. Almost the entire course is laid out below you, stretching across towards the Dublin Mountains. And mountainous might well describe the 1st hole, a par 5 of 555 yards that glides up and over the hill.

The first eight holes follow the perimeter of the course in a rectangular shape, and you can see the farthest corner (the 5th) from the 1st tee. This makes it sound very open, and it is. For now. Heavy tree planting in long, dense thickets will soon define the holes and separate them more substantially.

This is a long course – there are five par 5s – and at 580 yards, hole 16 is Index 1. Large ponds and the River Liffey running down one boundary (the 5th, 6th, 7th) make a huge difference to the appeal and the danger of the course. But it is straightforward, with wide fairways and plenty of forgiveness. Holes 6, 7, 11, 12 and 13 are deliciously dead straight and flat. The greens are wide open ensuring easy access, and the putting surfaces are large and tame.

While it is not a stunning course, it offers more than enough to keep you entertained. The real challenge is the length, despite a few short par 4s. The indices are interesting, too.

An inviting, good value course that will get considerably more tetchy with age.

FAVOURITE HOLE
Par 4 5th. 316 yards. A tempting short hole that curves wonderfully around a large pond to a slightly elevated green. It is the most picturesque and individual hole. A tough choice of club off the tee.

TOUGHEST HOLE
Par 5 16th. 580 yards. Not only is this long but you'll be playing off a sloping fairway that will push you close to the water. Three serious blows needed. The 17th is a tough, wet and wonderful par 3.

POINTS								
CD	A	G/F	B/W	L	F	V	G Ex	Total
12	7	6	7	7	6	8	14	67

THE COURSE
- Par 73
- Length: 6,712 yards
- Millicent Golf Club, Millicent Road, Clane, Co. Kildare
- Tel: +353 (0) 45 893 279
- www.millicentgolfclub.com
- Green Fees: €25–€35

COURSES NEARBY
Bodenstown
K Club
Killeen
Naas
Woodlands

MILLTOWN   Established 1907

SIMPLY SUBURBAN PARKLAND

Milltown is straightforward and short – a 'what you see is what you get' type of place. It won't set your pulse racing, but it is a pleasant, effortless and relaxing round of golf. Like Elm Park, its location near Dublin city is its main attraction, but it is superior to its city neighbour and better value.

The course has recently been upgraded and the once flat ground now has more shape and interest – both in terms of aesthetics and playability. Holes slide between avenues of trees and most head straight for distant flags on attractive greens. Even so, with its short length, you should bring in a back-slapping score. The 16th, 17th and 18th are strong finishing holes which require serious concentration or you might score 38 points and not 42.

Be aware that you have to cross a road four times, which complicates things, and there are no weekend visitors. If you are after slightly more intrigue, try Castle or Grange.

TOUGHEST & BEST HOLE
Par 4 17th. 394 m. A long dog-leg hole. You need to position your drive perfectly if you are to make the green around the corner. If you are short or left, some big evergreens will block your progress. The 16th is a long par 3 that often needs a driver.

POINTS								
CD	A	G/F	B/W	L	F	V	G Ex	Total
13	6	8	7	5	9	6	14	68

THE COURSE
- Par 71
- Length: 5,423 m
- Milltown Golf Club, Lower Churchtown Road, Dublin 14
- Tel: +353 (0) 1 497 6090
- www.milltowngolfclub.ie
- Green Fees: €65–€80

COURSES NEARBY
Castle
Edmondstown
Elm Park
Grange

MITCHELSTOWN   Established 1908

SOME STUNNING HOLES

Come and play the 4th hole. It's Index 1 and it reminds me – don't laugh – of Augusta. The hole drops to a flat fairway around a few lone pines and the green sits behind the river in the shadows of majestic trees. In evening sunlight, it is captivating. The 15th (see below) is just as good, with the 13th, 14th and 16th coming close. The rest of the holes vary widely.

After a long walk from the 5th, past a nasty mermaid fountain, you reach an outer loop of six new holes (the 6th to 11th, three of them par 5s) cut into the slope of an open field. Huge mounds separate gently curving fairways and accuracy is required or your views will be blocked. They are challenging but not that attractive. The oustanding feature is the view of the Galty Mountains right above you.

On the other side of the road, the mature trees and river provide far more interest. The 13th and 14th greens sit side by side on opposite sides of the River Funshion. They are right on the edge and this is not a river from which to retrieve balls. Along with the 4th, 12th and 15th, these are the outstanding holes. The remainder are straightforward parkland stuff, and the change of pace is erratic.

Personally, I'd start at the 4th (next to the 1st tee), then play the 13th (next to 5th tee) to the 18th. Repeat.

FAVOURITE HOLE
Par 4 15th. 272 m. Trees are everywhere around and over you on a treacherously difficult dog-leg. Your landing area is tiny if you want a good line in. If you have time, hit a few different clubs to figure it out. A hidden pond waits for the foolish.

TOUGHEST HOLE
Par 4 12th. 349 m. Another dog-leg that requires a well-judged tee shot. Then it's sharp right and down into a tricky grove of beautiful oak. Two difficult shots.

POINTS								
CD	A	G/F	B/W	L	F	V	G Ex	Total
14	7	7	9	7	8	9	15	76

THE COURSE
- Par 70
- Length: 5,493 m
- Mitchelstown Golf Club, Gurrane, Mitchelstown, Co. Cork
- Tel: +353 (0) 25 24072
- www.mitchelstown-golf.com
- Green Fees: €20–€25

COURSES NEARBY
Ballykisteen
Fermoy
Mallow
Tipperary

MOATE Established 1900

MORE THAN MEETS THE EYE

'This looks dull', you'll think when you arrive at the clubhouse on the outskirts of Moate. The holes on show look flat and uninteresting. But don't be fooled: there are some great holes at the other end of this rural-looking course. These make up the original nine and the clubhouse used to be down by the 8th green. This is the best 'field' on the course, with deep rollers moving across open fairways. It's not a serious, quality course, but it plays perfectly into the hands of societies and sociable golfers.

The opening holes and last six don't offer huge excitement. They are too flat to be called interesting and they are still settling in. As new parkland holes they are a bit predictable. That said, holes 1 and 2 require thread-like shots between big ash trees.

The best holes start after the amusing 99-m 4th with its postage-stamp-type raised green. Then come Indices 1, 3 and 5. A tough run along the perimeter with some colourful trees and even a fairy fort.

Fairways rock along and greens are left to lie fairly naturally on the landscape. They provide some sharp slopes and tricky banks. Including the 8th hole, these are the best four holes.

Assuming you don't go OB, there is not too much difficulty inside the course. It delivers a pleasing and quiet round of golf.

FAVOURITE HOLE

Par 4 7th. 348 m. Index 3. A great par 4. After a short walk you get to a tee that reveals a completely new landscape. You can see the green over the ridges. Two lovely, inviting shots and a dangerous green.

TOUGHEST HOLE

Par 4 6th. 350 m. Index 1. A dog-leg right that will test your distance judgement as OB lies ahead. The second drifts along before a bank drops to the green, with the fairy fort on the right. A tricky, narrow green to see and stay on.

POINTS								
CD	A	G/F	B/W	L	F	V	G Ex	Total
14	7	7	7	6	8	7	14	70

THE COURSE

- Par 72
- Length: 5,716 m
- Moate Golf Club, Aghanagrit, Moate, Co. Westmeath
- Tel: +353 (0) 90 648 1271
- www.moategolfclub.ie
- Green Fees: €20–€25

COURSES NEARBY
Athlone
Esker Hills
Glasson
Mount Temple

MONKSTOWN Established 1908

EMBRACING PARKLAND GOLF

When you need a splash of wonderful, charming golf, Monkstown would be the place to start. I would almost say relaxing, but the drop down the 3rd and the corresponding climb up the 5th are in sharp contrast to the playful shapes elsewhere. There is great maturity here, and the holes flow through acres of big trees with a subtle routing that rarely crowds you. It has an embracing and vibrant atmosphere (and in the big, glossy clubhouse, too).

The course is not long. Five holes are under 300 m, and Index 1 is a straight hole of just 370 m. But it's all about strategy here and a 3 wood/iron will be your tee shot of choice if you hit the ball big. As at Douglas, this constraint gives the short hitters greater opportunities to attack greens with lofted irons, and makes the game far more equal. I like strategic courses because you have to use your head, and despite many flags being out of view around dog-legs and behind trees, tee shots are rewarding. Driving down the 3rd is the highlight – a soaring shot at the hillside (and factory) opposite. As you descend, Cork Harbour appears as a remarkably complex view. Elsewhere, views are limited, but this is another club where the course has everything you need. Some strong water features appear on the more standard back nine, where a couple of small waterfalls tumble down from the par 3 16th and the water runs across the 10th, 11th and 15th. More water awaits left of the 18th green.

When you walk down to the 7th, look left at Monsktown Castle (built in 1636). This used to be the old clubhouse.

FAVOURITE HOLE
Par 4 8th. 347 m. Straight at the flag, the hole is nicely captured between the trees. There is good shape to the fairway and the bunkers are farther than they look. A big bunker also props up the right side of the green. The 6th, 7th and 8th are a good run.

TOUGHEST HOLE
Par 5 3rd. 490 m. Index 14 is madness. As a visitor you will have no idea where your second is to go and it is a steep, steep drop to a green that has gorse behind it. Staying on the green is also very tough, but you must land on it.

POINTS								
CD	A	G/F	B/W	L	F	V	G Ex	Total
15	8	8	8	6	10	8	17	80

THE COURSE
- Par 70
- Length: 5,370 m
- Monkstown Golf Club, Parkgarriff, Monkstown, Co. Cork
- Tel: +353 (0) 21 484 1376
- www.monkstowngolfclub.com
- Green Fees: €37–€50

COURSES NEARBY
Cork
Douglas
Fernhill
Mahon
Water Rock

MOOR PARK   Established 1993

NEEDS MORE

Moor Park does not generate any great passion. A lot of work is needed to tidy up a course that simply slips back and forth across the top of an easy hillside. There are no trees of any maturity and the young plantings are scattered about quite sparsely. The water features (ponds and wide, attractive ditches) are surprisingly good and, combined with the shape of the land, indicate that Moor Park offers some entertainment. But not a lot. It will need time and money to satisfy the standards of most golfers, and that applies to the basic clubhouse and facilities too.

Its openness means you can see lots of the course around you and I imagine it's risky to play when it is busy, especially with holes that invite big wind-ups as well as some blind drives. Very short for a par 72: two of the par 5s measure 408 m and 417 m.

An interesting quirk is the 9th and 18th which sit side by side and are almost identical holes – the 18th is a metre longer. They hit down onto a flat fairway, divided by a decent stream, before moving on sedately to the green. Basically, if you don't get it right first time, you'll have a second chance.

FAVOURITE HOLE
Par 4 5th. 346 m. Good shape as the hole drifts around the OB on your left. The tee box is tucked in the corner and you are forced to drive towards a pond you can barely see.

TOUGHEST HOLE
Par 4 10th. 350 m. Index 1. A good drive that will find a stream in just the wrong spot. There is also a pond on the right which will catch the big hitters. The hole then rises sharply to a bunker directly in front of the green.

POINTS								
CD	A	G/F	B/W	L	F	V	G Ex	Total
11	5	6	7	6	2	7	11	55

THE COURSE

- Par 72
- Length: 5,607 m
- Moor Park Golf Club, Mooretown, Kentstown Road, Navan, Co. Meath
- Tel: +353 (0) 46 902 7661
- Green Fees: €15–€20

COURSES NEARBY
Glebe
Headfort
Killeen Castle
Knightsbrook
Navan

MOUNTAIN VIEW   Established 1995

ENDLESS VIEWS

The name says it all. After a narrow drive through overhanging trees and past a couple of holes you arrive at the functional clubhouse. The views around you are endless, stretching off to Slievenamon and the Comeragh Mountains in the distance, and across fields of green and gold. If you're lucky enough to have a clear day then you are in for a treat.

And the golf's not bad either. Mountain View knows it's not going to attract premier league golfers, and has designed the course accordingly. It's very short, with six par 4s under 310 yards and only two par 5s. There is no great style, but there are good changes in elevation and some nice touches. The pond behind the first green affects four holes, and the water and wildlife add tremendously to your start. Old stones stand like lost soldiers in the middle of fairways, marking your line when you can't see the green. The greens are creative and there is no 'one size fits all', with some hovering on banks and others lying quietly at the fairway's end.

The course is wide open, and on the short par 4s you will want to have a crack at the green (the 2nd, 4th and 14th especially). There's not much difficulty. The tough holes are the 15th and 18th (the only par 4 close to 400 yards) which run in parallel on the lower section of the course. They have angled slopes, narrower fairways and rise all the way to high greens.

The most exciting holes start at the 13th (see below), and you have to negotiate a miniature chicane to reach the thrilling 14th.

FAVOURITE HOLE
Par 3 13th. 141 yards. A straight downhill hole with an endless backdrop of Ireland's beauty. You hit at a distant mountain and then follow the ball descending across the landscape. Don't be long. The 14th is just as good.

TOUGHEST HOLE
Par 4 1st. 336 yards. Dog-leg left. Short it may be, but I've never seen so much water so close to a 1st green. The hardest green to hit. Index 2 for a very good reason.

POINTS								
CD	A	G/F	B/W	L	F	V	G Ex	Total
11	5	6	7	8	5	8	13	63

THE COURSE
- Par 71
- Length: 5,685 yards
- Mountain View Golf Club, Kiltorcan, Ballyhale, Co. Kilkenny
- Tel: +353 (0) 56 776 8122
- www.mviewgolf.com
- Green Fees: €15

COURSES NEARBY
Callan
Gowran Park
Mount Juliet
New Ross
West Waterford

MOUNT JULIET Established 1991

PICTURE-PERFECT GOLF

What is golf if not a gloriously relaxed and inspiring day out? The 1,500-acre Mount Juliet estate is an idyllic setting for the perfect break. Everything a golfer (and other half) could ask for is right here, including a luxury eighteenth-century hotel, excellent practice facilities, a par 53 putting course (with water and bunkers) and – no cliché – a warm welcome. They're good people here and it starts you off in the right mood.

This course has real pedigree (Jack Nicklaus designed it, and it has held the Irish Open and the WGC American Express Championship), and just being here feels like a special occasion.

The broad 'American style' design is not to everyone's taste, but Nicklaus worked with a picturesque parkland landscape to create something that is rightly ranked as one of Ireland's best golf experiences. It is always in perfect condition and despite three lacklustre holes (the 6th, 9th and 15th), you're always left wanting more.

In spite of its length, it is difficult only occasionally so you will feel like opening up the shoulders, right from the first hole. There are welcoming fairways, big, contoured greens and bunkers that can easily be avoided. It finds a perfect pace for everyone. Trees are well spread out and come to the fore at the 10th (see below) and 17th, while water threatens often. Three par 3s (the 3rd, 11th and 14th) promise thrilling tee shots, with the water-fronted 3rd tricking you into playing one club too short.

Tiger Woods played four championship rounds here in 2002, and only bogeyed the 18th. Try and go one better before enjoying the 19th.

Allow a few minutes to get to the 1st tee from the practice areas.

FAVOURITE HOLE
Par 5 10th (see photo). 553 yards. It doesn't matter where your brilliant drive lands, the green simply isn't on, tucked completely behind glorious tree sentinels. And whether you go left or right on the split fairway the green is well and truly bunkered. A beauty.

TOUGHEST HOLE
Par 4 18th. 474 yards. It is long, and a watery grave awaits your second shot all along the left. So, whether you fade or draw the ball, it's a nerve-wracking approach.

POINTS								
CD	A	G/F	B/W	L	F	V	G Ex	Total
17	9	10	10	6	10	9	20	91

THE COURSE
- Par 72
- Length: 6,926 yards (whites)
- Mount Juliet Golf Club, Thomastown, Co. Kilkenny
- Tel: +353 (0) 56 777 3064
- www.mountjuliet.com
- Green Fees: €65–€90

COURSES NEARBY
Callan
Gowran Park
Kilkenny
Mountain View

MOUNTRATH Established 1929

ANOTHER HIGH ROLLER

Big rolls, like waves, sweep across the landscape and you'll find yourself being tossed around by them. On some of the longer holes you have to contend with two of them and it adds difficulty and drama. It might, just might, be a bit frustrating and monotonous from time to time as there is that 'blind drive' element, but the way the fairways rise in front of you means you have a big target. Plenty of golfers won't reach them. I'm being picky because Mountrath is tremendous fun. The peripherals – the tee boxes, shrub beds, the walks and bridges – add significantly and woodland walks to the 12th and 13th are enchanting. When that is combined with a good course, you are in for a treat. Some of the greens are spectacular, the par 3s are lovely, and the par 5s are short. The 17th and 18th are the only real dog-legs, both short, but this is a driver's course. Getting over those mounds is sheer pleasure as your ball can just keep running.

Greens are surprisingly good. The 1st and 2nd are not very interesting, but then they really switch gear and there are some greens (the 8th and 17th) that must be lethal in summer. The 15th is scandalously narrow on top of a hillock.

There's also a great switch of pace on the completely flat 13th and 14th. But here the River Nore is a serious threat, with the 14th being a tricky par 3 of 174 m.

If you don't mind this kind of landscape then Mountrath offers a riveting round of golf. You start between the clubhouse and a fairy-tale wood.

FAVOURITE HOLE
Par 5 11th. 458 m. A great high tee box in the trees shows off the green. You hit out over a mound, down into a hollow, up again, down again then up to the green. Fun.

TOUGHEST HOLE
Par 4 1st. 380 m. A tricky start. Even a good drive is unlikely to reveal the green over an enormous mound that curves all the way over and down to the green. Then the 3rd is Index 2 and the 4th is Index 1. Good luck.

POINTS								
CD	A	G/F	B/W	L	F	V	G Ex	Total
14	8	8	7	6	8	10	16	77

THE COURSE

- Par 71
- Length: 5,984 m
- Mountrath Golf Club, Knockanina, Mountrath, Co. Laois
- Tel: +353 (0) 57 873 2558
- www.mountrathgolfclub.ie
- Green Fees: €25

COURSES NEARBY
Abbeyleix
Portlaoise
Rathdowney
Roscrea

MOUNT TEMPLE   Established 1991

A COUNTRY GOLF ADVENTURE – BUT NO MORE

Look, I don't get satisfaction out of criticising a course, but this golf club gets a bit carried away: 'Mount Temple Golf & Country Club with Golf Academy' and 'traditional Irish Championship course' sound very grand and elegant, but it doesn't live up to the hype. If it promoted itself as a good, fun, country course for players of all abilities, that would be accurate, because Mount Temple is built from farmland. It lacks any great design flair or structure and eight holes run straight back and forth, albeit on very different levels.

There are good points, of course: some old lichen-smothered walls appear sporadically to give a dash of colour; water/marsh appears on a few holes; two ring forts add a historical flourish (the 6th/7th and 17th); the land has some interesting movement (the 7th, 11th and the closing stretch); and woods are scattered about. The final four holes really raise the temperature with tough tee shots and very difficult approaches to the 16th (uphill) and 18th (out of sight), and these are the best holes by a country mile.

Greens sit flat on the land and are cut from the fairway. They are hard to hold with some severe slopes and shapes. Bunkers are just holes in the ground. Oh, and beware the model bunny rabbits on the tee boxes.

Clearly there is a loyal contingent of golfers, and it is perfect for societies, but you won't come here for a quality golf experience – try Athlone, Glasson or New Forest.

FAVOURITE HOLE
Par 3 17th. 143 m. On the top of the course (housing development on the course to your left), this hits up to a green sitting well above heavy rough and in the trees.

TOUGHEST HOLE
Par 4 10th. 397 m. The only serious dog-leg hits from under the clubhouse and up between a line of trees before it breaks left for the green. A nest of bunkers waits short of the green which is steeply sloped. Beware players teeing off the 8th to your right.

POINTS								
CD	A	G/F	B/W	L	F	V	G Ex	Total
11	6	6	5	7	6	5	11	57

THE COURSE
- Par 72
- Length: 5,927 m (medal)
- Mount Temple Golf Club, Mount Temple Village, Moate, Co. Westmeath
- Tel: +353 (0) 90 648 1841
- www.mounttemplegolfclub.com
- Green Fees: €20–€25

COURSES NEARBY
Athlone
Glasson
Moate
New Forest

MOUNT WOLSELEY   Established 1996

IMPRESSIVE BUT OVERCOOKED

The positive things I had heard about Mount Wolseley had me salivating: 'long', 'tough', 'gorgeous', 'beautifully maintained', 'a real test'. And the buzz continues on arrival, too, with the drive up to the colourful hotel running alongside the impressive dog-leg 18th. Once you start this muscle-bound championship course, you will encounter endless elaborate hillocks – many stuffed with bunkers – water aching to catch your ball, and tough inaccessible greens. There are dog-legs of some degree on almost every hole. Even with big greens and generous fairways, this is a long and tough challenge, so high handicappers beware.

With its multitude of hillocks and thick clumps of young trees – never mind the holiday homes scattered about – the front nine have been overdone. That is not to say they aren't good but, by adding too much, something has been taken away. Charm, namely. (Compare it with nearby Carlow.) Fortunately Mount Wolseley's back nine are more natural and relaxed, with flowing countryside and an excellent run of holes starting at the 13th.

Golf writers rave about the 11th, but from the everyday tees it is an average par 3 (so slip across and play from the back tees). Mount Wolseley has all the space and drama to be a 'big' course but it tries too hard. Society and high-handicap golfers will find it hard going.

FAVOURITE HOLE
Par 4 13th. 409 yards. A flat and pretty dog-leg that leaves the green accessible from anywhere on the fairway. But the second, over gorse, is a tough shot to a viciously sloping green. The 14th, across a valley, is a close second.

TOUGHEST HOLE
Par 4 3rd. 435 yards. The ball will be below your feet for your long second, making the water to the right of the green all the more menacing. The green is heavily tiered.

POINTS

CD	A	G/F	B/W	L	F	V	G Ex	Total
14	7	9	9	6	8	7	15	75

THE COURSE

- Par 72
- Length: 6,763 yards
- Mount Wolseley Golf Club, Tullow, Co. Carlow
- Tel: +353 (0) 59 915 1674
- www.mountwolseley.ie
- Green Fees: €40–€50

COURSES NEARBY
Bunclody
Carlow
Coollattin
Killerig Castle

MOYOLA PARK   Established 1977

GLAMOUR ON THE ESTATE

Like any great course, Moyola Park hits you right between the eyes. The 1st introduces you to the enormous trees that lace this parkland estate into a wonderful roller coaster of character, beauty and excitement. Massive beeches seem to be everywhere, accompanied by oaks and pines, yet despite the trees and deep woods, there always seems to be plenty of room to play. It makes it a thrilling and rewarding experience for everyone. And I haven't even mentioned the dark Moyola River that divides the course and creates the two best holes (see below). The flow of the land is perfect and several tee boxes and greens are perched tantalisingly at the top of slopes. The backdrop to greens – on later holes especially – is dense trees that capture the imagination and the flight of the ball. And some lengthy walks through pretty woods build the anticipation – some people complain they are too long, but it is more idyllic than taxing. You have to admit, it's some setting.

Despite all the trees and a couple of wicked dog-legs (the right-angled 15th is a love/hate hole) the course is not too difficult. Only the 8th, 10th, 14th and 15th present any trouble. Unfortunately, the 6th and 7th sit rather lamely over the road and lack the same spirit, while the driveway slices the 5th in half and is very dangerous. Solve these problems, add some finesse, and Moyola Park might be able to play with the big boys. Then again, the 'rough-around-the-edges' feel adds to the occasion.

Quirky clubhouse too.

FAVOURITE HOLE

Par 3 17th. 128 yards. An absolute peach. Very short but a downhill shot that does everything right: the tee box, the trees towering all around, the shrubs tumbling down to a dipping green and the river running behind. Superb.

TOUGHEST HOLE

Par 4 8th. 421 yards. Index 1 and thrilling. It's not hugely enticing off the tee, but you need to be in a good spot to open up the green that sits in a channel of big beeches and over the wide river. A seriously daunting approach and a beautiful walk over the bridge.

POINTS								
CD	A	G/F	B/W	L	F	V	G Ex	Total
16	8	7	8	6	9	10	18	82

THE COURSE

- Par 71
- Length: 6,299 yards (yellow tees)
- Moyola Park Golf Club, 15 Curran Road, Castledawson, Co. Tyrone, BT45 8DG
- Tel: +44 (0) 28 7946 8468 (048 from Rep. of Ire.)
- www.moyolapark.com
- Green Fees: £24–£30

COURSES NEARBY
Dungannon
Gracehill
Killymoon
Loughall

MOYVALLEY   Established 2006

PERFECT RHYTHM

There is a sensuous rhythm to Moyvalley. The roll of the open landscape is matched by the roll of the fairways, greens and bunkers. This is a wonderful creation by Darren Clarke and the quality of the venue is just what you would expect: exceptional. The greens were pristine in February when I visited. Not only do they look the part on approach shots but they play so sweetly you may not want to move to the next tee. Trees are rare (the 1st, 10th and 12th only) and it is wide open and barren. You may not like this, but I found it captivating. The rough grasses – a sandy gold – define the holes and all that you see. It is a striking contrast to the rich green fairways, and the patches of gorse that have been planted will light up the course in spring.

Moyvalley is the full package with the classy finesse associated with these big, new developments. A long driveway brings you through Balyna Estate and past the large hotel. There are comparisons with Montgomerie's creation at Carton House, but Moyvalley is far easier – perhaps too easy. The bunkers are less harsh and fairways wider. As a result you

will relish the tee shots presented to you and every shot thereafter.

The water features are mostly for appearance, although they are significant hazards on the 9th, 16th and 18th. Only the 16th and 18th pose a serious threat and these are the best holes as a result. Moyvalley is about beautiful, relaxed, almost elegant golf. If you want a comfortable, easy-paced round you'll love this.

The blue tees add another 700 yards to an already long course.

FAVOURITE HOLE

Par 4 16th. 407 yards. Index 1. Water lies ahead to the left, below the tee. It is the toughest drive (but not that tough), which then sets up a glorious approach. Fire over the water, all the way to the green, or sneak in from the right if you've driven far enough.

TOUGHEST HOLE

Par 5 18th. 567 yards. A challenging enough drive, but your second is far harder as you have to decide how to avoid the water that runs along your left all the way to the green. The green is well protected so your third shot is no easier.

POINTS

CD	A	G/F	B/W	L	F	V	G Ex	Total
16	9	10	9	5	10	10	18	87

THE COURSE

- Par 72
- Length: 6,645 yards
- The Champions Club, Moyvalley, Balyna Estate, Moyvalley, Co. Kildare
- Tel: +353 (0) 46 954 8080
- www.moyvalley.com
- Green Fees: €25–€35

COURSES NEARBY
County Meath
Kilcock
Knockanally
Rathcore

MULLINGAR   Established 1894

A ROLLER COASTER OF A CLASSIC

Mullingar is blessed on two fronts: it is known for its friendliness and it has some cracking parkland holes. The reason I love older courses is that they don't over-egg the pudding in terms of design: simplicity wins the day. Stand in the smartly refurbished clubhouse, from where you can see several holes, and you'll see what I mean. Yes, the course might have been surpassed by the swathe of new courses and their fancy designs, but Mullingar has a charm and maturity that newer courses lack. Then again, Mullingar did take a step forward with the addition of dramatic and punishing new green complexes.

Many of Ireland's great golfers have honed their game here (the Scratch Cup is a significant event), yet little is made of this pedigree. Mullingar doesn't seem to believe in boasting about its reputation, which makes the course even more endearing.

The front nine are strong – particularly the two excellent par 3s (the 2nd and 5th) and the rolling par 5 4th that curves over the hill – but the homeward run is superior, with nine colourful, well laid out holes that weave around lovely wooded countryside. The big trees give holes so much distinction it will be hard for you to pick out a favourite. The course is 6,412 yards and doesn't give up many scoring opportunities. Anything over 30 points is good when you consider the curves and twists. This is tactical golf, where bunkers are well placed and the tricky greens are often perched above you, making club selection difficult.

What makes Mullingar is its attractive setting and a brilliant flow of holes. The par 3s are some of the best around and only the 18th lets it down.

FAVOURITE HOLE

Par 4 11th. 389 yards. The prettiest hole with a scattered and tree-lined fairway and a rise in the middle. The green is tucked in the corner of the course and offers a real birdie chance.

TOUGHEST HOLE

Par 3 2nd. 197 yards. Mullingar's most famous hole, this one-shotter has to be played with every ounce of confidence because anything off target will result in a bogey – at best. A perfect surrounding of trees and a green that sits up and tantalises.

POINTS								
CD	A	G/F	B/W	L	F	V	G Ex	Total
16	9	9	8	5	9	9	18	83

THE COURSE

- Par 72
- Length: 6,412 yards
- Mullingar Golf Club, Belvedere, Mullingar, Co. Westmeath
- Tel: +353 (0) 44 934 8366
- www.mullingargolfclub.com
- Green Fees: €40–€45

COURSES NEARBY
Ballinlough Castle
Castle Barna
Delvin Castle
New Forest

MUSKERRY   Established 1897

THE REASON FOR THIS BOOK

I set out on this journey to find the unsung courses of Ireland: the ones that sparkle and enthral; the ones that every golfer would want to play. You simply don't realise how many there are, and Muskerry, with its twenty-three holes, is one.

Before I start, here is a short safety announcement: it has two serious climbs and the defibrillator in reception is not for show. Look left from the 5th fairway and you'll see the heights you have to scale. Holes 7 to 10 are so solitary on the heavily wooded hillside it's as if there is no one else on the course. The 9th is particularly steep. The 14th and 15th (132 m) are steeply downhill and offer soaring tee shots and sweet relief.

Everything has shape and intrigue, and gorse and big woods give it a real wildness in places. Even the last three holes on the flat have a special character with the River Shournagh running in front of the 17th and 18th greens. You might think that means an easy finish but it's not. This is parkland blended with woodland.

The least exciting holes are at the start.

They introduce you to the width of the fairways, show you that there's room to move around, and prepare you for the bunkering and the laser-sharp greens. They also give you a taste for the slopes to come: the 5th drops down steeply to a rising fairway and the par 3 6th hits over a valley and the river to a precariously perched green.

I am docking points for the criss-crossing – the 18th is crossed twice by the 6th and 15th – and a couple of dangerous tee boxes.

FAVOURITE HOLE
Par 4 11th. 344 m. You drive over the corner of OB towards the countryside. It is a gentle downhill shot. You're then left with a very steep hill down to the green that sits a trolley-width from the aforementioned OB.

TOUGHEST HOLE
Par 4 13th. 351 m. You will probably be tired by now. Take heart, it's the last climb. Uphill all the way to an unseen surface. Energy-sapping as opposed to tough.

POINTS								
CD	A	G/F	B/W	L	F	V	G Ex	Total
16	8	8	9	6	9	9	17	82

THE COURSE
- Par 70
- Length: 5,506 m (white tees, yellow course)
- Muskerry Golf Club, Carrigrohane, Co. Cork
- Tel: +353 (0) 21 438 5297
- www.muskerrygolfclub.ie
- Green Fees: €30–€35

COURSES NEARBY
Blarney
Cork
Fota Island
Lee Valley
Mahon

NAAS   Established 1896

PERFECT DRIVING

It is not often you get so many great driving holes in one round. Dynamic changes in elevation will do that, although the flatter section has good driving holes too. Naas is another course that has slipped under the radar. It is in excellent condition and the new, tamer nine (the 2nd to the 10th) have settled in very well. True, the par 3s, 8th and 10th, feel squeezed in and drainage lines across some fairways remain, but the holes still work effortlessly. The mature trees scattered about help things along nicely and you'll have plenty of space to play. It all puts a smile on your face. The run home from the 11th is excellent.

Naas should be treated with respect and the flashes of finesse emphasise this, with pretty shrub beds, strong tee boxes and other little extras. Water appears only twice (the 11th and 16th) and it is both charming and challenging. Approaches to long, lilting greens are inviting and not too difficult, so you reap the rewards for good driving – and if you drive well you will reduce the threat from the trees which give you a surprising amount of room.

The course is not that long for a par 71 and there are plenty of ways to score. But be close to the pin because you won't 2-putt very often from 30 feet.

I found Naas even more enthralling than Beech Park because it has that extra shape that shows the holes off more glamorously. Stand on the tee at the 1st, 2nd, 6th, 9th, 12th, 13th (see photo), 15th and 18th and tell me you don't want to get stuck in.

FAVOURITE HOLE
Par 4 12th. 359 yards. Gently dog-legging uphill, the green sits tucked into an amphitheatre under the clubhouse. The 9th is not dissimilar, while the 13th looks picture-perfect from the high tee box. The best par 3 is the 17th, with a dangerous pond.

TOUGHEST HOLE
Par 4 1st. 417 yards. A dog-leg is a tough start. Not only do you have to figure out how much you can take on (a big tree on the right causes problems), but you may well be blind for your second over the crest.

POINTS

CD	A	G/F	B/W	L	F	V	G Ex	Total
16	8	8	8	5	8	10	18	81

THE COURSE
- Par 71
- Length: 6,173 yards (blue tees)
- Naas Golf Club, Kerdiffstown, Naas, Co. Kildare
- Tel: +353 (0) 45 874 644
- www.naasgolfclub.com
- Green Fees: €35–€40

COURSES NEARBY
Bodenstown
Craddockstown
Killeen
Palmerstown

NARIN & PORTNOO   Established 1930

WALK THIS WAY

Fractionally shorter than nearby Donegal, this par 73 will feel longer. Three consecutive par 5s will destroy a mortal human on a windy day and some of the fairways sway so much it's like being at sea. It is a links course to be reckoned with, especially from the 4th on. The quiet, flat start will fool many, but stand on the 2nd tee and look high into the far dunes on your left. Yes, that is a flag you see and it will send a tingle down your spine. It belongs to the 14th.

The holes caught up in the big dunes (the 5th to 11th and the 14th to 16th) are of a quality you cannot appreciate until you play them. The 7th to 11th may be the best run of holes in Ireland, dancing around the dunes and along the water's edge – it starts and finishes with tremendous par 3s. The 7th hits from dune top to dune top. Holes 2, 3, 4, 12 and 13 are dull by comparison and, to be blunt, let the course down.

It is too difficult for high handicappers. Drives need good carries, considerable thought and accuracy, and heavy danger surrounds greens. Frustrations may rise, so just enjoy the incredible sea and mountain views instead.

The 8th and 9th mark this course for greatness, while the two new par 5s – the 14th and 15th – are superb: the 14th rocks its way between lines of dunes while the 15th, above the beach, is mouth-watering.

Despite its remoteness, there is vision here, including a new clubhouse. Drive down to the beach and through the mobile-home park to reach the club.

FAVOURITE HOLE
Par 4 8th. 301 m. A downhill hole from the highest tee box (and best all-round views) on the course. The hole tumbles down to a green right on the water, with the 9th tee box sitting on the rocks just beyond.

TOUGHEST HOLE
Par 5 10th. 475 m. As with several holes here, placing the drive in the right spot makes all the difference. A chaotic fairway sweeps to the right, down into a hollow in the dunes, that makes the approach to a sloping green very hard to judge.

POINTS								
CD	A	G/F	B/W	L	F	V	G Ex	Total
17	10	10	8	10	8	10	19	92

THE COURSE
- Par 73
- Length: 6,016 m
- Narin & Portnoo Golf Club, Narin, Portnoo, Co. Donegal
- Tel: +353 (0) 74 954 5107
- www.narinportnoogolfclub.ie
- Green Fees: €30–€60

COURSES NEARBY
Donegal

NAVAN   Established 1997

A RACETRACK PARKLAND

Navan has two great things to offer that you don't get at many parkland courses: a racetrack that holds nine holes (the 2nd to the 10th) and lots of wind. It is situated on top of a hill where the wind apparently never stops, which means your opening downhill drive will be hitting straight into the wind. When you look at the indices you'll figure out where the prevailing winds come from. And all of the holes, bar the 7th and 14th, hit either directly into it or away from it, with the 7th the only dog-leg.

The racetrack holes are very open and well spaced out. Small clumps of trees and shrubs are scattered about giving it a huge garden feel. If you lose a ball here then you're doing something very wrong – shots into the large pond between the 3rd and 6th excluded. And if you think that the inside of a racetrack is flat, you'd be wrong there, too. Great contours and a dip across the middle give fairways some really good shape.

It is a lot of fun and the only difficulties come from the wind and the big, sharply contoured greens. It's also long enough to keep golfers of all levels happy.

Holes 11 to 17 are quite different. Three tame holes go up and down a gentle hill, while the 12th to 15th are the most colourful. The 13th is the only testing drive of the day.

Greens are excellent. They sit up nicely for attacking approach shots and it all adds up to an entertaining day.

FAVOURITE HOLE
Par 3 14th. 155 m. You'll probably have a cross wind on Navan's prettiest hole. There is a pond on your right (swans included), a tree in the middle of the fairway and a tempting green. The 15th is just as good but far harder.

TOUGHEST HOLE
Par 4 1st. 378 m. Index 3. In terms of getting your par, this is a nightmare hole to start. Downhill, but into the prevailing wind, your approach will be impossible to judge so early on.

POINTS

CD	A	G/F	B/W	L	F	V	G Ex	Total
13	7	7	8	7	9	9	15	75

THE COURSE
- Par 72
- Length: 6,056 m
- Navan Golf Club, Proudstown Park, Navan, Co. Meath
- Tel: +353 (0) 46 907 2888
- www.navangolfclub.ie
- Green Fees: €20–€25

COURSES NEARBY
Headfort
Killeen Castle
Knightsbrook
Moor Park
Royal Tara

NENAGH   Established 1929

WORKING ALL OVER

Nenagh works on a number of levels. It is out in the country, up high and creative. Therefore it is peaceful, has pleasant views and offers many tempting shots. The clubhouse follows in the same vein: nothing too fancy and a little rough around the edges . . . and that's meant in a good way. I love this kind of golf course. It doesn't take itself too seriously, but it has smart design, plenty of thrills, and plenty of opportunities to score or make a fool of yourself.

The course is an easy roller that tilts you up and down, on fairways and greens as you play between the trees. Excellent fairway bunkers prove very distracting as you try to calculate where to position your ball on the many gentle dog-legs. Usually the sand is in the exact spot you want to be, and from the many high tee boxes it taunts you all the more.

Nenagh is spread over a landscape that has variety and space. Holes take different forms as a result, so every hole comes as a surprise. Perhaps only the 4th and 18th are similar: curving, uphill dog-legs between evergreens that take you back to the clubhouse. The 14th is a perfect par 4

wedged into the side of the hill, while the drive off the 15th is perfect and lethal (see below).

Nenagh doesn't follow a rhythm and that works to its advantage. You'll certainly need an accurate driver – I lost two balls in the dense rough and my partner, Tom, caused consternation in neighbouring counties with some huge, wild drives.

The showers are so strong, they'll leave a mark.

FAVOURITE HOLE

Par 5 12th. 439 m. A downhill drive that tempts you to bite off more than you can chew, as it dog-legs left and up to the green. Anything too far left is gone. The par 3s, the 6th and 8th, also deserve a mention.

TOUGHEST HOLE

Par 4 14th. 316 m. The high tee box (good views behind) hits down over rough to a fairway scattered with trees and bunkers. For a newcomer this is impossible to judge, and the approach to the green is well bunkered.

POINTS								
CD	A	G/F	B/W	L	F	V	G Ex	Total
15	7	8	9	7	8	9	15	78

THE COURSE

- Par 71
- Length: 5,691 m
- Nenagh Golf Club, Beechwood, Nenagh, Co. Tipperary
- Tel: +353 (0) 67 31476
- www.nenaghgolfclub.com
- Green Fees: €30

COURSES NEARBY
Birr
Portumna
Roscrea

Hole 15
Westport Golf Club
Par 5, 498 yards, Index 9
The imposing Croagh Patrick looks down or the golf course as you drive over Westport Bay and then play around the water. (© *Golf Image*)

Hole 16 'Shipwreck'
Tralee Golf Club
Par 3, 179 yards, Index 9
There is drama a-plenty at Tralee, but the 16th combines a thrilling, short, dune-side hole with views and golden beaches. (Courtesy Tralee Golf Club)

Hole 17
The European Club
Par 4, 389 yards, Index 4
Pure elegance. A straight links hole that drifts down between lines of dunes. (© Gerard Ruddy)

Hole 18 'Log 'a Fola'
Carne Golf Club
Par 5, 486 m, Index 7
The deep hollow that awaits your second shot makes this a tough and dramatic 18th. (Courtesy Carne Golf Club)

NEWBRIDGE   Established 1997

SIMPLE, PRETTY AND FUN

Newbridge is an interesting and young little course. If I said it was exciting, you'd arrive on the 1st and think I was crazy. Yes, it does look very flat and uninteresting from here, but it hides a few absolute beauties. Holes 2 to 5, 8, 14 and 15 are wonderful. They use the ponds (and wildlife) and mature trees to create real interest on all shots. And the ponds are glorious affairs – the approach to the 2nd is captivating with large beeches marshalling you over the pond.

The planting of 40,000 trees has enhanced the experience everywhere as you find yourself walking through young woods of birch, beech, conifers and others.

On such a flat landscape it was aways going to be difficult to maintain momentum and the holes fall into two categories: the very good and the rather dull. That said, you won't find that all-too-common fallback of typical golf designers – endless mounding. And perhaps that is one of the other advantages of Newbridge – it was mostly designed by the owner and his son (Eddie and Jamie), so you'll find a nice few quirks along the way. And the greens are really excellent, with great shapes and good backdrops.

It's not a difficult or particularly long course, but on the good holes a little care is required, and the line of mature beech trees that crosses the opening holes can cause problems (the 2nd and 5th particularly). You walk under a railway bridge to reach the final six holes – a quirk in itself, as you'll discover.

This is an accessible course that will attract many with its low green fees. New clubhouse added in 2009.

FAVOURITE HOLE
Par 4 2nd. 300 yards. So unexpected after the 1st, the 2nd curls between tall trees and over a pond. There is more water to the right and it is a very pretty setting. No more than a 3 iron off the tee, and aim right. The 14th is a beauty too.

TOUGHEST HOLE
Par 4 10th. 455 yards. It's all about length. The hole curves gently left but club golfers will find it a long way with bunkers to contend with.

POINTS								
CD	A	G/F	B/W	L	F	V	G Ex	Total
13	7	7	8	5	7	8	14	69

THE COURSE
- Par 72
- Length: 6,214 yards
- Newbridge Golf Club, Barretstown, Newbridge, Co. Kildare
- Tel: +353 (0) 45 486 110
- www.newbridgegolfclub.com
- Green Fees: €25–€30

COURSES NEARBY
Curragh, The
Dunmurry Springs
Naas
Woodlands

NEWCASTLE WEST Established 1938

GENTLE PARKLAND GOLF

Newcastle West is a young course (it moved location recently) with an old stone clubhouse surrounded by mature trees. It is a very attractive spot that sits above the course. Holes 8, 9 and 10 use it to the best advantage. Farther away the holes feel newer, although mature trees still appear frequently. This is flowing countryside that rolls around you and you will find good changes in elevation without ever having to climb – the par 3s all offer shots from a height, while the 8th and 9th wind sideways across the hillside.

It is not a difficult course. The generous fairways are rarely hidden and Index 1 is only 372 yards – an uphill dog-leg that requires you stay well right of the line of mature trees. The longest par 4 is 414 yards, and the longest par 5 is just 496 yards.

The water features should only threaten on a few holes: the par 3s – the 3rd and 6th – your drive on the 5th and the dangerous par 4 11th. But bunkers are surprisingly snappy, and around the green you will find some unexpectedly tall faces to conquer.

Newcastle West offers a relaxing round of golf, with some nice touches. It is not challenging enough or dramatic enough for very low handicappers but, other than that, it rarely puts a foot wrong. Even when tee boxes seem to drive over greens, it's the green you've just come off, so there's no danger. The 12th and 17th stand out.

Not that easy to find.

FAVOURITE HOLE
Par 4 12th. 346 yards. You're on the flat, the green clearly visible, with two trees acting as sentries 80 yards from the tee. Because of their position, you have to aim at the mature wood on the right, which runs to the green.

TOUGHEST HOLE
Par 4 11th. 381 yards. A downhill hole with water on the front left of the green. Big hitters have to worry that they'll find it off the tee; everyone else will worry about their approach – you can bail out and go right.

POINTS								
CD	A	G/F	B/W	L	F	V	G Ex	Total
13	7	7	8	6	9	7	14	71

THE COURSE
- Par 71
- Length: 6,141 yards
- Newcastle West Golf Club, Rathgonan, Ardagh, Co. Limerick
- Tel: +353 (0) 69 76500
- www.newcastlewestgolf.com
- Green Fees: €25–€35

COURSES NEARBY
Adare
Adare Manor
Charleville
Limerick

NEW FOREST   Established 2006

SWEEPS THROUGH THE ESTATE

A new, plush and beautifully manicured golf course that winds its spacious way around an elegant eighteenth-century manor (club)house. While similar to Moyvalley, New Forest has more drama and more adventure than its 'sister' course. It doesn't have the sensuous rhythm or flashing gold grasses of Moyvalley, but it has creative mounding that steers fairways into explosively bunkered greens in what is, essentially, a natural setting.

The course is well routed along the dense perimeter, over ponds, streams and bridges, around marshland and even through a walled garden (par 3 9th). The perfect greens sit in nests of bunkers and fall-offs, and the bunkered fairways move in such a way that they are deceptive. When you discover that Index 17 is a 207-yard par 3, you will appreciate that there are no easy holes. You don't see many flags either. And if you know what's good for you, play the par 4 4th as a 5: a deep ditch sits under a narrow green and laying up is the best option. Holes 14 to 16 are separate and are more open. They

come after the most beautiful approach of the day to the 13th green which sits in a dell of giant beeches, fronted by a dark pond.

I suspect that it will be a little over-manicured for some and, in places, it feels a bit aloof and loses its rhythm. But this is the new breed of tough, modern course and it has a perfect setting. And the apple crumble is sensational.

FAVOURITE HOLE
Par 4 12th. 421 yards. Index 1, and probably the most natural hole on the course. It's flat and long and has two streams, one running diagonally across your landing area which is perfectly blocked by a tree. The 17th has a superb finish.

TOUGHEST HOLE
Par 4 7th. 407 yards. Only Index 10, but a horrible drive over the marsh that swings into an alley of bunkers, and not much fairway to be seen. Get the drive wrong and it could be in serious trouble. A difficult hole to play well.

POINTS

CD	A	G/F	B/W	L	F	V	G Ex	Total
17	8	10	9	6	10	10	17	87

THE COURSE
- Par 72
- Length: 6,571 yards
- New Forest Golf Club, Higginstown, Tyrrellspass, Co. Westmeath
- Tel: +353 (0) 44 922 1100
- www.newforest.ie
- Green Fees: €20–€45

COURSES NEARBY
Castle Barna
Esker Hills
Moate
Mullingar
Tullamore

NEWLANDS   Established 1926

SUPERB CLUBHOUSE

Newlands falls into two categories – flat holes and gentle hillside holes. Not surprisingly it is the latter that are more interesting on this suburban parkland course. The corner that hosts the 3rd, 4th, 5th, 10th and 11th is the best section by far, with dense, mature trees, good shape to the land and an old wall that runs along the perimeter. That, though, is about it.

As it is located on the edge of Dublin city, you don't get any views – even from the towering drive down the 13th that hits towards the city. And the course ignites only rarely as most holes simply slip up and down between lines of trees. Most of what you need to know is laid out in front of you and greens are accessible. Trees can get close but you'll find more room than you would expect. It is straightforward and not overly tough. In fairness, Newlands have added some fine touches: the lovely raised tee boxes amongst colourful shrubs are an appealing distraction. But more fire is needed, tee to green. The bunkers feel a bit slapdash, forming the main danger on many holes.

The best stretches are the 3rd to 5th and the 9th to 13th, all focusing on the aforementioned top part of the course. This is when it gets interesting: huge beeches wreak havoc over the greens on the 5th and 8th, and several oaks and beeches squeeze fairways and hang over tee boxes. Elsewhere the many different varieties of trees are scattered about and promise plenty of colour.

From the 18th green you have to cross the 10th fairway to reach the big, flash clubhouse.

FAVOURITE HOLE
Par 3 9th. 169 m. A good one-shotter, with a lovely tee box and a green that is sharply raised in front of a thicket of heavy trees. Index 5 shows how difficult it is. The 5th and 13th are lovely downhill drives.

TOUGHEST HOLE
Par 4 7th. 354 m. Nothing like as long as indices 1 and 2 (holes 5 and 17), but this hole sweeps right and judging your distance is very hard off the tee. It is not a big drive, but you then have a putting surface that hides out of sight. Aim for the lone gorse bush.

POINTS

CD	A	G/F	B/W	L	F	V	G Ex	Total
13	7	6	7	4	9	6	13	65

THE COURSE
- Par 71
- Length: 5,683 m
- Newlands Golf Club, Newlands Cross, Dublin 22
- Tel: +353 (0) 1 459 3157
- www.newlandsgolfclub.com
- Green Fees: €30–€50

COURSES NEARBY
Beech Park
Citywest
Grange Castle
Lucan

NEW ROSS   Established 1905

COUNTRY CANTER

There simply aren't enough courses to choose from in these parts, so New Ross has it easy. As parkland courses go, this has enough quirks, oddities and fun to make it an enjoyable round of golf. And the attractive views of the Blackstairs Mountains (and others round about) make it a captivating day out. New Ross sits on a hilltop and several holes promise beautiful tee or approach shots. The 11th and 16th are outstanding.

The course is too short to be called challenging and you'll lap it up in short order. The back nine are stronger, more dramatic and more entertaining. Being on the side of a gentle hill and festooned with evergreens and mature pines (replete with rookeries) makes all the difference. You'll also find better golf holes, and by that I mean that the flatter front nine have a couple of inferior holes and three rather daft holes: on the 6th and 8th you might be tempted to hit at the wrong green, and you won't know where huge bunkers lie in wait for you, even if you can figure out where to cut the dog-leg. And the par 5 10th leaves you completely

bemused for your second – aim at the bunker.

In short, there's no stunning design (the 11th, 12th and 15th are the best) and no great difficulty (the 4th and 18th are the only long holes), but there is a lot more fun than you would expect and little things like trees sitting on mounds add character to holes. The views are tossed in for free.

FAVOURITE HOLE
Par 3 11th. 173 m. A sensational backdrop to a green that sits far below you. Watching your tee shot soar is the moment of the day. The green is perched on the slope with bunkers snug to the left hand side so it's not easy.

TOUGHEST HOLE
Par 4 15th. 343 m. Demands the most accurate drive as the trees squeeze you and offer little room for error. It is a good approach with the flat green under evergreens, but judging the distance is made tougher by the bunkers across the front.

POINTS								
CD	A	G/F	B/W	L	F	V	G Ex	Total
13	7	6	7	8	7	7	13	68

THE COURSE
- Par 70
- Length: 5,568 m
- New Ross Golf Club, Tinneranny, New Ross, Co. Wexford
- Tel: +353 (0) 51 421 433
- www.newrossgolfclub.ie
- Green Fees: €20–€30

COURSES NEARBY
Faithlegg
Mountain View
Scarke
Waterford

NEWTOWNSTEWART   Established 1914

LET IT ROLL

If you like roller-coaster golf then this quiet country course is for you. It's never hilly, but you do have dips and hillocks that create blind holes. In fact, the only climbs are from greens to tees: the 10th, 13th and 14th spring to mind. Usually I am not a fan of blind drives, but there is so much going on here that it doesn't matter. The course is divided by an achingly pretty woodland stream that you cross high above, creating two distinct sets of holes. The wonderful curves of the land never let up and neither do trees that squeeze your drives. But the outer nine (the 9th to 17th) are younger and more open. Lots of trees still, but you will find room off the tee. On the other hand you're likely to find more sloping lies for second shots. The inner holes are excellent woodland holes. That feeling is cemented on the 1st tee, which sits underneath two enormous beech trees. If you're lucky, you'll see a pair of red squirrels scampering about.

Of the thirteen long holes (there are five par 3s – the 7th and 13th are superb), nine of them have to show you the way with direction stakes. It is a course for everybody, even if it is quite short. Big hitters will need to be smart as the curves go left and right as well as up and down. Several greens are tucked just out of sight or have shoulders hiding them. So, as well as intriguing and pretty, it's challenging. And cheap.

FAVOURITE HOLE
Par 3 13th. 175 m. Long and downhill from a raised tee box. Beautiful woodland views stretch into the distance. A gorse-covered shoulder juts in from the right, halfway down the hill, hiding some of the green, and a bunker sits left.

TOUGHEST HOLE
Par 3 7th. 190 m. A long hole. It is flat and trees drift inwards in a pincer movement, squeezing the green, with one particularly nosey beech.

POINTS								
CD	A	G/F	B/W	L	F	V	G Ex	Total
15	8	7	6	8	8	10	16	78

THE COURSE

- Par 70
- Length: 5,320 m
- Newtownstewart Golf Club, 38 Golf Course Road, Newtownstewart, Co. Tyrone, BT78 4HU
- Tel: +44 (0) 28 8166 1466 (048 from Rep. of Ire.)
- www.newtownstewart golfclub.com
- Green Fees: £17–£25

COURSES NEARBY
Ballybofey & Stranorlar
Omagh
Strabane

NORTH WEST   Established 1891

THE SUBTLE ART OF LINKS GOLF

Usually I don't dwell on a course's age but at North West, coastal erosion has stolen 100 to 150 yards of coastline over a century. The rock barrier that now braces against the onslaught came too late. With a busy road on the other side, North West had to deal with an ever smaller space. Inevitably some holes are close together and some cross. On a windy links course that spells trouble.

But you don't see many links courses like this any more. It is the subtlety that is true to golf's roots, not the muscularity now in vogue. It may look flat and open but there is far more than meets the eye, with tricky fall-offs, creeks and bunkers that, while not punishing, are well placed. This is particularly true on the few (and best) holes where mounds ripple across fairways.

It is not dramatic (not like nearby Ballyliffin) but it promises lots of fun – assuming you don't slice the ball. On the first eleven holes that hug the shoreline and the road, OB is on your right.

The fairways are smooth and crisp, the greens are fast and sit comfortably on the land. You'll have ample opportunity to master low shots and bump-and-run. Three par 3s are 82 m to 139 m, but they hit into the wind and may well balloon.

It is a beautiful location with the sea and mountains across Lough Swilly. It feels old and there are things that could be updated. But why would you want to?

Limited parking around clubhouse. More is available on the road.

FAVOURITE HOLE

Par 4 11th. 324 m. Back towards the clubhouse. Climb to the main back tee as it sits right on the beach and offers great views. The drive is a daunting one over a stretch of gorse and impossible grass and a creek leaks across the front of the green.

TOUGHEST HOLE

Par 4 12th. 395 m. The land rises slightly showing a fairway but not a line. A good drive will drop away over the slope to leave another blind shot to the green. The fairway buckles ahead of you and it's not an easy green to hit.

| POINTS | | | | | | | | |
CD	A	G/F	B/W	L	F	V	G Ex	Total
14	7	8	7	9	7	9	15	76

THE COURSE

- Par 70
- Length: 5,620 m
- North West Golf Club, Lisfannon, Buncrana, Co. Donegal
- Tel: +353 (0) 74 936 1715
- www.northwestgolfclub.com
- Green Fees: €30–€35

COURSES NEARBY
Ballyliffin
Foyle
Greencastle

NUREMORE   Established 1991

A COUNTRY PLEASURE

With Concra Wood just opened nearby, Nuremore has stiff competition. The course is, or was, the main player in these parts, but it still offers a professional touch and the green fees are well apart. For such a young course, it is maturing comfortably. Young trees are integrating easily with the many mature specimens and it has that spacious, parkland estate feel that takes you all around the clubhouse and hotel. Water appears time and again, and you've got to love a course that has a sign by the entrance declaring 'Slow Please, Ducks Crossing'. This is the pond by the 2nd green and the ducks are vociferous. Lakes appear again at the 5th, 6th, 7th, 9th and, magnificently, at the 10th, where you drive through a tiny gap in the trees, over a lake to a green 289 m away.

A lot of mounding shapes the fairways and holes, but because the landscape curves so sweetly, you won't notice after the opening holes. The 1st tee sits up high and it is a smart way to show you what lies ahead, yet there are far higher points on the other side of the hotel. Back-to-back par 5s (the 14th and 15th sit

noticeably on their own) offer the best views over the countryside, and the tee box on the 18th towers above the clubhouse; combined with the huge drop down the 17th, it's a tremendous finish.

It is challenging, tantalising and full of variety. The eighteen holes feel disjointed at times – not quite a full set – but you won't put a foot wrong coming here.

FAVOURITE HOLE

Par 3 6th. 157 m. The scorecard suggests you to take an extra club: make sure you do. A lovely setting for the tee deep in trees that hits out over a pond, rising sharply to a green set in trees. One-shot wonder. The 10th and 17th are also superb.

TOUGHEST HOLE

Par 4 18th. 385 m. It's Index 2 and calls for a perfect drive from a high tee, over the sloping hillside down onto the fairway. You'll be blind for your second as the fairway rises up by a huge dead tree, before dropping down to the green and four bunkers. A stunning finishing hole.

POINTS								
CD	A	G/F	B/W	L	F	V	G Ex	Total
15	8	8	9	7	9	9	16	81

THE COURSE

- Par 71
- Length: 5,536 m
- Nuremore Golf Club, Carrickmacross, Co. Monaghan
- Tel: +353 (0) 42 966 1438
- www.nuremore.com
- Green Fees: €35–€45

COURSES NEARBY
Ardee
Concra Wood
Mannan Castle
Rossmore

OLD CONNA   Established 1986

LACKS SPARKLE, BUT SOME GOOD HOLES

I could not warm to Old Conna: the practice green and nets are shoddy and the 1st is a dreadfully dull opening hole. It starts you off in the wrong frame of mind. This is what I'd call a 'worker' parkland course, where good holes are interspersed with a few duds and the design lacks punch (holes 1, 5, 13, 15 and 16 spring to mind). There is not enough of a 'wow' factor, despite some big trees.

Located on the side of a mountain, it has sea views and some nice rises and falls, but this only emphasises the course's shortcomings. The best run is the 6th to 12th, where the excitement of golf finally comes to life. The 11th is a strong dog-leg par 4 that hits into a pretty uphill green, and the 12th is a great downhill par 3 surrounded by bunkers.

While the greens are slick and difficult to read, the tee shots are not sufficiently challenging. I am tempted to say that the course is too forgiving, but that's what some golfers want. At least holes 17 and 18 offer a strong par 3/par 5 finish, with the 18th green nicely located amidst trees and beside the attractive wooden clubhouse.

FAVOURITE HOLE
Par 4 7th. 379 yards. A short but serious dog-leg left that is a great-looking hole and a tempting tee shot. Your second is to an elevated green. If you feel brave (or mad), take the more direct approach over tall trees.

TOUGHEST HOLE
Par 4 10th. 340 yards. With this hole's punishing angled fairway, your drive will end up in rough. A large green awaits, but there is serious trouble behind. Locals play short and let the ball run in from the left.

POINTS

CD	A	G/F	B/W	L	F	V	G Ex	Total
13	7	7	6	6	7	6	13	65

THE COURSE

- Par 72
- Length: 6,519 yards
- Old Conna Golf Club, Ferndale Road, Bray, Co. Wicklow
- Tel: 00 353 (0) 1 282 6055
- www.oldconna.com
- Green Fees: €25–€50

COURSES NEARBY
Bray
Dun Laoghaire
Glen of the Downs
Greystones
Powerscourt
Woodbrook

OLD HEAD   Established 1997

DRAMA YOU WON'T BELIEVE

A blistering ball of sun rises from the ocean, sculpting shadows out of cliffs that bear one of the world's most dramatic golfing landscapes. A narrow peninsula takes you to this golfing heaven and, once you find the 2nd tee box, you will be in raptures, standing on the cliff's edge with a churning chasm separating you from a green perched on the edge of oblivion.

OK, enough of my attempts at literary worthiness but you get the idea. Old Head is the most remarkable golf destination. Yet I arrived with knives sharpened, ready to champion the cause of walkers who struggle to gain access, to criticise the manufactured feel of the course and the way it has been over-Americanised; not to mention the huge green fees. But I came to one conclusion: this is the kind of golf experience that can never be repeated. It will leave you speechless!

The argument that the course design is average is nonsense – how can it be when it is so intrinsically sewn into the fabric of the landscape, with sheer drops bordering many holes and greens teetering on the brink? Sure, the inner holes lack the same excitement but fairways still swing sweetly between ancient ruins, rocks and pampas grass. They are a bit of respite as the cliff-side holes demand so much bravery that your adrenaline will be mere vapours by the time you stand under the lighthouse on the 18th.

It is not a true links course and you are over-cossetted from start to finish – it's that 'American experience' with greeters and the Stone of Accord – but it is truly unforgettable.

FAVOURITE HOLE

Par 4 2nd. 376 yards. Your first taste of what inspires this course. A dog-leg left that shows you the green across the cliffs. Not long, but still terrifying. The 4th is a thing of pure beauty.

TOUGHEST HOLE

Par 4 18th. 385 yards. Not dissimilar to holes 2 and 4 (see photo) in shape and tackling vast chasms, but this one rises to a raised green that will throw most approaches into treacherous grass. Two big shots are needed. Venture back to the black tees for a professional's perspective.

POINTS								
CD	A	G/F	B/W	L	F	V	G Ex	Total
18	9	10	10	10	10	7	19	93

THE COURSE

- Par 72
- Length: 6,493 yards (white tees)
- Old Head Golf Links, Kinsale, Co. Cork
- Tel: +353 (0) 21 477 8444
- www.oldhead.com
- Green Fees: €160–€200

COURSES NEARBY
Bandon
Kinsale

OMAGH   Established 1910

TALE OF TWO NINES

There are many courses that could justify this heading, but Omagh is particularly obvious as it is sliced apart by a road. The outer nine (the 2nd to 10th) are flat. OK, the 2nd, 3rd and 5th are not entirely flat, but this is an alluvial plain and the rest of the holes could not be flatter. Three of them run alongside the River Drumragh, the 8th being particularly nerve-wracking as the hole dog-legs around the river's path. These are not particularly interesting or difficult (the 5th excepted) and you'll look forward to crossing the road for better thrills.

The inner, hilly nine are lined with mature trees and offer some great drives to rising fairways and attacking shots to greens below. The 1st hole is a beautiful down-and-up opener and this is repeated on the 11th, 12th and 14th. They're all good holes although the 12th hits dangerously over the 11th green. The two par 3s are tantalising downhill shots and the 18th is a relaxing finish.

Overall, there is not too much trouble so it works beautifully for club golfers and societies. The greens are tame but they are merely subtle with some good slopes and smooth surfaces.

The design and appeal of this quiet course is old school. It gets on with the business in hand, and is perfectly pleasant, unpretentious golf. The changing rooms could do with a revamp.

FAVOURITE HOLE
Par 4 1st. 316 m. A great down-and-up start. It is one of those tantalising views from the tee as the green is on eye level. The challenge is to see how far up that hill you can get.

TOUGHEST HOLE
Par 4 5th. 348 m. Devil's Elbow. Nothing special off the tee, but it needs to be an accurate drive if you are to see the flag up the hill and a long way around the dog-leg. Your second is almost blind and is character-building stuff.

POINTS								
CD	A	G/F	B/W	L	F	V	G Ex	Total
14	6	7	6	7	6	7	14	67

THE COURSE

- Par 71
- Length: 5,365 m
- Omagh Golf Club, 83 Dublin Road, Omagh, Co. Tyrone, BT78 1HQ
- Tel: +44 (0) 28 8224 3160 (048 from Rep. of Ire.)
- www.omaghgolfclub.co.uk
- Green Fees: £20–£25

COURSES NEARBY
Castle Hume/Lough Erne
Dungannon
Newtownstewart
Strabane

OUGHTERARD   Established 1973

HOW IT SHOULD BE DONE

I liked Oughterard so much that I'll start this review with the negatives to get them out of the way: a lot of holes go straight up and down and are slightly too tight together, separated by single lines of trees. You can imagine the risk of stray shots on a busy day. The same applies to some tee boxes. And there are eight holes all around the 370-m length.

Now for the good stuff. Oughterard is a blast, with greens that sit up and beg to be bombed. The braver you are the more you will be rewarded as weak shots will run into bunkers or tumble off fairways. Every green complex is well designed and the quality of the surfaces makes putting a real pleasure. The rest of the hole, tee to green, is basic stuff but, once the green comes into view, there is a sense of anticipation. Five of your first seven drives have to reach the top of the curving landscape that hides the greens, so it's a joy walking over the crest to see what awaits.

Oughterard has done everything right, with nice touches everywhere. There is a course map fitted into a dead trunk by the first tee, the hole information boards are well presented and include a drawing of the hole, and water on the 9th, 10th and 11th adds interest and danger.

The course may be a straightforward design (only one dog-leg) but everything else makes it a pleasure. It takes off at the 4th hole and never really stops. The 7th, 8th and 9th are the best, with the 17th and 18th offering a strong close. There's something for everyone here.

FAVOURITE HOLE

Par 5 8th. 444 m. A walk through woods to reach the tee, and then a drive that hits straight at more trees with an old wall all along the left. The hole dog-legs left, and then almost dog-legs right, with a well-protected green tucked away.

TOUGHEST HOLE

Par 4 4th. 376 m. A great drive between flanking silver birches, but the downhill second presents problems with a fairway tree, a very misleading bunker well short of the green and trouble behind. Cleverly designed.

POINTS

CD	A	G/F	B/W	L	F	V	G Ex	Total
13	7	8	8	6	7	9	16	74

THE COURSE

- Par 70
- Length: 5,876 m
- Oughterard Golf Club, Oughterard, Co. Galway
- Tel: +353 (0) 91 552 131
- www.oughterardgolf.com
- Green Fees: €25–€30

COURSES NEARBY
Bearna
Cregmore Park
Galway
Galway Bay

PALMERSTOWN   Established 2006

PERFECT STORM

Ask someone to describe Palmerstown's main feature and it's a one-word answer: 'water'. Thirteen holes are resplendent with it, and the lakes are wrapped up with reeds and wildlife. You cross several bridges to reach tees or greens and it brings a luxurious dimension to what must be one of Ireland's most immaculate parkland courses. Water threatens drives and approaches alike so expect to get wet.

Located just off the N7, facilities and clubhouse are first rate. Holes flow around the old estate house and most are wonderfully isolated. And level. Gentle undulations give smooth curves that look good to the eye and it is all enhanced by mature trees and meandering mounds that hold bunkers and help steer your shots. It feels big and at times it is like a painting – on the front nine especially.

It's tough too. The water and some enormous bunkers (the par 3 10th is surrounded) are always in your face, and there are some very tricky drives. And pick the right tee box. The back gold tees measure 7,419 yards and sane people will play off bronze. It will depend on your driving abilities. Big hitters may find problems as fairways narrow or run into water in all the wrong places, particularly on the four par 5s (the lowest indices) which are intimidating S-shapes around water.

Horse-filled fields coast alongside you on the less dramatic back nine, showing the course's origins, and emphasising how heavily Palmerstown has invested to create this beauty. The trees and shape of the front nine make them more attractive than the back, but it's all impressive.

FAVOURITE HOLE
Par 4 4th. 396 yards. You drive out of trees onto a generous fairway. The green is fronted with red brick and drops straight into the water, a few feet from the putting surface. To reach it you walk over a bridge and through a small wood.

TOUGHEST HOLES
Par 5s. All four of them. Long and twisting around water that will taunt you no matter how far you hit the ball. Sensible golf required. The 9th has a wall of bunkers rising to the green. It looks frightening until you realise the fairway is to your right.

POINTS								
CD	A	G/F	B/W	L	F	V	G Ex	Total
17	9	9	10	6	10	7	18	86

THE COURSE
- Par 72
- Length: 6,468 yards (bronze tees)
- PGA National Ireland,
  Palmerstown House, Johnstown,
  Co. Kildare
- Tel: +353 (0) 45 906 901
- www.palmerstownhouse.com
- Green Fees: €50–€80

COURSES NEARBY
Castlewarden
Craddockstown
Killeen
Naas

PORTADOWN   Established 1900

SLOW AND COMFORTABLE

You can sum up Portadown easily: it is a classic and straightforward parkland course. The trees have had long enough to grow up and add structure and, while the course is cramped in places, the trees do enough to dispel the feeling.

In terms of design it is relaxing and gentle. It is a pleasing course that doesn't stretch the imagination, and sometimes that is exactly what you want from a round of golf. At par 70, with two par 4s under 270 yards and three par 3s under 150 yards, there are plenty of opportunities to score. The greatest challenge is finding the right spot to place your ball on three of the flat dog-legs (the 7th, 8th and 11th). It is also worth mentioning that gauging distances to the flag on the flattest section of the course (holes 7 to 17) is never easy, with bunkers often placed across your line. The difficulty is compounded by the flatness of the greens. There's no fuss about them and that works very nicely indeed.

The hillier part of the course has a good hump that is used across the middle of several holes: the 1st, 2nd, 3rd, 5th and 18th. Holes 5 and 18 are side by side (don't mistake the 18th for the 5th) and the hump means you will be completely blind for your second.

Portadown is a simplistic type of course that is fun and accessible. The clubhouse setting is entertaining too. The showers are almost too powerful for the relaxing golf you've just played.

FAVOURITE HOLE
Par 5 9th. 472 yards. The best drive, hitting over the River Bann into a gentle dog-leg. You have plenty of room and this should be a birdie opportunity. You can have a real wind at the par 4 255-yard 14th – Index 18, allegedly.

TOUGHEST HOLES
Par 4 11th. 360 yards. It's all about getting your drive into position 'A' on this strong, endlessly curving dog-leg. A bunker blocks the left half of the green. The 5th is a brute: 425 yards, driving into a rise with a blind second.

POINTS

CD	A	G/F	B/W	L	F	V	G Ex	Total
13	7	7	6	6	8	8	14	69

THE COURSE

- Par 70
- Length: 5,786 yards
- Portadown Golf Club, 192 Gilford Rd, Portadown Co. Armagh, BT63 5LF
- Tel: +44 (0) 28 3835 5356 (048 from Rep. of Ire.)
- www.portadowngolfclub.co.uk
- Green Fees: £18–£22

COURSES NEARBY
Banbridge
County Armagh
Lurgan
Tandragee

PORTARLINGTON   Established 1908

'THAT WAS BETTER THAN THE K CLUB'

So said the man standing at the clubhouse bar, who winked at me as I prepared to go out and play. 'Now, do I get my free drink?' he asked the barman. He didn't get his drink, but he certainly raised my expectations.

And he wasn't wrong. I'm not comparing design or finesse or grandeur, but Portarlington is an absolute thrill. I was overwhelmed. It is a level but very shapely course that has gloriously big, vibrant trees defining holes. They cause all kinds of havoc – even if only because you know they're there – nowhere more so than on the 13th and 14th where they almost block your way. On the 7th (Index 1) and 15th, the trees are one long channel, tee to green. For me, that is bliss.

It is not long, and it is not too tough. Yes, if you go off-line the trees will trap you, but apart from the three subtle dog-legs you will always have room, and you can see the flag from the tee box – another big bonus. The 14th is the only serious dog-leg (see below).

It is green and lush and wonderful. Tee boxes sit in and under the trees, greens have some superb backdrops. There aren't any views but your surroundings are simply enchanting. And when the River Barrow appears on the 16th and 17th, that's the icing on the cake.

The only niggles I have are that holes cross (the 10th and 13th drive over the 18th fairway), some tee boxes are a bit close to greens. And two of the par 5s should be par 4s.

FAVOURITE HOLE

Par 4 14th (see photo). 348 m. The only real dog-leg, with a big oak dead centre of the fairway, woods left and right. Three iron left of the tree or go for a big one right of it? A pretty second shot in.

TOUGHEST HOLE

Par 4 7th. 402 m. Index 1. The longest par 4 and the most intimidating drive, straight down between dense woods of beech. Looks beautiful but you must be accurate to tackle the green in two.

POINTS								
CD	A	G/F	B/W	L	F	V	G Ex	Total
15	9	7	8	6	9	10	19	83

THE COURSE

- Par 71
- Length: 5,723 m
- Portarlington Golf Club, Garryhinch, Portarlington, Co. Laois
- Tel: +353 (0) 57 862 3115
- www.portarlingtongolf.com
- Green Fees: €25

COURSES NEARBY
Castle Barna
Dunmurry Springs
Heath, The
Heritage, The

PORTLAOISE Established 2005

PLENTY OF THREES

At least two people told me that Portlaoise was a par 3 course. It is not. It has moved on and is now a par 67. What's more, some of the longer holes are surprisingly attractive. It is too short to be a serious attraction but it does contain one of the hardest par 3s around (see below) and some good, fun shots. On the flip side, there are some bland holes and the quality is decidedly average. I have had the conversation more than once that there are many nine-hole courses that are better than some eighteen-hole courses I've played. Portlaoise proves the point. It will appeal to those shaping their game and looking for a laugh, but it is not challenging enough for the serious golfer.

Its location between a couple of roads doesn't give it huge appeal, but there are ponds, woods on the back nine, and some good rises and falls. These don't start until the 6th – Index 1 – which arrives very unexpectedly, with a green perched up high.

The 6th, 7th, 8th, 11th, 12th and 15th are strongest and play like real parkland holes. Ironically, some of the par 3s let it down.

Three tee boxes double up, which may prove chaotic, and you could easily drive off the par 3 12th, and then drive off the 13th before heading to the 12th green.

Not worth going out of your way for, but it's good for your short game.

FAVOURITE HOLE
Par 4 15th. 299 m. A sharp dog-leg that offers two options: over the trees with a driver (the mad option), or a 4 iron down the middle. It's a steep green (like some others) and the prettiest hole on the course.

TOUGHEST HOLE
Par 3 12th. 151 m. The narrowest tee shot you will face in the county – the country, even. Up high, you hit between a narrow gap of tall pines. No fade, no draw, just dead straight.

POINTS								
CD	A	G/F	B/W	L	F	V	G Ex	Total
11	6	6	5	5	5	7	12	57

THE COURSE
- Par 67
- Length: 4,794 m
- Portlaoise Golf Club, Abbeyleix Road, Portlaoise, Co. Laois
- Tel: +353 (0) 57 866 1557
- www.portlaoisegolfclub.com
- Green Fees: €15–€20

COURSES NEARBY
Abbeyleix
Heath, The
Heritage, The
Mountrath

PORTMARNOCK   Established 1894

THE REPUTATION OF KINGS

Portmarnock comes across as the old, distinguished gentleman: highly regarded, dignified and a bit superior. It has a reputation and history that few can equal but, for me, it lacks drama. Strategic, yes, but thrilling, no. It is a beautifully crafted course that changes direction constantly as it runs through low- and medium-sized dunes. These dunes allow you to see most of the hole and the dangers that await. It is not a common trait of links and perhaps that's why it is less exciting than somewhere like The Island. The gorse and isolated pines are startling but, with so much of the level landscape on show, it still feels muted. Your views are restricted to Dublin city and Howth.

Now don't get me wrong: this is a severe challenge. Strategy and cunning are required to avoid horrible rough or nests of gorse. Driving is the easier part of the day although deep bunkers are perfectly placed and offer only recovery shots. It is coming into greens where you will be tested magnificently. Green complexes dazzle with their arsenal of links defences and you will be foolish to attack greens from anywhere but the fairway, because your short game will need to be brilliant.

The best holes are close to the beach: the 14th is superb, and the famous par 3 15th will ruin many cards – my partner put two balls on the beach (in play at The European, but not here).

Portmarnock remains one of the 'must play' courses for links fanatics, so if you want the kudos of saying you played it, then go ahead. But for a bigger thrill, at smaller green fees, go to The Island.

FAVOURITE HOLE
Par 4 14th. 387 yards. A perfect links hole that deceives the eye all the way. It is Index 2 and it dog-legs up to the beach. A nest of bunkers left and a yawning bunker on the right threaten drives, but the green is so inaccessible it's perfectly terrifying.

TOUGHEST HOLE
See above. Also, Par 5 6th. 583 yards. This kind of length calls for three big, accurate shots. On a windy day, that's a big challenge, and the bunkers and water (left and hidden) show no mercy.

POINTS								
CD	A	G/F	B/W	L	F	V	G Ex	Total
17	7	10	10	7	10	6	16	83

THE COURSE

- Par 72
- Length: 6,934
- Portmarnock Golf Club, Golf Links Road, Portmarnock, Co. Dublin
- Tel: +353 (0) 1 846 2968
- www.portmarnockgolfclub.ie
- Green Fees: €120–€180

COURSES NEARBY
Deer Park
Howth
Malahide
Portmarnock Links
Royal Dublin
St Anne's

PORTMARNOCK LINKS   Established 1996

UNSYMPATHETIC, TOUGH LOVE

What do you want from links golf? Do you want stunning views and massive dunes, or do you want to play golf and tame a brute? If it's the latter, Portmarnock Links has every challenge you can imagine (as does Portmarnock alongside). This is not about appealing golf that gives you time to admire the scenery. Rather, it is a rugged, tight and low landscape with dunes that give the course an interrupted, raw appearance. Personally, I felt it lacked charisma early on despite the yellow blaze of gorse. But I did enjoy it. It is completely unsympathetic to poor shots: the 100 steep-faced bunkers do not forgive; greens are heavily protected; and putting surfaces are large, fast and twisting. If you're not plum centre on the fairway, there is no hope of bump-and-run. And even if you are, approaches can sweep your ball away. A par, and even a bogey, will feel like victory.

The best holes are closer to the sea – rarely in view – where fairways move more enthusiastically between heavier dunes. This begins at the 8th, which is also when you start to find some elevation. Holes 1 to 7 are open and flatter, with relatively straightforward drives. The 8th dog-legs dramatically into the dunes, and the fairway is almost invisible. And so it continues, with almost every tee shot calling for precision and common sense. Even the excellent par 3s are slotted on nerve-wracking plateaus. Holes 16 and 17 are the highlight.

Oh, and if your drive ends up in the graveyard off the 1st tee, take the hint and go back to the warm hotel for a pint instead.

FAVOURITE HOLE
Par 4 8th. 342 m. Just when you were settling in to your drives, the 8th comes along and smacks your impertinence. Little to see but a yawning bunker and that 'hit-and-hope' feeling as the hole angles left to a green that sits in steep dunes.

TOUGHEST HOLE
Par 4 16th. 360 m. The 16th has an elevated view across a dog-leg to the green. For some, this will be a big carry to reach a small landing area that swings right and down to the green. The bunkers on the elbow are almost magnetic, and more surround the green.

POINTS								
CD	A	G/F	B/W	L	F	V	G Ex	Total
16	7	9	9	7	9	9	17	83

THE COURSE
- Par 72
- Length: 6,005 m
- The Links Portmarnock, Strand Road, Portmarnock, Co. Dublin
- Tel: +353 (0) 1 846 1800
- www.portmarnock.com
- Green Fees: €40–€60

COURSES NEARBY
Deer Park
Howth
Portmarnock
Royal Dublin
St Anne's

PORTSALON   Established 1891

GOOD ENOUGH TO EAT

Another delicious links course in a beautiful location, and one of Ireland's oldest. So expect certain old features that make a classic links. Such as the greens, which sit easily on the landscape with no effort at all – not rivetingly exciting perhaps (despite two double greens), but they fit so perfectly you wouldn't want them any other way. So, too, the little bunkers. The course oozes colour and excitement – though it may not look like it from the clubhouse. Compared with nearby Rosapenna, it is a more charismatic round of golf.

Portsalon uses every inch of the dunes available, and the first seven holes are sheer heaven with high tee boxes showing off the course and scenery beautifully. They stretch along the most gorgeous beach towards Knockalla Mountain, and throw you all over the place, without ever getting too violent. The best views, however, are from the 13th and 14th when you're up high on the very inland edge of the course. You get to see the early holes with new clarity, and you'll want to nip over and play them again.

You start with a fairway that simply erupts up the hill. It doesn't stay so rumbustious but you're taken through lilting valleys that throw your ball. Driving is particularly tough to start, with slightly obscured fairways and, even after the 8th, when fairways give you more room, your judgement is tested. You will encounter a great variety of holes too. Compare the closing stretch with the start and you have a combination that teases you. There are streams and trees, and the sea can be heard all day.

FAVOURITE HOLE

Par 4 2nd (see photo). 361 m. No better 2nd hole in Ireland. A beauty that drives over a sliver of beach and a river flowing to the sea. This river also fronts the green and it is wide. Your landing area for your drive is tiny and angled. And stunning views.

TOUGHEST HOLE

Par 4 14th. 366 m. Named 'Matterhorn', the hole is all on view from the highest point on the course. The fairway reaches a ledge and then tumbles down with trouble left and right. Drive at the lone gorse bush to find the down slope.

POINTS

CD	A	G/F	B/W	L	F	V	G Ex	Total
18	10	9	8	9	7	10	19	90

THE COURSE

- Par 71
- Length: 5,986 m (yellow tees)
- Portsalon Golf Club, Fanad, County Donegal
- Tel: +353 (0) 74 915 9459
- www.portsalongolfclub.com
- Green Fees: €40–€50

COURSES NEARBY
Dunfanaghy
Letterkenny
North West
Rosapenna

PORTSTEWART (OLD)   Established 1894

ENTERTAINING HOLIDAY GOLF

The Old course at Portstewart is exactly that, for this is where the club started. It is located at the opposite end of the town to the other two courses and has a very basic clubhouse. You can use the main clubhouse. It does not introduce you to rip-roaring design or huge challenges – rather, it is a course for perfect holiday entertainment. At Par 64 (eight par 3s and no par 5s) that's not exactly surprising. There is fun to be had, especially on the opening five holes that are so close to the seashore and rocks, you're likely to get wet. Little dunes rumble along, throwing up good shapes in a stretch of land that is squeezed between the sea and the road – holes 2 and 17 share the same wide fairway. The holes are quirky and basic links type holes with small, simple greens. The 16th to 18th are also on this stretch but are 'uphill', close to the road.

The remaining holes are over the road and on a quirky hilltop. It is very easy, barren and straight. There's not much to grab you. The 6th, however, is a brute (see below) and the 9th is a par 4 of 454 yards. Overall these are dull holes and it is the natural element of the seaside holes that tempts you most. The par 3s can be a bundle of laughs in the wind.

Odd, odd indices.

FAVOURITE HOLE
Par 4 4th. 190 yards. You must hit over the sea, and it's a fairly hefty carry to reach the other side – let alone the green. Watch out for idiot tourists who don't realise that a flying white ball can be very painful.

TOUGHEST HOLE
Par 3 6th. 236 yards. Index 4 is the first hole over the road and it is all uphill. Only the flag appears on the skyline and, while it is all very open, this is one tough tee shot. The green is tiered and small. The 17th is index 8, with the nastiest, blindest approach you can imagine.

| POINTS | | | | | | | | |
CD	A	G/F	B/W	L	F	V	G Ex	Total
11	6	6	6	8	5	8	13	63

THE COURSE
- Par 64
- Length: 4,822 yards
- Portstewart Golf Club, 117 Strand Road, Portstewart, Co. Derry, BT55 7PG
- Tel: +44 (0) 28 7083 2015 (048 from Rep. of Ire.)
- www.portstewartgc.co.uk
- Green Fees: £10–£15

COURSES NEARBY
Ballycastle
Castlerock
Gracehill
Roe Park
Royal Portrush

PORTSTEWART (RIVERSIDE) Established 1894

A GENTLE RIVERSIDE LINKS

With its more impressive, powerhouse sibling alongside, the Riverside course is not going to impress you in the same way. But play them months apart (as I did) and you'll find it has charm and character all of its own.

Riverside is not about mountainous dunes, pothole bunkers, tee box dilemmas or awe-inspiring shots – it is about a pretty and short course that will be enjoyed by everyone. It starts and finishes up by the clubhouse where you'll find the best views, but the holes that drop gently towards the River Bann form the backbone of the course. It is a tranquil, open setting with gorse scattered about fitfully and water features adding some sparkle to the middle holes.

It has links features and quality, and bump-and-run is nearly always an option, but this is almost a relaxing education. It is not difficult: you have more than enough room on fairways and around big, well-shaped greens. Most flags are on view, which adds to the sense of gentleness, and while bunkers are well placed they are not deep. You'll settle into an easy rhythm in no time. The run from the 9th to 11th sparkles, with the 9th and 11th promising the most dramatic water features, and the 10th being Index 1.

Views are of the river and the gentle river valley – the only par 5 (the 6th) runs beside the water – but the daunting dunes of the Strand course are never far away.

A huge new clubhouse (open in 2009), enhances the facilities.

FAVOURITE HOLE
Par 4 9th. 268 yards. A beauty (so play from the back blue tees) that will tempt big hitters into hitting over reeds, field and low trees to find the green that sits in a gentle bowl. But water lurks – twice – so play the easy route and aim left onto the fairway.

TOUGHEST HOLE
Par 4 1st. 412 yards. Even tougher than the lower indices because this is the opener. It is a semi-blind drive and, at this point, you don't know how much room you have to play with. A good bumpy run down to the green also plays its part.

POINTS								
CD	A	G/F	B/W	L	F	V	G Ex	Total
14	7	7	8	8	9	9	15	77

THE COURSE

- Par 68
- Length: 5,497 yards
- Portstewart Golf Club, 117 Strand Road, Portstewart, Co. Derry, BT55 7PG
- Tel: +44 (0) 28 7083 2015 (048 from Rep. of Ire.)
- www.portstewartgc.co.uk
- Green Fees: £20–£25

COURSES NEARBY
Ballycastle
Castlerock
Gracehill
Roe Park
Royal Portrush

PORTSTEWART (STRAND)   Established 1894

IRELAND'S FRONT NINE

Stand on the first tee and tell me you are not blown away by this links course. The views over the beach, the sea and the dunes towards Mussenden Temple on the distant headland make this the best opening drive in Irish golf. As you look into the heart of the towering dunes you will feel a shiver of anticipation at what is to come, so pause and absorb this remarkable moment. The opening dog-leg emphasises that, despite its beauty, this relatively short links course requires a strategic approach.

Driving is never simple: there are eight dog-legs in the first eleven holes, so trust your clubs, your swing and your distances. And second shots are no easier, with several greens protected by severe banking (notably the lethal postage-stamp-type par 3 6th – see photo). There is nothing more humbling (or amusing for your companions) than chipping a ball only to see it roll back behind you because you were weak. The fairways are tossed violently, and the dramatic changes in elevation are inspiring. Such challenges are partially offset by the scarcity of bunkers (most evident on the par 3s), which are small and deep.

After the excellent 10th, 11th and 12th, the course starts to lose its impetus. Nowhere is this more noticeable than on the uninspiring final three holes. It is a disappointing end.

Holes 2 to 8 are located in Thistly Hollow known as 'God's Own Country'. Added in 1990, they are as natural and raw as you could hope for, with elevated tees and flowing valleys. They are justifiably regarded as the best front nine in Ireland, and not something you will forget. There are two other, gentler courses here as well.

FAVOURITE HOLE
Par 4 8th. 372 yards. A perfect roller-coaster dog-leg. You can land your drive on an idyllic plateau surrounded by an amphitheatre of dunes, or you can take on the corner and almost reach the green with the downslope. Beauty comple-mented by precision.

TOUGHEST HOLE
Par 4 2nd. 360 yards. Not one shot is easy here. From a high tee you drive over the shoulder of a dizzyingly tall dune. Then it is up to the narrow green, with the same tall dune overshadowing you. Land short and you could find the ball back at your feet.

POINTS								
CD	A	G/F	B/W	L	F	V	G Ex	Total
17	8	10	10	9	9	8	18	89

THE COURSE

- Par 71
- length: 6,467 yards
- Portstewart Golf Club, 117 Strand Road, Portstewart, Co. Derry, BT55 7PG
- Tel: +44 (0) 28 7083 2015 (048 from Rep. of Ire.)
- www.portstewartgc.co.uk
- Green Fees: £80–£95

COURSES NEARBY
Ballycastle
Castlerock
Gracehill
Roe Park
Royal Portrush

PORTUMNA   Established 1913

IDYLLIC

Superb parkland. I can't say it any simpler. No two holes are alike as you work your way around this lazy estate. It is resplendent with big oak, beech and ash and you are completely ensconced in woods, which protect every perimeter. The land moves significantly to provide some stunning tee boxes and greensites, to hide putting surfaces and to give the course beautiful character. You are often walking through trees to get to tee boxes, and the 12th sits between huge pines with bare trunks that are stark and captivating.

It is a good length and you need to keep your head to score well. Your driver will be well used, but look carefully at what lies ahead – an upslope may be preferable to a downslope. Portumna likes you to see lots from the tee, which adds significantly to the experience. As do the many deer that call the woods home.

Greens are tricky, with a few dangerous curves turning long putts into nightmares (the 7th, 10th and 12th) and the bunkering is very effective. One of the things I really like is the simple approach that has been taken to presenting greens.

There is no great mounding to interrupt the beauty around you and it complements the landscape perfectly.

Even when you reach the relatively open, middle area of the course, you will find big trees making a dramatic statement. The dog-leg 3rd – Index 1 – is a case in point.

And look out for the round, stone watchtowers. When this was an estate, the ladies used to climb these to watch the horse races.

Even the practice range is pretty.

FAVOURITE HOLES
Par 3 5th. 177 m. None of the par 3s is short. This sits in a dense wood, with the green well below. Picture-perfect stuff. The 11th, 14th and 16th deserve a mention, too.

TOUGHEST HOLE
Par 5 17th. 488 m. A beautiful drive that heads between the trees and over a crest. Once you are over the top it is both majestic and lethal. A lake runs all along the right, propping up the green, with trees curving in from the left.

POINTS								
CD	A	G/F	B/W	L	F	V	G Ex	Total
18	9	9	9	7	8	10	19	89

THE COURSE

- Par 72
- Length: 6,100 m
- Portumna Golf Club, Ennis Road, Portumna, Co. Galway
- Tel: +353 (0) 90 974 1059
- www.portumnagolfclub.ie
- Green Fees: €30–€35

COURSES NEARBY
Birr
Curra West
Loughrea
Nenagh

POWERSCOURT (EAST)   Established 1996

GOOD AT BOTH ENDS, BUT A BIT FLAT IN THE MIDDLE

If ever an entrance was going to get your juices flowing, then this is it. Ancient beech trees line the road to one of Ireland's grand estates, the Great Sugar Loaf pierces the skyline and three glorious holes will fill you with anticipation. Powerscourt is much lauded and has hosted two major Irish championships. So, is it that good? Honestly? No. The course is perfectly maintained and the greens are spectacular – they are beautifully presented, quick and devilishly contoured – but Powerscourt made the mistake of putting the best and most exciting holes early on (the 2nd to 5th) and at the end (the 16th to 18th). For example, the opening five holes have a feast of trees and avenues; the next four have just one. It's wooded parkland combined with open parkland, and the latter does not provide the same intrigue. I'm not saying they are bad, simply that they lose that early excitement.

From the 6th to the 15th, there are good, long holes that roll lazily across the open estate (the 7th, 8th, 13th and 14th stand out). They offer great views of the countryside and Powerscourt House, but the holes don't grab you in the same way; by the time you stand on the tee box at the par 3 16th, with the green perfectly wedged above a pond, you will have forgotten how good the opening holes were. Big hitters will love the par 5 17th where you can foolishly attempt to carry water on your second.

The East course is a real scoring challenge and, with the West course alongside, you can make a 36-hole day of it.

FAVOURITE HOLE
Par 5 2nd. 444 m. A serious tree-lined dog-leg that runs alongside the driveway. Your approach to the green is blocked by majestic trees, and you go left or right. Either way, it is a tough shot that calls for distance control.

TOUGHEST HOLE
Par 4 8th. 401 m. A long links-like hole that demands a seriously good second shot. Bunkers and banks channel the fairway all the way to a green with a hidden putting surface. A par is a struggle.

POINTS								
CD	A	G/F	B/W	L	F	V	G Ex	Total
14	7	10	8	7	10	5	13	74

THE COURSE
- Par 72
- Length: 5,930 m
- Powerscourt Golf Club, Enniskerry, Co. Wicklow
- Tel: +353 (0) 1 204 6033
- www.powerscourt.ie
- Green Fees: €50–€120

COURSES NEARBY
Bray
Druid's Glen/Heath
Dun Laoghaire
Glen of the Downs
Greystones

POWERSCOURT (WEST)   Established 2003

GREAT VIEWS AND GREAT CLIMBS

All in all, I prefer this course to its more highly regarded East sibling. The scenery is more dominant and impressive, and the differences in elevation make it more entertaining. Weave in some big trees, woods, ponds and streams and it's an idyllic setting that promises lots of variety around this parkland estate. And despite some significant climbs, it is more fun. The excellent finish helps – the 16th to 18th are all downhill, with the par 3 17th sharply so, providing the most dramatic hole on the course.

The quality is excellent. Some superb bunker complexes light up fairways and they are designed to impress as well as threaten. Water appears frequently too: a pretty stream crosses the 4th, 6th, 7th and 10th, and the pond on 9th is a treacherous affair, threatening drive and second alike. Greens are large, fast and difficult to read. It all combines to make the course more enticing, and, while the lengths of the courses are the same, the wider fairways mean the West plays more freely than the East course.

The Great Sugar Loaf stands beside you and the surrounding hills are with you constantly. Nowhere is this more obvious than the 15th which stretches across the top of the course under a pine wood.

You must drive straight if you're to avoid the unforgiving fairway bunkers and if you want to attack well-protected flags. Yes, it is tough in places, but driving is a real pleasure as balls soar against great backdrops. And for your seconds, trust the yardage, trust your irons and go for your shots.

FAVOURITE HOLE
Par 3 6th. 132 m. The 17th is a beauty, but the 6th offers a more attractive tee shot, dropping to a wide green, over a stream, with trees piercing the sky behind. The bunkers add extra drama.

TOUGHEST HOLE
Par 4 12th. 327 m. A difficult dog-leg with trees along the right. Hit it straight if you're to have any shot at the green, which is elevated and jealously guarded by a bunker directly in front.

POINTS								
CD	A	G/F	B/W	L	F	V	G Ex	Total
16	8	8	9	8	10	6	17	82

THE COURSE

- Par 72
- Length: 5,955 m
- Powerscourt Golf Club, Enniskerry, Co. Wicklow
- Tel: +353 (0) 1 204 6033
- www.powerscourt.ie
- Green Fees: €50–€120

COURSES NEARBY
Bray
Druid's Glen/Heath
Dun Laoghaire
Glen of the Downs
Greystones

RATHBANE   Established 1998

MUNICIPAL ON THE CLOCK

Rathbane is squeezed by a main road and getting to the course is not exactly attractive as you drive through an industrial estate and then heavy security gates. The course spreads out like the face of a clock with the clubhouse at the centre. Holes go out and then come back, in what can only be described as a basic design style. It is immersed in mature trees but these fade to younger plantings as the holes stretch away from the clubhouse. Standing in the car park you will see many greens, tees and people. It is all a bit confusing.

Be in no doubt: it is a popular course that appeals to many of the golfing fraternity, but it won't attract serious golfers or those looking for a real challenge. It doesn't have enough charisma for that. It is more a 'what you see is what you get' type of course. But like so many of these less impressive courses, it fits a niche that will always encourage novice golfers and those looking to bash the ball about.

It is young and, as it matures, it will improve. And because it is a municipal course it is well maintained.

FAVOURITE & TOUGHEST HOLES
Par 4 17th and 18th. 326 m and 371 m, and Indices 4 and 2 respectively. On a course that packs few surprises, two of the serious challenges are left until the end. Both dog-legs, they call for well-judged tee shots to open up the green.

POINTS

CD	A	G/F	B/W	L	F	V	G Ex	Total
10	6	5	5	4	5	6	10	51

THE COURSE
- Par 70
- Length: 5,349 m
- Rathbane Golf Club, Crossagalla, Limerick, Co. Limerick
- Tel: +353 (0) 61 313 655
- www.rathbanegolfclub.com
- Green Fees: €20–€25

COURSES NEARBY
Adare Manor
Castletroy
Limerick
Limerick County

RATHCORE   Established 2004

BEAUTIFUL, CHALLENGING, THRILLING

The beauty of Rathcore is that it is seriously good and so completely unexpected . . . except that now you expect it.

This is farmland hardly touched by the designer's hand. It is a short, quality, parkland paradise with gorse, trees and water in abundance. The landscape tosses superbly and erratically and hides greens time and again. Take the par 5 13th: you drive from a tight, high corner onto and over a shoulder, turn right and repeat, then down into a huge hollow that rises to the green.

The centrepiece is the gorse-drenched hill that hosts several tees and greens, as well as great views of the course. There is rural charm at every turn, which makes it prettier than the preened courses that grab the headlines. Approach the green on the terrifying par 4 270-yard 3rd and you'll find sheep evaluating your effort.

The routing is superb and the artistry of the design is magical. But the most enjoyable thing of all is the number of options you have. Besides the excellent par 3s, you will face a variety of choices from the tee box or for your approaches.

Water – great ponds of the stuff – adds a whole new dimension to your round. There are five short par 4s, yet on three of these you are stumped by water. The golf is about common sense and bravery, and on several occasions your ball will disappear over the hill, you know not where. This was one of the most enjoyable three hours I've spent on a golf course.

Rathcore offers the best value golf in Ireland.

FAVOURITE HOLE

Par 3 11th. 154 yards. Set on the hilltop, amidst the gorse. The hole hits out and down into marshland, where a raised green waits. It is the huge tree on the right that makes the hole, forcing you to take on the water. The 5th, 14th, 15th and 18th are all superb.

TOUGHEST HOLE

Par 4 3rd. 270 yards. A tee shot to jangle the nerves. You have a sliver of fairway to aim at. Anything short is water, anything left is hillside gorse, anything long is bunker or OB. The approach is easier but there is more water on the right.

POINTS

CD	A	G/F	B/W	L	F	V	G Ex	Total
18	10	9	9	6	7	10	20	89

THE COURSE

- Par 72
- Length: 6,008 yards
- Rathcore Golf Club, Rathcore, Enfield, Co. Meath
- Tel: +353 (0) 46 954 1855
- www.rathcoregolfandcountry club.com
- Green Fees: €20–€35

COURSES NEARBY
County Meath
Kilcock
Knockanally
Moyvalley

RATHDOWNEY   Established 1930

A STEADY HEARTBEAT

The word I'd use for Rathdowney is 'comfortable'. Everything about it satisfies that word: the views, the clubhouse, the golf course. It may not be exhilarating but it's never dull. I would even say it's the perfect course for societies and club golfers. There are plenty of generous, rolling fairways and not too much difficulty. The fairways are lined with a wide variety of tree types – sometimes to the point of messiness (the 11th) – but generally it adds to the appeal and gives the holes extra definition as they tumble along.

After Castlecomer and Abbeyleix on previous days, the straightness of Rathdowney was reassuring. On what is a fairly standard parkland course the landscape has been used brilliantly, with greens often on the rise or at the top of ridges.

One thing that jumps out at you is that even though holes go back and forth, you will rarely know which hole is beside you. The routing is intriguing and only the trip to the 7th tee, across the 13th fairway, is dangerous.

Plenty to enjoy, nothing to excite. Holes 2, 8, 9, 14 and 17 stand out.

FAVOURITE HOLE
Par 4 14th. 363 m. You see the flag and the fairway weaves its way towards it. Big evergreens tower on the right while a couple of lone trees sit in the rough on the left.

TOUGHEST HOLE
Par 4 15th. 375 m. A large bank rises directly in front of you, with a white direction stone on top. It is totally blind and the land hitches again on the other side, and then again to the green. A good drive is essential.

POINTS

CD	A	G/F	B/W	L	F	V	G Ex	Total
13	7	7	6	7	7	8	14	69

THE COURSE
- Par 71
- Length: 5,593 m
- Rathdowney Golf Club, Coulnaboul West, Rathdowney, Co. Laois
- Tel: +353 (0) 505 46170
- www.rathdowneygolfclub.com
- Green Fees: €25

COURSES NEARBY
Abbeyleix
Mountrath
Roscrea
Thurles

RATHSALLAGH   Established 1994

TESTING, TREE-LINED AND TEMPTING

How wonderful it must be for Rathsallagh to be the envy of clubs all over the country – to have the wealth of mature trees that others can only aspire to and to be able to boast that not one tree was felled in the course's design. Golfers will undoubtedly wish otherwise on holes 3, 6, 9, 14 and 16, where you have to thread your ball past majestic beauties. This is lush and rolling countryside where the grass seems greener than elsewhere, and where trees form the backbone to every hole – sometimes up close and personal, other times just setting the scene along fairways and around greens.

Rathsallagh is a long and spacious parkland course that makes the heart flutter. There are two long walks and a couple of climbs (the 9th and 18th), which will sap your energy, but there's a terrific sense of anticipation as you head from one tee to the next.

Water appears a few times and, as with any great course, the variety makes it special. The length and the danger call for all kinds of shots and every club will be used. The 6th says it all (see below): you could hit different clubs off the tee and a

variety of shots for your second. Smart thinking is needed.

For me, Rathsallagh and nearby Tulfarris are the most superb pairing of parkland courses. Tulfarris is longer and more picturesque, while Rathsallagh has a certain majesty with greens that are more difficult to attack.

The beauty of the clubhouse is its simple layout. That and the burger. Stay at Rathsallagh House (which dates back to 1798) for a truly special occasion.

FAVOURITE HOLE
Par 3 13th. 134 yards. A sweet walk up through trees brings you to a raised tee. A sweet, short shot takes you down to a sloping green that implores you to land on it. Watch out for the slope front left.

TOUGHEST HOLE
Par 5 6th. 490 yards. Trees jut out to block off the fairway, stifling long hitters, while the lake and wall in front of the green complicate club selection on your second. It's an easy hole if you play it the sensible way, but why would you do that?

POINTS								
CD	A	G/F	B/W	L	F	V	G Ex	Total
17	9	9	8	6	10	9	18	86

THE COURSE
- Par 72
- Length: 6,499 yards
- Rathsallagh Golf Club, Dunlavin, Co. Wicklow
- Tel: +353 (0) 45 403 316
- www.rathsallagh.com
- Green Fees: €45–€55

COURSES NEARBY
Baltinglass
Curragh, The
Kilkea Castle
Tulfarris

RINGDUFFERIN   Established 1993

ROLLER COASTER: LITTLE AND LARGE

Ringdufferin may be short but it will take all your energy to finish. The back nine have some steep climbs and less hardy golfers will want to take a buggy or play the front nine again. Not that the front nine are flat (don't let the 1st fool you), awash as they are with stormy, natural mounding. The interest and excitement of this course is all about the mounding, the changes in elevation and the views on the back nine. The greens are small and lie simply on the land (slopes and all) but they are difficult to approach. Greens on the 10th, 13th, 14th and 16th are perched so high up that, from 100 yards , you can't see a thing – just sky. Is that good or bad? It depends on what you like.

The course is rudimentary in terms of quality but this is a natural landscape and sometimes you just can't knock it. When you pause for breath after the 10th you can look east and be revitalised by Strangford Lough and beyond. Believe me, you'll need the time to recover. Please note, the 10th is a dog-leg left, and not right as indicated on the card.

Club selection poses a few challenges and irons may well be the best choice early on (the 2nd, 3rd, 5th and 7th) as holes dog-leg and twist to hide greens. The rolling fairways (the 5th particularly) will see balls stall or fly.

The course is open and most of the trees have been around for a while (there's a lovely walk through a wood after the 6th). Check your bearings on the 3rd and 7th (they share a tee box).

FAVOURITE HOLE

Par 5 5th. 463 yards. Walk left off the 4th green to see the two huge dips that await – they're not visible from the tee. It's quite captivating. Your second has another mound to clear. Two rather blind shots, but worth it.

TOUGHEST HOLE

Par 4 10th. 319 yards. The fairway tilts right, taking you away from the green high above the dog-leg. It is a long shot up to a small green protected by a slim bunker. The 13th and 14th are tough, too, hitting over yawning valleys to invisible greens.

POINTS

CD	A	G/F	B/W	L	F	V	G Ex	Total
13	7	6	6	8	6	9	14	69

THE COURSE

- Par 68
- Length: 4,993 yards
- Ringdufferin Golf Club,
  36 Ringdufferin Road, Toye,
  Killyleagh, Co. Down, BT30 9PH
- Tel: +44 (0) 28 4482 8812
  (048 from Rep. of Ire.)
- Green Fees: £14–£16

COURSES NEARBY
Ardglass
Bright Castle
Downpatrick
Spa

RING OF KERRY   Established 1998

OVER THE ISLANDS

Ring of Kerry works its way across a big hillside in a series of shapely holes. As you can imagine, fairways move dramatically, greens are often perched and flags remain hidden. There is a fresh, mountain airiness to proceedings, while the views of the Kerry Mountains, and the Greenane Islands that sit playfully in Kenmare Bay are spectacular. There's also a great, wild Irishness around the heath-like fringes.

The par 3s are brilliant holes – dramatic to look at and tough to play. And holes like the 7th and 14th (see below) are perfect in their appearance and emphasise that this is a tough and, at times, beautiful course. But considering its location it should capture you more. It might be some scruffiness about the place or that some holes lack definition, or perhaps it's the holiday homes that add to the slightly disjointed feel.

And yet there is plenty to impress. Several holes reveal lots of deceptive movements and hidden difficulties under and around greens (bunkers, water, slopes).

It is a good length that requires strong driving to give views of the green.

Otherwise, if you leave yourself blind, it is almost impossible to find the greens.

Of course, there are some climbs (the hardest being up to the clubhouse after 18th) and it challenges your golfing brain all day. I suggest you look at the legends on the tee boxes, and also figure out where the open spaces are off the tee – you'll find one side is usually very forgiving. With the wind making a big impact that may not be easily done.

FAVOURITE HOLE
Par 3 3rd. 148 yards. Uphill, between two shoulders of gorse that border an amusing waterfall, which reveals just the flag. The long par 3 13th is a beauty too, hitting down over a stream at the islands beyond.

TOUGHEST HOLE
Par 4 14th. 404 yards. Index 1 drives up a gentle hill. It is quite isolated and well flanked by dense trees, particularly around the green. Bunkers hold the left of the fairway, and even a brilliant drive won't reveal the bunker in front of the green.

POINTS								
CD	A	G/F	B/W	L	F	V	G Ex	Total
14	7	8	8	9	8	6	15	75

THE COURSE
- Par 72
- Length: 6,353 yards (white)
- Ring of Kerry Golf Club, Templenoe, Kenmare, Co. Kerry
- Tel: +353 (0) 64 42000
- www.ringofkerrygolf.com
- Green Fees: €25–€60

COURSES NEARBY
Bantry Bay
Kenmare
Killarney
Skellig Bay
Waterville

ROCKMOUNT   Established 1995

ROCK-SOLID FARMLAND

Rockmount is a good, short, fun test of golf. You need to be tidy without being too accurate, and you can get away with some bad shots.

This is farmland that has been nurtured into a natural-feeling parkland. There are lovely touches and clever challenges: several tee boxes are fronted by traditional stonework or railway sleepers, and some have immaculate beds of shrubs (the 10th stands out for both reasons and a sycamore hovers over you for added drama); a small stream runs across numerous holes defending greens, and the stone bridges are a quaint feature. The stream empties into a daunting pond that fronts the 11th green. Fairway bunkers are plentiful and dangerous with their open-mouthed appearance.

There are places where the course tries a little too hard (e.g. open-sided huts) and the desired result is just out of reach. But from an enjoyment perspective it makes no difference. For instance, the course lacks consistency from time to time with some amazing fairways that simply erupt up the slopes, but then switch back to the flat and open variety. Does it matter? I prefer the tumbling fairways as they are more attractive to hit at, especially with the tantalising changes in elevation. This is particularly true on holes 5, 7, 10 and 18 where greens are visible and it looks like a sheer thrill to reach them.

An excellent clubhouse is let down by weak changing facilities.

FAVOURITE HOLE

Par 5 5th. 513 yards. Drive of the day. An attractive and high tee box hits over the stream below and onto a rising fairway. There's OB right so care is needed, but the distant green – set in a bowl – beckons.

TOUGHEST HOLE

Par 4 18th. 412 yards. The tumbling fairway returns, with the distant flag wedged in the hillside. Two well-placed bunkers add risk to a long hole and your approach must carry the stream and a steep upslope. A great finish.

POINTS								
CD	A	G/F	B/W	L	F	V	G Ex	Total
13	7	7	8	6	7	7	14	69

THE COURSE

- Par 72
- Length: 6,079 yards
- Rockmount Golf Club, 28 Drumalig Road, Carryduff, Co. Down, BT8 8EQ
- Tel: +44 (0) 28 9081 2279 (048 from Rep. of Ire.)
- www.rockmountgolfclub.com
- Green Fees: £12–£30

COURSES NEARBY
Castlereagh Hills
Lisburn
Malone
Spa

ROE PARK   Established 1992

YOUNG, OPEN, SEARCHING

Roe Park is attached to the SAS Radisson hotel, so facilities are excellent. But it raises a warning light as the success of hotel/golf course developments can be hit and miss. Roe Park is more hit than miss, but it will need time to establish itself. The trees are young and struggling to add character to holes, and there are many opportunities to enhance the course – a few big banks behind greens are begging for a bunker, or something to give them a more enlightening backdrop. As a result, the course feels bland in places. And yet because of the good turning landscape, there is plenty to enjoy. The rises and falls have been used to good effect, and the more interestingly shaped back nine are a lot more entertaining.

A nice downhill drive greets you on the 1st, but the course only starts to show some flair on the scaling-the-heights 6th (you walk past it on the way to the 1st) and then settles into its stride on the impressive and sloping 10th. The holes in between are good holes but they don't deliver any knock-out blows. It's all a little open for that, but you can drive a bit wildly and get away with it. And the course is short enough so that it's enjoyable for short and big hitters alike.

There are pleasant views all around you (7th tee box) and these become more prominent on the back nine, nowhere more so than on the impressive downhill par 3 17th, which hits at the rocky outcrops of Binevenagh.

FAVOURITE HOLE
Par 4 15th. 266 yards. Starting the best run of holes, the 15th is a huge risk-v.-reward hole. From a high tee box to a high green you have a big tree directly in your line. It hides a pond and the sensible option is an easy iron down to the visible fairway.

TOUGHEST HOLE
Par 4 10th. 381 yards. The fairway slopes down from left to right, with an uphill approach to a high green and a hidden putting surface. Two tough shots. If you feel adventurous, the high back tees make the hole far more thrilling.

POINTS								
CD	A	G/F	B/W	L	F	V	G Ex	Total
13	6	7	6	8	9	7	14	70

THE COURSE

- Par 70
- Length: 5,984 yards (white tees)
- Roe Park Golf Club, Radisson SAS Roe Park Resort, Limavady, Co. Derry, BT49 9LB
- Tel: +44 (0) 28 7772 2222 (048 from Rep. of Ire.)
- www.roegolf.com
- Green Fees: £25–£30

COURSES NEARBY
Castlerock
Faughan Valley
Portstewart

ROGANSTOWN   Established 2004

YOUNG AND KEEN

Take a quietly undulating, farming landscape on the edge of Dublin, put a hotel, spa and leisure centre on it, add a few houses (shame about that) and a golf course around the perimeter. Mound the areas between fairways, plant them with trees and lace them with bunkers. Create well-presented greens with swift twists and turns and tricky fall-offs into well-shouldered bunkers. Then just add water. Here's one Roganstown prepared earlier.

First off, Roganstown is not a dramatic course. There are no views and the rather lifeless landscape means holes are predominantly flat. But don't think that means it's not good, because it is. And it will improve: all the right ingredients are here. The mounding along fairways is everywhere but it is not excessive and the trees give it a natural feel. The result is straight fairways (there's not one real dog-leg), with the mounding appearing like welcoming arms along the sides. There is also a tremendous amount of bunkering. Some holes look as if one entire side is a small beach, but they keep a low profile so they don't dominate.

You can swing away with your driver since most of the trouble is on green approaches. Here, bunkers will fray the nerves – several come right across the front – and raised greens are often deceptive, being farther than they look, with low dips rising to the attractive putting surfaces and sneakily placed bunkers. The scatterings of mature trees are also used very well, often guarding greens or leading you onto fairways.

There are several pretty ponds, with the 6th, 9th and 12th hitting over lots of them.

FAVOURITE HOLE
Par 3 6th. 182 yards. A beautiful hole with a large pond from tee to green. The water is lovely but particularly dangerous (as on the 9th and 12th), snatching anything short. A bunker rises out of the pond to front the green.

TOUGHEST HOLE
Par 4 16th. 417 yards. Probably the most imposing and impressive hole. It glides upwards over a stream and then swings left between two bunkers. It demands the perfect drive if you want to see the green, and even then the putting surface is hidden by a bunker.

POINTS								
CD	A	G/F	B/W	L	F	V	G Ex	Total
15	7	9	8	5	9	6	16	75

THE COURSE

- Par 71
- Length: 6,588 yards (whites)
- Roganstown Golf Club, Swords, Co. Dublin
- Tel: +353 (0) 1 843 3118
- www.roganstown.com
- Green Fees: €40–€55

COURSES NEARBY
Corrstown
Forrest Little
St Margaret's
Swords

ROSAPENNA (OLD TOM MORRIS)   Established 1893

TRADITIONAL, QUIRKY, INTRIGUING

Chances are, if you come to Rosapenna you're coming to play Sandy Hills. It's the sexy, modern and muscular links course that many dream about. Yet much of the Old Tom Morris course comes from a different age entirely. Perhaps the golf experience can be summed up in one word: respect. Respect for tradition and one of the greatest names in golf.

Old Tom Morris designed this back in the 1890s. The back nine ('Valley') are still his. The new front nine ('Strand'), opened in 2009, are Pat Ruddy's. It's old versus new and they sit side by side remarkably well. Pat's holes remain true to the spirit of Old Tom. They're not too grand or too showy; they are subtle and glide easily between low dunes. The challenges are subtle too, with pins tucked just out of sight, below the eyeline or interrupted by the shoulder of a dune. Fairways dip and leap, especially short of the greens, and the greens themselves offer little hope for the wayward.

When you move to the back nine, you'll discover an older style but a similar pace and rhythm. These holes follow the flow of the land even more naturally. It presses up against the Sandy Hills course (which looms above you the entire time). Some holes are almost flat, while others suddenly flick up to lend drama: the 14th has a huge mound that rises up beside Tramore Beach and then swerves down to the green. Definitely an old links education and one that you should treat with respect.

Tom Morris's old and distinctly quirky Coastguard nine are still here too.

FAVOURITE HOLE
Par 4 10th. 414 yards. The tee box by the clubhouse overlooks the sea, and the wide fairway runs beside it towards the Sandy Hills course. The simplicity of the hole makes this a beauty.

TOUGHEST HOLE
Par 4 11th. 450 yards. A flat hole that plays tricks on the eye. It is also long. Now, throw in the wind . . . Index 1

POINTS								
CD	A	G/F	B/W	L	F	V	G Ex	Total
17	7	8	8	8	10	7	17	82

THE COURSE
- Par 71
- Length: 6,206 yards
- Rosapenna Hotel & Golf Resort, Downings, Letterkenny, Co. Donegal
- Tel: +353 (0) 74 915 5000
- www.rosapenna.ie
- Green Fees: €35–€70

COURSES NEARBY
Dunfanaghy
Letterkenny
Portsalon

ROSAPENNA (SANDY HILLS) Established 2004

FIELDS OF SILVER

Donegal is the luckiest spot on the planet. Remote, beautiful, and the golf is superb value for money. This glamorous resort, with a pavilion (aka clubhouse) and plush hotel, has forty-five holes. Sandy Hills is the main event.

Designed by Pat Ruddy, it has many high greensites, fairways that slip away into hollows and dunes that have the most sensuous rhythm. They feel alive and, when you come up for air, tee boxes promise stunning views – not only of the surrounding mountains and sea, but also the course. Pause and look around you before you drive to appreciate how completely immersed you are. (You'll see the defunct St Patrick's Links nearby.) Play in sunshine and the marram grasses turn to a brilliant silver. It's like being in the ocean and, with the excellent routing, you rarely know where you are. Interestingly, the easy, continuous rhythm of the course makes some holes forgettable. It's not a criticism – I love the course – but when the shapes are similar and you're down in the dunes for so long, some holes slip the memory. In that way it is similar to Ballyliffin's Glashedy.

Ruddy is a master of deception. He obscures fairways (dunes, changes in elevation), making you think you have less to play with than you actually do. Claustrophobic dunes, fall-offs and steep slopes around the greens mean you often need to attack the putting surface itself. The bunkers are difficult to avoid despite their scarcity. Unfortunately for you, they are often hidden and always punishing.

It is astounding. Play Portsalon to appreciate the brilliant differences.

FAVOURITE HOLE
Par 4 10th. 365 yards. No hole deserves to be ignored, especially the par 3s but, with its drive down into the bottom of the dunes, followed by a second to the green above, the 10th lets you see all the beauty of the hole. Leave the driver in the bag.

TOUGHEST HOLE
Par 4 6th. 390 yards. Index 1, yet six par 4s are longer (hole 1 is 461 yards). A drive straight up the dune, before the hill crests and sends you tumbling down a narrow dune alley to a treacherous green. One of the toughest second shots in Irish golf.

POINTS								
CD	A	G/F	B/W	L	F	V	G Ex	Total
18	9	9	9	10	10	10	19	94

THE COURSE

- Par 71
- Length: 6,383 yards
- Rosapenna Hotel & Golf Resort, Downings, Letterkenny, Co. Donegal
- Tel: +353 (0) 74 915 5000
- www.rosapenna.ie
- Green Fees: €30–€70

COURSES NEARBY
Dunfanaghy
Letterkenny
Portsalon

ROSCOMMON   Established 1904

SIMPLICITY

There is nothing at Roscommon that will get you too excited. It is a simple parkland course that flows back and forth over a very gentle hill, with fairways separated by semi-mature trees, and a few mature ones appearing here and there. There are no great hazards off the tee and you can drive pretty wildly, like I did, and not find too much trouble. There are plenty of golfers who will embrace that with open arms. Greens tend to be long and narrow, becoming more generous on the back nine (added in 1996). Water comes into play at the 9th and 13th (very good par 3s) and the 15th.

There is little character to the holes as they are all very straight and, until the trees gain more presence, this will remain the case. Even so, the younger back nine are the better. The variety of hole length is good. It's not a course you'll go out of your way for but pleasant if you're in the neighbourhood.

FAVOURITE HOLE
Par 3 13th. 132 m. This hole really stands out from the rest. It plays over a large pond to a green sheltered by mature trees. A really attractive tee shot, although I'm never sure about fountains.

POINTS								
CD	A	G/F	B/W	L	F	V	G Ex	Total
11	5	6	7	4	6	6	11	56

THE COURSE
- Par 72
- Length: 5,937 m
- Roscommon Golf Club, Mote Park, Roscommon, Co. Roscommon
- Tel: +353 (0) 90 662 6382
- www.roscommongolfclub.ie
- Green Fees: €15–€20

COURSES NEARBY
Athlone
County Longford
Glasson

ROSCREA   Established 1892

SOMETHING FOR EVERYONE

In Roscrea's clubhouse I was informed by a member that the course was on a par with Rathdowney. Buy that man glasses. Roscrea is far more of an adventure with great variety, great trees and a sense of maturity. Even the newer holes (added in 1991) that are located on two separate peninsulas (the 9th to 11th and the 16th to 18th) have a positive, young parkland feel.

The fairways are rugged and some kick quite dramatically – the 6th and 7th match any links – and they add flair to holes. Trees define the course and these fall into a number of categories: big evergreens dominate the interior of the course; beeches dominate the holes from the 2nd to the 6th; and semi-mature varieties stretch around the new holes. Generally, it's a combination that works gloriously.

Holes are predominantly straight, and with the undulating fairways it is thrilling to stand on the tee box with your driver in hand. The scorecard indicates a few dog-legs, but only the 16th will tax you. Other than that, it's about straight hitting and you usually have enough room off the tee to play your fade or draw. But as you know full well, evergreens rarely forgive an errant shot.

The best stretch of holes is the 3rd to 6th where it feels a bit wild, with deep rough around tee boxes and the pretty wood beside the 4th and 5th. The toughest holes come near the end with some very low indices over the last six holes.

Greens are smooth and swift and the dark, peaty earth ensures the course is playable all year round.

Good clubhouse and a great little bar.

FAVOURITE HOLE
Par 5 5th. 445 m. Known as 'Burma Road', the fairway stretches straight and true between a long bank of inspiring beeches on the right and a dense wood (OB) on the left. It looks perfect from the tee.

TOUGHEST HOLE
Par 4 13th. 396 m. Index 1. Dense evergreens line this long right-to-left hole. One large beech hovers along the right and inside this is your line if you want to see the green. Two big shots.

POINTS

CD	A	G/F	B/W	L	F	V	G Ex	Total
14	8	8	7	6	6	9	16	74

THE COURSE
- Par 71
- Length: 5,594 m
- Roscrea Golf Club, Millpark, Roscrea, Co. Tipperary
- Tel: +353 (0) 505 21130
- www.roscreagolfclub.ie.
- Green Fees: €25–€30

COURSES NEARBY
Birr
Mountrath
Nenagh
Rathdowney

ROSSLARE   Established 1905

AN UNHERALDED, BEAUTIFUL LINKS

Rosslare is a beauty. This is classic links that has everything you expect or want, and not one weak hole in the bunch. Sea views are mostly hidden behind a single line of coastal dunes and they are not overly dramatic in terms of size, but these are only minor quibbles. It is superior and more entertaining than many of the more heavily touted superleague courses. And better value.

It is a dynamic course, beautifully routed, that will thrill you and test you. In terms of elevation there is little change but that doesn't mean you won't get tossed from hole to hole. They fall into three types: the 4th to 7th are the most exciting, where fairways have buckled over the dunes offering blind drives and nerve-wrenching moments when you have no idea if your ball has bounded into tricky rough or if you have the perfect lie; the 1st to 3rd and the 8th to 14th are still punctuated by bumbling fairways but the dunes are not as aggressive or as embracing – the 11th is the exception – and the 15th to 18th have serene fairways that promise open, clear drives. But all offer great, low-running opportunities into greens that just fade out of the fairways. When I played in December, they were immaculate, fast and smartly protected by hollows, swales and bunkers. It is testament to the course that numerous golfers were roaming the fairways on a cold morning.

Apart from the 14th, which hits directly at the sea, all holes go out or back. There's the twelve-hole Burrow course, too.

FAVOURITE HOLE
Par 5 7th. 550 yards. From a seaside dune, the hole arcs gently inland before returning to the coast. It's the best-shaped fairway, dropping and then rising out of the dunes. From the green check out the Burrow course.

TOUGHEST HOLE
Par 4 11th. 469 yards. The drive looks simple, but your long second is completely blind over a large dune in the middle of the fairway, so use the direction post on top. The green sits in a bowl of low dunes. Hole 12 is three yards longer and is a par 5.

POINTS								
CD	A	G/F	B/W	L	F	V	G Ex	Total
17	9	10	9	7	10	10	18	90

THE COURSE
- Par 72
- Length: 6,597 yards
- Rosslare Golf Club, Rosslare, Co. Wexford
- Tel: +353 (0) 53 913 2203
- www.rosslaregolf.com
- Green Fees: €35–€40

COURSES NEARBY
Enniscorthy
St Helen's Bay
Wexford

ROSSMORE   Established 1916

WEAVING GENIUS

What a find! This is superb hillside golf that challenges the legs as well as the brain. The routing can take you anywhere and there are eight dog-legs which send you all over. As much as I enjoy trying to kill my drives, there are times when cunning feels so much more rewarding. On several dog-legs a tee shot of 200 m will serve you well. Any less and you'll be blocked by a variety of obstacles; any more and fairways run out. The 6th and 7th are perfect examples: the first dog-legs left and up, around an old wall of beech trees; the second heads down with a mammoth hillside on the right. They're right angles and call for intelligent golf. This is repeated several times but you will get to open your shoulders and enjoy holes like the 9th and 17th where drives swoop down majestically.

You will have nothing but fun. Yes, it's hilly, but it is a short and charming course in wide open countryside – a great touch on the 16th tee is a map showing many distant mountains – so there's a lovely sense of peace. In the middle, some of the holes flatten out (hard to believe), and there are streams and ponds to maintain interest and danger. The 9th, 10th and 14th holes cross two streams and the 11th has two ponds (one hidden).

The greens are big and mostly flat, which is quite a feat on this landscape, as too are the tee boxes. Two flat holes, the 12th and 13th, are the tamest of the bunch while the 1st, 2nd and 3rd build you up nicely. The 18th is a touch too quirky.

FAVOURITE HOLE
Par 5 9th. 417 m. A truly soaring tee shot onto a flat, slightly hidden plain below. There are two streams to cross on the way to the green but many will fancy their chances of getting on in two.

TOUGHEST HOLE
Par 4 5th. 357 m. There are many tough holes, but the 5th stands out with its flat fairway that drops sharply just after 200 m, with trees all along the left. The green is below and left. Only a perfect tee shot up the right will do.

POINTS

CD	A	G/F	B/W	L	F	V	G Ex	Total
16	9	8	9	8	7	10	18	85

THE COURSE
- Par 70
- Length: 5,331 m
- Rossmore Golf Club, Cootehill Road, Monaghan, Co. Monaghan
- Tel: +353 (0) 47 71222
- www.rossmoregc.com
- Green Fees: €25–€30

COURSES NEARBY
Concra Wood
Clones
County Armagh
Mannan Castle
Nuremore

ROUNDWOOD   Established 1995

VIEWS AT IRELAND'S HEART

Location adds so much to any golf experience. Take a links course with sea, islands and coastline, and already it's special. Roundwood matches these with the glorious Wicklow Mountains and the coast. It is set high on a hillside with the colours of Ireland's beauty stretching out around you. You'll feel like you're in the heart of the mountains and there are dramatic backdrops to many holes.

The course has some excellent drama – the run from the 5th to 8th is superb – but several greens lie lifeless to approach shots and detract from the overall appeal. It is, in the grand scheme of things, a minor complaint, as Roundwood is all about the views and walks that open up the landscape beyond. The highlight is exiting the coniferous tree-lined avenue on the 5th, when the sea beckons in the distance. This is the most romantic corner of the course. The 11th promises more of the same, while the panorama from the superb par 3 13th green is breathtaking.

Playing on a hillside means you will have sloping lies – the 16th is the only one that truly terrifies – and don't be surprised if what you can see of the course on arrival fails to inspire, especially after the dull start.

The trees and slopes provide the difficulty, creating some blind drives and hidden greens. It ensures good variety in shot selection and difficulty. A pond between the 12th and 15th greens is a nice touch, as is the dark and silent walk between the 7th and 8th.

FAVOURITE HOLE

Par 4 6th. 324 yards. Perched on the edge of the course, above ferns, gorse and the distant sea, this is a stunning and tricky hole. The shot to the green is the most intimidating of the round and one of the most stunning.

TOUGHEST HOLE

Par 4 4th. 387 yards. Anything more than a 230-yard drive will put you in trouble on this blind hole, as the fairway suddenly switches left and sharply downhill. It then corrects itself and heads up to the green. An odd hole and a tough one for visitors.

POINTS

CD	A	G/F	B/W	L	F	V	G Ex	Total
14	6	6	6	10	9	8	15	74

THE COURSE

- Par 71
- Length: 6,175 yards
- Roundwood Golf Club, Newtownmountkennedy, Co. Wicklow
- Tel: +353 (0) 1 281 8488
- www.roundwoodgolf.com
- Green Fees: €25–€40

COURSES NEARBY

Bray
Delgany
Druid's Glen/Heath
Greystones
Powerscourt

ROYAL BELFAST   Established 1881

ALL ABOARD

The drive in gives a tasty little appetiser. This is the 'top' of the course, which sits beside and above the impressive clubhouse, which dates back to the 1850s. These are good, attractive and mature parkland holes. Their shape is excellent, creatively using a hillside that works its way down to the sea. It promises many inspiring shots and views across Belfast Lough.

The perimeter is dense woods or sea. In the centre are younger trees and a few smaller woods. It gives the course a peaceful character while leaving it relatively open. If you think that means you can drive wildly on a short course, you'll be wrong. Placement is the key. You will find many fairway bunkers at 250 yards, so it actually favours shorter hitters.

The par 3 4th is a beauty (in the classic parkland sense), but as you slide down the 5th towards the sea things get even more interesting. Ignoring the 6th, 13th and 14th (squeezed together and uninteresting), driving gets harder as the fairways find heavier undulations and you are faced with blinder shots (the 5th, 8th, 10th, 13th and 15th). With the backdrops of sea or woods, they are tempting and quite different.

With three holes right on the sea, and a rich history, Royal Belfast delivers wonderful golf that lifts it comfortably above 'good parkland' status. The variety of holes is a big plus, greensites are lovingly presented and the green bunkering is excellent. It is tough without being long so everyone gets a kick out of it.

Not easy to find, but definitely worth the effort. Great showers and clubhouse facilities.

FAVOURITE HOLE

Par 3 11th. 170 yards of pure thrill. Your tee box sits above the water and you hit up through an aisle of dense trees, over a rag-tag of humps and gorse. No fairway and, seemingly, no forgiveness.

TOUGHEST HOLE

Par 4 10th. 303 yards. Index 14 dog-legs left around trees on the rocks above the sea. It needs a perfect tee shot up onto the rise, because only then can you fire at the severely protected green that sits against a wild bank and a sheer drop. The 15th feels enormous.

POINTS

CD	A	G/F	B/W	L	F	V	G Ex	Total
16	8	9	8	8	10	7	16	82

THE COURSE

- Par 70
- Length: 6,185 yards (whites)
- Royal Belfast Golf Club, Station Road, Craigavad, Co. Down, BT18 0BP
- Tel: +44 (0) 28 9042 8165 (048 from Rep. of Ire.)
- www.royalbelfast.com
- Green Fees: £35–£70

COURSES NEARBY

Bangor
Blackwood
Carnalea
Clandeboye
Holywood

ROYAL COUNTY DOWN   Established 1889

PERFECTION EVERY STEP OF THE WAY

Royal County Down rightly ranks as one of the best in the world. It is a fine-tuned masterpiece, lacking only a decent visitors' bar and restaurant. Perhaps what makes this Royal unique is the purple heather, the blazing gorse, the backdrop of Slieve Donard and the blind drives (some people love; some hate). Add this to a perfect links landscape of rolling golden dunes and this is an occasion you'll be aching to experience and one you won't forget.

After your first drive, walk up the slope that looks over the sea. Now look back to the magnificent Mourne Mountains and tell me you're not inspired.

The course, the second oldest in Ireland, is famous for names like Old Tom Morris, Vardon and Colt, and also for its remarkable blind shots. Drives on the 9th and 11th will leave you speechless, with the latter demanding an excellent drive (and prayer) to clear a dune that can be appreciated – and feared – from as far back as the 10th tee. Intriguingly, designing holes this way is now regarded as outdated, which is a shame as it adds a whole new dimension. The course should be played twice to be fully appreciated and understood.

It is a beautiful links course with fabulous green complexes, cunning dog-legs, mischievous fairways and deep bunkers that are topped by bearded wisps of grass (stunning, but best avoided). Royal County Down, strategically, is not as challenging as Royal Portrush (club selection off the tee) or Portstewart (approaches need more guile) but it is more dangerous than either. Here it is a question of positioning and relishing a world beater.

The 17th and 18th provide a tame finish.

FAVOURITE HOLE
Par 4 13th. 422 yards. A gorse-enclosed driving hole that comes as a surprise, but is all the more attractive for it. It dog-legs right with a sharp shoulder. The green is steeper than most and has a dune backdrop with steps climbing to the next tee.

TOUGHEST HOLE
Par 4 9th (see photo). 428 yards. The 9th is mesmerising as you hit straight and blind over dunes towards the mountains. The revelation comes when the fairway (80 feet below) and green appear from the dune top. A long second must overcome a narrow entrance and bunkers.

POINTS								
CD	A	G/F	B/W	L	F	V	G Ex	Total
19	10	10	10	10	7	9	20	95

THE COURSE
- Par 71
- Length: 6,881 yards
- Royal County Down Golf Club, Newcastle, Co. Down, BT33 0AN
- Tel: +44 (0) 28 4372 2419 (048 from Rep. of Ire.)
- www.royalcountydown.org
- Green Fees: £50–£180

COURSES NEARBY
Ardglass
Bright Castle
Kilkeel
Royal County Down (Annesley)

ROYAL COUNTY DOWN (ANNESLEY)   Established 1900

SHORT AND OH SO SWEET

To appreciate fully the art and craft of links golf, you could go nowhere better than Annesley (aka Mourne Golf Club). The benefits are enormous: first you have a terrific little course (six par 3s, and no par 5s) where a driver should never be considered and your links short game will be tested to the extreme; you have heather, gorse and dunes that are captivating and a death knoll for errant shots; the Mourne Mountains hover above you; and, lastly, you have the mighty Royal County Down course alongside.

Essentially, the two courses are on the same land – to get to the 8th, and then back to the 13th, you have to cross the championship course – so Annesley is the perfect warm-up for the main event. Many Americans play it this way as it introduces you to the heaving fairways that can twist infuriatingly, casting tee shots aside like swatting at flies. Five and six irons may well be the tee shot of the day, especially as second shots typically need to be low and running. Endless trouble around the small, hard putting surfaces – some visible, some hidden – make high shots a risky strategy. Consider then, how you play the six par 3s.

The 1st to 4th holes and the 16th to 18th are farthest from the sea. They are also the flattest, lacking the beauty and drama of the 5th to 15th. In a way, these middle holes are like the championship course in miniature, with shorter, narrower fairways and smaller greens, but with all the twists and challenges and those same awesome bunkers. The best sea and mountain views are from the 10th and 11th tees.

FAVOURITE HOLE

Par 4 10th. 251 yards. A high tee to a low green and a cascading fairway that rocks its way to the green. Great sea views but don't be distracted – you need to watch your ball bounce.

TOUGHEST HOLE

Par 4 15th. 339 yards. Lots of fairway to see with the now familiar undulations leading to a small, visible green. It is pushed up against gorse and protected by the most startling pot bunkers: the heather grows over and down into them.

POINTS								
CD	A	G/F	B/W	L	F	V	G Ex	Total
17	8	8	9	9	7	10	18	86

THE COURSE

- Par 66
- Length: 4,322 yards
- Annesley Links, Royal County Down Golf Club, Newcastle, Co. Down, BT33 0AN
- Tel: +44 (0) 28 4372 3314 (048 from Rep. of Ire.)
- www.royalcountydown.org
- Green Fees: £20–£25

COURSES NEARBY
Ardglass
Bright Castle
Kilkeel
Royal County Down

ROYAL DUBLIN   Established 1885

FLAT AND WINDY

Knowledge is power. Stand on the 1st tee at Royal Dublin and know this: if the wind's behind you, you're blessed for the first nine holes, and cursed all the way home. Yep, nine classic links holes out and nine back. The course runs flat between low dunes and the wind pummels you all day. There is nowhere to hide.

Drives ran for miles at the start. 'This is easy', I thought, only to struggle to stay upright after the turn and despair as second shots threatened to balloon behind me. Then there's the immensely deep rough which has to be avoided to save hours of ball-searching. This is really tough, hard-graft, links golf. You'll leave the 18th green either defeated or defiant.

Royal Dublin sits in the curve of Dublin Bay on Bull Island – an island formed thanks to Captain 'Mutiny on *The Bounty*' Bligh's survey of the bay in 1800. It is reached via an old wooden bridge and the scenery is cityscape. It is oddly captivating.

From an enjoyment point of view, it's hard to get carried away. Royal Dublin is a great links challenge, promising a remarkable pedigree (it has hosted the Irish Open and many other major events),

beautiful quality and wonderful green complexes. It doesn't lack in those departments. If you want to say you've played one of the most famous links courses, then fire ahead. But if you're after a golfing adventure, then it isn't worth the green fee when you have courses like The Island and The European not far away – they are far more dramatic and exciting.

It is very impressive and smart, but just too flat for me.

FAVOURITE HOLE
Par 5 6th. 510 yards. A gentle dog-leg that requires real accuracy to steer it around the bend – it's perfect if you draw the ball. A nicely raised green looks very welcoming over the bumbling fairway if you fancy a go.

TOUGHEST HOLE
Par 4 10th. 417 yards. This is typically your first foray into the wind and you have to lower your expectations, and shots. There is a ditch right in front of the green that complicates the carry and the green has some tough slopes. Index 1.

POINTS								
CD	A	G/F	B/W	L	F	V	G Ex	Total
15	7	10	8	7	9	6	15	77

THE COURSE
- Par 72
- Length: 6,465 yards (yellow)
- The Royal Dublin, North Bull Island Nature Reserve, Dollymount, Dublin 3
- Tel: +353 (0) 1 833 6346
- www.theroyaldublingolfclub.com
- Green Fees: €90–€125

COURSES NEARBY
Clontarf
Portmarnock
Portmarnock Links
St Anne's

ROYAL PORTRUSH (DUNLUCE) Established 1888

A BIG, OPEN AND BEAUTIFUL LINKS

Royal Portrush has a completely different feel to Royal County Down (RCD). The dunes are less intrusive and this promises spectacular views of the course and sea. Gone are the gorse and heather that give RCD that golden texture. In their place are the silver dune grasses you expect and fear. There are no blind shots here, yet strategy and club selection are crucial, especially with intricately protected greens.

As the only course to host the British Open outside Great Britain (in 1951), its reputation and history shine brightly. Everything feels perfect and, like all great links courses, it will draw you for its reputation, the quality and the experience.

Royal Portrush is blessed with two of the best holes in Irish golf: the 5th and 14th. Others, like the 8th, 13th and 15th, come close but it is your arrival on the 5th tee after a slow start that will take your breath away. It is an amazing vista that takes in cliffs, sea, the hills of Donegal and the forbidding Skerries reef. Before you lies a large swathe of the golf course, jealously protected from the encroaching sea by an army of dunes. It looks, sounds and smells perfect. From here on the holes are cleverly routed and cunningly designed, despite only minor changes in elevation. Fairways move easily between the dunes and you might mistakenly believe that you have room to manouevre, but find the rough and par will evaporate before your eyes. The 17th and 18th offer a tame finish.

Tips: drive from the east, from Bushmills (home of the great Irish whiskey), for inspiring views of the course. Play the Valley course too.

FAVOURITE HOLE

Par 4 5th (see photo). 379 yards. From an elevated tee you can see the green sitting above the Atlantic Ocean. It's a deceptive dog-leg, so your drive has to be exact (check yardages in the excellent Yardage Guide). Do not go over the back of the green.

TOUGHEST HOLE

Par 3 14th. 202 yards. 'Calamity Corner.' A remarkable-looking, aptly named, hole. A long tee shot has to carry a chasm that descends to the Valley course below. If you fade the ball it's hard to keep your head down. The green is perched on the edge of the world.

POINTS

CD	A	G/F	B/W	L	F	V	G Ex	Total
18	8	10	10	9	10	8	19	92

THE COURSE

- Par 71
- Length: 6,641 yards
- Royal Portrush Golf Club, Dunluce Road, Portrush, Co. Antrim, BT56 8JQ
- Tel: +44 (0) 28 7082 2311 (048 from Rep. of Ire.)
- www.royalportrushgolfclub.com
- Green Fees: £60–£140

COURSES NEARBY

Ballycastle
Castlerock
Gracehill
Portstewart

ROYAL PORTRUSH (VALLEY)   Established 1947

IN THE VALLEY I WALK

Valley. Does that mean it's flat? Not likely.

The Valley gets very friendly with its more illustrious sibling – the Dunluce – and from several spots around the course you get to see the famous Dunluce 14th, its green fluttering high up in the dunes. But if you come here only to play the Dunluce then you're missing out. Indeed, some locals prefer the Valley – perhaps because it is shorter and better protected from the wind. But it is not easy. Fairways may look wide but the rough is horrible stuff and approaches to greens can get narrow and rugged. Here, bump-and-run will serve you well with deep bunkers being mercifully scarce, but don't expect a good result every time.

This is a terrific par 70 course (despite what you might think upon arrival) sitting low in dunes that rise up around you on all sides. Holes that look flat are far from it and the elevated tee boxes show the course off in the best possible fashion. The fact that so many flags are visible helps a lot too.

Even if there's no wind, there are testing drives (the 3rd, 10th, 14th, 16th)

with some hefty carries, but your approaches are more dangerous, especially with colourful rose bushes crowding the backs of greens. With big putting surfaces and the stunning backdrops, the aerial route always looks good.

No, it doesn't have the charisma of Dunluce, but it is still a quality course and excellent value for money. Go to the big course for the facilities.

Good par 3s.

FAVOURITE HOLE
Par 4 5th. 324 yards. Picture-perfect, high tee, beckoning fairway, deep bunkers, endless dune backdrop. And the 231-yard par 3 6th (Index 9) is a beautiful brute.

TOUGHEST HOLE
Par 4/5 10th. 472/496 yards. Index 2 and a choice of tee/par. Either way it's a tough drive to judge over dunes that jut into the fairway. Your second has a dune on the left and a huge dip you can't see. Needs excellent accuracy on your first two shots.

POINTS								
CD	A	G/F	B/W	L	F	V	G Ex	Total
16	7	8	7	7	10	10	17	82

THE COURSE
- Par 70
- Length: 6,054 yards
- Royal Portrush Golf Club, Dunluce Road, Portrush, Co. Antrim, BT56 8JQ
- Tel: +44 (0) 28 7082 2311 (048 from Rep. of Ire.)
- www.royalportrushgolfclub.com
- Green Fees: £25–£40

COURSES NEARBY
Ballycastle
Castlerock
Gracehill
Portstewart

ROYAL TARA Established 1906

AS SOLID AS THE BENCHES

What a pleasure to play a mature parkland course that is this relaxing and will keep you entertained for twenty-seven holes, if you so choose. And despite seeing other holes, you feel nicely cocooned. From the moment you arrive you know everything is going to be done properly. The clubhouse is big and gives the place a great start as you walk around it to get to the opening tee boxes (Red and Blue). The original nine (Yellow) are the least interesting nine.

The course has all the necessary ingredients for a great day's golfing. It has a strong design that offers good variety and challenges as the course weaves through mature trees and over sloping terrain. There are plenty of trees to consider off the tee boxes and while fairways are generous enough, you will find that placement is crucial on the gentle dog-legs. Tee boxes are nicely set and wooden benches give you a chance to take the weight off. Sometimes it's the little things that make all the difference. Since there are no views to speak of (despite the rich history being ripped open by the

construction of the M3 nearby), the paths, walks under trees, stone walls and little woods make the course visually appealing.

The Blue nine are the longest (par 37) with three short par 5s, and feel more interesting than the Red nine as drives are more rewarding. Red, however, is more difficult (par 35 and only 60 m shorter).

This area is one of the richest archaeological sites in northwestern Europe, now marred by the M3 motorway development.

FAVOURITE HOLE
Par 4 Blue 6. 291 m. The hole is set up for a mighty bash. There is a sharp hollow that drops from the tee and then rises on the other side, before heading right around trees. You will really, really want to smack your drive.

TOUGHEST HOLE
Par 4 Blue 7. 387 m. A gentle dog-leg around enormous evergreens that are much farther than they look. They will block most of us from the green so aim well left. An attractive green is also deceiving.

POINTS

CD	A	G/F	B/W	L	F	V	G Ex	Total
14	8	8	7	6	10	8	16	77

THE COURSE
- Par 72
- Length: 5,668 m
- Royal Tara Golf Club, Bellinter, Navan, Co. Meath
- Tel: +353 (0) 46 902 5508
- www.royaltaragolfclub.com
- Green Fees: €30–€35

COURSES NEARBY
Black Bush
Killeen Castle
Knightsbrook
Moor Park
Navan

ST ANNE'S   Established 1921

A NICE FEW BIRDIES

In Dublin Bay, in the palm of Dublin city's grasp, lies an island of sand. On it rests a bird sanctuary and two golf courses, separated by no more than a pitching wedge. When you butt up against the renowned Royal Dublin, it's hard to compete.

A huge new clubhouse, additional mounding, new greens and tees are the result of a busy few years at the club as it adds more style to a natural, flat links. Now the truth is that some of the mounding looks out of place and the course is never going to pack in the excitement of the big dune-lined courses elsewhere, but be prepared for the terrors of the wind. Its openness means the wind will rip into you at every opportunity: into your face (the 7th is a par 4, 465-yard brute), or at your back (at 506 yards the par 5 1st is reachable with a drive and a mid iron). Fairways and greens are clearly visible from the tee, making driving sweeter and there are few design tricks here. You can see the challenges and hone your shots to meet them. Ultimately, it is

you against the wind. Greens are big, undulating – sometimes sharply so – and wonderful. It promises a good bump-and-run education, without delivering the 'wow' factor of its immediate neighbour.

The big disappointment was the sensational, tossing fairway on the opening hole, which then wasn't repeated until the 16th. Please pay attention to the many birds you won't have seen before, as they whip around you or leave friendly deposits on fairways and tee boxes. At least they ignore the greens.

FAVOURITE HOLES
Par 3 10th and 17th. The 10th hits into the wind alongside the marshes of the sanctuary. It has a large water feature in front of a well-presented green. The 17th is downwind with the green set among dunes. Nice tee box, great tee shot.

TOUGHEST HOLE
Par 4 7th. 465 yards. A flat, curving hole into the wind. What more needs to be said?

POINTS								
CD	A	G/F	B/W	L	F	V	G Ex	Total
14	7	8	7	7	8	6	14	71

THE COURSE
- Par 71
- Length: 6,443 yards
- St Anne's Golf Club, Bull Island Nature Reserve, Dollymount, Dublin 5
- Tel: +353 (0) 1 833 6471
- www.stanneslinksgolf.com
- Green Fees: €40–€50

COURSES NEARBY
Deer Park
Howth
Royal Dublin

ST HELEN'S BAY   Established 1993

A LATE RUSH

It's a winding country lane that brings you to this parkland club (resort) and you pass several holes on the way. As you play your round, you cross this lane a number of times. It adds to the vitality and interest of St Helen's Bay.

When you step out of the car you hear the sea. Unfortunately, you only get to enjoy its splendour on the last three stunning holes. It's a long time to wait but there is plenty to keep you occupied before you get there. I wouldn't call St Helen's particularly attractive – it has more of a windswept look – but there are some strong water features (streams and ponds on six holes), old stone walls that bracket tee shots and approaches, and palm trees – I kid you not. The land has gentle curves and, despite the fairway bunkers, it is definitely a driver's course. The 12th and 13th are long, tough holes and start a tricky run for home that brings this course to life.

Sometimes the course feels a bit erratic on the eye, like there's too much going on, but that may be down to some scrappy tree planting and the flat landscape on certain holes – and these are the least rewarding. Greens are good, varying considerably in size and difficulty, which means you can't take anything for granted. The 15th is minuscule.

It is a perfectly enjoyable course without ever stretching the imagination. At least not until you arrive on the 16th where the course changes dramatically: fifteen parkland holes, then three excellent links holes to finish (see below).

FAVOURITE HOLE
Par 4 18th. 250 yards. A terrifying hole for Index 15. There's no fairway to be seen beyond the scattering of dunes (aim at the palms) and your eye is dragged unerringly to the curve of the cliffs and sea that sweep under the tiny green.

TOUGHEST HOLE
Par 3 17th. 203 yards. The 12th is deservedly Index 1 but hole 17 is a one-shot demon. Long, dramatic and difficult. From a raised tee the small green seems almost hidden (and protected) by a hungry dune. A wall to the right is preferable to the steep drop left.

POINTS								
CD	A	G/F	B/W	L	F	V	G Ex	Total
13	7	7	8	7	7	7	14	70

THE COURSE
- Par 72
- Length: 6,446 yards
- St Helen's Bay Golf Resort, Kilrane, Rosslare Harbour, Co. Wexford
- Tel: +353 (0) 53 913 3234
- www.sthelensbay.com
- Green Fees: €25–€40

COURSES NEARBY
Courtown
Rosslare
Wexford

ST MARGARET'S   Established 1992

ROLLING AND MUSCULAR

St Margaret's presents an interesting dichotomy: it is a fine parkland course that lies on an uninteresting, open landscape. If you look at the hole you're playing, it has good shape and flow, but, if you zoom out and look around, it doesn't captivate in the same way. This happens at many courses around the country but St Margaret's has a substantial reputation to live up to. I found it an entertaining course, although I didn't warm to it. Perhaps having heard such great things I expected it to be more dramatic, like Druid's Glen. But there are enough strong holes to make it worth a visit and it is still maturing. Located in such a peaceful setting, so close to Dublin Airport, it will remain a favourite.

Big hitters will be in paradise, with only the 6th and 11th needing guile. I hit only two out of fourteen fairways but was never severely punished, so despite some narrow fairways, you will find room. Fast greens are often elevated so you can see what awaits your second shot. I found length to be quite deceptive, even from the 100-yard marker: take care.

St Margaret's is a manufactured landscape, with a lot of rolling mounds sweeping all around you. There are many water features, too, and these add hugely to the appeal, nowhere more so than on the impressive par 3s which all have water. And some serious ponds appear on the 8th and 18th.

The 18th is Index 2 and a superb finishing hole. Overall, it is surprisingly generous for a par 73.

FAVOURITE HOLE
Par 3 5th. 159 yards. Strikingly different from what comes before, this downhill hole threads between trees around the green, and water on the left. A perfect setting for the green.

TOUGHEST HOLE
Par 4 6th. 431 yards. Long, obviously, but the drive is the hardest part as you can't see enough of the fairway before it dog-legs right. My best drive of the day went straight in the water. Then it's a long approach to a hard and fast green.

POINTS								
CD	A	G/F	B/W	L	F	V	G Ex	Total
15	7	8	8	6	10	8	15	77

THE COURSE

- Par 73
- Length: 6,629 yards
- St Margaret's Golf Club, St Margaret's, Co. Dublin
- Tel: +353 (0) 1 864 0400
- www.stmargaretsgolf.com
- Green Fees: €25–€40

COURSES NEARBY
Corrstown
Forrest Little
Roganstown
Swords Open

SCARKE   Established 2004

FIELD DAY

Scarke is a classic example of farmland golf. From a driving range and pitch-and-putt course, an eighteen-hole golf course has materialised. The front nine are plastered across a huge field on an easy hillside; the back nine are more of the same but with more maturity and more inventiveness. Water appears periodically, but on holes 2 and 14 it is with spectacular effect. The 2nd is a downhill par 3 with an almost island green that is nerve-wracking, and the 14th is a par 5 that has ponds along the left-hand side all the way to the green. Both holes are at the bottom of the course and so capture all the water naturally. The other water features are not so good.

It is all enjoyable if basic stuff, with some good mountain views thrown in. It's not about quality, but there is enough of that quirky, home-made design to keep things alive – like the distance marker posts standing in the middle of the fairway. Once the trees grow up on the front nine especially they will gain more definition – and add some much needed protection from wayward hitters – but there's nothing here to tempt you away from nearby New Ross. The 'clubhouse' is a shop/check-in kind of place.

Very short for a par 72.

FAVOURITE HOLE
Par 3 2nd. 125 m. Looks good, plays tough. Water is the key ingredient, surrounding the green on three sides. A pleasure to find the putting surface.

TOUGHEST HOLE
Par 5 14th. 432 m. Yes, it's short, but the water is along the left, almost the entire way. And, if that wasn't enough, the slope of the fairway will drag you that way too.

POINTS								
CD	A	G/F	B/W	L	F	V	G Ex	Total
10	5	5	6	7	4	7	10	54

THE COURSE

- Par 72
- Length: 5,594 m
- Scarke Golf Club, New Ross, Co. Wexford
- Tel: +353 (0) 87 237 4444
- www.scarkegolf.com
- Green Fees: €18–€22

COURSES NEARBY
Enniscorthy
Mountain View
New Ross

SCRABO   Established 1907

BEAUTY AND THE BEAST

One word: extraordinary. There is simply no end to the drama and the challenge of this short course. Situated on Scrabo Hill, on slopes covered with gorse and heather, this is quite probably the greatest inland test of golf you will face on this island, and also one of the most beautiful. The views from almost every hole are astounding and the panorama from the clubhouse balcony is perfection. On a clear day you can see the Isle of Man and Scotland across Strangford Lough. Closer to home is Scrabo Tower, a magnificent nineteenth-century turret that rises high above the 1st green and serves as a centrepiece.

Scrabo will test every skill and wit you possess. Staying on fairways and finding small putting surfaces is always tough. It can be frustrating as good shots are not always rewarded and it might break a lesser golfer – take that as a challenge.

The course plunges up and down the hillside, sliding through gorse-covered mounds and over tumbling rock. Drives of breathtaking proportion greet you at every turn and 100 per cent concentration is needed. Even shots into uphill greens may require bump-and-run.

I must stress that the 8th introduces you to a lethal junction of holes, so be careful. And there are some tough climbs and descents.

I am deducting points for crossing fairways, lack of directions and two crazy holes (the 15th – where the fairway ends blindly at 230 yards – and the 7th), which are simply unfair.

FAVOURITE HOLE

Par 4 1st (see photo). 404 yards. Play from the back tees (459 yards) to appreciate fully the best opening hole in Irish golf. You hit over a valley onto a narrow, rising fairway that is squeezed by hills of gorse. Then to a heavily protected green above with Scrabo Tower alongside.

TOUGHEST HOLE

Par 4 12th. 441 yards. The 7th and 15th are so blind you'll cry, but the 12th is another monster that hits over the 8th and 9th to a fairway that resembles a corrugated steel roof. A long shot uphill with no room for error.

POINTS

CD	A	G/F	B/W	L	F	V	G Ex	Total
17	10	8	9	10	8	10	19	91

THE COURSE

- Par 72
- Length: 6,130 yards
- Scrabo Golf Club, 233 Scrabo Road, Newtownards, Co. Down, BT23 4SL
- Tel: +44 (0) 28 9181 2355 (048 from Rep. of Ire.)
- www.scrabo-golf-club.org
- Green Fees: £19–£24

COURSES NEARBY

Blackwood
Castlereagh Hills
Clandeboye
Shandon Park

SEAFIELD   Established 2002

SEA AND FIELD

Seafield has done itself no favours. The development's overbearing housing estate swamps the opening holes, offering an unpleasant reminder of what modern golf courses aspire to. Build the course, the houses and the hotel, and people will flood in. The aesthetics of golf are secondary – the par 3 4th has a backdrop of drab houses and you walk through them to reach the 5th. What was the developer thinking? Here is a seaside golf course that introduces you to the sea only after the 8th. It is ever-present after that as the holes are very open, with the 11th and 17th running above the beach and sharing the same green. The 16th and 17th offer the best views on the difficult and exposed back nine, although there's a pretentious new house that comes in to play on the 16th.

The course is good and bad: the best part is hitting into devilishly tricky greens. They are superbly presented, they're small, and they are usually at odd angles requiring laser-like accuracy. And they are well protected, either by bunkers, water or trees (particularly the 1st to 4th). The 5th is a perfect example: a very dull drive is saved by a terrific approach shot over water. The 2nd, 7th, 8th, 13th and 15th are also saved by good approaches.

The par 70 has a good mix of short (300 yards) and long (420+ yards) par 4s, and there is no doubt that, with its narrow fairways and small greens, it is a challenge, but I found it captivating only occasionally. A lot of work is being done, and let's hope this will make all the difference.

FAVOURITE HOLE
Par 4 1st. 326 yards. A great, if tricky, start. A high tee drives between old trees over a stream to a very tight fairway that rises and then heads left into the green. Precision required.

TOUGHEST HOLE
Par 4 15th. 423 yards. A mad, bad hole. A blind drive over the hilltop leaves what looks like a simple shot into the green. Wrong green. Yours is way left, through a tiny gap in a small conifer wood. Only a perfect drive gives you access.

POINTS								
CD	A	G/F	B/W	L	F	V	G Ex	Total
13	7	8	7	7	9	6	11	68

THE COURSE
- Par 70
- Length: 6,165 yards
- Seafield Golf Club, Ballymoney, Gorey, Co. Wexford
- Tel: +353 (0) 53 942 4777
- www.seafieldgolf.com
- Green Fees: €25–€45

COURSES NEARBY
Ballymoney
Courtown

SEAPOINT   Established 1993

AVENUES OF GORSE

It is surprising to find two back-to-back courses (Seapoint and Baltray) with such different fairways and dunes. Seapoint's fairways are far flatter and the dunes, even by the sea, are less imposing. But that makes it more playable and you get better sea views from the high tee boxes: the 16th to 18th is a great closing stretch.

And yet the start is tame. Parkland-style holes take you into a den of unattractive houses. They are decent holes with good water features, trees and strong bunkering but they don't have much bite. It's the back nine where the course finds its teeth. Holes 7 to 9 do a good job of joining the two sets of holes and the houses disappear from view shortly afterwards.

The back nine are easier to compare with Baltray. At Seapoint you are less likely to see balls kick off fairways or run down steep greenside slopes, so it feels easier. That said, Seapoint has more gorse-flanked holes, giving them definition and danger – the 11th to 13th are excellent. It makes the back nine more colourful, interesting and, for many golfers, more enjoyable.

The back nine have many deep bunkers to contend with and greens that are presented with a dash of flair. It makes you want to attack them but, as with any good links, consider other options too. The final holes throw you into the biggest dunes as you head straight back towards the spanking new clubhouse and great food.

FAVOURITE HOLE
Par 4 11th. 344 m. Good sweep to the fairway as it drifts slightly upwards around a corner of bunkers. It just looks great. The 14th (384 m), which is half-links and half-parkland, promises two great shots on another sweeping hole that ends in trees.

TOUGHEST HOLE
Par 4 5th. 353 m. The hole is flat with trees all along the right. You are required to hit around them – a fade if you can – which leaves a long shot to a green surrounded by water on three sides. The 16th is also tough.

POINTS								
CD	A	G/F	B/W	L	F	V	G Ex	Total
15	7	9	9	8	9	8	16	81

THE COURSE

- Par 72
- Length: 6,075 m
- Seapoint Golf Club, Termonfeckin, Co. Louth
- Tel: +353 (0) 41 982 2333
- www.seapointgolfclub.com
- Green Fees: €40–€55

COURSES NEARBY
Bellewstown
County Louth
Laytown & Bettystown

SHANDON PARK   Established 1926

ENJOY BEING FOOLED

I have always enjoyed courses like Shandon Park. It has a relaxed pace that embraces the trees, the surroundings and the parkland holes themselves. There are few holes that truly stand out as being exceptional (the 6th, 10th and 15th) but the eighteen work in perfect harmony.

When you stand on the 1st, it all looks very gentle, flat, tidy and green. A perfect stroll of golf, if you will. And that's what I like even more – you have been fooled. Shandon Park has a handful of flat holes but there are far more with great rises and falls. It gives several holes a real buzz, but the course never loses that comfortable pace. You are always striding along tree-lined fairways and other holes are often on view – bar the 14th (see below). It makes driving a pleasure and big hitters will be in their element. But don't think that excludes short hitters because Shandon Park is a perfect length and straight enough to give everyone a fun and testing game. The two par 5s use angled hillsides brilliantly and you'll need all the run you can find on the 543-yard 3rd.

Considering the course's suburban location, with views over Belfast to the hills beyond, you are well ensconced in trees. And some green settings are glorious, even if the road is only a few yards behind them. A smile-a-minute golf course that is elegantly simple.

FAVOURITE HOLE
Par 3 15th. 174 yards. Perfect tee, perfect green, perfect backdrop and perfect dip in between. It looks so appetising but the slope up to the green will ruin any shot that's short. And the bunkers are deep.

TOUGHEST HOLE
Par 4 14th. 372 yards. A blind-ish drive into a dog-leg that sweeps right and up. The tee shot needs strength if the green is to be seen, but the putting surface is out of sight and the sharp fall-off left makes it a difficult approach.

POINTS								
CD	A	G/F	B/W	L	F	V	G Ex	Total
14	7	8	7	6	9	9	17	77

THE COURSE

- Par 70
- Length: 6,336 yards (white tees)
- Shandon Park Golf Club, 73 Shandon Park, Belfast, BT5 6NH
- Tel: +44 (0) 28 9080 5030 (048 from Rep. of Ire.)
- www.shandonpark.net
- Green Fees: £30

COURSES NEARBY
Belvoir Park
Castlereagh Hills
Knock
Malone
Rockmount

SHANNON   Established 1966

FLIGHTS OF FANCY

An easy review to write. Shannon is a perfectly gentle parkland experience. Cosy, in fact. I'm sure some people would say that it's too close to the airport, it's heavily tree-lined and it's flat, but that would be to miss so much that is enjoyable about Shannon. Yes, planes fly overhead sporadically, but that adds to the entertainment. (No, really!) And you drive right by the airport to reach the course.

Dark, tree-lined fairways look very average from the 1st tee, but they have a great rhythm, they step in and step back and they add important character and danger all over the place. Yet, if you're smart, you will find room around them. And the fairways have rhythm too. A 3 iron should often be considered off the tee with short holes and tricky dog-legs causing problems for longer hitters. You need to think your way around and that adds interest and enjoyment. Play it twice: once sensibly, and once with a dash of recklessness.

The great condition of the course covers all elements of your day's golf, from attractive tee boxes to well-bunkered greens with lovely, straightforward surfaces that lean towards you.

The course is squeezed in neatly enough so don't expect big expanses of space. Wander too far off-line and the trees will not be the only threat. There are some strong water features, drenched in reeds, and you finally get to the sea's edge on the 17th, for a terrifying par 3.

What makes the golf experience is the rhythm, the generous feel and the simple design that delivers one good hole after another.

FAVOURITE HOLE
Par 4 9th. 455 yards. Long and straight, this is Index 1 and it's a beauty. No bunkers, just a cavorting fairway that must be found if you're to reach the green in two.

TOUGHEST HOLE
Par 3 17th. 213 yards. Play from the whites or blues for the best effect alongside the sea. The best views are from here (the airport is at the other end) and, at 213 yards, plenty of people will find the sea short of the green.

POINTS								
CD	A	G/F	B/W	L	F	V	G Ex	Total
14	7	9	8	7	9	7	17	78

THE COURSE
- Par 72
- Length: 6,448 yards
- Shannon Golf Club, Shannon Airport, Shannon, Co. Clare
- Tel: +353 (0) 61 471 849
- www.shannongolfclub.ie
- Green Fees: €25–€65

COURSES NEARBY
Castletroy
Dromoland Castle
Ennis
Woodstock

SILVERWOOD   Established 1984

AN IDYLLIC GOLFING LANDSCAPE

Silverwood has all the finesse of a doner kebab at 2 a.m. And it's just as enjoyable. But unlike the kebab, Silverwood has serious potential. And I mean 'serious'. This is a stunning, natural landscape, rich in specimen trees and woods, with holes leading you a merry dance up and down and rarely impinging on each other. There are surrounding views, and water too. Considering this is a pay-and-play facility, with an unimpressive car park and walk to the 1st tee, you will be quite amazed when you arrive at the opening hole. It's a great drive down onto a rising fairway that swings away to the right. The dog-legs are a popular theme, using the trees and the gentle hills to maximum advantage. Time and again, you will be eager to get up and blast the ball when you see the hole before you. And that, for me, is one of the joys of golf: the anticipation.

The course satisfies the important niche of beginner and occasional golfers, but if a serious designer was brought in with serious money behind him, Silverwood would be up there with the best. As it is, you're still going to have tremendous fun on holes of all different shapes and sizes.

The biggest let-down is the greens. They have no shape and they sit on the land with scant bunkering and little danger around them. It is what you would expect of a basic-quality course but it still disappoints.

You have room to be aggressive, and the venue comes with a ski slope and a par 3 course. Good luck reading the scorecard map.

FAVOURITE HOLE

Par 4 10th. 314 yards. From one of the many high tees you are presented with a difficult drive. There is water on the left, below, and a scattering of big trees on the right. A tough drive in a picturesque setting.

TOUGHEST HOLE

Par 4 14th. 422 yards. Index 1 requires a big drive up the left on this relatively flat hole that then dog-legs easily around trees. The 5th (Index 2) is similarly shaped, although it drops to a stream and then goes up to the green.

POINTS

CD	A	G/F	B/W	L	F	V	G Ex	Total
15	8	6	6	7	6	8	15	71

THE COURSE

- Par 72
- Length: 6,188 yards
- Silverwood Golf Club, Turmoyra Lane, Silverwood, Lurgan, Co. Armagh, BT66 6NG
- Tel: +44 (0) 28 3832 5380 (048 from Rep. of Ire.)
- www.silverwoodgolfclub.com
- Green Fees: £18–£21

COURSES NEARBY

Banbridge
Edenmore
Lurgan
Portadown

SKELLIG BAY   Established 2005

WONDER WALL

Skellig Bay is a unique experience. It is defined both by its beauty across a gently moving hilltop, under the shadow of larger mountains, and by its long, drystone walls that lead you a merry walk over this wonderfully open golf course. Over 8,000 m of walls give this course a remarkable character, starting in the car park. Even on the plain and wide holes, it is the walls (and views) which give it that extra-special something. You drive either at mountains or at Skellig Bay itself, and the 14th and 15th put you right on the cliffs (peek over the side at the 14th tee).

You will find a few hidden hazards (water under the green on the 1st and 4th) but, with its open fairways, it is a straightforward course, designed to please more than to hurt. The par 3s are another matter, with three over 168 m and tough bunkering or water. And if it's windy, that's another matter entirely.

Holes 3, 4, 5 and 18 are the most thrilling and most dangerous, rising up the valley of the Fionnglassa River, with wild swathes of gorse, great colour and good carries over the river. Down below is the famous Butler's Pool where Tiger Woods and Mark O'Meara once fished.

Since it is a modern course with American touches, you can expect long, sweeping fairways, mounding and banking (but neither too noticeable nor severe), and perfect greens that sit up high or down low – offering different attacking opportunities.

It is relaxing, beautiful and fun. The perfect foil for Waterville.

FAVOURITE HOLE
Par 3 3rd. 168 m. A high tee hits down through the gorse, over the river and onto a flat green that sits in a hollow. Perfect to look at and perfect to play.

TOUGHEST HOLE
Par 4 5th. 326 m. Target golf, hitting over a hollow of gorse, trees and the river. Good length required to see a claustro-phobic green that will destroy you if you go left or long (river) or right (thick rough rising up the bank).

POINTS								
CD	A	G/F	B/W	L	F	V	G Ex	Total
16	8	8	8	10	6	8	18	82

THE COURSE

- Par 72
- Length: 6,150 m
- Skellig Bay Golf Club, Waterville, Co. Kerry
- Tel: +353 (0) 66 947 4133
- www.skelligbay.com
- Green Fees: €35–€70

COURSES NEARBY
Ring of Kerry
Waterville

SKERRIES Established 1905

A SLOW START, A RUMBLING FINISH

With Balbriggan up the road, there doesn't seem to be much to choose between these two courses. But there are significant differences: Balbriggan is delightfully steady – one good hole after another – while Skerries doesn't really get going until the 8th, after which there are some terrific holes; and while both are covered with pine trees, a shallow hollow at Skerries throws up some impressive beech trees. These add an extra dimension, especially as they define the hill corner that hosts Skerries' best holes (the 1st, the 9th to 12th and 18th). But there are definitely a few weak holes on the 'outer' ring: the 3rd is an uninspiring Index 1 beside the railway line; the 4th is a ridiculously short par 5 of 395 m (the course is a short par 73); and the 6th and 14th are par 5s that dog-leg right at 90 degrees.

From the 8th on, the drives are delicious, firing between the pines mostly, but also up the corrugated hillside or down the slopes in the top corner of the course. Greens are entertaining with some clever angles and some good defences.

The maturity of the course undoubtedly gives it something extra and the back nine find better variety as they move away from their dependence on the pine trees. Fairways open up and you see more of the holes. The 16th, 17th and 18th are a great finish on a mature and diverse track that promises flashes of real fun.

FAVOURITE HOLE
Par 4 9th. 283 m. A driver's dream. The drive fires between the beech trees and up the hillside to an inviting pin that you imagine you can reach. Plenty of room so why not have a go?

TOUGHEST HOLE
Par 4 18th. 363 m. An almost mirror image drive of the 9th, but you need to keep left if you want to see the green, which dives away quickly from the top. Trees short and right of the green are a tough defence if your drive strays.

POINTS								
CD	A	G/F	B/W	L	F	V	G Ex	Total
14	7	8	7	6	8	8	15	73

THE COURSE
- Par 73
- Length: 5,844 m
- Skerries Golf Club, Hacketstown, Skerries, Co. Dublin
- Tel: +353 (0) 1 849 1567
- www.skerriesgolfclub.ie
- Green Fees: €20–€30

COURSES NEARBY
Balbriggan
Beaverstown
Hollywood Lakes
Laytown & Bettystown
Turvey

SKIBBEREEN   Established 1935

A FINE, FRIENDLY CLUB

Converted from nine to eighteen holes in 1993, Skibbereen offers up some interesting holes. The original nine have a wild heathland/parkland feel, with pines and evergreens lining some good rugged fairways, and gorse and dense scruff appearing frequently. The 2nd is a remarkable little par 3, the green completely hidden in a depression behind gorse and wild rough. With the open space around you, you can't believe there's a hole at all. It is all on a gentle hillside and, while it looks quite spacious, you will find greens are long and narrow, so off-line drives will create problems for approaches. There's a good feeling here.

One hundred and fifty yards across the road are the new holes. This is a steeper hillside and five of the holes really shine. Their wild touches and shapes are fantastic. Standing on the 10th, it seems straightforward, a short dog-leg around a lone tree, then the 11th is even shorter, over an angled rise and up to a perched green. The par 5 12th (427 yards) is blind, up and over the hilltop with gorse everywhere, including the middle of the fairway. The best views are from here, and it is an enticing shot down onto the green. The 13th is even better but still blind, and the 14th is a strong par 3 to finish this dynamic stretch.

It is a short, country course (five holes under 300 yards) with narrow, tough greens and plenty to worry about off the tee if you're wild. The clubhouse could do with a revamp, but it's friendly inside.

FAVOURITE HOLE
Par 4 13th. 337 yards. A post marks your line over the hill with gorse and scruff beside you. The fairway turns to rough after 230 yards, then rises sharply to a green that sits on the skyline. It is tricky to approach and harder to putt on.

TOUGHEST HOLE
Par 4 1st. 402 yards. The 13th is harder, and the 8th is a tough Index 1 with water left of the green, but the 1st is a tricky start, especially as you have yet to 'meet' the greens, and this one lies below your eyeline. A difficult approach.

POINTS								
CD	A	G/F	B/W	L	F	V	G Ex	Total
14	7	8	7	7	6	8	14	71

THE COURSE
- Par 71
- Length: 5,728 yards
- Skibbereen Golf Club, Licknavar, Skibbereen, Co. Cork
- Tel: +353 (0) 28 21227
- www.skibbgolf.com
- Green Fees: €20–€30

COURSES NEARBY
Bandon
Bantry Bay

SLADE VALLEY   Established 1970

BRING YOUR CLIMBING BOOTS

For some serious hiking and views over Dublin, Slade Valley is the place to go. You will love it or hate it. Personally, I thought it was fun: it is short, there are plenty of thrilling shots (your drive off the 1st for starters), and you definitely need to think your way around. Do I fire it on or run it down the hill? Is it a driver or a 3 iron? You get the idea, but being straight is crucial if you want to get at the greens because the trees are thick and well placed, the changes in elevation can be severe and the dog-legs very precise – the 3rd, 6th, 8th, 10th, 15th and 16th demand precision placement into the elbow.

There is no spectacular hole, but it is consistently good as it winds around the clubhouse. Several par 4s – three of them sharp dog-legs – are just a drive/3 iron and a flick of a wedge. Of these the 3rd stands out: it is a right-angled dog-leg that requires no more than a 3 iron off the tee as hitting your driver may put players on the 9th tee at risk. Then it's a lovely punch shot downhill towards the views beyond.

On the other hand, these are countered by six tough par 4s (the 1st, 9th, 10th, 11th, 17th and 18th) and some mightily amusing greens – the 16th and 17th have swings that defy belief.

It all comes together to offer a bit of everything. It's a simple design and cramped in places (be careful around the 4th green/18th tee box which are practically one and the same) but the elevation changes provide exercise and fun.

FAVOURITE HOLE
Par 4 15th. 282 m. An uphill, gentle, but tight, dog-leg that really demands a lot of your second shot, especially with the sweeping green and the trees immediately behind.

TOUGHEST HOLE
Par 4 18th. 372 m. It is a long climb up to the clubhouse and you might well be exhausted at this point. The 9th is almost identical. Beware players on the 6th who drive over the fairway from your right.

POINTS								
CD	A	G/F	B/W	L	F	V	G Ex	Total
13	6	7	6	7	8	9	15	71

THE COURSE
- Par 70
- Length: 5,448 m
- Slade Valley Golf Club, Lynch Park, Brittas, Co. Dublin
- Tel: +353 (0) 1 458 2183
- www.sladevalleygolfclub.ie
- Green Fees: €30–€35

COURSES NEARBY
Beech Park
Castlewarden
Citywest
South County

SLIEVENAMON   Established 1999

SHORT, OPEN, FARMLAND GOLF

Slievenamon can be described in one sentence: if you think of golf as a car, then Slievenamon spends its time stuck in second gear, very occasionally slipping in to third – Dundrum, played earlier in the day, is comfortably in fourth gear, with several smooth switch-ups to fifth – and really it is not what golfers would call a golf course, although, having said that, it serves a purpose, which is to accommodate families, teenagers needing some place to try out their swing and men who want a good laugh while they bash the ball about, because there is no class here, with the most basic of tee boxes and brick-like greens (long and narrow and sloping towards you), and fairways that have clearly never met a real fairway in their lives, an amusing collection of dog-legs, a few old trees, a ditch that is, well, a ditch, and a length and openness that ensures you can spray shots hither and thither without ever worrying about the end result.

I think you'll find that's one sentence. Slievenamon has no pretensions to being a great course and it appeals to a niche market of golfers who are not catered for by other courses. From that point of view, it's perfect.

FAVOURITE HOLE
Par 4 15th. 286 yards. A good driving hole up a gentle hill. A mature oak watches over the tee box while a further tree lingers up the fairway.

POINTS								
CD	A	G/F	B/W	L	F	V	G Ex	Total
5	3	3	4	7	6	5	6	39

THE COURSE
- Par 67
- Length: 4,874 yards
- Slievenamon Golf Club, Lisronagh, Clonmel, Co. Tipperary
- Tel: +353 (0) 52 6132213
- www.slievenamongolfclub.com
- Green Fees: €15–€20

COURSES NEARBY
Cahir
Callan
Carrick-on-Suir
Clonmel
Dundrum

SLIEVE RUSSELL   Established 1992

VARIETY IN EVERYTHING

What a cracking parkland course! Yes, a little too manufactured, but every ingredient you could ask for is here: lakes, mature trees, bunkers of white sand, hills, elevated tees. It all ensures tantalising drives, awesome approaches and beautiful holes. And, while each hole has its own unique character and sits unassaulted by other holes, you can still see plenty of the course and the surrounding countryside. The view from the 4th green is outstanding, as it looks across and down on several holes including the 12th and 13th, which wrap themselves around Lough Rud in an intimate embrace. It's lengthy (6,600 yards) but you will be so busy enjoying yourself you won't care. Imagine what it will be like when it matures fully.

Two lakes divide the course with a broad stream stretching between them. Four holes play over this stream, most notably the 2nd (see below) and the par 3 11th which needs a perfect shot to avoid getting wet or sandy. All in all, the six holes that involve water are among the best, but that would be unfair to holes 3 (see below), 5, 15 and 17. In fact, the 1st is the only poor hole on a course that has acres of space in which to express itself. There are plenty of little extras too.

There is a big hotel and health spa so it's a good destination for everyone. It is a touch pricey but you can easily see the amount of work that goes into such an immaculate course.

FAVOURITE HOLE
Par 4 3rd. 371 yards. Almost a dog-leg that drops down into a valley before rising to the green, which is about level with the tee box. The green is just visible through the trees and it's a demanding tee shot. The uphill second is to a narrow two-tiered green.

TOUGHEST HOLE
Par 4 2nd. 407 yards. After the poor 1st this seems almost unfair: a dog-leg around the lake and bunkers strategically placed which make a driver a dangerous proposition. But without it you'll have a 200-yard+ shot to a high green. Then there's the stream just out of view.

POINTS

CD	A	G/F	B/W	L	F	V	G Ex	Total
17	9	9	10	7	9	9	18	88

THE COURSE
- Par 72
- Length: 6,607 yards
- Slieve Russell Golf and Country Club, Cranaghan, Ballyconnell, Co. Cavan
- Tel: +353 (0) 49 952 5090
- www.quinnhotels.com
- Green Fees: €30–€49

COURSES NEARBY
Clones
County Cavan
Enniskillen

SOUTH COUNTY   Established 2002

IT'S ALL HERE

The walk up the 18th is just cruel. You've played a long round of golf and then there's this killer steep climb to finish. Worth it? Definitely.

The countryside around you – the forests and the sweeping starkness of the Dublin Mountains – could only be Irish, and the course sits in the valley. I played early in the morning, sunlight sparkling off the dew, breath billowing, peaks hidden in mist.

It's not that there are two nines, but that their challenges are on different levels. On the front nine the holes sweep easily ahead of you making driving a thrill on gentle slopes (the pretty par 3 3rd excepted). Fairways are wide and the dangers off the tee are not too severe: fairway bunkers, thick rough and some OB (holes 5 to 9). But you'll be lucky to find an even lie which makes hitting the impressive greens all the more difficult. From the 7th tee box look across the course. It appears barren, with few mature trees (oak and hawthorn), but the designer had plenty of space to work with and all the holes stand on their own It will age very nicely.

The second nine are more exciting and dangerous with water, more trees and more changes in elevation. Accurate driving is crucial, which you'll notice on the 10th as it disappears down the hill, opening up the countryside beyond. The 12th is a beautiful drive from a high tee to a sharp dog-leg. How much you take on depends on the nest of bunkers below. The 17th may be Index 1, but the hardest holes for visitors are the totally flat par 5s, the 13th and 15th.

FAVOURITE HOLE
Par 4 10th. 392 yards. After the openness of the previous holes, much of this hole is hidden. You have to hit and hope. Halfway down the fairway the green appears far below you – it is the best second shot you'll have.

TOUGHEST HOLE
Par 5 13th. 533 yards. Index 15. Water appears three times and the challenge is where to land your shots on this nasty, flat dog-leg. You have no idea how much to bite off on each shot.

POINTS								
CD	A	G/F	B/W	L	F	V	G Ex	Total
16	7	8	8	8	10	8	17	82

THE COURSE

- Par 72
- Length: 6,657 yards
- South County Golf Club, Lisheen Road, Brittas Village, Co. Dublin
- Tel: +353 (0) 1 458 2965
- www.southcountygolf.com
- Green Fees: €25–€50

COURSES NEARBY
Beech Park
Dublin City
Dublin Mountain
Slade Valley

SPA   Established 1907

GREEN COMPLEXES TO BE RECKONED WITH

There is a lot going on here and all of it good. The course has an enthralling shape with big trees, slopes and banks leading you a merry dance. It is a fascinating blend of all things parkland. The back nine are a touch better and there is a wonderful meeting of paths and tees around the 9th and 18th.

The course is not long (front tees) but it is testing, especially your approaches to greens. After a brief, dry spell, greens will be rock hard. If you see the ball kick off the opening greens then you'll have to change your game plan. And it is no easy matter to run the ball in as bunkers often lurch in front of the green, steep banks are ever-present and views can be restricted. The 5th is Index 3, at 350 yards, but the banks around the green could send a good iron shot 30 yards back towards you. The 17th (see below) is harder still. It's a popular feature and every approach needs lengthy consideration and, preferably, local knowledge. I hooked up with Frank after eleven holes and it made a huge difference.

Driving is a real pleasure as fairways and greens are usually visible – only the 15th is truly blind. Two of the hidden greens are on short dog-leg par 4s. Big hitters will be tempted but you won't gain anything. That's the nature of this course: it is pretty and short but it will hurt you if you don't respect it. Highly recommended and superb value for money.

Be sure to ask about the exasperated golfer who cut down a tree in the middle of the night.

FAVOURITE HOLE
Par 4 9th. 372 yards. Bobby's Bridge, named after the bridge in the middle of the fairway, far below the tee. It then rises sharply to the green. A big drive is required to clear the stream. Achieve that and it's a lazy 9 iron.

TOUGHEST HOLE
Par 3 17th. 165 yards. One shot. On first glance it looks innocuous, but look again. Forget that the green is tiered because the slope up to the green is severe and any weak shot will be punished harshly. A real card-wrecker so late in the day.

POINTS								
CD	A	G/F	B/W	L	F	V	G Ex	Total
15	8	8	7	6	10	10	17	81

THE COURSE
- Par 72
- Length: 6,130 yards
- Spa Golf Club, 20 Grove Road, Ballynahinch, Co. Down, BT24 8PN
- Tel: +44 (0) 28 9756 2365 (048 from Rep. of Ire.)
- www.spagolfclub.net
- Green Fees: £20–£25

COURSES NEARBY
Downpatrick
Lisburn
Rockmount
Royal County Down

STACKSTOWN   Established 1975

CREATIVE HILLSIDE GOLF

It would be very easy to compare Stackstown with Slade Valley. They're both short, sit on mountainsides and look down over Dublin City. The latter has the advantage of being farther away, with better views, but Stackstown is closer to the city and has more thrills and challenges. Don't get me wrong: I like Slade Valley, but Stackstown has quirky character: the little white cottage on the 3rd fairway stands out with nothing behind it but pine forest; the 17th hits over a small gorge with a stream tumbling along; and the 9th and 18th are almost identical holes, side by side. There's no huge passion to the design but it is a fun and exhausting day's golf. And two words that might sway the argument for you: Padraig Harrington.

Hillside golf means you will be faced with uphill and downhill drives. You can't always see where you are going and hidden putting surfaces abound. Does that sound enticing or infuriating? Whatever your answer, Stackstown is an exuberant course with natural streams, good woods and plenty going on all around you. The well-set greens are not easy to hit and the surfaces will trick you constantly. The fairways can also send balls rolling away into the trees so you'll understand when I say this is tactical golf. Index 1 and 2 are par 5s, and the toughest drive of the day is the 15th, which is Index 18.

Both Stackstown and Slade Valley are cursed by tight space which creates several dangerous holes. At Stackstown, the 8th drives over the 5th tee box, and the 3rd drives over the 2nd green.

FAVOURITE HOLES
Par 3 17th. 175 yards. This is a lovely setting. You are hitting up to the forest, over a hollow with running stream, and it's a single, challenging shot. The 2nd, 6th and 15th also deserve a mention.

TOUGHEST HOLE
Par 5 7th. 489 yards. It shouldn't be difficult, but with the fairway slope, which doesn't look severe, you could easily run across onto the 5th fairway and be blocked by trees. The green is deceptive to the approach too.

POINTS								
CD	A	G/F	B/W	L	F	V	G Ex	Total
14	8	8	7	8	8	9	16	78

THE COURSE

- Par 71
- Length: 5,811 yards
- Stackstown Golf Club, Kellystown Road, Rathfarnham, Dublin 16
- Tel: +353 (0) 1 494 1993
- www.stackstowngolfclub.com
- Green Fees: €30–€40

COURSES NEARBY
Castle
Edmondstown
Grange
Milltown

STRABANE   Established 1908

DOWN BY THE RIVER

You're in for quite a surprise when you come to Strabane. The car park, the opening hole and the other holes you see indicate that this is flat, short, parkland golf, but not a lot more.

The 1st is a good opening hole: wide with plenty of good trees watching you go by. The 2nd and 3rd pass similarly. Then you cross the road and the fun begins. The 4th comes as a real shock and such a treat. You drive out at the hills as the fairway drops out of view, and it drops and drops. You have to put the brakes on as you descend to the distant green. From flat to hilly in one fell swoop, and doesn't it make a difference? The curve on the holes makes an immediate impact as you dog-leg uphill for the 5th, and then roller-coaster across for the 6th. There's real shape and character and, despite some short holes, they are all difficult to read off the tee. The 7th is a glorious downhill par 3 through a tiny gap in the trees.

And then comes the river. Big and wide and the 9th tee hanging above it. It's a brave and beautiful drive down onto the plain. The 11th races up again, and the 13th and 14th are both short par 4s where flags may just be visible over the curves.

It's a marvellous adventure, all the more so because of that tame start. The 17th and 18th are back on the flat and make for a leisurely finish. A basic clubhouse.

FAVOURITE HOLES

Par 4 4th, 5th, 6th, 9th, 11th and par 3 7th. All for the reasons listed above. They have their difficulties and their beauty and you'll love every one of them.

TOUGHEST HOLE

Par 4 11th. 347 m. The hole rises across the hillside with a huge shoulder leaning in from the left. Your second will fade off the slope, which doesn't help as the green has an impenetrable thicket on the right. The green is long and double-tiered.

POINTS

CD	A	G/F	B/W	L	F	V	G Ex	Total
14	8	7	7	7	6	10	16	75

THE COURSE

- Par 69
- Length: 5,542 m
- Strabane Golf Club, 33 Ballycolman Road, Strabane, Co. Tyrone
- Tel: +44 (0) 28 7138 2271 (048 from Rep. of Ire.)
- www.strabanegolfclub.co.uk
- Green Fees: £16–£20

COURSES NEARBY
Ballybofey & Stranorlar
City of Derry
Letterkenny
Newtownstewart

STRANDHILL   Established 1931

AN UNSUNG HERO

Pay attention: come to Strandhill and bring your brain. This super links may only be a par 69, and somewhat overshadowed by County Sligo across the bay, but it goes to the heart of your golfing prowess. County Sligo gives you free rein with the driver but here you have to be smarter and more restrained, especially on the back nine where a couple of tricky dog-legs (the 13th and 15th) will perplex you. Fairways can be so tumbling that your ball will go anywhere, and firing at greens is a riot as they are either tucked behind these amazing fairways, slipped between dunes or perched up high. Bump-and-run is always on but don't expect them to run straight. The best holes are the 5th to 7th and the 12th to 16th, but it's a good opening and a tough finish – the 18th is Index 1.

Strandhill sits on an open landscape between a giant dune and Knocknarea. Sea laps on two sides and you play alongside the beach for the 2nd, 3rd and 4th. From the elevated 7th tee, on the opposite side, you can watch surfers taking on the ocean waves. The routing weaves you around beautifully, sliding across the open terrain and then in and out of dunes. It doesn't have the spectacular views of its neighbour but it is still beautiful.

If you come this way to play Sligo and/or Enniscrone, do not pass Strandhill by. It is every bit as good, if only in a different way. And that comes down to the course architects: the club members.

The 8th to 11th are tame and cramped by houses, but change is in the air.

FAVOURITE HOLE
Par 4 13th. 333 m. Of the best holes this one, The Valley, takes the honours. A disorienting blind shot to a valley below, which then whips right between imposing dunes. Your second must bisect two guardian dunes, which channel you into a very small, amphitheatre green.

TOUGHEST HOLE
Par 4 15th. 306 m. A sweeping uphill dog-leg with the flag hanging on to the sky. Your tee shot is about distance and bravery as a wall of dunes awaits. Then it's straight uphill and a steeply sloping green.

POINTS								
CD	A	G/F	B/W	L	F	V	G Ex	Total
17	9	10	8	10	9	10	19	92

THE COURSE
- Par 69
- Length: 5,467 m
- Strandhill Golf Club, Strandhill, Co. Sligo
- Tel: +353 (0) 71 916 8188
- www.strandhillgc.com
- Green Fees: €30–€40

COURSES NEARBY
Castle Dargan
County Sligo
Enniscrone

SWORDS OPEN   Established 1995

ALWAYS ACCESSIBLE

This is right next door to Roganstown. The 17th tee box sits beside Roganstown's putting green, separated only by the Broadmeadow River. In fairness, it is also separated by class. Swords does not have the charisma or quality of Roganstown, and this is reflected in the green fees. That said, Swords presents some interesting challenges. It is designed for a different golfer too. Here you will find people who want lots of fun and don't take the game too seriously. Judging by the numbers on the course, there are lots of such golfers.

There is an outer circuit of holes (the 10th to 15th), and these resemble the holes of its neighbour, with flattish fairways flanked by continuous mounding. They are the least interesting on the course, situated as they are on a flat, open landscape. And from there you move to the main attraction – hole 16.

Broadmeadow River lends itself nicely to the character of the course. A bridge takes you to the 2nd tee and back again to the 5th, with the latter running along the river's edge. It also features up by the 16th green.

While you might infer from all this that Swords is basic, it still presents challenges. There are some tricky drives and some sneaky fall-offs that will catch first-timers. The 1st green is a case in point. Trees are growing strongly and the bunkering is smartly placed. Greens have good shapes with the 16th, again, standing out.

FAVOURITE HOLE

Par 4 16th. 351 m. What a bolt out of the blue. A fairway that kicks and rolls like a links. It's gorgeous. There is trouble off the tee and then you have to hope the ball sits up for you. The green is a great shape and just sits beyond the bucking fairway.

TOUGHEST HOLE

Par 5 6th. 461 m. It's a straight hole, but difficulty awaits on both sides and all the way to the green. It might feel claustrophobic to hookers and slicers.

POINTS								
CD	A	G/F	B/W	L	F	V	G Ex	Total
12	6	6	6	5	5	7	13	60

THE COURSE

- Par 71
- Length: 5,435 m
- Swords Golf Club, Balheary Avenue, Swords, Co. Dublin
- Tel: +353 (0) 1 840 9819
- www.swordsgolfclub.ie
- Green Fees: €20–€25

COURSES NEARBY
Corrstown
Roganstown
St Margaret's

TANDRAGEE   Established 1911

TALL AND COLOURFUL

The Duke of Manchester's old estate offers plenty of colour, a feeling reinforced when you drive under the archway and through the entrance gates. And, when you walk up to the 1st tee under a big oak and look down towards the first green, you know it's going to be an adventure.

It is not dissimilar to nearby Banbridge but there is a touch more traditional parkland finesse to Tandragee. It lacks that quality touch of a big course, but it promises some fine holes and features. Perhaps with a good designer's eye (and fee) Tandragee could rise up the rankings because the key elements are here. The course has big shapes and big trees, and enough challenges to keep you focused.

The holes go back and forth with big trees separating fairways effectively. They channel holes and their rhythm changes constantly so, while some holes have dense thickets that make driving tough (the 10th, 11th and 17th), others have scatterings of trees in all shapes and sizes. There is also an old stone wall that divides the 10th and 11th with some panache,

and the large ash trees around this part of the course make it particularly colourful. It does mean you have to pay attention, even on a course as short as this. And the endless curves that take you up, down or over crests make it tough to maintain your driving rhythm.

Hopefully they'll have applied a new lick of paint before you get here.

FAVOURITE HOLE
Par 4 2nd. 256 m. The only dog-leg of note, this is a perfect length for the brave. The hole rises calmly through the oaks and then shifts right down to the green. It's a good setting for the green with some sharp-faced bunkers.

TOUGHEST HOLE
Par 5 3rd. 487 m. Index 2 takes you up a good hill. You're blind for your second over the crest, and blind again for your shot down to the green. There is plenty of room but, like a few holes, it's not easy to know exactly where to aim.

POINTS

CD	A	G/F	B/W	L	F	V	G Ex	Total
14	7	7	6	6	8	9	15	72

THE COURSE
- Par 71
- Length: 5,578 m
- Tandragee Golf Club, 11 Markethill Rd, Tandragee, Co. Armagh, BT62 2ER
- Tel: +44 (0) 28 3884 1272 (048 from Rep. of Ire.)
- www.tandragee.co.uk
- Green Fees: £15–£25

COURSES NEARBY
Banbridge
County Armagh
Lurgan
Portadown

THURLES   Established 1909

CLASSIC, ELEGANT PARKLAND

I had heard much about Thurles before my arrival. A good course that rightfully claims 'championship' status, yet it has none of those airs and graces: it is calm and unpretentious. The big clubhouse is immediately off the busy N62 road and it, too, is unfussy.

So even before you walk through the tunnel on your way to the 1st you know what kind of golf awaits. A par 5 Index 18 is a leisurely start to be sure. The flatter, more open front nine are out here and they have considerable variety as they curve around a whole mixture of young and mature trees and woods. Big bunkers fill elbows, water is a serious threat on four holes (ponds and a river) and greens are shapely and well protected – they have been created to allow bunkers to sneak underneath (front) and above (behind). The charming 122-yard 3rd is a perfect example. Off the tee, the 8th is odd (see below) while the 9th is out of context with its tossing fairway.

Back by the clubhouse, the 10th is Index 1 and starts a run of classic parkland holes that gently rise and fall between big oaks and beeches. There is that lovely greenness that tempts you every step of the way. Bunkers are less dangerous and the greens are flat and lie calmly on the land, making them surprisingly tough to attack as you can't see enough of them.

Thurles promises great golf, where your driver will be well used on the front nine (bar the 4th), and where you will feel more relaxed on the back nine. A good combination.

FAVOURITE HOLE

Par 3 11th. 201 yards. Downhill off a stone-sided tee box, to a green cupped in majestic trees. An old ruin lies halfway down the fairway, partially buried in the ground. It gives a dramatic touch. The 7th is a sweeping beauty with a giant beech in the fairway.

TOUGHEST HOLE

Par 5 8th. 529 yards. Bunkers lie straight ahead, implying you have to go right of the line of evergreen trees. In fact, you can also go over them as the evergreens split the fairway. Water on the left fronts a narrow and tricky downhill green.

POINTS								
CD	A	G/F	B/W	L	F	V	G Ex	Total
15	8	8	9	6	8	9	16	79

THE COURSE

- Par 72
- Length: 6,377 yards
- Thurles Golf Club, Turtulla, Thurles, Co. Tipperary
- Tel: +353 (0) 504 21983
- www.thurlesgolfclub.com
- Green Fees: €30

COURSES NEARBY
Ballykisteen
Dundrum
Rathdowney
Slievenamon

TIPPERARY   Established 1896

QUICK DRAW

As courses go, this one is a gentle stroll. It is not exciting, not dramatic, but it is a pleasant round of golf in a peaceful bit of countryside. There are easy fairways and placid greens, and little trouble to catch you out, but you don't want to come here with a big hook. Several holes, notably the 1st to the 3rd, will crucify you as there is no room off the tee. The 1st tee is tucked in against a long line of trees, and the 2nd and 3rd have out of bounds and more trees to confront. Not the kind of start hookers want. The positive side is that there is lots of room on the fairways and despite trees all over the course you can quickly recover from any trouble.

The greens were being hollow-tined and sanded when I visited, and it's the mark of a popular course when members volunteer to do the hard work: half a dozen of them were scattering sand with gusto.

The course has little distinction until you hit the 6th. Fairways present themselves more enticingly and driving becomes more interesting. This is especially true of the holes after the 13th.

What are rather flat fairways suddenly find a bit of backbone, hitching themselves into nice contours and sharp bumps. Trees stretch along the fairways and the sausage-roll evergreens down the 6th and 9th are most peculiar. Water on the 11th (see below) is a genuine hazard and a stream runs beside the 12th. All of these extra elements make the back nine a better run of holes.

Some signposts to the place would help.

FAVOURITE HOLES

Par 4 14th. 345 m. A good-looking hole from the tee. The fairway rises slowly and drifts right to a green you want to attack. There's a hollow at 220 m to add some punch. The pretty 15th is a promising understudy with a large bowl in front and steep fall-offs.

TOUGHEST HOLE

Par 4 11th. 391 m. Straight as a die. Long, with trees closing in to create a narrower approach to the green. Water to the right of the green compounds things.

POINTS								
CD	A	G/F	B/W	L	F	V	G Ex	Total
12	6	6	6	6	8	7	12	63

THE COURSE

- Par 70
- Length: 5,858 m
- Tipperary Golf Club, Rathanny, Tipperary, Co. Tipperary
- Tel: +353 (0) 62 51119
- www.tipperarygolfclub.com
- Green Fees: €20

COURSES NEARBY
Ballykisteen
Cahir
Dundrum
Mitchelstown

TRALEE   Established 1896

A TOUCH OF GENIUS

Stand by the clubhouse and Tralee hints slyly at the wonders to come. A huge dune away to the right, cupping a green in its palm, and another green below, sitting in the sea. The bait has been laid. That's what makes Tralee such an amazing golf experience and it was the genius of Arnold Palmer that created it.

The course sits over a beautiful coastline that offers a rocky harbour, a castle ruin, beaches, sand spits, old drystone walls and an old round tower. You will be drawn to the views all day, especially on the eight holes that bring you back to the sea. Of these, the 2nd is a huge dog-leg par 5 around a gorge that drops to the beach and the par 3 3rd sits delightfully on top of the rocks in front of the round tower.

Tralee is very peaceful, which may be why some prefer it to the nearby and busier Ballybunion. The golf is far from peaceful, but it comes down to the simple rules of links golf: find the reasonably flat fairways and make the right choice in approaching the greens. And when it comes to choice, Tralee will make you a master craftsman of float, punch and bump-and-run.

The front nine are gentler (if that's possible), with holes 2, 3 and 8 being absolute beauties. The back nine are a different matter, with dunes so big you are thrown about like a rag doll. On the 12th (Index 1) you're so far down that you can even go under the green. Holes 12 to 17 are too spectacular for words – huge dunes with flashes of fairway and some sky-high greens.

FAVOURITE HOLES
Holes 12 to 17. It's just as well that there are some tame holes here (the 4th, 5th and 9th) because if they were all as good as the 12th to the 17th it would overwhelm a mere mortal. The 13th and 16th (see photo) are two of the most punishing and thrilling par 3s into massive dunes.

TOUGHEST HOLE
Par 4 8th. 391 yards. The 12th deserves Index 1, but it is manageable. The 8th will scare the living daylights out of you off the tee: sea left, dunes right and seemingly no fairway to find with a driver. The green is above the water.

POINTS

CD	A	G/F	B/W	L	F	V	G Ex	Total
17	9	9	10	10	9	8	19	91

THE COURSE
- Par 72
- Length: 6,678 yards
- Tralee Golf Club, Barrow, Tralee, Co. Kerry
- Tel: +353 (0) 66 713 6379
- www.traleegolfclub.com
- Green Fees: €90–€180

COURSES NEARBY
Ballybunion
Castleisland

TRAMORE   Established 1894

ALL CHANGE ON A GLORIOUS PARKLAND

With all the big new courses out there, Tramore decided it was time to keep up – after all, it has a reputation to maintain. Nine new holes have been introduced, along with eighteen new greens. This is a stunningly appealing parkland course that roves through dense trees, over pretty ditches and across the gentle landscape. It's one surprise after another and there is good space to play. The extra touches around tee boxes and the attractiveness of fairways make a huge difference too. When you walk onto the tee, Tramore gives off a richness that every golfer will enjoy.

It hits you on the 1st tee from where you see three of the best holes. Almost every hole has something: prickly gorse-lined ditches appear directly in front of tees and greens; trees pressing in to force your hand (the 11th and 12th); and sweeping dog-legs that curve tantalisingly around the trees. Only the 4th stands on its own as a tight and severe dog-leg that calls for no more than a 220-m drive.

Fairways are soft and smooth, and greens have attractive backdrops. When you step up to your shot it all looks so tempting and challenging, especially as pins are invariably protected by steep-faced bunkers.

Now with twenty-seven holes and the addition of lakes (most notably in front of the 16th green), Tramore continues to deliver a great experience.

FAVOURITE HOLE

Par 4 12th. 315 m. You can see the green but an obstructive tree lurks nearby. How about a 200-m carry with fade over a nasty ditch (180 m)? No? Then play short and enjoy the colourful hydrangeas along the fairway.

TOUGHEST HOLE

Par 4 11th. 344 m. Another daunting drive, this time out of trees to a fairway that runs straight towards the clubhouse. Your second is uphill to a green surface you can't see.

POINTS

CD	A	G/F	B/W	L	F	V	G Ex	Total
16	8	7	8	5	9	8	17	78

THE COURSE

- Par 72
- Length: 5,923 m
- Tramore Golf Club, Tramore, Co. Waterford
- Tel: +353 (0) 51 386 170
- www.tramoregolfclub.com
- Green Fees: €30–€50

COURSES NEARBY
Dungarvan
Dunmore East
Faithlegg
Gold Coast
Waterford Castle
Williamstown

TUAM   Established 1904

EAGER TO PLEASE

Tuam is a strong, if basic, parkland course. The land is flat and the fairways are lined with trees as holes slip up and down. You can see several from the clubhouse. As a result, there tends to be some monotony, but you will have plenty of scoring opportunities and holes vary in length to keep the interest going. There are few hazards in the landing areas and plenty of fairway to aim at so you can swing freely. Personally, I think the course would really come to life if the flat greens could be presented in a more interesting way, even if it's just to use better flagsticks. Greens are very good – they are fast and true – but there's not enough appeal when you are hitting approach shots (the 13th is best). There are bunkers and nice backdrops but giving them a bit more lift, a bit more shape, would work wonders (see Oughterard). Not a simple or cheap solution, and I paid the bargain price of €15 to play in an open competition with John and Martin, so I shall make no more criticisms.

The best stretch starts at the par 3 11th and runs to the 17th. There is far more interest off the tees and you need to be careful with drives. It makes a good score all the more rewarding.

Holes 6 and 8 are Index 3 and 1 respectively, sandwiching a very tricky par 3, and it's another good run of holes. Hole 8, a dog-leg left, has a pond to the right, and big drivers need to be cautious.

FAVOURITE HOLE
Par 5 12th. 462 m. After so many benign driving holes, you encounter 80 m of real trouble in front of the tee and there's OB to the left. You will need three good blows to reach a green that is tucked behind a gentle ridge with a good backdrop of trees.

TOUGHEST HOLE
Par 4 6th. 363 m. This used to be Index 1 and the green is lethal. It's another gentle dog-leg – stay right – but you have to be directly below the hole as the green slopes viciously.

POINTS

CD	A	G/F	B/W	L	F	V	G Ex	Total
13	6	8	7	5	7	8	14	68

THE COURSE

- Par 72
- Length: 5,885 m
- Tuam Golf Club, Barnacurragh, Tuam, Co. Galway
- Tel: +353 (0) 93 28993
- www.tuamgolfclub.com
- Green Fees: €20

COURSES NEARBY
Athenry
Ballinrobe
Claremorris
Cregmore Park
Galway Bay

TULFARRIS   Established 1989

A GLORIOUS SETTING AND GREAT, GREAT GOLF

Mark Twain once said that 'golf is a good walk spoiled'. Not here, it's not. There are some great courses in these parts (Rathsallagh and Carlow) and Tulfarris is right up there with them. It is certainly the most scenic of the three and the course has everything a golfer could wish for as it moves gracefully around Blessington Lakes. The lakes are always in view, becoming very prominent on the back nine, and the trees and mountains make it an idyllic setting.

Every swing of the club is a pleasure . . . and at 6,745 yards you will be swinging a lot. There is a tough par 5/par 3 start which illustrates perfectly how challenging and pretty this course is. There are more good holes to follow – the par 3 6th is picture-perfect over a deep pond – but, for me, the course really takes off at the 9th where you have to fade your drive around trees (something which is repeated on the 14th) as you hit towards the lakes. And from then on the lakes are ever-present. The last ten holes are spectacular, with mature trees crowding in on you at the 10th, 12th, 13th and 14th, and, while the fairways remain gentle and generous, far more is demanded of your drives and accuracy. As a result, the holes and your shots are more satisfying, nowhere more so than on the tricky dog-leg 17th and the wonderfully intimidating, water-laced 18th.

This is another course where playing to your handicap is tremendously rewarding. I recommend you play this and Rathsallagh to experience two of Ireland's great parkland tracks.

FAVOURITE HOLE
Par 5 15th. 501 yards. A long, picturesque hole with a smart drive out of trees. There is heavy danger (woods and deep rough) all the way to the green, which drifts slowly left and out towards the lake.

TOUGHEST HOLE
Par 4 10th. 434 yards. A big dog-leg that swings left out into the lakes. Wherever you land your drive, the ball will be above your feet. It makes your second shot the most daunting of the day. There is no room for error around the green below. Index 1.

POINTS								
CD	A	G/F	B/W	L	F	V	G Ex	Total
17	9	8	9	9	8	10	19	89

THE COURSE

- Par 72
- Length: 6,745 yards
- Tulfarris Golf Club, Blessington Lakes, Blessington, Co. Wicklow
- Tel: +353 (0) 45 867 600
- www.tulfarrishotel.com/golf
- Green Fees: €30–€40

COURSES NEARBY
Craddockstown
Curragh, The
Rathsallagh
South County

TULLAMORE   Established 1908

WOODED PARKLAND ADVENTURE

A red squirrel ran across the fairway and climbed a huge pine as I played the 16th. It confirmed the wonderfully mature nature of the highly regarded Tullamore. You get completely wrapped up in the oak and beech woods as you drift between them (there are some glorious tee box settings), and they cause absolute chaos on many holes. Dog-legs throw huge trees or water at you, making for great risk-v.-reward drives. It's all thoroughly enjoyable as you have to figure out exactly what you're capable of. The variety in shapes, lengths and difficulty of holes keeps you off balance and certainly demands concentration.

You can be adventurous off the tee, but not wild, as the trees will punish you severely. A big drive definitely helps to beat dog-legs and you need to exploit the generous amounts of room, which is not always visible, to get the most out of the round. Once you start playing the course, you'll learn quickly.

Excellent greens have good shapes and are very well protected by punishing bunkers. But most greens are accessible.

The notable exceptions are Indices 1 (steep and bunkered rise) and 3 (perched green with water in front).

The 5th to the 8th are on a barren lower plain (the driving range slips between the 5th and 7th). It is more manufactured and less interesting despite lots of water. They just feel out of tune.

Holes cross twice which is a shame as the course feels so spacious and mature.

FAVOURITE HOLE
Par 4 13th. 377 yards. A high tee hits straight to the flag, with heavy trees left and right above a stream. A good drive is needed to avoid them and then straight in to the green.

TOUGHEST HOLE
Par 4 14th. 455 yards. Trees line the right, from tee box to the dog-leg, and a bunker at the end indicates the turn. No room for error if you want a second shot at the green which is up a short, bunkered rise. The 16th and 18th are very good and tough dog-legs (Index 3 and 5).

POINTS

CD	A	G/F	B/W	L	F	V	G Ex	Total
16	8	8	9	6	10	9	17	83

THE COURSE
- Par 70
- Length: 6,196 yards
- Tullamore Golf Club, Brookfield, Tullamore, Co. Offaly
- Tel: +353 (0) 57 932 1439
- www.tullamoregolfclub.ie
- Green Fees: €25–€48

COURSES NEARBY
Castle Barna
Esker Hills
Moate
New Forest
Portarlington

TURVEY   Established 1984

GREAT ROUTING AROUND THE HOTEL

Turvey falls into that category of appealing courses that always entertain. It's a pleasant round of golf mixing in all the essential elements, with a few more besides. There are good ponds on the 17th and 18th, and an enchanting oak wood brings to life the 2nd, 3rd, 13th, 14th, 16th and 17th – the 3rd and 13th are the best of these. The oaks appear elsewhere, just not in the numbers that Turvey would have you believe. A beauty sits on the right of the 1st fairway but, apart from the wood, they are scarce.

The thing that jumped out at me was the good routing which tries to keep you close to the mature trees, especially around the perimeter. There is no huge danger off the tee with wide fairways and generous rough. But bunkers and trees often require your tee shots to hit away from the green. The smallish greens are nearly always accessible. In fact, where there are bunkers around the green they stand off a reasonable way, giving you plenty of room to work with. Mounding

appears from time to time although it seems a bit forced on the 16th and 17th. This is because Turvey is such a natural course with a good pace that golfers enjoy. Fairways bumble along or offer slopes to make second shots tougher and they are presented in such a way that driving is fun and rewarding. On a flattish course, that's not easy to achieve.

FAVOURITE HOLE

Par 3 13th. 166 m. Everything works here. The green sits in a lovely setting of oaks that almost surround the hole. The fairway slopes down and then rises again, making a perfect presentation of the green.

TOUGHEST HOLE

Par 4 8th. 383 m. This is the only blind drive and it is a long hole. It is also a dog-leg so knowing where to place your drive is impossible for visitors. After the rise, the fairway bounces to the turn before heading left around tall trees. Aim right from the tee.

POINTS

CD	A	G/F	B/W	L	F	V	G Ex	Total
14	7	7	6	5	7	8	14	68

THE COURSE

- Par 71
- Length: 5,824 m
- Turvey Golf Club, Turvey Avenue, Donabate, Co. Dublin
- Tel: +353 (0) 1 843 5169
- www.turveygolfclub.com
- Green Fees: €20

COURSES NEARBY
Balcarrick
Beaverstown
Corballis
Donabate
Island, The

WARRENPOINT   Established 1893

A LONG START

A par 5, 3, 5, 5 start is enough to unnerve any golfer. Fortunately, or perhaps unfortunately, the holes stretch across a very flat, tree-lined landscape so no great effort is required. And it's not very interesting either. The quality and maturity are fine, but there is not much life to the front nine. Only the 5th, 6th and 7th find some serious spark with better shapes, bigger trees and more intrigue off the tee.

The back nine are a different story entirely, offering a brilliant stretch from the 11th to the 17th. It's the dynamic parkland you've been waiting for (and will make you think of nearby Kilkeel). Super holes with mature trees get close and personal, fairways find some life and tee boxes and greens deliver some real oomph to your day. Several tees have three or four sets of steps, which add a burst of interest. The 12th and 14th hit out of great wooded settings, while some shots into greens are really tough. These holes are made all the better by the gentle start, while the 17th is made tougher by the 7th and 11th, which cross it dangerously. On this stretch you need to pay attention as it is tricky off the tee and the punishment for stray shots is far more severe.

Views are of hillsides on the other side of the road beside Carlingford Lough. Not particularly prominent but nice to have.

It is a course that looks well, has plenty of big bunkers and mature trees, but the juicy bits come a little too late.

FAVOURITE HOLE
Par 4 13th. 354 yards. Difficult to tell where or how far to hit. Your shot must fall between 210 and 240 yards on a lopsided plateau if the lovely looking green is to be accessible. Trees flank the sides and your ball must avoid steep fall-offs around the green.

TOUGHEST HOLE
Par 4 7th. 412 yards. It's Index 1 and the toughest two shots, with a green defended by a hidden set of banks. Your tee shot, ideally, has to fade through a narrow channel, hold the fairway and be far enough right to give you a shot at the green.

POINTS

CD	A	G/F	B/W	L	F	V	G Ex	Total
13	6	6	7	7	8	5	12	64

THE COURSE

- Par 71
- Length: 6,001 yards
- Warrenpoint Golf Club, Lower Dromore Road, Warrenpoint, Co. Down
- Tel: +44 (0) 28 4175 3695 (048 from Rep. of Ire.)
- www.warrenpointgolf.com
- Green Fees: £24–£28

COURSES NEARBY
Ballymascanlon
Greenore
Kilkeel
Royal County Down
Royal County Down (Annesley)

WATERFORD Established 1912

DIGNIFIED

The arrival always makes so much difference: Waterford has a narrow lane that winds up between holes to the clubhouse. There are lots of trees and slopes, which starts you off on the right foot. And you never get off it. This is a simply designed, shortish and very effective parkland course that you'll enjoy the whole way around. The holes occasionally go back and forth, but you don't notice as they are well separated by lines of mature evergreen, hawthorn, oak and more recently planted varieties.

The trees definitely make the course, promising enough space to give the course that relaxed, inviting feel. They embrace fairways and sometimes nudge farther in to cause problems – the 4th, 5th and 6th – while they also create attractive backdrops for greens. The strong holes (the 1st, 5th, 6th, 7th, 10th, 13th, 14th and 18th) are perfectly spaced out and keep the momentum flowing. It means you find a good rhythm despite the variety of holes.

At the start, fairways have subtle undulations before changing to the rolling version, as the 12th to the 18th are on the side of a gentle hill. Here you'll find good tee boxes that make driving more exciting and rewarding. It is not difficult off the tee and, after the opening holes, the trees are far enough back that they shouldn't cause problems.

There are views but you will need a good day to appreciate the Comeragh Mountains in the distance and the colourful countryside. Closer to home, there are houses and Waterford town. The high point, literally and metaphorically, is the 18th tee box.

FAVOURITE HOLES
Par 4 6th. 340 m. A nice tree-lined dog-leg that will swallow long drives. You need to keep right and hit around 210 m to find the fairway before it narrows and then rises left to a tricky green. Par 3 7th is very enticing too.

TOUGHEST HOLE
Par 4 18th. 360 m. The only tough drive you'll face, and it is very tough. A long carry over gorse and rough to a barely visible fairway downhill. If you are too short you can't see the green far below. Shame about the Lego houses which ruin the view.

POINTS								
CD	A	G/F	B/W	L	F	V	G Ex	Total
14	8	6	8	6	8	7	15	72

THE COURSE
- Par 71
- Length: 5,491 m
- Waterford Golf Club, Newrath, Waterford, Co. Waterford
- Tel: +353 (0) 51 876 748
- www.waterfordgolfclub.com
- Green Fees: €35–€45

COURSES NEARBY
Faithlegg
Waterford Castle
Williamstown

WATERFORD CASTLE   Established 1992

WORTH THE FERRY RIDE

What an introduction: a private ferry to an island surrounded by the River Suir. There's a castle, a hotel and a golf course. If that doesn't sound grand, I don't know what does. From the 1st tee it all looks good too, as you hit down towards the river and the landscape beyond. It is a great setting that lasts the entire round.

In time, when the course and young trees mature, Waterford Castle will live up to its start. But, for now, several of the holes don't quite match the setting – particularly on the more open back nine. The mass planting of trees is erratic – the drive on the 5th is bewildering (aim at the blue conifer) – and putting surfaces are a bit plain. But it has the right ingredients with good changes in elevation, colourful woods and a strong routing through this idyllic setting. There is plenty for you to enjoy, that's for sure. You'll face good and tricky drives over crests of hills and around dog-legs, which then reveal the beauty beyond.

Sometimes a course comes down to the nice touches and the individuality of holes.

The 2nd and the 16th are par 3s beside the river with their own water features. The 346-m 3rd – Index 1 – has a walk over a bridge to the tee and a delightful drive over water and between tall trees. And the 13th is dramatic (see below).

Greens are big (up to 40 paces) so ask for the day's pin positions. Fairway markers are in metres to the front of the green.

FAVOURITE HOLE
Par 5 13th. 427 m. The best hole by far overlooks the river and dog-legs right around mature trees. The fairway runs up the hill and looks delicious. There are bunkers and gorse but you have to give it a lash. The green is in a beautiful wooded setting.

TOUGHEST HOLE
Par 4 12th. 397 m. The longest par 4 is a gentle downhill dog-leg towards the river. It has the added danger of fairway bunkers and a well-protected green. A good driving hole.

POINTS

CD	A	G/F	B/W	L	F	V	G Ex	Total
14	7	6	7	8	8	8	15	73

THE COURSE
- Par 72
- Length: 5,827 m
- Waterford Castle Golf Club, The Island, Ballinakill, Co. Waterford
- Tel: +353 (0) 51 871 633
- www.waterfordcastle.com
- Green Fees: €30–€50

COURSES NEARBY
Dunmore East
Faithlegg
Tramore
Waterford
Williamstown

WATER ROCK   Established 1994

MOVING DAY

This is a family-run, pay-and-play course. You might think that means a lesser quality. Not true.

Sure, it is a bit short and it doesn't have the design delicacies of a 'great' parkland course, but it takes you on a roller-coaster ride over heaving countryside with excellent water features on the spacious back nine. Huge work has gone into the banking that creates and separates fairways. It provides havens for well-placed bunkers and rises up around the greens to steer your approach. It all works and it looks great. There are natural inclines too. They rise (the 7th and 18th are best) or fall (the 10th is as good a par 5 as you will find) and the 18th is straight uphill with a green so steep errant putts could roll 20 yards down the fairway.

It is not so much a driver's course as a thrasher's course as you try to reach some par 4s. It is difficult in places, but pleasantly so. And there is plenty of room to manouevre. Anyone and everyone can play here and, with its wide open spaces and lots of movement, it's perfect for all golfing abilities. Perhaps that's what I like about the place: it has made itself completely accessible to every level. Eoin, my partner, had played six times in his life and was having a great time. You'll have to try hard to lose a ball unless you're in water or playing the 12th from the back tee.

Very popular with UK golfers.

FAVOURITE HOLES
Par 4 16th. 361 yards. The fairway curves around a lake all the way to the green and you get to decide how much you take on. The ultimate driving test. The 7th, 10th and 12th are also beauties.

TOUGHEST HOLE
Par 3 12th. 219 yards. Please play this from the back tees (240 yards), with an old ball. You stand on the tee, with a lake in front of you that reaches all the way to the green. Hit right, forget it; hit left, you might get away with it. Beautiful and terrifying.

POINTS

CD	A	G/F	B/W	L	F	V	G Ex	Total
15	7	8	9	6	5	10	17	77

THE COURSE
- Par 70
- Length: 5,880 yards
- Water Rock Golf Club, Midleton, Co. Cork
- Tel: +353 (0) 21 461 3499
- www.waterrockgolfcourse.com
- Green Fees: €27–€33

COURSES NEARBY
Cobh
Cork
East Cork
Fota Island

WATERVILLE   Established 1889

THE MOST PICTURE-PERFECT LINKS

There are always courses where you hold your breath as you arrive. Waterville is one, and it hides its beauty until you stand on the 1st tee. A strong, straight hole gets things started: the wispy-lipped bunkers look ominous; the fairway surprisingly wide and flat; the green enticing; and the backdrop dramatic. And as you romp your way through the dunes, along the River Inny estuary, every hole is picture-perfect. From raised tee boxes, being able to see the flag time and again tucked away behind cascading dunes makes the holes so much more attractive. But even on the few occasions when you can't (the 11th comes to mind), the holes have beautiful shape and symmetry.

Early on, the wide fairways ensure that you can fire at the greens from almost anywhere, as the dunes are not too severe, but the back nine are tougher as the dunes put up greater defences and fairways throw more shapes. And as the dunes get higher, so do the tee boxes, and this gives spectacular views over the course and of the MacGillycuddy's Reeks and Caha Mountains. When you come to the 16th, 17th and 18th, the sea makes a dramatic appearance, nowhere more so than on the long, par 5 18th back to the clubhouse.

A round of golf is pricey but you won't be disappointed by what Waterville has to offer. The wide fairways make this long course seem forgiving. And even though approaches to greens are more troublesome – the bunkers are not just for show – it is not as difficult as nearby Dooks, because so much of the hole is visible and the greens are big and smooth.

The par 3s are stunning.

FAVOURITE HOLES
Most of them. The par 4 3rd curls around the river estuary with one of those terrifying approach shots. The par 3 12th hits over a big hollow to a green that offers no escape route. And the par 5 11th, 'Tranquillity', dives down into the deep peace of the dunes.

TOUGHEST HOLE
Par 5 18th. 556 yards. If you've played well, this long, straight hole beside the sea is a dangerous finish; if you've played badly, it's a long and tiring walk home.

POINTS
CD	A	G/F	B/W	L	F	V	G Ex	Total
20	10	10	10	10	9	8	19	96

THE COURSE
- Par 72
- Length: 6,794 yards (white tees)
- Waterville Golf Links, Waterville, Co. Kerry
- Tel: +353 (0) 66 947 4102
- www.watervillegolflinks.ie
- Green Fees: €60–€170

COURSES NEARBY
Ring of Kerry
Skellig Bay

WESTMANSTOWN   Established 1988

NICE AND TIDY

Golf at Westmanstown is of the flat and honest variety. The landscape has been mounded along some fairways and around the greens, but it is not intrusively done as can so often be the case. This parkland track will work for everyone. It is not long and the dog-legs are gentle affairs that invite full drives (bar the 1st, 10th and 11th). Big hitters will find plenty of opportunity to smash their way around and there is little serious rough to worry about. On a few holes tree pairings present sterner tests off the tee, but nothing too threatening.

Westmanstown is undoubtedly relaxing and pleasant golf. With the flat landscape and limited views it is not dramatic, nor does it ooze character, but it is simple enjoyment. Shots into greens are the highlight with most surfaces well presented to your approach and the mounding giving them good shape. Around them you will find plenty of well-placed and attractive bunkers – an island with two trees sits in a bunker by the 1st – but they are rarely deep. It's the

kind of course that will reward you frequently and punish you seldom. Yes, of course you might end up in water, or blocked by a tree, but they won't destroy your card. The large, reed-bound pond adds hugely on the side-by-side par 3s, the 6th and 16th, and the 18th has a good pond to finish – not to mention the best green of the day.

It is part of a large leisure complex and conference venue.

FAVOURITE HOLE
Par 3 6th. 143 m. A large pond runs up to the green from the right and swings across under the front. The green has a stone front, making this the most inviting shot of the day.

TOUGHEST HOLE
Par 4 15th. 394 m. Toughest only because it is the longest par 4. With a gentle right-to-left sweep it also demands an accurate drive or the two trees on either side of the fairway, short of the green, will make your second difficult.

POINTS

CD	A	G/F	B/W	L	F	V	G Ex	Total
13	7	7	8	4	6	5	14	64

THE COURSE

- Par 71
- Length: 5,613 yards
- Westmanstown Golf Club, Clonsilla, Dublin 15
- Tel: +353 (0) 1 820 5817
- www.westmanstowngolfclub.ie
- Green Fees: €25–€40

COURSES NEARBY
Hermitage, The
Lucan
Luttrellstown

WESTPORT Established 1908

CROAGH PATRICK LOOMS LARGE

I don't think anyone would disagree that Westport gets off to a poor start: the first six holes are decidedly average parkland fare that go back and forth in front of the clubhouse. But at least you can use these holes as a warm-up as you enjoy the views. Then you walk across the driveway to the 7th and it's all change: from bland fairways and features, you hit holes with individuality, shape and intrigue. Fairways, while wide, start to become increasingly sloped and dog-legged – I'd tell you how good they are if I'd managed to hit one – and your driving has to be accurate.

It turns into a great parkland course at the flick of a switch. Hills, walls, water, bridges, pathways and trees are beautifully complemented by the sea and mountains. And all the while you have Croagh Patrick looming over you, something to look at when you need inspiration. Not that you'll need any more inspiration than the run of holes that begins at the 12th. These use the landscape to perfection. The 12th is a long par 3 that drops dramatically to a green on the water. The 14th, another par 3, hits

majestically out of trees straight at Croagh Patrick. And then comes the 15th tee and the spectacular climb up the 16th.

The par 5 18th green is the only one that has any difficulty and finishes off a round that just gets better and better.

There are great views from the clubhouse too. Be sure to order one of their superb scones (made fresh).

FAVOURITE HOLE

Par 5 15th (see photo). 498 yards. You drive over a large stretch of water that then curls with the fairway away to the left. With the fairway slope, the farther you hit your drive, the harder your second shot will be. The green is perched on the edge of the inlet.

TOUGHEST HOLE

Par 4 11th. 420 yards. The 13th is Index 1, but I think the 11th is harder, with a huge shoulder in the middle of the fairway that makes it all but impossible to stay on it. You are unlikely to see the green, so judging the length of your second shot is harder still.

POINTS								
CD	A	G/F	B/W	L	F	V	G Ex	Total
16	8	8	7	9	8	9	18	83

THE COURSE

- Par 73
- Length: 6,724 yards
- Westport Golf Club, Carrowholly, Westport, Co. Mayo
- Tel: +353 (0) 98 28262
- www.westportgolfclub.com
- Green Fees: €20–€40

COURSES NEARBY
Ballinrobe
Castlebar
Claremorris
Connemara

WEST WATERFORD   Established 1993

NOT A FOOT WRONG

Even the weaker holes (the 6th to the 9th) work really well here. They are separated from the rest of the course by a gentle hill and they go back and forth. As you walk down the long and dark path to the 6th tee box these holes look similar – but they're not. They are of different lengths and offer different tests. The 9th green, by the clubhouse, offers the best views of the Comeragh Mountains.

It is the holes on the other side that are so wonderful where the creativity focuses on simplicity. West Waterford has used the hills and trees perfectly, nowhere more effectively than holes 2 and 3, two reverse dog-legs. The 2nd hits down and demands a draw; the 3rd goes back up and needs a fade. Both are tight, need exact shots, and are enticing: they are beautiful holes.

Like Tramore, this is a driver's paradise. The variety of holes, both in terms of beauty and difficulty, will keep you excited all day and standing up on the next tee box never disappoints. The 12th, 14th and 15th run alongside the River Brickey, which is as natural and peaceful as the course itself. It warms the heart.

The 17th and 18th (see below) are two long and tough holes that will rattle the best golfers. When you climb that final slope, remind yourself that this course opened only in 1993. It is maturing spectacularly.

I was sitting in the restaurant when the President's prizes were being handed out. The winning visitor remarked how warm the welcome was at West Waterford and I couldn't agree more.

FAVOURITE HOLE

Par 5 12th. 464 yards. The first hole beside the river. It may look flat but the fairway has good undulations and there are two ditches, which challenge your drive and your second. The bridges add nicely and it offers a good birdie chance.

TOUGHEST HOLE

Par 4 18th. 455 yards. The fairway dog-legs gently against the slope of the hill, so finding the fairway is tough. Your long second is then well below your feet, with a bunker in exactly the wrong place in front of the green.

POINTS

CD	A	G/F	B/W	L	F	V	G Ex	Total
16	8	8	8	7	8	10	18	83

THE COURSE

- Par 72
- Length: 6,476 yards
- West Waterford Golf Club, Dungarvan, Co. Waterford
- Tel: +353 (0) 58 43216
- www.westwaterfordgolf.com
- Green Fees: €25–€35

COURSES NEARBY
Dungarvan
Gold Coast
Youghal

WEXFORD   Established 1960

TOO MANY COOKS

There is a sense that too many people have fiddled with this course. Put some trees here, mounds there, some fancy walls beside that, and where are we going to put the water? As a result, Wexford stutters and starts and never settles down. It constantly changes gear. The most obvious example is the bunkering: it is well positioned but their fancy shapes don't fit the nature of the course. It feels interrupted and busy.

There are good holes, to be sure. The 7th to 11th are excellent and call for serious skill. They rise and fall on an outer hillside loop, with views over Wexford Harbour and the coast. The rolling fairways and natural dangers are thrilling and you'll find plenty of trouble if you are too aggressive. The two par 3s both have high tees – the 8th rises steeply on a huge knoll behind the 7th green – this must be the best spot on the course, not only for views but to see how the players behind you tackle the tricky 7th, a downhill 225-m par 4. The 9th and 10th descend towards the sea with a magnificent backdrop.

The 15th and 17th are good dog-legs that run in opposite directions and are separated by evergreens: one heads down (great drive), the other up (tough approach). Perhaps the shift in styles works in Wexford's favour: one stretch of holes or the other is bound to appeal to you.

Overall, a little too erratic.

FAVOURITE HOLE

Par 4 15th. 395 m. The big downhill drive is the best tee shot of the day: hit straight at a distant spire. It dog-legs on its way down and the bunker is well placed if you try for too much. The green has water to the left.

TOUGHEST HOLE

Par 4 18th. 407 m. Realistically you have to go over the trees down the left if you want any reasonable chance of hitting the green in two. A driver might push you all the way down a steep slope you can't see. The green is well perched and protected.

POINTS								
CD	A	G/F	B/W	L	F	V	G Ex	Total
13	6	6	6	7	8	6	12	64

THE COURSE

- Par 71
- Length: 5,635 m
- Wexford Golf Club, Mulgannon, Co. Wexford
- Tel: +353 (0) 53 914 2238
- www.wexfordgolfclub.ie
- Green Fees: €30–€35

COURSES NEARBY
Rosslare
St Helen's Bay

WHITEHEAD   Established 1904

FROM THE MOUNTAIN TO THE SEA

I played Whitehead before Cairndhu, which certainly is the way to do it. Whitehead has a steep little lane leading you up to the clubhouse, and you know the views will be spectacular. They are, but you have a tough climb up the 1st, 2nd and part of the 3rd before you get the full 360-degree masterpiece. County Down, Belfast Lough and views across to Ailsa Craig and Scotland make the walk down to the 3rd green one of the highlights of the round.

The front nine bound up, down and around a hilltop. There are endless clutches of gorse and stands of pine trees, but it still feels bright and open. There are blind shots, long drops to greens and plenty of character. In terms of difficulty, there are some tough shots (drives on the 3rd and 8th) but there is room to move around, and greens are big and accessible. The design is straightforward and the quality good, but at the end of the day the views take most of your attention.

Down below, the back nine drop a gear or two. The 10th is an excellent par 5

heading down towards the sea, but these are younger, less interesting parkland holes with simpler lines of trees. They're formulaic and straight. The 15th used to be a right-angled dog-leg, but it has been reduced to a good uphill par 3 owing to the big house.

It's a short course and worth a visit for the hilltop nine.

FAVOURITE HOLE
Par 4 8th. 364 yards. It is worth looking for the 8th green (left) as you walk off the 7th. It shows you what is required since the hole curves right as it heads sharply downhill. Hard to judge but a peach of a drive.

TOUGHEST HOLE
Par 4 7th. 390 yards. It's Index 2 and you need a good drive onto a sloping fairway if you want to see one of the better bunkered greens over the crest and below. It is the tier on the green that may cause the most problems.

POINTS								
CD	A	G/F	B/W	L	F	V	G Ex	Total
13	6	6	5	10	8	9	14	71

THE COURSE

- Par 69
- Length: 5,643 yards
- Whitehead Golf Club, McCraes Brae, Whitehead, Co. Antrim, BT38 9NZ
- Tel: +44 (0) 28 9337 0820 (048 from Rep. of Ire.)
- www.whiteheadgolfclub.com
- Green Fees: £20–£24

COURSES NEARBY
Ballyclare
Cairndhu
Carrickfergus
Fortwilliam

WICKLOW   Established 1904

ABOVE THE SEA

Wicklow Golf Club hovers tantalisingly above the sea and the rocks. Nearby Blainroe may have more continuity but Wicklow has more excitement. From the first tee you have great views out to sea and across to the Wicklow Mountains (please ignore Wicklow town). There's a lighthouse and cannons down behind the green and a bouncing fairway to get there. It's an impressive start, if a dangerous one with houses close to the left and the 2nd fairway to the right.

The sea is a thrilling companion as the course rises and falls along the coast. It presents some wonderfully challenging drives: the 2nd and 6th (off blue tees) take on the sea in no small measure, while the 13th, 14th and 15th (par 5 Index 1) are on steep slopes. The shape also makes for thrilling shots into greens – even when they're hidden. Dog-legs are often difficult to gauge with well-placed trees and traps, so you certainly need to think your way around. Just because it is short doesn't mean it's easy.

There are several steep climbs – too steep for some, perhaps – but it's all worth it. This is a vibrant course that oozes energy. Just play the attractive gorse-drenched par 3 7th if you don't believe me. Gorse separates and defines many of the holes so playing in spring ensures a blaze of colour.

It is a bit disjointed and busy in places: the recent planting of palm trees on the 4th looks good but feels odd.

FAVOURITE HOLE
Par 4 12th. 383 yards. Practically the first straight hole and all of it wonderfully visible. The fairway tilts left as it slides down from the tee towards the green (with the sea along the left). Gorse lines the hole as well as rising impressively behind the green.

TOUGHEST HOLE
Par 4 2nd. 388 yards. The hole curves around the sea making it a nightmare for golfers with a draw. The drive to a tilting fairway is lethal, but the second is no easier with the green tucked behind a large rocky mound.

POINTS

CD	A	G/F	B/W	L	F	V	G Ex	Total
15	8	7	6	8	8	9	16	77

THE COURSE
- Par 71
- Length: 5,657 yards
- Wicklow Golf Club, Dunbur Road, Wicklow, Co. Wicklow
- Tel: +353 (0) 404 67379
- www.wicklowgolfclub.ie
- Green Fees: €30–€35

COURSES NEARBY
Arklow
Blainroe
Druid's Glen/Heath
European Club, The

WILLIAMSTOWN   Established 1997

DON'T BE PREJUDICED AGAINST 'MUNICIPAL'

Considering your arrival and the Portakabin clubhouse, you are not going to walk on to the first tee and go 'wow' – but don't turn your nose up quite yet. For those who say 'pah' to municipal courses, half of the holes here would sit comfortably on any good parkland course. There are crafted tee boxes, crisp greens that sit up invitingly, strategically placed bunkers and a whole chorus of ditches – although they remained stubbornly empty despite heavy rains. It is mostly open and level ground so there's lots of the course on view.

If you can ignore some scruffy fairways and grotty bunkers then you are in for an unexpected and long eighteen holes. The constantly lurking ditches and reed-infested ponds on the 2nd, 3rd and 8th are all real threats and make the course that bit longer. Eddie Hackett certainly did a great job with what was available to him and he has worked the greens very well into the available flat landscape.

Two of the par 3s are over 200 m and there are excellent driving holes. Your drives on the short dog-legs at the 2nd, 3rd and 8th are excellent risk-v.-reward

shots.

Of course there are some lacklustre holes (the 7th, 13th and 14th) but the good holes make up for them. You are also likely to get dizzy with the course routing – at any one time you won't have a clue which hole you're beside.

Don't expect much from the clubhouse, but do expect to be surprised by the course.

FAVOURITE HOLE

Par 4 8th. 317 m. It looks great from the tee box: the corner of the green peeks out from behind the trees as the hole swings around a large pond. There's a hidden ditch too, but you will probably go for the full carry.

TOUGHEST HOLE

Par 4 2nd. 337 m. If you hit the sensible 180-m shot, then the hole is easy, but why not take on the dog-leg, over the line of trees and the ditch and put it close to the green. There's very little room but it is fun.

POINTS

CD	A	G/F	B/W	L	F	V	G Ex	Total
13	6	6	6	3	3	8	14	59

THE COURSE

- Par 72
- Length: 6,053 m
- Williamstown Golf Club, Waterford, Co. Waterford
- Tel: +353 (0) 51 853 131
- Green Fees: €15–€20

COURSES NEARBY
Dunmore East
Faithlegg
Tramore
Waterford
Waterford Castle

WOODBROOK   Established 1921

A RICH HISTORY, BUT IT HAS FALLEN BEHIND

Lawn-like fairways, magnificent roller-coaster greens, a seaside location and a golf history that litters famous names like confetti. But: there's a 'but'. The land is too flat to give holes any flair. Even the huge, remoulded greens with their glorious shapes and bunker complexes, which make them the best and most challenging feature of the course, are simply not enough. If you played it on a still day it would be a tame golf experience. Trees are scattered about but it still feels open, whichever side of the railway track you find yourself on. Even the holes beside the low sea cliffs fail to build real excitement.

Of course there are some strong holes (the 6th, 7th, 10th, 13th and 15th), while the two par 3s, the 9th and 11th, hit straight out to sea to create some drama. It is also long enough to challenge most golfers, and generous enough off the tee to give societies and visitors plenty of second chances.

This may sound rather negative for a course that is in such good condition but, when you consider Woodbrook's history and reputation, you expect the course to jump out and thrill you. On this uninteresting landscape, it can't do that.

Woodbrook held the Irish Open in 1975, and numerous other Irish events, but history is not enough to keep this as a main attraction.

FAVOURITE HOLE
Par 5 14th. 526 yards. All along the cliffs, this straight hole needs a couple of great shots before your third has to negotiate a tricky, narrow green that slopes sharply away from you.

TOUGHEST HOLE
Par 4 7th. 456 yards. It all comes down to the second shot on this strong dog-leg, which means your drive has to be perfect. Err on the left side. From the middle of the fairway the green is a tough ask, so imagine what it's like from the rough.

POINTS								
CD	A	G/F	B/W	L	F	V	G Ex	Total
14	6	10	8	8	9	5	13	73

THE COURSE
- Par 72
- Length: 6,582 yards
- Woodbrook Golf Club, Bray, Co. Wicklow
- Tel: +353 (0) 1 282 4799
- www.woodbrook.ie
- Green Fees: €40–€80

COURSES NEARBY
Bray
Dun Laoghaire
Glen of the Downs
Old Conna
Powerscourt

WOODENBRIDGE   Established 1884

A TRULY COLOURFUL DAY OUT

You really could not ask for a more beautiful inland setting. Nestled in a deep valley of mature trees cascading down the hillsides, a clear, pure river follows you around all day. There is something very poetic about the place. And even before you get to the large clubhouse, you walk over an old railway line and the Avoca River. Talk about whetting the appetite.

So, does the course match up? For the most part, yes. You will feel cramped on the first few holes but, after that, you'll find more space, creating a relaxing round where enjoyment and camaraderie are the key ingredients. The course is flat, open, short and straight, and therefore accessible to everyone. There are plenty of trees but they give you room. Most of the trouble is on the long roller-coaster greens and in the bunkers jealously guarding them. Check the mini-flags that tell you the hole's location or you will be 3-putting all day.

The design is good, straightforward stuff – especially considering the limited space – with the river and location adding that extra something. The 7th and 10th are the only really tough holes and these are tempered by some very short par 4s – eagle possibilities perhaps. The 9th and 18th are two excellent par 5s, the latter with a big drive over water.

Better tee directions would help.

FAVOURITE HOLE
Par 4 14th. 284 yards. Reachable from the tee, perhaps, if it wasn't for that lone tree in the fairway. The river runs beside and then behind the green, but try not to think about that too much.

TOUGHEST HOLE
Par 3 4th. 174 yards. A long hit uphill to a small, valley-shaped green, heavily protected by bunkers. Land short and let it run in.

POINTS

CD	A	G/F	B/W	L	F	V	G Ex	Total
14	7	8	7	9	7	7	16	75

THE COURSE

- Par 71
- Length: 6,093 yards
- Woodenbridge Golf Club, Vale of Avoca, Arklow, Co. Wicklow
- Tel: +353 (0) 402 35202
- www.woodenbridgegolfclub.com
- Green Fees: €50–€60

COURSES NEARBY
Arklow
Coollattin
European Club, The
Macreddin

WOODLANDS   Established 1990

A QUALITY, BASIC COURSE

Ireland has very many of this type of course. To say 'painting by numbers' would be derogatory, but if I said 'it ticks all the boxes', you'd be satisfied. And it does. The course's two nines sit on either side of a road and there is a distinct difference. The first nine are younger, flatter and – for the most part – more open. Mounding is also more distinct (and rather unflattering on the 2nd and 9th). The second nine have more shape and maturity. They roll a lot more over gentle slopes, which gives the holes more character.

Ponds play a significant part, appearing on nine holes and quite dramatically on the 5th, 9th, 12th and 16th. The 9th tee box sits out in a pond that curves around it like a heart. The 12th and 16th are strong par 3s.

The holes are not hugely difficult. Golf here is about a pleasant day out and having fun. The greens are accessible and inviting with wide entrances and bunkers set well back. There are plenty of trees, although Woodlands is a misnomer (for now), and it really is a very enjoyable design that doesn't tax the brain or the wallet.

FAVOURITE HOLE
Par 3 16th. 146 m. A nicely raised tee hits over a pretty pond to a green, also raised and set into the slopes.

TOUGHEST HOLE
Par 4 5th. 354 m. The tee sits between two wild ponds. The fairway has real character as it twists and jumps around a line of trees that stick out from the left. That's the hard shot. A nice approach is mildly threatened by a poplar leaning over the green.

POINTS								
CD	A	G/F	B/W	L	F	V	G Ex	Total
13	6	7	8	5	8	8	14	69

THE COURSE

- Par 72
- Length: 5,924 m
- Woodlands Golf Club, Cooleragh, Coill Dubh, Naas, Co. Kildare
- Tel: +353 (0) 45 860 777
- www.woodlandsgolf.ie
- Green Fees: €25–€35

COURSES NEARBY
Bodenstown
Dunmurry Springs
Millicent

WOODSTOCK   Established 1993

COMING ON

The course has a lot of mature woodland around the place and it gives a smart parkland feel, despite Woodstock's youth. Younger trees have also been planted as small dense woods and they look good. It ensures a positive future for the club as it will really stamp the holes' individuality in years to come. There is also a brilliant and wild hillside at the bottom of the course, and you tackle it repeatedly between holes 5 and 11. It's a whole array of tough and thrilling shots. There are three par 3s in this stretch between 160 m and 170 m, and two are lovely bombs down onto greens. The 10th is a short par 5 and offers a similar approach. These are the best of the bunch, but the others are still good and there is enough space to give it that leisurely feel.

Woodstock will only get better. It has everything you want on a parkland track and will leave you feeling sated. Fairways have great movement and landing areas are often squeezed to make driving a challenge, although you usually have room before the trees swallow you up. Approaches to greens are exciting, too, as they vary in size and shape, and punitive bunkers are sunk into the sides of the well-created complexes.

I found plenty of holes and tee shots that brought a smile to my face, all done without any startling design or superior quality. It simply uses the pretty location (the hillside and lake) to please and challenge you in equal measure.

FAVOURITE HOLE
Par 3 8th. 134 m. A sweet tee shot over the lake with water fronting the stone-walled green and easing around the left. A good dense backdrop gives it a great feel.

TOUGHEST HOLE
Par 4 7th. 373 m. Index 1 drives from a gentle elevation over the corner of the lake towards a lone fairway tree. How much you take on as the hole dog-legs around the water is up to you. It's over water for the approach too.

POINTS

CD	A	G/F	B/W	L	F	V	G Ex	Total
15	7	8	8	7	7	7	16	75

THE COURSE

- Par 71
- Length: 5,813 m
- Woodstock Golf Club, Shanaway Road, Ennis, Co. Clare
- Tel: +353 (0) 65 682 9463
- www.woodstockgolfclub.com
- Green Fees: €20–€30

COURSES NEARBY
Dromoland Castle
East Clare
Ennis
Shannon

YOUGHAL   Established 1898

BEWARE THE LADYBIRDS

Youghal is hit and miss. As you play the first four holes you will favour the 'miss' approach as you drive on some unexciting holes and very dangerous holes. The 2nd and 18th tee boxes play pistols at dawn, the 3rd green is threatened from the 17th, and tee boxes on the 4th, 11th and 16th, combined with the 10th green, are other hot spots.

Still with me? Good, because now comes the 'hit' part: the greens are perfect – their speed and quality completely unexpected; and the 5th to the 9th on the other side of the road (a good 150-m walk) are my idea of superb parkland holes. Standing on the 5th tee is a revelation. The 5th and 9th are two super dog-legs (see below), and the 7th offers the best drive you'll hit, with a stunningly bunkered fairway swinging out of sight beyond a lone tree. The par 3 8th green is set beautifully alongside a stream in a wooded setting.

Back across the road again, it's the same as the start with blind drives taking you up and over, or over and down. I don't mind the occasional blind drive but there are too many at Youghal and they all hit between conifer-lined fairways. Tricky but not exciting enough.

The course sits high above the town, so long uphill climbs are accompanied by impressive sea, coast and mountain views. The 11th and 16th hit downhill with Cabin Point on the far side of the Blackwater Estuary as a backdrop.

On Mondays, watch out for the Ladybirds. Aged fifty-five and over, these ladies are a friendly bunch – thank you, Moira and Juliet.

FAVOURITE HOLE
Par 4 5th. 309 m. An attractive tee shot hits down towards a stream and bridge, the green just out of sight. You are left with a steep, downhill lie, but facing a perfectly bunkered green that is roughly level with you on the other side of the valley.

TOUGHEST HOLE
Par 4 9th. 371 m. The same as above, only longer and tougher as the fairway is barely visible and the stream has sprouted tall trees which partially block out the green.

POINTS

CD	A	G/F	B/W	L	F	V	G Ex	Total
12	6	7	7	8	8	7	13	68

THE COURSE
- Par 71
- Length: 5,789 m
- Youghal Golf Club, Knockaverry, Youghal, Co. Cork
- Tel: +353 (0) 24 92787
- www.youghalgolfclub.ie
- Green Fees: €20–€30

COURSES NEARBY
East Cork
Water Rock
West Waterford